# A Sense of Place

## DESIGN GUIDELINES FOR YOSEMITE NATIONAL PARK

For my dear friend Rusty,
who shared the loading dock
at Camp Curry a long time ago
with me
George Hounsley october 2012

PREPARED BY

THE NATIONAL PARK SERVICE

YOSEMITE NATIONAL PARK

CALIFORNIA

**MAN-MADE STRUCTURES CAN SCARCELY ADD TO YOSEMITE'S MATCHLESS BEAUTY.**

**RATHER WE MUST STRIVE THAT THEY NEITHER INTRUDE**

**UPON THIS SPLENDOR NOR SEEM TO RIVAL IT IN PERMANENCE.**

HILMER OEHLMANN • GENERAL MANAGER OF THE CURRY COMPANY

AT DEDICATION OF YOSEMITE LODGE • JUNE 1956

# CONTENTS



PAGE 2 *Sentinel Rock (1945) YRL-RA*
OPPOSITE *Nevada Fall (1938) YRL-RA*

# FOREWORD

JOHN J. REYNOLDS • (RETIRED) NATIONAL PARK SERVICE

I FIRST CAME to Yosemite in an official capacity in 1975. I was Team Captain for what was to become known as the 1980 Yosemite General Management Plan. It was a time of great controversy about the park, so much so that 62,000 people participated in the planning process. I shall never forget the headline in *Rolling Stone* that blared "Why Are They Golfing in the Cathedral?"

> THE QUEST, THE NEVER-ENDING QUEST, IN YOSEMITE IS FOR AN ALMOST SPIRITUAL OR SUPER-HUMAN QUALITY IN DECISIONS ABOUT PRESERVING AND ENJOYING IT. IT IS LESS A PLACE THAN AN EXPERIENCE. EVERY DETAIL COUNTS—NOT JUST A LITTLE, BUT A LOT. THIS IS THE CHALLENGE OF DESIGN OF ANYTHING IN YOSEMITE, BE IT THE VALLEY OR ANY OTHER PLACE IN THE PARK. YOSEMITE—ITS AURA, ITS UNIQUE PLACE IN OUR MINDS AND SOULS—DEMANDS THE ULTIMATE IN RESPECT FOR WHAT NATURE MADE AND THE AWE IT IMPARTS.

*Rolling Stone* weighing in about a national park? Unbelievable! But it happened. The "cathedral" was (and is) Yosemite. "Golfing" referred to the since-removed 9-hole pitch-and-putt course then in place behind The Ahwahnee. The headline has stuck with me ever since as I have engaged in the great ongoing intellectual and ethical adventure and struggle of what to do, and not to do, in Yosemite National Park."Cathedral" almost universally connotes extraordinary beauty and connection to a creating spirit. Yosemite evokes the same feelings of quality and connectivity to a greater life force, a greater reason for being. It is a sacred place, to many the most sacred symbol of sublimity and beauty anywhere in the world.

"Golfing" in such a place often symbolizes a level of separation dividing mankind from nature that could hardly be more stark unless it were industrial. The contradiction between golfing and cathedral in my experience with Yosemite National Park defines more clearly than any other metaphor the roots of controversy and feeling that are the basis for discussion about everything that happens or is proposed to happen in Yosemite.

OPPOSITE *El Capitan (1938) YRL-OW*

The quest, the never-ending quest, in Yosemite is for an almost spiritual or super-human quality in decisions about preserving and enjoying it. It is less a place than an experience. Every detail counts—not just a little, but a lot. This is the challenge of design of anything in Yosemite, be it the Valley or any other place in the park. Yosemite—its aura, its unique place in our minds and souls—demands the ultimate in respect for what nature made and the awe it imparts.

During the first 100 or so years of the existence of national parks, design professionals worked entire public service careers perfecting what was appropriate design in national parks. They learned by being immersed in the natural feel of the place. They came to know and respond to the rhythms and patterns nature imparts, unique to each place yet as related as trees and flowers, birds and bears, air and water are related one to another. These professionals dedicated their working lifetimes to creating the design ethics for which the National Park Service was and is known worldwide.

That cadre of public service professionals dedicated to studying and designing in response to the parks themselves no longer exists. Those who remain mostly manage the contracts and expectations of the private contractors hired from afar to do the work.

And so the need for this marvelous and essential book, *A Sense of Place: Design Guidelines for Yosemite National Park*. Its reason for being is to pass on at least the basics of the special and unique considerations that undergird excellence of design in Yosemite. It is a humbling undertaking, striving to convey to landscape architects, architects, and engineers the beginning basics they need to be sensitive to in Yosemite.

Very often in our culture, as places develop, we lose our sense of place. We lose the sights, sounds, smells that most positively impressed us as children. The farsighted men who wrote and passed the act creating the National Park Service understood that Americans would need places that were touchstones of their existence as a culture, places where wildness and history are paramount. More and more the national parks are the symbols for our national history and natural identity. Reverence and excellence in the stewardship and development of national parks is part of America's heritage.

*A Sense of Place* raises the standards for the next generation of designers. These design guidelines require designers to absorb the essence of Yosemite and employ that understanding in their work. Only then will the resulting design become worthy of Yosemite.

In closing, I am compelled to make a personal comment. I was given the gift of working for the future of Yosemite in many ways, off and on, for nearly 30 years. My experience in striving to give equal to what I got from working in and on Yosemite has compelled me to constantly question what more I could do to protect national parks and open them to the hearts of visitors. I am deeply and emotionally indebted to the authors of these guidelines and the leadership of Yosemite National Park for giving me the opportunity to write a foreword for it. If those of you who use this book will open yourselves to the same opportunity for growth that Yosemite gave to me, then you will be worthy of attempting to design for this most wonderful of places. You must do so with the absolute humility that you have been afforded an opportunity that only a very few will have. You must "buy into" the idea that you are important to Yosemite only insofar as your work deeply and honestly reflects what Yosemite is itself. Your design will affect millions of visitors who come to experience Yosemite. If it detracts in any way, you will have golfed in the cathedral. If it is true to Yosemite, you will have joined the eternal chorus.

JOHN J. REYNOLDS
Retired, National Park Service
Fellow, American Society of Landscape Architects
March 2011

---

*John J. Reynolds had a long and distinguished career in the National Park Service. During his 39 years of service, he served as Deputy Director of the National Park Service, Regional Director of the Pacific West and Mid-Atlantic Regions, Manager of the Denver Service Center, Superintendent of North Cascades National Park, and Assistant Superintendent of Santa Monica Mountains National Recreation Area. In addition to these positions, he spent 15 years as a Landscape Architect/Planner, during which he was Team Captain for the studies leading to the establishment of Bering Land Bridge National Preserve and Kobuk Valley National Park in Alaska, and was Team Captain of the Yosemite General Management Plan. He led the United States Delegation to the World Heritage Committee for three years. As Manager of the Denver Service Center, Reynolds began the sustainability movement in the National Park Service, leading the effort to publish the book* "Guiding Principles of Sustainable Design."

# INTRODUCTION

YOSEMITE NATIONAL PARK is unlike any other place in the world. Its breathtaking scenery has inspired many to describe this singular setting as a masterpiece of nature and Yosemite Valley, its centerpiece, as "the Incomparable Valley." This extraordinary park exhibits a grand assemblage of natural wonders composed of glacially sculpted mountains, immense rock forms, thundering waterfalls, pristine wilderness, serene meadows, and ancient groves of giant sequoias. Cliffs climb 4,000 feet, while soaring granite monoliths and a multitude of domes punctuate the landscape. The park encompasses hundreds of lakes and cascading rivers featuring some of the tallest waterfalls in the world, including Yosemite Falls, which appear to leap from the sky as they descend almost half a mile to the Valley floor. Millions of people from around the globe have made the pilgrimage to experience the park's wonders. Its sublime beauty has galvanized preservationists and inspired painters, poets, and photographers. Yosemite struck John Muir as the "sanctum sanctorum of the Sierra" and the "grandest of all the special temples of Nature." John Muir felt that in Yosemite, "Nature had gathered her choicest treasures" into this one mountain mansion. "No temple made with hands can compare with Yosemite," he exalted.

For thousands of years humans have dwelled in Yosemite. It was the first natural area set aside by the federal government for protection of outstanding scenery and has served as a profound inspiration for preservation philosophy in American and world history. Managed as a park since 1864, Yosemite Valley and The Mariposa Grove of Giant Sequoias are landscapes that reflect the complex interplay in the environment between the natural and the human-made. As places set apart, the park and its wondrous settings continue to evoke reverence and awe in all who visit.

How do people build on what many consider sacred ground? This has been an ongoing challenge for all who have designed facilities in the park. Within this grand setting, people have created a built environment to protect the park's resources and to facilitate enjoyment of them by generations of visitors. Hundreds of historic buildings and structures complement the natural setting and have become part of the total park identity and visitor experience. The National Park Service (NPS) recognizes that to uphold Yosemite as a special place, new facilities must be designed to be compatible and respectful of the park's natural and cultural setting.

OPPOSITE *Half Dome from Sentinel Bridge (1942) YRL-RA*

Today, as park managers continue to influence the park, there is the desire to harmonize the built environment with the natural landscape. These design guidelines have been developed to document, interpret, and understand what has already been built in the park and to provide careful direction for future designs that are compatible with the surroundings. The ultimate goal is to enhance the unique sense of place embodied by this extraordinary park called Yosemite.

## SETTING

Yosemite includes scenery and sights ranging from the spectacular to the sublime. At 1,169 square miles and 748,160 acres, the park is nearly the size of Rhode Island. Yosemite is located in the heart of the Sierra Nevada, a 400-mile-long mountain range that stretches along the eastern flank of California. It constitutes the longest and highest single mountain range in the contiguous United States. The park ranges in elevation from 2,000 feet above sea level at the western foothills to more than 13,000 feet at the crest of the Sierra Nevada to the east. This large park encompasses a wide range of natural environments which each require a unique sensitivity in design. The park includes two major watersheds: the Merced River in the south, passing through Yosemite Valley and Wawona, and the Tuolumne River to the north, flowing through Tuolumne Meadows and feeding the Hetch Hetchy reservoir. Much of the park is a granite wonderland, with sculpted mountain ranges, deep canyons, and hundreds of lakes carved by ice during past episodes of glaciation. Vegetation ranges from the foothills grey pine–chaparral belt in the low elevations to the west, through belts of yellow pine and lodgepole pine–red fir, up to the subalpine and alpine belts with short-growing-season plants above timberline to the east.

The most famous and highly visited portion of the park is Yosemite Valley. Most of the park's development is located within the seven square miles of this area. However, the Valley makes up less than one percent of Yosemite National Park. Beyond Yosemite Valley are several other scenic landscapes and destinations and smaller clusters of facilities, including lodging and campgrounds. Most of the park is undeveloped with 95% of the park being designated wilderness. Visitors enter the park through the three entrances to the west: Arch Rock, Big Oak Flat, and Hetch Hetchy; the entrance to the south: South Entrance; and the entrance from the east: Tioga Pass.

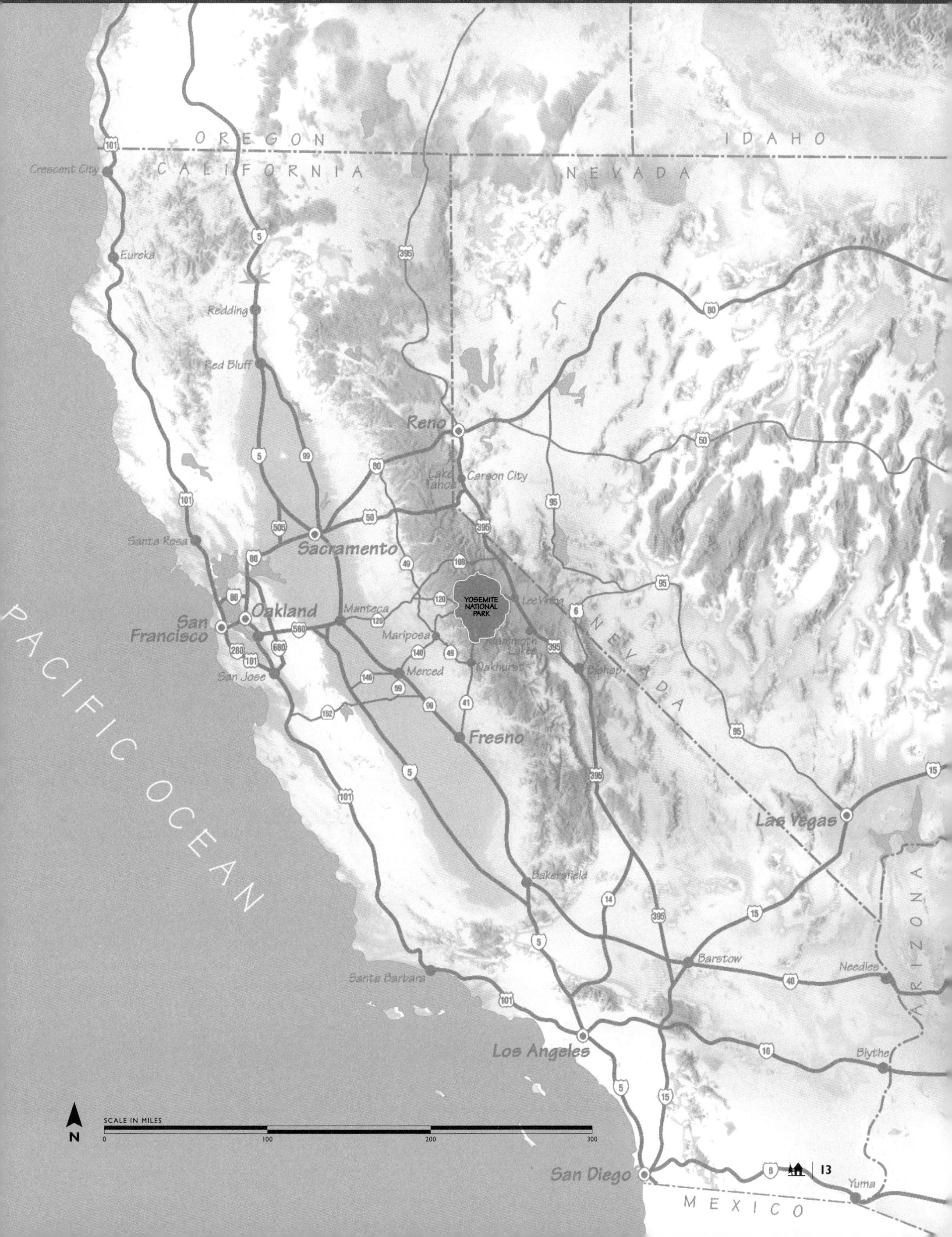
OREGON
CALIFORNIA
IDAHO
NEVADA
ARIZONA
MEXICO
PACIFIC OCEAN
Crescent City
Eureka
Redding
Red Bluff
Reno
Lake Tahoe
Carson City
Sacramento
Santa Rosa
Oakland
San Francisco
San Jose
Manteca
Mariposa
Merced
Oakhurst
YOSEMITE NATIONAL PARK
Lee Vining
Mammoth Lakes
Bishop
Fresno
Las Vegas
Bakersfield
Barstow
Needles
Santa Barbara
Los Angeles
Blythe
San Diego
Yuma
SCALE IN MILES
0
100
200
300
N

Highway 395
Sachse Springs Cabin
Wilma Cabin
YOSEMITE WILDERNESS
Lake Eleanor Reservoir
Frog Creek Cabin
Lake Vernon Cabin
Miguel Meadow Barn
Hetch Hetchy Reservoir
Mt. Conness
Highway 120
Tuolumne River
HETCH HETCHY ENTRANCE
Hetch Hetchy Road
Glen Aulin High Sierra Camp
TUOLUMNE MEADOWS
TIOGA PASS ENTRANCE
White Wolf
Tioga Road
May Lake High Sierra Camp
Tioga Road
Tuolumne Meadows Campground
Tuolumne Meadows Lodge
Highway 120
Snow Flat Cabin
Tenaya Lake
BIG OAK FLAT ENTRANCE
Hodgdon Meadow Campground
Yosemite Creek Campground
Mt. Lyell
HODGDON MEADOW
Porcupine Flat Campground
Olmsted Point
Tuolumne Grove
Snow Creek Ski Hut
Sunrise High Sierra Camp
Vogelsang High Sierra Camp
CRANE FLAT
Tamarack Flat Campground
Merced Grove
YOSEMITE VALLEY
Big Oak Flat Road
Crane Flat Campground
Half Dome
GLACIER POINT
Merced Lake High Sierra Camp
Merced Lake Ranger Station
Tunnel View
Valley Loop Road
Half Dome View
ARCH ROCK ENTRANCE
El Portal Road
EL PORTAL
Merced River Canyon
Highway 140
Glacier Point Road
BADGER PASS
Chinquapin
Bridalveil Creek Campground
YOSEMITE WILDERNESS
Wawona Road
Ostrander Ski Hut
Section 35
Buck Camp Cabin
Wawona Campground
WAWONA
South Fork Merced River
SOUTH ENTRANCE
Mariposa Grove
Highway 41
N
SCALE IN MILES
0
2.5
5
7.5
10
15

*Parsons Memorial Lodge, north facade, Tuolumne Meadows, (2007) GH*

Two hundred and sixty miles of roads connect the various developed areas and allow visitors to explore the park by vehicle. The major through-corridors are an integral part of the visitor's experience of the park: the Wawona, El Portal, and Big Oak Flat Roads and the Tioga Road, a National Scenic Byway. Two other roads are addressed in these guidelines and lead to—and end—at the destinations of Glacier Point and Hetch Hetchy.

Major visitor-use areas in the park outside of Yosemite Valley include Wawona, the giant sequoia groves, Glacier Point, Hetch Hetchy, Tuolumne Meadows, and the highcountry. Wawona, at the southern end of the park, originally served as an overnight stop for visitors traveling from Oakhurst to Yosemite Valley. Architecturally, it features the Wawona Hotel, which is the largest Victorian hotel complex in the national park system and is a designated National Historic Landmark. Nearby is The Mariposa Grove of Giant Sequoias, part of the original 1864 Yosemite Land Grant. It is the largest sequoia grove in the park and arguably the most famous sequoia grove in the world. Two other sequoia groves, the Tuolumne and Merced Groves, are located close to Crane Flat. Glacier Point is east of Chinquapin, and the access road passes by the winter ski area at Badger Pass. The panoramic view from Glacier Point of the Sierra Nevada and Yosemite Valley, over 3,200 feet below, is one of the most spectacular in Yosemite. Hetch Hetchy is accessed by a road branching north near the Big Oak Flat Entrance and features another glacially carved valley similar to Yosemite Valley. Much of it is filled by the reservoir created by the O'Shaughnessy Dam. Tuolumne Meadows, at 8,600 feet, is the largest subalpine meadow in the Sierra Nevada. Tuolumne Meadows is a 55-mile drive from Yosemite Valley and is a favorite starting point for backpacking trips and day hikes, providing easy access to the backcountry, including the six High Sierra Camps arranged along a loop trail.

## PURPOSE

These design guidelines are intended to provide a framework for determining the appropriate architectural and landscape character of new buildings, site work, and alterations. Based on the assumption that the most accomplished and creative practitioners will be tasked with the sensitive requirements of working within the park's setting, these design guidelines go beyond basic universal principles of good design and focus on the "character" qualities that are reflected in and contribute to the distinctiveness of Yosemite.

*Stone wall under construction at Lower Yosemite Fall area (2004) RF*

These guidelines build upon and supersede those of the original 2005 *A Sense of Place: Design Guidelines for Yosemite Valley*, which were critical for the implementation of the many projects in the Valley. This volume expands upon the previous guidelines and covers all of the developed areas in the entire park.

When visitors come to see and experience the magnificent natural beauty of Yosemite, their stay and activities often occur within the developed areas of the park. Their experiences are affected, negatively or positively, by the character and quality of these areas. These guidelines have been established to ensure that the park avoids a piecemeal approach to facility development that would create visual clutter or incoherence in the park. Appropriate design ensures supports a setting in which the values of the park are clarified and reinforced.

The built environment must complement the natural and historic setting, blending in as though part of it, but at the same time being distinctive in a way that emphasizes the special nature of the place. New facilities should be designed in a way that establishes compatibility and continuity with the most successful design elements of the past; there should be a respectful consistency between old and new. The resulting built environments should enrich and become part of the evolving poetry of the Yosemite landscape.

In general, the goals of these design guidelines include:

- Retaining natural site character, including setting, materials, and ecological processes.
- Designing new buildings and facilities to blend with the natural environment, emphasizing nonintrusive design that is sensitive to the site. Facilities fit in with their sites rather than dominate them, and buildings are subordinate to the environment.
- Designing structures and facilities to be compatible with the historic context in which they are located.
- Coordinating and integrating the design of individual structures with those of the site as a whole.
- Enhancing unifying architectural and landscape themes and elements.
- Emphasizing simplicity and restraint in design and respect for past building character, traditions, and practices.
- Recognizing established principles of rustic design within the park and identifying those aspects of rustic design that retain validity today, while allowing for contemporary interpretation of those principles.

IN THE CONSTRUCTION OF ROADS, TRAILS, BUILDINGS, AND OTHER IMPROVEMENTS, PARTICULAR ATTENTION MUST BE DEVOTED ALWAYS TO THE HARMONIZING OF THESE IMPROVEMENTS WITH THE LANDSCAPE. **NPS STATEMENT OF POLICY • 1918**

## HOW TO USE THESE DESIGN GUIDELINES

These design guidelines are a reference for anyone affecting the design of the built environment within the park boundary, including architects, planners, landscape architects, engineers, concessioners, administrators, maintenance personnel, design review staff, and park managers, as they work to create contextually and environmentally appropriate structures and landscapes.

These guidelines are provided to ensure that new park facilities will be compatible with the park's natural and cultural resources. The guidelines will be used by park management, becoming part of a project review process that ensures compatibility of design solutions for buildings and site work as they are proposed. They provide background information on the development and most important design characteristics of the built environment as well as direction for which design strategies and themes may be suitable for a particular area. The guidelines recognize that buildings and the landscape setting are closely interrelated and need to be considered in an integrated fashion to attain a successful solution. The objective is to develop parkwide design themes that are interwoven into specific guidelines for each area of the park, ensuring that the built environment harmonizes with the resources. Park managers can use this manual to reinforce broad visual concepts from one end of the park to the other. Designers should translate parkwide and area themes into project-specific solutions. These themes will be important for guiding design decisions.

The descriptions of the settings within Yosemite and the guidelines in this document are organized by:

- Overarching and unifying parkwide design principles and themes
- Significant developed areas with unique qualities and characteristics
- Significant or dominant characteristics and site-specific characteristics within each distinct geographic area, including common elements and site specific details and features; and
- Resource sensitivities; compatibility issues; and historical patterns

These guidelines are not meant to provide direction in every facet of the visual image of the park, nor are they meant to be a substitute for comprehensive design work by professionals, nor provide for every decision by park management and maintenance personnel. They will serve, however, as a tool to tie the varying areas of the park together into a compatible visual whole.

While protecting recognized values, these guidelines provide sufficient flexibility to accommodate changing times, circumstances, and technologies. They are aids to decision-making and are not intended to be so rigid as to stifle creative expression or reinterpretation of existing design themes and detailing.

Implementation of these design guidelines will contribute to the fulfillment of the overall park goals of resource protection and visitor enjoyment. The results should be the design and construction of buildings and landscapes that integrate seamlessly within the existing landscape of Yosemite. What is added to the setting should provide visual unity and further enrich the visitor experience. The resulting built environment, which will become part of this magnificent setting, should ultimately enhance the remarkable sense of place within Yosemite National Park.

## AGENCY POLICIES + STANDARDS

### National Park Service Management Policies

Familiarity with and understanding of NPS policies and standards will assist designers in implementing the guidelines. Many of those policies articulate how the built environment should protect natural and cultural resources and enhance visitor enjoyment of those resources. The *NPS Management Policies* (2006) provide direction under the "Park Facilities" heading, which echoes the purposes and intent of the design guidelines.

*The Ahwahnee and Half Dome (1941) YRL-RA*

*[F]acilities will be integrated into the park landscape and environs with sustainable designs and systems to minimize environmental impact. Development will not compete with or dominate park features or interfere with natural processes.... If a cohesive design theme is desired, recommended, or required, the theme will reflect the purpose and character of the park, or in a large park...an individual developed area.* NPS MANAGEMENT POLICIES 2006, 9.1.1.2

Curry Village tent cabins
(2004) RF

*Designs for park facilities, regardless of their origin (NPS, contractor, concessioner, or other), will...be harmonious with and integrated into the park environment. They will also be subject throughout all phases of design and construction to the same code compliance; the same high standards of sustainable design, universal design, and functionality.* NPS MANAGEMENT POLICIES 2006, 9.1.1

The most important statutory directive for the National Park Service is provided by interrelated provisions of the NPS Organic Act of 1916 and the NPS General Authorities Act of 1970. The key management-related provision of the Organic Act states:

*[The National Park Service] shall promote and regulate the use of the Federal areas known as national parks, monuments, and reservations hereinafter specified by such means and measures as conform to the fundamental purpose of the said parks, monuments, and reservations, which purpose is to conserve the scenery and the natural and historic objects and the wild life therein and to provide for the enjoyment of the same in such manner and by such means as will leave them unimpaired for the enjoyment of future generations.*

Accordingly, the NPS *Management Policies* directs that "the impairment of park resources and values may not be allowed by the Service unless directly and specifically provided for by legislation or by the proclamation establishing the park." It is important for the planner or designer to produce designs that will not harm the integrity of park resources or values, including the opportunities that otherwise would be present for the enjoyment of those resources or values.

All construction must be accomplished in accordance with applicable codes and accepted standards. This is a federal area, and designers need to consult with the National Park Service about prevailing codes that apply within the park.

## Sustainability

Sustainability is an approach that recognizes that every design choice has an impact on the natural and cultural resources of the local environment as well as regional and global environments. As an agency whose central mission is the protection of both the natural and cultural resources entrusted to it, the NPS has made sustainability an integral part of its design and management philosophy. The agency has an obligation, as well as a unique opportunity, to demonstrate leadership in environmental stewardship.

Vernal Fall (2002) RF

Sustainable design concepts should be incorporated into new construction as well as alterations to historic structures. These concepts include design solutions that seek to minimize long-term impacts to the environment through strategies such as historic preservation and rehabilitation (often the most sustainable option); recycling; reducing material and water consumption; ensuring energy efficiency; providing life-cycle cost analysis; planning for long-term operations; and using vernacular or local construction methods and materials.

The National Park Service is committed to ensuring that the agency remains a leader in implementing sustainable design policies in any park development. Current resources that are helpful include the 2009 Executive Order 13514: *Federal Leadership in Environmental, Energy and Economic Performance*, the NPS publication *Guiding Principles of Sustainable Design* (and other federal and state energy conservation requirements), *The Secretary of the Interior's Guidelines on Sustainability for Rehabilitating Historic Buildings*, and the U.S. Green Building Council's Leadership in Environmental and Energy Design (LEED) program. For larger projects, the National Park Service has used the LEED process to evaluate, rank, and make decisions as part of the design process to optimize the levels of sustainability.

## Historic Buildings, Structures, and Landscapes

The treatment and management of buildings, structures, and landscapes that are on, or determined eligible for listing on, the National Register of Historic Places are covered by NPS policy (Director's Order 28), the National Historic Preservation Act (1966, as amended), and *The Secretary of the Interior's Standards for the Treatment of Historic Properties.*

Planners and designers need to be cognizant of the National Register status of any property as well as the historic property's significance and contributing features.

*Vernal Fall bridge (2011) RF*

*The Secretary of the Interior's Standards for the Treatment of Historic Properties* provides historic preservation guidance for the treatment of historic resources, applicable to all new construction within a historic property, including infill, add-ons, modifications, and replacement of all historic buildings, structures, and other associated landscape features. For new construction in historic areas, a key standard to follow is: "New additions, exterior alterations, or related new construction shall not destroy historic materials that characterize the property. The new work shall be differentiated from the old and shall be compatible with the massing, size, scale, and architectural features to protect the historic integrity of the property and its environment" (NPS 1995c). This requires a sensitive balance between new development that does not exactly mimic yet is still compatible with the historic precedent.

## ACCESSIBILITY + UNIVERSAL DESIGN

The National Park Service is committed to providing access to facilities and programs to as wide an audience as possible. Its policies on accessibility are articulated in Director's Order 42: *Accessibility for Park Visitors*, which states:

> *The NPS will design, construct, and operate all buildings and facilities so they are accessible to, and usable by, persons with disabilities to the greatest extent reasonable, in compliance with all applicable laws, regulations, and standards. This means that all new and altered buildings and facilities will be in conformance with appropriate design standards.*

One fundamental component of this Director's Order is that the National Park Service will seek to provide the highest level of accessibility that is reasonable, and will not simply provide the minimum level required by law. It encourages the implementation of "universal design" principles, whereby everyone enjoys the same form of access instead of being provided separate or special facilities or programs. For historic structures, special consideration must be given to ensure compatibility of any changes with *The Secretary of the Interior's Standards for the Treatment of Historic Properties*.

Additional information on accessibility requirements may be obtained from the NPS project manager and the United States Access Board, which publishes the *Accessibility Guidelines for Outdoor Developed Areas*, along with other accessibility standards.

## PLANNING CONTEXT

Several existing plans provide broad direction for future development within the context of protecting resources and providing for visitor enjoyment of the park. In addition to establishing overall goals, these plans describe parameters for development at specific locations within the park.

In the mid-1970s, the National Park Service began a comprehensive planning process in Yosemite that was completed in 1980 with the approval of the *General Management Plan* and *Final Environmental Impact Statement*. This plan provides basic management direction for Yosemite National Park based on the 1916 Organic Act (the law that established the National Park Service); the park's enabling legislation (the laws that established Yosemite National Park); and the 1958 act that established the El Portal administrative site. The 1980 *General Management Plan* identifies Yosemite's purpose: firstly, to preserve the resources that contribute to Yosemite's uniqueness and attractiveness, and secondly, to make those resources available to people for their enjoyment, education, and recreation, both now and in the future.

The 1980 *General Management Plan* established the following five broad goals to guide the management of Yosemite National Park and perpetuate its natural splendor:

- Reclaim priceless natural beauty
- Promote visitor understanding and enjoyment
- Allow natural processes to prevail
- Markedly reduce traffic congestion
- Reduce crowding

Tunnel View, *Tom Killion, woodcut print, 1999*

Bird-walk group along Merced River (1936) YRL-Ralph Anderson

In support of these goals, the 1980 *General Management Plan* includes several developed area plans (including Yosemite Valley, Tuolumne Meadows, and Wawona) which recommend specific changes to these developed areas. These changes include the removal or modification of roads, buildings, and landscapes and the construction of some new facilities. The 1980 *General Management Plan* still guides planning in Yosemite National Park, and the design of all new facilities should be consistent with it or any subsequent park-approved planning/design documents.

# HISTORY OF DEVELOPMENT IN YOSEMITE NATIONAL PARK

FROM THE EARLIEST time of exploration and pioneer settlement, development at Yosemite National Park has occurred under differing influences and priorities. Sometimes decisions were made that tried to balance opposing goals, such as the expansion of profit and development versus the preservation of aesthetic values and the protection of park resources. The present is a time of great change in Yosemite, particularly in the redevelopment of facilities within the park. This history of the development of Yosemite is important for today's planners, designers, and park management. The lessons of the past call for a high level of responsibility today—to respect what has been accomplished and recognize timeless building principles on behalf of the future.

## AMERICAN INDIAN INHABITATION: PRIOR TO 1833

PRIOR TO 1833

Yosemite National Park has had an estimated 8,000 years or more of occupation by American Indians, represented through an impressive archeological record. They influenced, created, and cultivated much of the landscape encountered by early settlers in 1851.

American Indians, during their long occupation of the Yosemite Valley, built permanent villages in the Valley and winter villages and camps for seasonal hunting, gathering, and fishing. Most of the later-period homes in the Valley were "constructed of pine poles tied with grapevines and covered with overlapping layers of incense-cedar bark.... During the hot summer months, lean-tos covered with bark or brush were used as temporary shelters" (Bates and Lee 1990). The native people also built circular ceremonial houses with earthen roofs supported by oak posts, "forty to fifty feet in diameter, dug to a depth of three or four feet" (NPS 1987b). They built grinding houses of bark slabs, and they kept seed and nut crops like black oak acorns for winter use in chukah, or storehouses built of four or more cedar poles supporting a basket-like structure.

Information about the number of villages in Yosemite Valley is unreliable because it is limited to observations by early settlers, starting with Stephen Powers who in 1877 noted nine villages along the Merced River. Dr. C. Hart Merriam identified 37 past villages in his work from 1917 (Sierra Club 1917). The most important village in Yosemite Valley was just below Yosemite Falls and was known as *Koomine*. During occupation by early settlers, most of the Indian population lived in a village at the mouth of Indian Canyon, near the present-day Yosemite Medical Clinic. (Only six of the 37 villages Merriam counted were inhabited by 1898. Two other villages were located near what is now the NPS maintenance yard and near Sentinel

Rock.) The village at the mouth of Indian Canyon, *Yowatchke* (or the "Old Village"), was where the Mono Lake Paiute often camped, and was occupied by the Yosemite Miwok and Paiute until the mid-1930s. When a part of the village was needed for construction of the Yosemite Medical Clinic, residents were relocated to the "New Village," called *Wahhoga*, which was built in the NPS Rustic style. Eventually all the homes were removed. The last one was razed in 1969.

*Acorn granaries,* chukahs, *below Sentinel Rock (1901)*
*YRL-HW*

Throughout Yosemite, hundreds of archeological sites demonstrate the American Indians' rich association with the park and the region. Within the Valley, much of the archeological record has been damaged by park development. Evidence of American Indian culture is retained in bedrock mortars and pestles, midden deposits, lithic scatters, rock shelters, and an extensive oral history. The Indians of Yosemite still have vital cultural and spiritual ties to the Yosemite landscape, natural resources, and archeological sites.

## EXPLORATION + PIONEER SETTLEMENT: 1833–1864

1833–1864

The first sighting of Yosemite Valley by non-indigenous people was probably made by members of the Joseph Walker Party in 1833. After the discovery of gold in the Sierra Nevada foothills in 1849, thousands of miners came to the region to seek their fortune; their penetration into the native peoples' territory resulted in conflict with the local native groups, who fought to protect their homelands. Because of such interaction, the Mariposa Battalion was organized as a punitive expedition under the authority of the state of California to bring an end to the "Mariposa Indian War." The battalion entered Yosemite Valley while searching for Indians on March 27, 1851. The Indians, led by Chief Tenaya, fled from the Valley in the face of greater firepower. A second expedition in the same year ended in their surrender and relocation to the Fresno River reservation. Chief Tenaya made repeated appeals for the Indian people's return to the Valley, and eventually they were allowed to return to Yosemite, where they became partially integrated with settlers and concessioners.

Although not developed to the extent of Yosemite Valley, the rest of the park also saw expansion by settlers in the 1850s. The popular assumption is that development outside the Valley and on its rims was stimulated by development in the Valley. However, there is evidence of early development in other areas that predates development and the growth of tourism in the Valley. Wilderness studies indicate very early use of park areas by settlers after the gold rush. Before and during the establishment of the tourist trade in the Valley, cattlemen, sheepherders, and miners penetrated into the central and southern Sierra Nevada. In 1850, settlers entered Hetch Hetchy Valley, and soon thereafter cattlemen and sheepherders had explored the forests and meadows of the upland plateaus. In Mariposa, the gold rush brought an influx of miners, packers, businessmen, and camp followers. Following the gold rush, some miners, attracted to the high country south of the Valley, settled in the area, becoming stockmen and hunters.

In the 1850s, publicists, writers, artists, and photographers brought Yosemite to the nation's attention. This led Congress to recognize the value of the Valley and The Mariposa Grove of Giant Sequoias (or "Big Trees") as national treasures. As a result, a steadily increasing stream of visitors came on foot and on horseback. Realizing money could be made from tourism, James Hutchings became one of the first in a long line of Yosemite entrepreneurs. Other business owners contributed to the built environment in and around Yosemite by constructing hotels and residences, by bringing livestock in to graze in the meadows, and by planting orchards. Pioneer architecture was typically vernacular in style and was expressed in the utilitarian log cabins used by stockmen, miners, and loggers. Although V-notched corners prevailed, saddle-notched corners were also used by the pioneers. Roofs were generally covered in split shakes. Because of their availability and ease of splitting, sugar pine shakes were widely used by pioneers on the western slope of the Sierra Nevada. Used on both walls and roofs, and split from bolts averaging 32 inches in length, these shakes have a distinctive long appearance. Boards, if used, were often whipsawn from local trees.

Because the arduous and dusty journey to Yosemite made day visits impossible, early visitors clamored to the California state legislature for hotels with comforts and services similar to those offered at fashionable Atlantic coast seaside resorts. In the 1850s hotels were among the earliest tourist structures in the Valley and were located near the Merced River for the extraordinary views. Such accommodations initially were no more than large barns with stalls for rooms, dirt floors, and open windows. These eventually gave way to two-story framed wood structures constructed of lumber. An exception was J.C. Smith's Cosmopolitan House, which offered "a saloon, billiard hall, bathing rooms, barber shop, mirrors full-length, pyramids of elaborate glassware, costly service, the finest of cues and tables, reading-room handsomely furnished and supplied with the latest from Eastern cities and baths" (Demars 1991). Albeit slowly, hotels did improve and were built within and around Yosemite.

## FROM A STATE PUBLIC TRUST TO A NATIONAL PARK: 1864–1890

In 1864, the federal government ceded to the state of California the Yosemite Grant, which included the Valley and The Mariposa Grove of Giant Sequoias, as a public trust. Early written accounts indicate that the Mariposa Grove, six miles southeast of Wawona, was first encountered by settlers in 1849. Once served by a wagon road, this grove of ancient trees became a popular stopping place for visitors on their way into Yosemite Valley.

In 1865, Frederick Law Olmsted was appointed chairman (and one of eight commissioners) to manage the area protected in the Yosemite Grant. He first set about defining the philosophy of how to manage the grant—an action with consequences for the future Yosemite National Park and other national and state parks. An important element in Olmsted's report was his shaping of the reason for parks to exist, and that the establishment "by government of great public grounds for the free enjoyment of the people...is thus justified and enforced as a political duty" (Olmsted 1865). The Yosemite Grant set a national precedent by becoming the first instance of the government preserving an area for scenic values and public enjoyment. Thus, the Yosemite Grant is recognized as marking the beginning of the national park movement in America, as well as the birth of the California state park system and of other state park systems throughout the country.

*Lamon's log cabin: the first house in Yosemite Valley (date unknown) YRL-TH*

Olmsted's report included suggestions for campgrounds, trails, and accommodations in the park; a good road into the Valley and around the perimeter of the Valley floor with footpaths to scenic points; and a system for funding the park by contract and concession. At Mariposa Grove, he recommended a road to and around the grove as a fire barrier. His plan, however, was expensive and impossible to implement within the constraints of the slim government budgets of the day. The commissioners did rely on Olmsted's report and continued to circulate it in manuscript form at least through the turn of the century. Although they were unsalaried political appointees, most of the commissioners took a strong interest in the management of Yosemite Valley. To the extent there was funding and support, the commissioners planned and managed the resources and facilities of the Valley and frequently denied inappropriate permit requests.

During the 1860s, the commissioners instituted a policy of leasing land for 10-year periods to hotel owners, road and trail developers, and others; these people charged visitors a fee to recover their costs. In the commissioners' view, income from the leases helped offset other costs. After the Valley was made a state grant in 1864, toll roads were built into the park. In the early 1870s, companies constructing toll roads from the communities of Coulterville, Mariposa, and Big Oak Flat raced to be the first to reach Yosemite Valley. The Coulterville & Yosemite Turnpike won, opening in June 1874. The Chinese Camp & Yo Semite Turnpike reached the Valley from Big Oak Flat less than a month later. In 1875, a road from the town of Mariposa to Big Tree Station (Wawona) and on to Yosemite Valley was completed. Of the three toll roads, only Wawona was profitable. Stagecoach service replaced horses as soon as passable roads into the Valley were completed. North of Yosemite Valley, the Great Sierra Consolidated Silver Mining Company built a wagon road to its mines on the Sierra Nevada crest in 1882. The Great Sierra Wagon Road, later called the Tioga Road, was completed in 1883, although it was abandoned shortly thereafter.

With the completion of the Central Pacific Railroad into the San Joaquin Valley in 1869, Yosemite became more accessible to visitors. As early as 1871, developers had wished for rail service to Yosemite both for tourism and to facilitate business enterprise. The Stockton & Copperopolis line transported travelers partway to Yosemite, from Stockton to Milton, where they then transferred to stagecoaches for the rest of the trip. Taking advantage of the Southern Pacific Railroad, the California Lumber Company founded Madera in 1876, "from which a stage road ultimately led via Coarsegold, Fresno Flats (Oakhurst), and Fish Camp to Wawona" (NPS 1987b).

Of the 3,800 visitors to the Valley during the 1888 summer season, more than half stayed at the Stoneman House (1886), a quarter stayed at the Sentinel Hotel, and the rest camped out. In the decades that followed, the number of camping excursions increased, and camping grew in popularity in the Valley. Camping was restricted to parts of the lower Yosemite Valley because administrators had divided up portions of the Valley among permit holders for grazing. Aaron Harris established the first campground in the area of the Lamon's winter cabin, now the area of The Ahwahnee Hotel. Harris' campground lasted until 1886, when the area was leased to Coffman and Kenney for their stables (which were later removed and rebuilt at the current concessioner location). Although the commissioners tried to meet demands for campgrounds by clearing land and seeding it with perennial grasses, they found visitors left campgrounds littered with trash, defaced prominent rocks with inscriptions, cut down or destroyed trees and shrubs, and were careless in the use of fire.

John Muir, a young Scotsman, arrived in San Francisco in 1868 and made his way to Yosemite, where he explored, "studied the animals and weather,...formulated theories on glaciation and began molding his gospel of wilderness—the basic tenets of a philosophy of ecology and conservation that perceived wilderness as a necessity for the sustenance of human existence" (NPS 1987b). As the years passed, he became well known for his theory of the formation of Yosemite Valley by glaciation—as opposed to the popular theory of subsidence—and wrote extensively for national magazines on the origin, beauty, and use of America's wilderness. In 1889, Muir and the editor of The Century Magazine, Robert Underwood Johnson, visited Yosemite Valley and were appalled to find it "despoiled by commercialism and exploitation." Both men felt that the commission's management was inadequate and would ruin the Valley's landscape.

Eventually, sheepherders and the effect of their flocks grazing on the meadows provoked Muir and others to secure a forest reserve surrounding the Yosemite Grant. Muir's articles for *The Century Magazine* brought widespread public attention to the Sierra Nevada and fostered a growing awareness of the threats to the mountain environment. The effort prompted Congress to authorize the establishment of Yosemite National Park in 1890, in great part because of Muir's influence. More than 900,000 acres were thus set aside for the preservation of timber, minerals, meadows, and other "natural curiosities." (This area was reduced in later years when portions of the park were turned over to logging and mining interests.) Not included in the park at that time were the Yosemite Valley and the Mariposa Grove, which remained in the state grant until returned to federal management in 1906.

*Theodore Roosevelt and John Muir at Glacier Point (1903) YRL*

## UNITED STATES ARMY: 1891–1914

Following a congressional battle over civilian administration of Yellowstone National Park, U.S. cavalry were sent to manage Yellowstone in 1886. The cavalry became the park manager for Yosemite National Park a few years later. They were well-organized, equipped for long periods of field work, and needed a substitute for maneuvers in a time of few military conflicts. In May 1891, when the cavalry arrived in Wawona to administer the newly created park, their chief mission was to control access and to prevent intrusions by miners, loggers, trappers and hunters, cattlemen, and sheepherders. Responsible for the entire park except for the Valley and Mariposa Grove (which were still under state administration until 1906), the army was generally motivated by a policy of "patrol and control" (Farabee 2003). Initially, cavalry troops erected basic facilities for seasonal use and patrolled the park only in the summer months. Temporary summer quarters were established near Wawona, and in 1906 the army moved its headquarters and operations to the Valley after the Valley and the Mariposa Grove were both consolidated into the surrounding national park. There the army set up a post on the site of the American Indian village of *Koomine*, near Lower Yosemite Fall. In addition to a system of patrol cabins, roads, trails, and bridges, the army also constructed campgrounds and administration buildings. Their buildings were designed and erected either from Quartermaster Corps standardized plans or as vernacular buildings using local materials. The army knit together ancient trails to form patrol routes and developed new circulation patterns, "with most of the main features of today's system laid down by 1914" (NPS 1987b).

In 1897–98, in an attempt to manage the use of public campgrounds and prevent damage to the park's natural resources, the state erected a number of tents for rent. This marked the beginning of tent camps like Curry Village, established by David A. Curry in 1899, that offered tent accommodations to guests. After return of the Valley to federal control in 1906, the army conducted a study of the water, roads, and sanitation needs. Because sewage was dumped into the river below the Sentinel Hotel, campgrounds below the hotel were closed in 1908. The campgrounds east of the Sentinel were slowly developed with garbage pickup, drinking water, and sewer facilities. Eventually, 20 numbered campgrounds were located in the Valley; most of these have been given place names, removed, or replaced by other visitor facilities, with the exception of Camp 4.

Incorporated in 1902, the Yosemite Valley Railroad approached the park from Merced through the Merced River canyon and by 1907 reached El Portal. The company also built a stage road from El Portal into the Valley; travelers from El Portal transferred to a stage line for the final leg of their trip. Most visitors took this shorter route, causing the other stage lines to decline. In 1914, eight years after California receded control of Yosemite Valley and the Mariposa Grove to the federal government, civilian park rangers took over management of the park from the cavalry.

## NATIONAL PARK SERVICE PLANNING: 1914–1940s

1914–1940s

Planning for the National Park Service began in late 1914, when Stephen Mather was informally offered the leadership of a yet-to-be-formed agency to administer the nation's parks by Secretary of the Interior Franklin Lane. After formation of the National Park Service in 1916, Mather took time to meet his superintendents, conduct a national publicity campaign to educate the public about national parks, buy the long-abandoned Tioga Road as a gift to the federal government for Yosemite, and develop an organizational structure for the new agency. Under his leadership, the Rustic style of architecture was established by the National Park Service as the standard in the planning and development of park facilities from 1916 into the 1940s. It was "based on a canny combination of pioneer building skills and techniques, principles of the Arts and Crafts movement, and the premise of harmony with the landscape" (USFS 2001). The Rustic style relied on natural materials like native stone, timbers, shakes, and shingles. Buildings were designed to fit the topography of the land. Director Mather's desire to make Yosemite the showplace of the national park system, as well as his goal of relocating Yosemite Village to a new site on the north side of the Valley, precipitated a lengthy study on the design of new park structures. Other goals included establishing a strong landscape architecture division for the agency to ensure that structures would be in harmony with their surroundings.

*U.S. Cavalry at The Mariposa Grove of Giant Sequoias (1899) YRL*

Primary design features of the NPS Rustic architectural style in Yosemite included heavy hewn logs; carefully detailed river-washed cobble-and-boulder masonry work; heavy shake roofs; and natural colors. Picking up on the earlier pioneer theme, designers consistently used sugar pine shake on roofs and side walls of administration buildings, utility buildings, and residences in the Valley and throughout the park. They used a palette of shakes, lap siding, and stone to create banding patterns on side walls. Sugar pine shakes were used to create alternate bands of long and short lengths; alternating courses of sugar pine shakes and cedar shingles were also used on many residential structures in Yosemite Village. Other building features were often oversized to harmonize with elements of Yosemite's enormous cliffs and peaks. With dark-brown stained walls displaying foundation plantings and vegetation screening, these buildings were unobtrusive and blended well with their surroundings. The "log cabin in the wilderness" look evolved into a mature style and was emulated nationwide in other parks.

Within Yosemite Village is one of the largest and most significant collections of NPS Rustic-style buildings in the national park system. Early examples of the NPS Rustic style include the administration building (1924), the museum (1926), and the post office (1924). The Rangers' Club (1920) was a gift from Stephen Mather to the National Park Service and is an example of the Stick style, a variant within the NPS Rustic style. Mather's association with the building is significant in its own right and gains importance because the building represents his commitment to a national architectural style for park buildings. Refer to the "Development of a Design Ethic" section in the "Unifying Elements" chapter for a detailed discussion of the NPS Rustic style.

Although protection of natural resources was a concern, development for visitor use was also an issue of tremendous importance. Mather recognized that attracting visitors to the national parks meant building facilities to accommodate a wide range of visitors. He immediately understood that the National Park Service had to educate people about parks and that doing so would encourage them to fall in love with the parks. His philosophy of providing visitors with the chance to see the resources without hardships contributed to Yosemite Valley becoming the focus for most visitors. A promoter of Yosemite's premier lodging in the Valley, The Ahwahnee and its bungalows, Mather also supported continued development of Camp

*Yosemite Superintendent W.B. Lewis, Curry Company Director A.B.C. Dohrman, an NPS architect, Curry Company president Don Tresidder and architect Gilbert Stanley Underwood hold large rendering of The Ahwahnee (1925) YRL*

Curry (established in 1899) to offer tents and more modest accommodations. Until 1907, when the Yosemite Valley Railroad was completed, tourist operations were seasonal, with few winter occupants. (The Yosemite Valley Railroad stopped running in 1945 after lumber and mining operations along the route were closed down and the railroad's mail service contract was cancelled.) Following World War I, the National Park Service encouraged Yosemite's concessioner to develop and offer winter sports to sustain winter operations. Camp Curry offered an excellent location for such development. Located on the south side of the Valley, Camp Curry was the best place for long-lasting ice skating, tobogganing, and ski-joring (being pulled on skis by horses). Within the winter shadow, there is daylight but no direct sunlight, providing a consistently cool microclimate.

In 1916 the Desmond Park Service Company, later the Yosemite National Park Company, was granted a 20-year concession to operate camps, stores, and other services in the park. The company had also begun construction of mountain chalets, forerunners of the current High Sierra Camps. Until this time, visitors to the backcountry either carried their own gear or relied on pack trains. In 1924, in an attempt to lure visitors into the backcountry, the National Park Service began promoting the opening of the High Sierra Camps. Located within one day's walk of each other, the camps offered food and cheap lodging along a grand High Sierra loop that included Merced Lake, Boothe Lake, Tuolumne Meadows, Glen Aulin, and Tenaya Lake. Six camps remain: Tuolumne Meadows, May Lake (which replaced Tenaya Lake), Glen Aulin, Sunrise (established in 1961), Vogelsang (which replaced Boothe Lake), and Merced Lake.

The Big Trees Lodge was established in 1920 at the Mariposa Grove. Other hotel facilities constructed in the park during that time include the White Wolf Lodge on the Tioga Road, built in 1926 and operated privately by the John Meyer family until it was purchased for the park. The Wawona Hotel was acquired by the National Park Service, and new furnishings and equipment were purchased by the concessioner in 1932. The Glacier Point Hotel overlooked the Valley and was later destroyed by fire. At Hetch Hetchy, construction of the dam also attracted visitors who stayed at the Hetch Hetchy Lodge. Operated on U.S. Forest Service land at Mather by a concessioner, the City of San Francisco bought the lodge and opened it as Camp Mather, part of a summer resort.

In 1932 the concessioner and the Sierra Club pushed the National Park Service to develop a system of winter huts and ski trails, leading to the development of Badger Pass and the Chinquapin area for skiers. Eventually, the Ostrander Ski Hut, designed as a touring shelter and built by the Civilian Conservation Corps in 1940, became an integral part of winter recreation at Yosemite.

Earlier trails were extended on and around the Yosemite Valley rim and established overlooks. Backcountry trails were built by the army for patrolling and later by the National Park Service for visitor enjoyment. Using hand labor and with few explosives or heavy equipment, these early trails were designed and planned to blend with the environment and to follow the topography.

Although the first automobiles entered Yosemite in 1900, they were banned from the park in 1907 in response to increased road use and then readmitted in 1913. By the 1920s, auto tourism created the demand for better and more direct roads into the Valley. In 1926, the state completed the All-Year Highway to El Portal and improved the Arch Rock entrance into the Valley. In the 1920s and 1930s, the federal government reconstructed the major park roads for automobile traffic. The Wawona Road was rebuilt, and much of the Big Oak Flat Road was relocated and rebuilt for safety, heavier traffic, and higher speeds. Four tunnels were built to avoid scarring of the Valley walls, and overlooks were constructed for visitors to take in the scenery. Also in the early 1930s, the western portion of Tioga Road was relocated south, connecting White Wolf and Crane Flat, instead of farther north through Aspen Valley. The army, to some extent, and the National Park Service, in particular, took care to build tunnels, bridges, and stone retaining walls to blend with the land. Significant for engineering and aesthetic reasons, the roads in Yosemite harmonize with their natural surroundings in the use of natural materials for road-related structures built in the Rustic style.

Cascades Civilian Conservation Corps camp (since removed) (ca. 1930) YRL

## CIVILIAN CONSERVATION CORPS: 1933–1942

President Franklin D. Roosevelt's answer to the Great Depression was the initiation of New Deal programs in 1933. The Civilian Conservation Corps (CCC), one of the relief programs to grow out of the New Deal, was responsible for much of the development in Yosemite National Park between 1933 and 1942. During the years the CCC program was in place, the park enjoyed a boom period of development and construction. The six CCC camps established in Yosemite were among the first organized in the west. Their projects included road cleanup, signs, borders, bridges, stream channel cleanup, erection of telephone lines, insect and erosion control, fire protection, building construction, and trail building. All CCC work in natural areas of the national park system was "planned and overseen by landscape architects, park engineers, and foresters" (NPS 1983). Their activity was widespread and included all the park's developed areas, with particular attention given to the Valley, where their work was characterized by careful craftsmanship and the use of natural materials in the Rustic style. CCC projects emphasized harmonious design using natural, local materials like wood and stone. Soon, structures of log and stonemasonry outnumbered earlier vernacular structures. The labor-intensive CCC work focused on a beautification program in the Yosemite Village, which included removing deteriorated buildings; installing log curbing; extensively planting native ferns, trees, and shrubs around buildings and campgrounds; and maintaining trees. Although the Civilian Conservation Corps was very active in flood recovery after the 1937 flood, one of their main jobs was cleaning up after the Yosemite Lumber Company, which logged in the southwest part of the park, and the Yosemite Sugar Pine Lumber Company in the northwest. Forestry work led easily to insect work and the elimination of species like the gooseberry to help prevent blister rust in Yosemite forests.

Another New Deal program, the Public Works Administration (PWA), completed capital improvements such as bridges, culverts, roads, and buildings using skilled labor and NPS design standards. PWA projects were unique because they were based on master plans initiated by Director Mather. In Yosemite, PWA projects were completed in four main areas: park headquarters in Yosemite Valley; Glacier Point (overlooking the Valley); Wawona; and Tuolumne Meadows. Enlarging and raising the O'Shaughnessy Dam at Hetch Hetchy by 85.5

feet was another PWA project, albeit administered by the City of San Francisco. PWA designers also devoted a great deal of attention to housing at Yosemite, building a number of residences, apartments, and duplexes. Development extended to buildings and a campground at Tuolumne Meadows; cabins for the Indian Village; Chinquapin; and the construction of fire lookouts at Henness Ridge and Crane Flat.

## MISSION 66: 1956–1970

With the onset of the U.S. entering World War II in 1941 and the subsequent disbanding of the CCC camps, little development occurred in Yosemite from the 1940s until 1956. From its origins in the early 20th century until the development of the Mission 66 initiative, the National Park Service had relied on residential-scale administration buildings or structures in nearby towns to provide information to visitors. Mather's goals for the National Park Service also included establishing a strong landscape architecture division to ensure that structures would be in harmony with their surroundings. Although some ranger stations were located at entrances, others were located in the backcountry and thus were inaccessible to visitors arriving by automobile. Employee housing was of substandard quality, with inadequate living conditions. Most of the public facilities and services, including hotels, restaurants, and guided tours, were provided by concessioners. The sharp rise in park visitation by visitors freed from the constraints of World War II quickly placed natural and cultural resources at risk from overuse and mistreatment. In 1945, 11.7 million people visited the parks, and by 1956, this number jumped to 61.6 million visitors (Wirth 1980).

In 1956 Congress authorized a 10-year program of planning and construction known as Mission 66. This broad-reaching program of service-wide improvement was anticipated to be accomplished within 10 years, to coincide with the fiftieth anniversary of the National Park Service (giving rise to the program's name). The initiative, orchestrated by NPS Director Conrad Wirth, focused on a program of park development, infrastructure improvement, and resource protection that would "overcome the inroads of neglect and...restore to the American people a national park system adequate for their needs" (Wirth 1980).

The design philosophy of Mission 66 was a radical departure from the Rustic-style heritage of the National Park Service. The new style was based on a more contemporary, progressive architectural design and functionalism, employing the latest materials and technology. Mission

66 visitor centers used contemporary architectural forms and materials to fulfill a variety of functions, including providing spaces for interpretive talks, park administrative offices, and visitor services. Prominently sited at a major entry or other strategic point, the buildings became an instantly recognizable feature of the parks. Like visitor centers, ranger stations were also sited for easy automobile access and were the initial point of visitor contact and orientation in developed areas. The stations were designed to provide visitors with information, services, and orientation. They also provided an official presence in isolated areas of development and often served as the first official point of contact within the park boundaries.

Employee housing was an acute problem, as a projected doubling of the park's workforce was anticipated and, in other large western parks as well as Yosemite, the only available private-sector housing was an hour or more away. Standardized designs were developed for new housing, typically expressed by the NPS in this region as low, rectangular, horizontal forms similar to the low-cost housing found in suburban communities. Housing units had a shallow gable or flat roof with deep overhangs to accentuate the buildings' horizontal character. Carports or garages were common elements.

In the West, the variety of property types represented in the Mission 66 program included residential units, ranger stations, campgrounds, picnic shelters, maintenance areas, comfort stations, and circulation systems such as road networks, airstrips, and boat launches. The Mission 66 program at Yosemite created a new Valley Visitor Center and other visitor facilities and services. The program enlarged roads, parking areas, and campgrounds and constructed many new motel units. Visitation to Yosemite exceeded one million in 1954, and doubled that number by 1976. The post-war tourism boom continued unabated, and impacts in the Valley soon became apparent. To counteract these impacts, the NPS purchased the El Portal Administrative Site in 1958 with the expectation that park and concessioner administrative functions and employee housing could be removed from the Valley and placed in El Portal.

*Valley Visitor Center at Yosemite Village (2004) RF*

The last 21-mile stretch of the Tioga Road between White Wolf and Cathedral Peak was rebuilt in the late 1950s and was the largest Mission 66 project in Yosemite National Park. It became the focus of opposition by the Sierra Club and other activists who disagreed with the design and construction of a road that required blasting and scarring the glacially polished granite surfaces at Olmsted Point and Tenaya Lake. Despite the controversy, the road was "carefully designed to display to the fullest the dramatic assets of the Sierra Nevada. [It was]... well supplied with overlooks and interpretive signs" (NPS 1987b).

In the early 1970s, the National Park Service established one-way road traffic patterns, eliminated cars in the far-east end of the Valley, offered free shuttle bus transportation in the Valley, converted the parking lot in front of the Valley visitor center to a pedestrian mall, and generally encouraged visitors to enjoy the park on foot or by using public transportation.

## RECENT CHALLENGES: 1980 TO PRESENT

1980 TO PRESENT

Started in 1975 and completed in 1980, Yosemite's General Management Plan (GMP) articulated the need for parkwide visitor services, resource management, interpretation services, concessions management, and park operations. The GMP established a plan that called for the eventual removal of private vehicles from Yosemite Valley and a reduction in development by relocating nonessential facilities out of the Valley. After approval of the GMP, several projects occurred during the 1990s that implemented the goals of the plan. Two projects moved facilities out of Yosemite Valley by relocating them to the Rancheria section of the El Portal Administrative Site at the western edge of the park. These projects included the construction of the NPS Maintenance/Warehouse complex to enable removal of the old warehouse and maintenance shops in the Valley, and construction of new housing units consisting of a mix of single-family residences and apartments. Per the GMP, infrastructure was also improved in Wawona with the completion of new water and wastewater treatment plants on the hillside above the ranger station.

Early January of 1997 brought a major natural event in the history of Yosemite that had a profound effect on the built environment. A moisture-laden tropical storm brought warm, heavy rains that melted the deep snowpack in the Yosemite highcountry. The combination of torrential rains and melting snow resulted in a historic flood: the Merced River overflowed its banks and flooded much of the Valley, including lodging facilities, employee housing, campgrounds, and

*Flooding at Lower Pines Campground, Yosemite Valley, (1997) YRL-ST*

administrative offices. Portions of park roads, utilities, trails, and bridges were washed away during the devastation. The park was closed for two and a half months, during which time visitors were evacuated, temporary services were put in place, and damage was assessed.

A major effort was required to repair the damage from this flood event. The United States Congress, acknowledging the magnitude of the necessary work, appropriated $178 million to help Yosemite recover from the flood. This was the largest appropriation in history made to a single national park. A flood recovery team was assembled and worked with the rest of the park for the next several years on scores of simultaneous projects to remove damaged infrastructure and facilities and then replace, restore, relocate, and/or improve them. This major undertaking resulted in the repair or reconstruction of a variety of facilities, including miles of roads, trails, bridges, utilities, lodging, concessioner employee housing, and administrative offices. Some of the infrastructure, such as the utilities and employee housing, was relocated out of sensitive areas such as the floodplain, rockfall zone, meadows, oak woodlands, and the Merced River bed. A few of the noteworthy projects include the reconstruction of the heavily damaged El Portal Road from the park boundary to the intersection with Big Oak Flat Road, the rehabilitation of the deteriorating utility lines in Yosemite Valley, and construction of the 28-building Curry Village Employee Housing.

During this period of time, other funding sources were developed that had an impact on the rehabilitation or improvement of park facilities. The Recreation Fee program, covering the period from September 2004 through December 2014, was approved by Congress as the Federal Land Recreation Enhancement Act and was an outgrowth of the earlier successful Fee Demonstration Program authorized by Congress in fiscal year 1996. This program enabled the park to retain and use 80% of the entrance fees collected at the park gates to pay for programs and improvements that benefit park visitors. This translated to several million dollars per year, and the funds have been used for a multitude of projects that both address deferred maintenance and benefit park visitors, such as rehabilitating and improving the safety of the entrance stations into the park, rehabilitating the historic buildings in the core of Curry Village, and making improvements throughout the park to enhance universal accessibility.

The concessions Capital Improvement Fund was set up as part of the contract with the primary park concessioner to use a portion of the revenues to maintain, rehabilitate, and improve facilities managed by the concessioner. This program also generates several million dollars per year, and has been used to address capital improvement and component replacement needs at lodging facilities, stores, restaurants, utilities, and concessioner employee housing. Many of these properties are historic, so these projects often provide for the rehabilitation of culturally significant buildings and sites in the park. One of the noteworthy larger Capital Improvement Fund projects was the closure of The Ahwahnee Hotel for six weeks in 2011 to allow for improvements in fire and life/safety, such as fire detection/alarm/sprinkler systems and fire egress.

NatureBridge, the primary park educational partner, was founded in 1971 to offer an outdoor environmental education program for students, connecting them with the natural world and encouraging them to become future stewards of the environment. In 2002 NatureBridge embarked on planning and design for an environmental education center to replace the aging CCC era facilities at Crane Flat. A previously disturbed site at Henness Ridge was identified as an appropriate new location for a replacement facility that would provide an immersive outdoor education experience for young students. Plans were developed for a national role-model learning center that embodies sustainable strategies for materials, site work, and energy conservation. In addition to striving for a Gold LEED rating, the design minimizes grading by strategically working with the topography for circulation routes and placement of cabins and communal buildings. With reference to the Design Guidelines, the buildings will use simple forms with protected entranceways; materials will feature concrete bases, vertical wood siding, and metal roofs.

In 1988 the Yosemite Fund was established as the primary fundraiser for the park. By 2010 it had raised $55 million to support over 300 projects. In 2010 it merged with the Yosemite Association to become the Yosemite Conservancy. The Yosemite Association was founded in 1923 and was the nation's first "cooperating association," as well as the first nonprofit organization within a national park in the United States and the world. The Yosemite Conservancy has developed a program of providing donated funds to support the park in resource managment and improving park facilities heavily used by park visitors. The first large project was the 1997 Glacier Point restoration project. This was followed by the Lower Yosemite Fall project, a $13.5 million joint effort with the park service to improve the trails, viewing areas, bridges, signage, interpretive exhibits, universal accessibility, ecological restoration, comfort stations, and overall visitor experience at Lower Yosemite Fall, the most popular natural destination in the park. Renowned landscape architect Lawrence Halprin was commissioned to design the project, which was completed in 2005. The intent of the design was to retain the presence and character of the natural setting while accommodating large numbers of people. Several

Lower Yosemite Fall bridge (2005) RF

design objectives to improve the visitor experience and better protect the natural setting were achieved. They included replacing the parking area with a natural vegetated open area and picnic area; defining the edges of the walkways with stone edging; providing seating areas with granite pavers, boulders, and large wood-log benches; installing universally accessible footbridges that provide enough clearance to not hinder the flow of Yosemite Creek; replacing the cinder-block comfort station with a contemporary Rustic-style stone and wooden structure; improving views of Yosemite Falls, Yosemite Creek, Half Dome, and Sentinel Rock; adding a consistent wayside exhibit and signage system; and providing a one-mile scenic loop trail throughout the entire area.

2006 was the start of the Campaign for Yosemite Trails, a five-year program to restore miles of trails. Other completed projects included the remodeling of the Valley Visitor Center and bookstore, as well as the renovation of the exhibit hall to include new exhibits; and repairs and improvements to the viewpoints at Olmsted Point, Tunnel View, and Half Dome View. Currently, planning is under way to provide natural restoration and improve the visitor experience at two very popular visitor destinations—Tenaya Lake and The Mariposa Grove of Giant Sequoias.

All of the recent projects involving removal, repair, rehabilitation, reconstruction, or new design demonstrate the ever-changing nature of the built environment in Yosemite National Park. As of present, implementation of the *General Management Plan* continues, with several subordinate plans under development as well. Work is currently under way to develop plans for the two major rivers in the park: the Merced Wild and Scenic River and the Tuolumne Wild and Scenic River. The present time offers continuing opportunities and challenges, one of which is to bring about the changes outlined in the *General Management Plan* with the awareness that today's work will be critically judged by future generations. Designers can recognize the park's architectural and natural heritage in a manner that acknowledges and honors the work of those who came before, while learning from the past and improving park facilities appropriately.

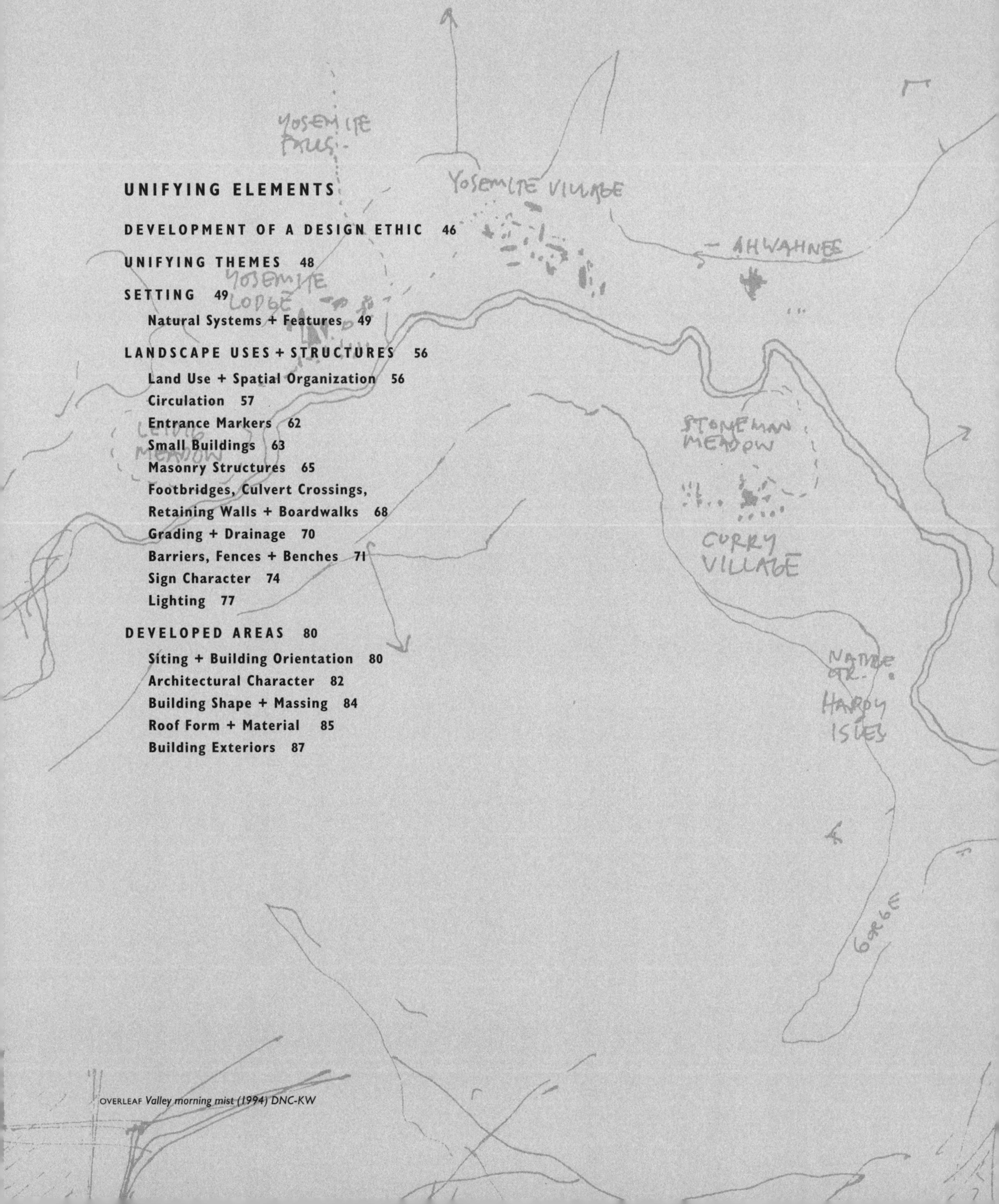


## UNIFYING ELEMENTS



OVERLEAF *Valley morning mist (1994) DNC-KW*

# UNIFYING ELEMENTS

THIS CHAPTER DESCRIBES unifying elements—both natural and human-made—that thread through the park and contribute to a unified sense of place. The guidelines that follow are recommendations for the design of new development that respects and builds upon the unifying elements.

This chapter includes three sections that address: Setting, Landscape Uses + Structures, and Developed Areas. Setting contains discussions of natural systems and features, views, and vegetation. The Landscape Uses + Structures section includes land use and spatial organization, circulation,

NEVER BEFORE HAVE I SEEN SO GLORIOUS A LANDSCAPE, SO BOUNDLESS AN AFFLUENCE OF SUBLIME MOUNTAIN BEAUTY...THE NOBLE WALLS SCULPTURED INTO ENDLESS VARIETY OF DOMES AND GABLES, SPIRES AND BATTLEMENTS AND PLAIN MURAL PRECIPICES—ALL A-TREMBLE WITH THE THUNDER TONES OF THE FALLING WATER. **JOHN MUIR**

and individual elements in the human-made landscape, including smaller structures. The Developed Areas section covers siting and building orientation, architectural character, and building appearance. In each section, these unifying elements are identified and described, and guidelines are identified.

Following this chapter, there are chapters on each developed area and recurring facility type in Yosemite National Park. The site-specific guidelines in those chapters flow from—and are supported by—the Unifying Elements.

## Development of a Design Ethic

From the earliest years of the national parks, design efforts were based on philosophical premises about the nature of the national parks themselves. Parks were separate from the surrounding world, and visitors to the parks expected to experience a different environment. Although there would be inevitable differences among the parks, the general goal was that across any particular park, all the developments had to share enough elements to give them a recognizable unity (NPS1989b). Architectural and landscape design contributed to realizing this premise.

Those charged with overseeing both protection and visitor use of Yosemite recognized early on that any design within the park required a different and measured approach. The chair of the Yosemite Commission, Frederick Law Olmsted, proposed farsighted guidelines for the management of Yosemite and the Mariposa Grove in a Preliminary Report dated 1865. Olmsted, regarded as the father of American landscape architecture, wrote the following:

> *The first point to be kept in mind then is the preservation and maintenance as exactly as is possible of the natural scenery; the restriction, that is to say, within the narrowest limits consistent with the necessary accommodation of visitors, of all artificial constructions and the prevention of all constructions markedly inharmonious with the scenery or which would unnecessarily obscure, distort or detract from the dignity of the scenery. (Olmsted 1865)*

In a similar spirit during the early years of the agency, Secretary of the Interior Franklin K. Lane wrote a letter in 1918 expressing an approach for park design to Stephen T. Mather, the first director of the National Park Service. This became a statement of NPS policy:

> *In the construction of roads, trails, buildings, and other improvements, particular attention must be devoted always to the harmonizing of these improvements with the landscape. This is a most important item in our programs of development and requires the employment of trained engineers who either possess knowledge of landscape architecture, or have a proper appreciation of the aesthetic value of park-lands. All improvements will be carried out in accordance with a preconceived plan developed in special reference to the preservation of the landscape.*

Mather was committed to developmental planning and believed in the importance of preserving the parks' natural scenery as much as possible while opening them to visitor use. One of his first steps was to establish a landscape architecture division to ensure that park structures would be in harmony with their surroundings. By the mid-1920s, Mather had instituted a program whereby park superintendents integrated and controlled new developments by planning them over a five-year period.

For Yosemite, Mather envisioned a cohesive park building program for rustic structures that included a grand lodge. He was concerned with the visual effects of the built environment on natural scenery. According to his vision for the park, buildings were not designed to be dominant elements in the landscape but instead were to blend with the natural environment.

Doctor's residence, Yosemite Village (2004) RF

LEFT *Stephen Mather, first director of the NPS, with a model of Yosemite Village (ca. 1925) YRL* RIGHT *Washington Lewis, first superintendent of Yosemite National Park, and Stephen Mather, Director of the NPS, in new Yosemite Village (1924) YRL*

Following Mather, Horace Albright, the second director of the National Park Service, agreed with preservationists that Yosemite Valley appeared overdeveloped and was filled with a hodgepodge of unsightly, unrelated structures. He ordered the relocation of administrative functions to a new Yosemite Village north of the Merced River, away from the floodplain. There was strong desire by park planners to rebuild Yosemite's facilities in an organized and aesthetic manner. Mather specified the use of rustic structures appropriate to the natural environment. These plans set the basic premises for park facility planning and aesthetics throughout the national park system. The park planners included a unified vernacular architectural theme; strong visual relationships between public spaces and nearby natural features; zoning of residential, public, and commercial areas; and a hierarchy of different street types (NPS 2004h).

The National Park Service was instrumental in creating an architectural vernacular of rough-hewn, rustic design using on-site materials such as boulders, cobbles, shakes, and peeled logs. Referred to as the National Park Service (NPS) Rustic style, it flourished between 1916 and 1942. The style was an expression of the philosophy that buildings should be in harmony with the landscape and in harmony with each other. Virtually everyone involved in early national park management agreed that proposed architectural development should blend and harmonize with the surroundings.

Buildings that are associated with the Rustic style may display individuality but include several similar characteristics. They often included adherence to a comprehensive plan; deference to the natural environment; and careful siting to develop strong visual ties with the surrounding setting, especially orientation to views. The physical characteristics of such architecture included natural materials and expression of texture, such as natural wood siding; wood-shingled roofs; heavily rusticated or boulder masonry; and peeled-log walls, columns, and trusses. Rustic buildings also often display hand craftsmanship, are small in size, and incorporate historical details. Within Yosemite Village, oversized stones and logs were used in construction to fit the mass of the buildings into the setting, horizontal lines were used to lower the profile of the structures, and vegetation was often massed along the foundations of structures to blend with the surrounding landscape.

The Rustic style grew out of and reinterpreted elements of several architectural movements, including the American Arts and Crafts movement, the Shingle style, the Adirondack style, the Prairie style, and regional styles of design. In Yosemite National Park, influences included the Bay Area and West Coast bungalow styles, including work by the architectural firm Greene and Greene.

The distinctive Bay Area style of architecture emerged around San Francisco during the first two decades of the 20th century and had a lasting influence on the design of park buildings. One of the leaders of this style was Bernard Maybeck, whose office was responsible for the design of two National Historic Landmark structures in Yosemite—the LeConte and Parsons Memorial lodges. The Bay Area style used local materials and followed principles of siting, hand craftsmanship, harmony with nature and structure, and presentation of scenic views (McClelland 1998). Many of these same features are reflected in Rustic architecture built in other national parks. By the 1920s, when NPS landscape engineers were working out a program of landscape design for national parks, there existed a well-established philosophy for park design drawn from the practices and precedents

El Capitan (1995) RF

Museum, Yosemite Village (1952) YRL-RA

in landscape architecture and architecture in California. During the 1930s, the Civilian Conservation Corps crews within Yosemite followed those practices in the construction of new buildings and structures.

The Mission 66 era of design heralded a rather severe departure from the earlier Rustic style. Mission 66 began in 1956 in response to the deteriorating conditions of national parks during the post-World War II boom in visitation. Mission 66 sought to not only rehabilitate the aging national park system but to modernize it. "Distinctive new buildings adapted various strains of postwar American modernism to the programmatic and aesthetic requirements of the national parks. Postwar park architecture made full use of steel, concrete, prefabricated elements, unusual fenestration, climate control, and other aspects of contemporary architecture" (Carr 2007). Here in Yosemite, Mission 66 projects included the Valley Visitor Center, employee housing, Degnan's Deli, and Yosemite Lodge. Projects in Yosemite also included campground improvements such as new amphitheaters and comfort stations, as well as road expansion—including the highly contentious rerouting of Tioga Road. (Refer to the "Mission 66: 1956–1970" section in the "History of Development in Yosemite National Park" chapter for more detail.)

The built environment in Yosemite National Park today contains examples from every phase of NPS architecture. A range of expression in Rustic design as well as Mission 66 design is represented by both concessioner and NPS-operated buildings.

## Unifying Themes

Several recurring general themes and elements in successful site planning and building design help unify the built environment within Yosemite National Park:

- Developments are planned in a holistic and integrated fashion.
- The patchwork of open meadows, woodlands, forests of varying density and darkness, and vast stretches of unvegetated granitic topography, ranging from level to ruggedly steep to vertical, dominates the built environment.
- NPS and concessioner facilities are typically separated by distance, topography, and/or vegetation.
- Historic structures and sites retain their original use or are compatibly reused.
- Natural systems such as flooding, rockfall, extreme climate, vegetation, and rich soils are important determinants for the location of physical development within the park.
- Siting and orientation of structures take advantage of scenic views as well as protecting important views from other vantage points.
- Buildings are sited to accommodate vegetation.
- Buildings are sited on level or gentle sloping topography to minimize need for grading.
- The design of buildings, landscape structures, and utilities does not dominate the natural setting.
- In general, the use of a Rustic style of architecture is typical of NPS design throughout the park and is an intentional response to the natural surroundings.

CLIMATE IS A MAJOR ECOSYSTEM DRIVER IN THE PARK, AFFECTING THE DISTRIBUTION OF FLORA, FAUNA, AND HUMANS. **NPS 1997**

# SETTING

## NATURAL SYSTEMS + FEATURES

### Climate

Located on the gently sloping west face of the Sierra Nevada, at the midpoint between the northern and southern extremities of the mountain range, Yosemite is characterized by hot, dry summers, cool winters, and deep snow packs at middle altitudes. Average temperatures range from 25 to 89 degrees Fahrenheit in Yosemite Valley (4,000 feet), and from 15 to 70 degrees Fahrenheit in Tuolumne Meadows (8,600 feet).

Most snow falls above 4,000-foot elevations between the months of October and April. Because most of the park's structures are in this zone, snow is a major influence on site design.

Within Yosemite Valley there are distinct microclimates. Curry Village, on the south side of the Valley, lies in the shadow of the adjacent 3,000-foot cliffs for much of the year. Although the winters at Curry Village are cold and damp, the weather is refreshingly cool during the summer. Most of the developed areas—Yosemite Lodge, Yosemite Village, and The Ahwahnee—are at the sunnier, north side of the Valley. The warmer exposures there are welcome during the winter, although it can be very hot during the summer.

**GUIDELINES**

- Building siting, orientation, and design detailing should respond to the unique microclimatic conditions at each site. For example, buildings on the cool, south side of the Valley should be oriented to maximize winter light. Buildings on the north side require shade in the summer. Designers should use passive strategies such as shade, ventilation, and insulation, and avoid a dependence upon the use of refrigerated air conditioning.
- Designers should consider the management of snow and ice for winter access, visitor safety, and structural longevity.

### Natural Light and Sound

The combination of light-colored granite, steep canyons, and the mostly barren slopes of the subalpine zones and peaks of the Sierra Nevada crest creates unique light phenomena. The sun reflecting off the granite on Clouds Rest, Half Dome, and other towering peaks outside the Valley has attracted artists, photographers, and visitors alike since the 1850s. The late afternoon sun occasionally bathes the steep, barren west faces and peaks of the Sierra crest in a famous orange-gold light called alpenglow. The reason John Muir called the Sierra "the range of light" is evident when the luminous, snow-covered crest is seen from California's distant Central Valley.

The absence of abundant artificial light at night provides opportunities to see the brilliant, star-filled night sky, especially away from developed areas. This is an important and integral part of the park experience that will take on increasing significance as California's Central Valley and Sierra foothills continue to urbanize.

In the Yosemite Valley, relatively quiet environments provide contrast to the Valley's roaring falls and the rushing of the Merced River in early spring. In more remote areas, one can take a short walk from the Tioga Road and experience solitude and the subtle sounds of wilderness. The park's natural soundscape is a critical part of the modern-day visitor experience and is important to document and protect.

**GUIDELINES**

- Any new design should ensure the minimization of the impacts of artificial light and sound.
- Refer to "Developed Areas—Siting and Building Orientation" in this chapter for guidelines on sound.
- Refer to "Landscape Uses + Structures—Lighting" in this chapter for guidelines on artificial light.

BUT NO TEMPLE MADE WITH HANDS CAN COMPARE WITH YOSEMITE. EVERY ROCK IN ITS WALLS SEEMS TO GLOW WITH LIFE. SOME LEAN BACK IN MAJESTIC REPOSE; OTHERS, ABSOLUTELY SHEER OR NEARLY SO FOR THOUSANDS OF FEET, ADVANCE BEYOND THEIR COMPANIONS IN THOUGHTFUL ATTITUDES, GIVE WELCOME TO STORMS AND CALMS ALIKE, SEEMINGLY UNAWARE, YET HEEDLESS, OF EVERYTHING GOING ON ABOUT THEM. **JOHN MUIR • THE YOSEMITE • 1912**

## River Systems

The Merced and Tuolumne rivers, with their network of tributary streams and unnamed ephemeral drainages, are central to the park's scenery, recreation, and ecological processes. Both are designated as "Wild and Scenic Rivers" and accordingly are protected for about a quarter mile on either side of the river. Ecological restoration along the rivers' beds and banks to encourage natural flows, channel formation, vegetation, and wildlife habitat is a high priority. Although protection from human impact is the general goal of the Wild and Scenic Rivers Act, facilities and recreation can be compatible. Much of Yosemite's development—Tuolumne Meadows, portions of the Valley, and Wawona—lies within these river corridors.

The Merced and Tuolumne rivers are subject to seasonal floods. On the Merced River there have been at least five severe floods in the last 100 years. Facilities near the rivers have been damaged by flooding at various times throughout the park's history.

*Horsetail Fall (2003) GH*

*Merced River with spring runoff (1943) YRL-RA*

The natural processes of flooding and the slow migration of river channels have resulted in a variety of associated landforms, such as low-lying wetlands and wet meadows. In some areas, bank erosion can temporarily damage or remove riparian vegetation. Valuable riparian and wetland vegetation has also been removed by trampling and riprapping in many places along the rivers, creeks, and other seasonal drainages.

**GUIDELINES**

- Locate new buildings and major landscape structures outside the 100-year floodplain.
- New development should be located to avoid the potential migration of rivers and streams and should be consistent with Wild and Scenic River plans.
- New development should not alter the alignment of natural drainages or cause erosion by altering surface flow.
- Buildings, structures, trails, and utilities should be sited and designed so that they do not interrupt groundwater migration and recharge.

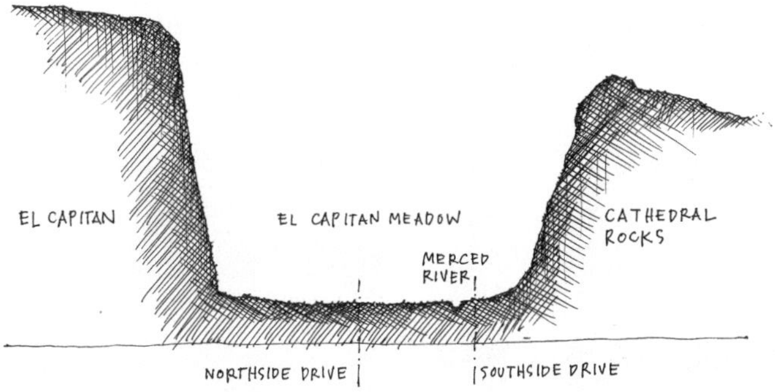


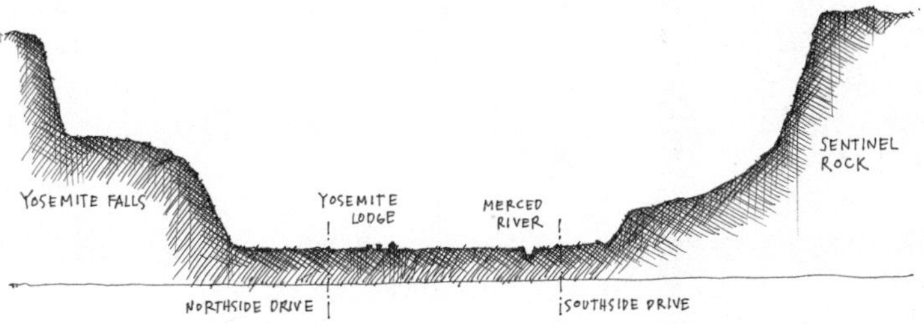


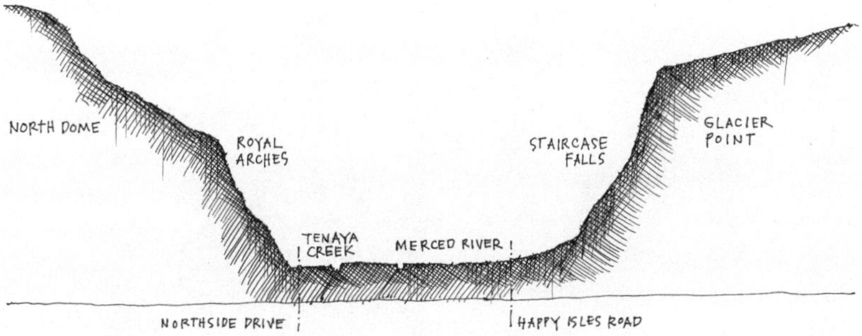


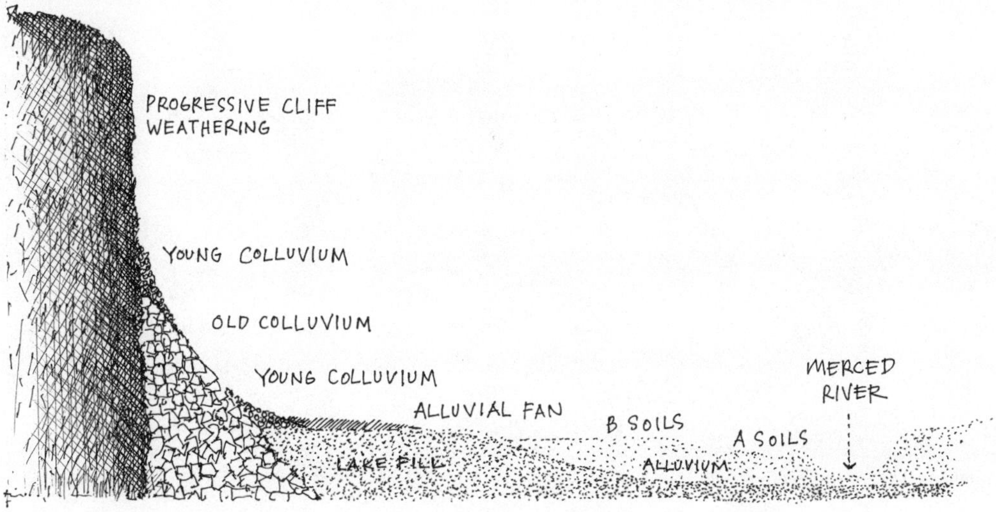


UPPER LEFT *El Capitan (2004) GH* MIDDLE LEFT *Cathedral Rocks with Merced River (2004) GH* UPPER RIGHT + BOTTOM *Cross sections of Yosemite Valley*

ENTERING THE VALLEY, GAZING OVERWHELMED WITH THE MULTITUDE OF GRAND OBJECTS AROUND US, PERHAPS THE FIRST TO FIX OUR ATTENTION WILL BE BRIDAL VEIL, A BEAUTIFUL WATERFALL ON OUR RIGHT. ITS BROW, WHERE IT FIRST LEAPS FREE FROM THE CLIFF, IS ABOUT 900 FEET ABOVE US; AND AS IT SWAYS AND SINGS IN THE WIND, CLAD IN GAUZY, SUN-SIFTED SPRAY, HALF FALLING, HALF FLOATING, IT SEEMS INFINITELY GENTLE AND FINE; BUT THE HYMNS IT SINGS TELL THE SOLEMN FATEFUL POWER HIDDEN BENEATH ITS SOFT CLOTHING. **JOHN MUIR • THE YOSEMITE • 1912**

*Civilian Conservation Corps at work (ca. late 1930s) YRL*

## Vegetation

The complex mosaic of vegetation communities that dominates the landscape of much of the park can be understood as a series of belts stacked along the west slope of the Sierra Nevada range. Although they respond to microclimates, the belts generally conform to elevational differences. The four belts most relevant to Yosemite (the foothill, mixed conifer, red fir, and subalpine belts) range in elevation from the 2,000- to 4,000-foot levels to the short-growing-season levels of 8,000 to 11,500 feet. Although the meadows may vary somewhat in species make-up, they are found in each of these vegetation belts. The meadows in Yosemite National Park are unique, fragile, and have great ecological, scenic, and historic value.

The park's primary policies and approaches related to vegetation management are embodied in the 1997 Yosemite National Park Vegetation Management Plan. The management issues and programs described in the plan include protection, fire, insect infestation and disease, hazard trees, nonnative and invasive species, and revegetation of disturbed sites, among others. This document continues to function as the general guide to vegetation management practices. All actions related to the removal of plants, modifications by trimming, removal of limbs, the addition of new plants, and irrigation and fertilization of plants must comply with this plan. National Park Service management policies regarding vegetation management, as well as the various vegetation studies (e.g., root rot studies, hazard tree removal guidelines, and wetland identification efforts), should also be consulted.

**GUIDELINES**

### *General Vegetation Guidelines*

- New buildings and structures should avoid or minimize the removal or damage of highly valued or healthy vegetation (such as deciduous oaks).
- Consider the age and health of plant communities when siting buildings and other structures. For example, consider locating new buildings and structures in areas where diseased or hazard trees might be approved for removal.

*Cluster of oak trees at meadow edge (1945) YRL-RA*

*Black oak in sunlight (2003) GH*

California black oak (*Quercus kelloggii*)

Winter in Yosemite Valley, *Albert Bierstadt, oil on paper, 1872. Garzoli Gallery, San Rafael, CA*

- Avoid locating new buildings or structures in plant communities where natural processes will be disrupted or disease accelerated.
- Structures to be located adjacent to meadows should be sited within the forest edge, adequately screened with plantings to blend with forest vegetation and reduce the visual impact on open meadows.
- Native vegetation impacted by construction projects should be salvaged for revegetation, when appropriate.

#### Guidelines for New Vegetation

- The plant palette for each developed area should be visually unified with the endemic plant community's associations and natural succession. All plant species used for landscape purposes should be appropriate to the plant community, as identified in the "Vegetation Management Plan" (NPS 1997).
- Selection, spacing, and massing of plant material for screening, restoration of disturbed areas, erosion control, or other design objectives should be modeled after and integrated with the natural plant mosaic found in the vicinity of the proposed work.
- Use deciduous trees for developments where winter solar gain is important, to reduce energy requirements.
- Where deciduous oaks have been identified as having special ecological value, new plantings should not include conifers if oaks would be negatively impacted.
- Planting projects should recognize the ultimate height and spread (among other characteristics) of the mature plants. When new trees are planted, care should be taken to ensure that they will not obscure important views when they mature.
- To minimize building maintenance and prevent damage to building foundations, the location and mature size and growth characteristics as well as anticipated maintenance levels of new trees and shrubs should be considered.
- Dense plantings of shrubs and trees adjacent to buildings are considered a fire hazard. New plantings should be in conformity with the "Yosemite National Park Fire Management Plan" (NPS 2004f).

### Scenic Views

The importance of Yosemite's outstanding scenery and its many associated views and vistas cannot be overemphasized. Early attempts to describe the scenery may have helped to shape modern definitions of scenic beauty. The early Romantic writings and paintings have evolved today into a sophisticated component of environmental analysis involving systematic documentation of scenic resources.

Broad, sweeping views of pastoral meadows, mountain landscapes and prominent peaks, towering geologic features, and the Valley's dramatic waterfalls have been

*Erosion of river bank near Yosemite Lodge (1929) YRL*

The Yohamite Falls, *Thomas A. Ayres, 1855. This is the first published image of Yosemite Valley. Courtesy of the California Historical Society*

recognized as some of the most revered scenic resources of the park. Human manipulations such as the periodic burning of vegetation by American Indians contributed to the development of broad, open meadows, allowing impressive vistas of the surrounding cliffs and falls. It is largely through the writings of early visitors to the parks, as well as the photographs and paintings of nationally recognized artists, that the beauty of the landscape came to the attention of the nation. These images helped make the case to Congress that Yosemite Valley was worthy of special protection, and later, of national park designation. It should be noted that other human manipulations that occurred after the park was established contributed to conifer encroachment on these meadows and scenic vistas. These manipulations included the removal of a large section of the El Capitan moraine that was acting as a natural impoundment of the Merced River (possibly resulting in a lowered water table in Yosemite Valley); the excavation of drainage ditches throughout meadows in the park; and fire suppression (allowing conifers to encroach on meadows).

From the earliest development of visitor facilities in Yosemite, views have been a major influence in the siting and orientation of structures. For example, the Lower Hotel, constructed in Yosemite Valley in 1856, was sited to take advantage of the view to Yosemite Falls. In the words of one visitor, "[C]omforts were at a minimum, but [the] surrounding beauty [was] so great that few lodgers complained." The siting of The Ahwahnee in 1926 was greatly influenced by the spectacular views from its site; the main axis of the dining room was purposefully oriented toward the view of Yosemite Falls.

Over the years, as the built environment in the Valley expanded, management of vegetation to retain significant views became an issue. In 1880 and again in 1886, the commissioner's report noted that dense underbrush in the Valley floor had begun to block the Valley's magnificent views. In 1890, trees were felled around the Stoneman House to permit views to Yosemite Falls. That same year, the commissioners announced a policy to clear the Valley of underbrush and restore the long vistas of the Valley's 1851 park-like setting.

Outside the Valley, the Wawona and Glacier Point hotels were sited with respect to scenic views. The former overlooks the verdant Wawona Meadow and the latter took in the spectacular panorama of the Sierra Nevada and Yosemite Valley.

During the preparation of the 1980 *General Management Plan*, the scenic resources of the Valley were analyzed to determine their historic and existing conditions. Lands within the Valley were classified according to three development categories. Scenic vistas to Yosemite Falls, Half Dome, El Capitan, Bridalveil Fall, Three Brothers, Cathedral Rocks, Sentinel Rock, Glacier Point, North Dome, Washington Column, and Royal Arches were identified as areas where development should not

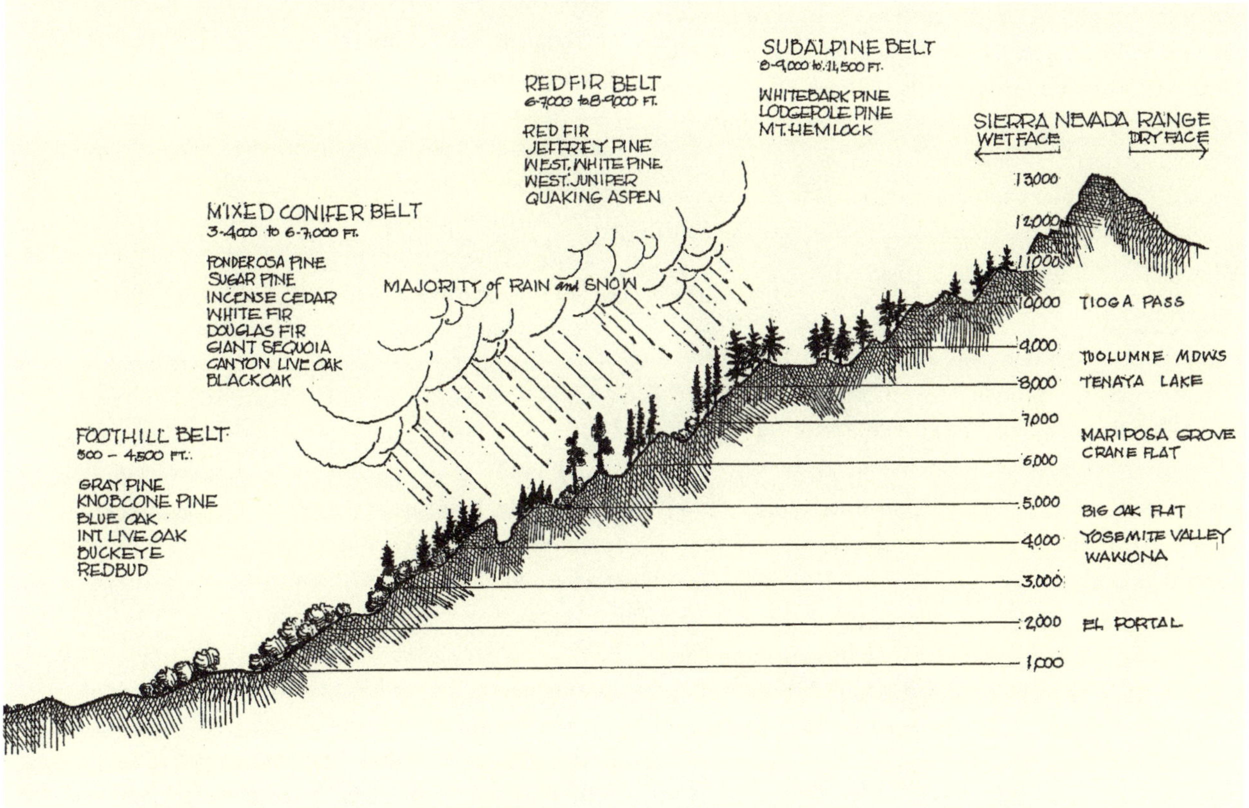


TOP LEFT *Meadow grasses, Yosemite Valley (2004) TP* TOP RIGHT *Upper Yosemite Valley from Rocky Point (1946) YRL-RA* BOTTOM *Yosemite's forest belts, adapted from Sierra Nevada Tree Identifier, Jim Paruk, Yosemite Press Association (1997)*

*Cascades cabins, 2003 (since removed)*

occur. The *General Management Plan* identified several points in the Valley that were consistently selected by 19th-century photographers such as Carleton Watkins, Eadweard Muybridge, George Fiske, and Charles Weed. The GMP attempted to reconcile the emotional response to these scenic resources with the need to objectively quantify scenery. The information gathered in this analysis was used to make recommendations about where to build, where not to build, and how to mitigate the visual impacts of the built environment.

**GUIDELINES**

- Align roads, overlooks, and pedestrian walkways to include views of prominent scenic features wherever possible. Views should be one of the important organizing elements for the site planning process.
- The siting, design, and arrangement of buildings and open spaces should recognize and maximize views to scenic resources.
- New buildings should not intrude upon or detract from significant views. Brightly colored finishes and reflective surfaces should be avoided. Multiple outbuildings, service areas, etc., should be sited and screened to minimize impacts on existing views.
- If creating a view: plant, trim, or clear trees and shrubs in a manner that blends with adjacent natural vegetation patterns.
- Refer to *Yosemite Scenic Vista Management Plan* (NPS 2011d) for further guidance.

## Landscape Uses + Structures

### LAND USE + SPATIAL ORGANIZATION

The establishment of permanent human development in Yosemite has always been constricted by the area's physical geography—be it the steep walls of the Valley, rugged river canyons, or the vast, exposed-granite slopes of the high country. Prior to the establishment of the park, development in Yosemite occurred with only limited access, due to rough wagon roads. Thus, early buildings and structures tended to be modest in size, finish, and detail—reflecting the harsh and rugged nature of their surroundings. After the establishment of the park, the beginning of master planning in the 20th century, and the initiation of the era of Rustic design, most development was limited to concentrated areas in a conscious effort to preserve the surrounding natural environment.

At the highest elevations, development was limited to widely separated log cabins. Later development at Tuolumne Meadows was sited in clusters primarily strung along the south side of Tioga Road. Some clusters were separated by distance and forest screening to create an impression of being isolated in a backcountry setting.

At Wawona, the concentrated cluster of historic hotel buildings sits on a small topographic shoulder, screened by forest from the nearby store and gas station. Administrative and maintenance facilities at Wawona are also located as distinct clusters.

Human activity in Yosemite Valley has been constricted by the steep walls of the Valley and the meandering course of the Merced River. Development has historically occurred in concentrated areas at the eastern end of the Valley. The six major developed areas—The Ahwahnee, Curry Village, Yosemite Lodge, Housekeeping Camp, Yosemite Village, and the campgrounds—support the needs of visitors and NPS administration. In spite of changes in the early days of development, the overall pattern of concentrated developed areas is well-established in the Valley and has remained in place over time. Although changes within individual developed areas have taken place (such as the redevelopment of Yosemite Village and Yosemite Lodge), these changes have generally occurred within the historic footprint of development since 1942 (NPS 2004h).

In addition to the primary developed areas in Yosemite Valley, there are day-use parking areas, campgrounds, picnic areas, interpretive wayside exhibits, trails, stables, multiuse paths, and other visitor resources. For more information, see separate chapters on developed areas outside Yosemite Valley, including Tuolumne Meadows, Wawona, and day use areas.

## CIRCULATION

Circulation within the park can be expressed as a hierarchy of routes ranging from paved highways to rocky foot-trails.

### Roads

Vehicle circulation in the park is limited and consists of five major road corridors: Tioga, Big Oak Flat, El Portal, Wawona, and Hetch Hetchy. Secondary roads include Valley Loop Road, Glacier Point Road, and Mariposa Grove Road. The roads often provide visitors with quintessential views of natural features while also orienting them to specific destination points. The scenic driving experience is paramount in the design of these roads.

*Cabins set in the trees, Curry Village*

*Ahwahnee Bridge with Half Dome (2004) GH*

Often curvilinear, oriented toward views, and designed for slower speeds of travel, these roads are intended to enhance the visitor's experience of the park's natural environment and not just provide a means of ingress and egress. A mixture of concentrated parking areas and informal turnouts are located along the roads.

In addition, a number of secondary paved roads provide public access to both major and minor developed areas. The most intense traffic is found in the highly developed Yosemite Valley. A number of other service roads are open only to authorized vehicles. Some of the latter are historic routes and still serve the public as hiking trails or cross-country ski routes.

Although the need for new roads is not anticipated, any modifications or relocation of roads in developed areas should conform to the NPS "Park Road Standards" and the following guidelines.

*Rangers' Club at edge of Cook's Meadow*

*Tioga Road at Tenaya Lake (2008) GH*

**GUIDELINES**

- In order to remain subordinate to the landscape, the design and alignment of road modifications should respond to natural conditions and features such as topography, boulders, healthy trees, and drainages. Graceful, curving alignments based on low speeds should be used to impart a sense of a scenic road fitting naturally in the landscape while conforming to applicable safety standards.
- Roadway width, paving type, and edge treatment should be designed to help the visitor distinguish a hierarchical circulation pattern and make wayfinding easy and logical for visitors, with a minimum of directional signs.
- Primary and secondary roadways should be sited with an emphasis on the driver's visual experience. As a new road approaches a developed area, it should be aligned to provide views of significant natural features where possible. Parking areas should not distract from this view opportunity.
- Within a developed area, the approach roads should be aligned to building entry points.
- Convenient access should be provided to park transit systems, shuttle bus stops, walkways, and hiking trails.

## Trails and Pathways

Trails provide the most intimate experience with the landscape. The park contains almost 800 miles of hiking trails, ranging in elevation from 2,000 to 13,000 feet, and connecting the most developed areas (Yosemite Valley) to the most remote corners of the Yosemite Wilderness. Yosemite's trail system includes long segments of the regional John Muir and Pacific Crest trails.

In the Valley, a network of biking, equestrian, and pedestrian routes connects visitor attractions with lodging, employee housing, administrative offices, and visitor services. Although the distinctions are not always clear within developed areas, circulation routes are typically hierarchical and include primary entries, pedestrian plazas and gathering areas, walkways, and footpaths. In less-developed areas, pedestrian access is informal in nature and typically along asphalt, packed decomposed granite, gravel, or dirt trails. In meadows or wetlands, boardwalks are frequently used to allow visitor access while protecting sensitive resources.

Pathways in developed areas vary in character, width, surface treatment, and edging. The following guidelines are intended to provide a uniform approach to trail and pathway design and maintenance, appropriate for the differing landscapes in the park.

**GUIDELINES**

- Design pedestrian and bicycle paths to be clearly distinguishable—through width, pavement type, and edge treatment—as non-vehicle routes.
- The design of new paths and walkways in developed areas should be compatible with existing materials, widths, and alignments. Widths should be the minimum required to accommodate anticipated usage.
- Design trails and pathways to be natural in character, following site contours and outside edges of vegetation and incorporating rock formations, trees, and views. Some trails and pathways may directly follow established desire lines, while others should provide for a relaxed pace, a sequence of experiences, surprise views, interpretive exhibits, seating, and places to pause and take in the scenery.
- Define vista or rest points by widening the path. Where feasible, provide log benches, boulders, or downfall logs for seating.
- Paths and walkways should be designed to meet current accessibility standards. Detail curbs, landings, and ramps to be rustic in character, which will reinforce the overall aesthetic character of the path.
- Where steeper gradients cannot be avoided, construct steps, stair runs, or step-ramps using materials that

*Trail to Lower Yosemite Fall (2004) RF*

*Snow on path, Yosemite Lodge (2004) GH*

match site conditions. Stair dimensions should accommodate average and comfortable-stride lengths and riser heights. Setting flattened faces up for stone treads is critical for safety. Provide for landings at reasonable intervals or as topography allows. Choose or treat tread materials to ensure adequate slip-resistance for safety.

- Paving for pedestrian routes in developed areas should be distinguished by material and edging variation from vehicle routes and should be continuous, clearly leading the pedestrian from the parking area to visitor services. Material should match site conditions so that the defined walking area presents minimal contrast to the surrounding matrix of soil and rock.

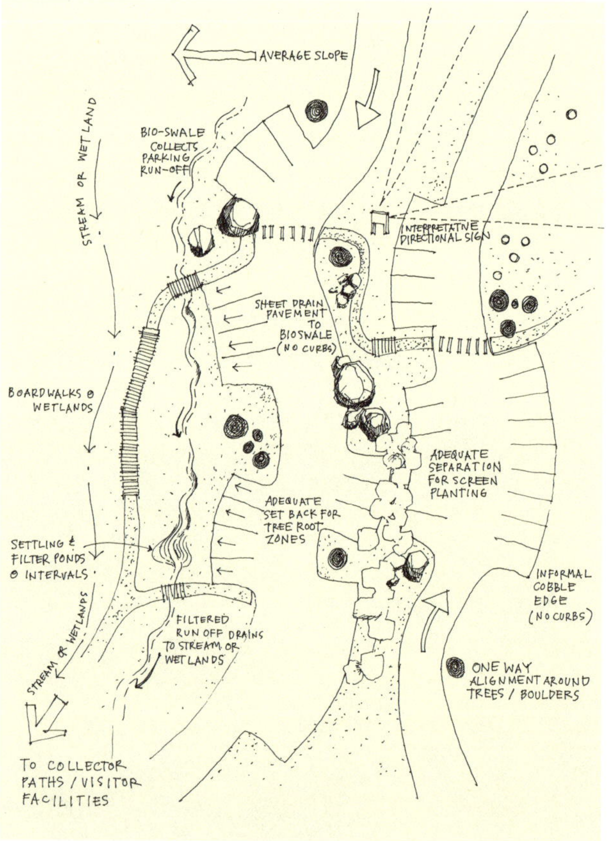


*Conceptual site-sensitive parking layout*

- In intensely used developed areas, earth-tone pigmented exposed aggregate, pigmented concrete, and surface-treated asphalt may be considered.
- If feasible, pathway paving should be a porous, compacted granular material placed on a compacted subgrade. In some cases, a stabilized granular material (using a resin or similar binder) may be acceptable to ensure accessibility. The design of all-season, hard-surfaced paths should specify materials that are readily maintained, durable, and easily cleared of snow and ice. In more isolated areas, decomposed granite, gravel, stabilized soil, or other hardened surfaces should be used, as appropriate.
- Use materials and details that are contextually appropriate to define the edges of trails and pathways. In wooded areas, use downfall logs, short split-cedar post and rope fencing, or low split-cedar log and pierced-post barriers to delineate pathway edges. Taller barriers such as zigzag fencing may be used where more substantial barriers are needed, where historically appropriate, and/or near dense vegetation where they will blend visually. In open or dry areas, particularly in rocky subalpine elevations, use local or matching rock, unevenly spaced and partially buried, to define path edges. Spacing of rocks may decrease to make the edge more obvious where protection of vegetated areas is needed, strive for a naturalistic look. Rounded, river-washed cobbles may be appropriate near rivers or streams. Refer to "Landscape Uses + Structures—Barriers, Fences, and Benches" in this chapter.

## Parking

The first automobile—a "Locomobile" driven by Oliver Lippincott—arrived in Yosemite Valley in June 1900. That year, Foley's *The Yosemite Tourist* announced that "the auto will soon become a prominent factor in Yosemite travel" (Johnston 1995). By the 1920s, automobiles filled the parking lot at Government Center (later Yosemite

Village), and photographs of the period depict visitors parked and camped on meadows.

Since then, relatively small parking areas were added where deemed necessary. Where more parking was needed, the additions were placed adjacent or close to existing parking areas to avoid trees, wetlands, trails, etc.

Today, with increasing visitation to Yosemite National Park, parking for private vehicles has become a major concern. Planning and siting for parking calls for careful site analysis and documentation of resources such as wetlands, drainages, healthy trees and vegetation, and wildlife habitats.

**GUIDELINES**

### *Siting*

- Site parking areas on dry, naturally well-drained soils.
- Site parking areas to be naturally screened from pedestrian areas and viewpoints.
- Parking areas should not be located where they would detract from views of significant natural or historic features from existing buildings or pedestrian areas.
- Siting new parking areas in meadows, oak groves, wetlands, or other sensitive areas is not appropriate.

### *Layout*

- Lay out parking areas to create small, partially separated clusters. Work with existing topography and vegetation (e.g., large trees) to separate parking areas.
- Include intervening grade-change strips sufficiently wide to support planting, use existing features such as trees and boulders to break-up continuous parking bays, and avoid long, straight rows of parked vehicles.
- Natural features (e.g., healthy shrubs and trees, boulders, trees, etc.) should be incorporated into parking areas to help break up the size of the parking areas and visually buffer them from developed and natural areas.

*Parked cars at new Yosemite Village (date unknown) YRL*

Grading and paving should not extend within the drip line of trees.

- Lay out pedestrian routes to clearly link parking areas to visitor services and take advantage of natural features such as boulders, views, and vegetation.
- Parking areas that are visible from elevated viewpoints (such as the Valley from Glacier Point) should be screened by tree canopy to minimize visual impacts.

***Details***

- Lay out non-porous paved areas so that runoff and snowmelt is guided to mechanical or biological filters (such as bio-swales, oil/water separators, and filter ponds). In areas where potential contamination of waterways is not a concern and where climatic conditions permit, porous pavements may be considered.
- Design parking areas to provide snow storage areas where winter use and plowing are anticipated, vegetation will not be damaged, and snowmelt runoff will be filtered.
- Because of the high potential for damage by plow blades, avoid the use of curbs in parking areas that are subject to snow removal.
- Refer to "Landscape Uses + Structures—Lighting" in this chapter for guidelines on lighting for parking areas.

*The Ahwahnee entrance marker*

*Camp Curry entrance marker*

## ENTRANCE MARKERS

Entrances to some of the major developed areas in Yosemite are announced with a visually significant marker in a style that is appropriate to that development. Historically, markers such as rockfall cairns marked the entrance to the park. The Ahwahnee has a masonry gate shelter set into a large granite block. Curry Village has a lighted, unpeeled-log welcome sign that acts as a gateway to the Curry Village commons.

**GUIDELINES**

- Entrance markers should be inspired by the surrounding natural setting and the architectural character (e.g., the granite used at The Ahwahnee gatehouse or the logs used in the Camp Curry welcome sign).

## SMALL BUILDINGS

Small buildings throughout the park accommodate visitor activities away from the main centers of developed areas. They include comfort stations, shower houses, kiosks, storage sheds, and miscellaneous shelters. (Shuttle bus shelters are addressed in a separate chapter.) These buildings are often solitary structures in locations such as campgrounds or trails, and they may also be used as ancillary structures within a development where the character is defined by larger buildings. This building type should be designed to adapt to local site conditions.

Entrance kiosks, comfort stations, and shower houses are visitor service facilities found in campgrounds and other developed areas within the park. In keeping with traditional NPS design principles, these buildings are typically designed with a consistent architectural character. In campgrounds, a comfort station may be the largest building, but it is seen as part of a larger developed area that includes picnic tables, benches, barriers, amphitheaters, and footbridges. Because all of these elements contribute to the character of the site, they typically share character-defining features such as materials and workmanship.

During the 1920s and 1930s, the National Park Service recognized the importance of small buildings and related landscape elements. Standard designs were developed and included in portfolios that were circulated throughout the National Park Service as well as in state parks. In 1938, a compilation of illustrated examples from national and state parks was published in an influential book by NPS Architect Albert Good, entitled *Park and Recreation Structures*. This publication continues to be a useful reference.

The standard design for comfort stations in Yosemite consisted of simple, rustic, wood-frame buildings with gable roofs and shake roof covering. These buildings were typically rectangular, with entrances at each end. This basic design was adapted to different sites using variations of rustic treatments including a stone base, exposed wood posts, infill wall panels of wood boards, exposed rafters, gable roofs, wood shingle or shake roof covering, and muted colors. The comfort stations in the park typically used a wood frame with exposed posts, exposed rafters, and no gutter or fascia. The comfort station built at Yosemite Falls in 2004 shares many features with the standard design of the 1920s, including entrances at both ends, a gable roof, muted colors, wood siding, and a stone base.

Shower houses and comfort stations have similar functional requirements, and they are typically designed as companion buildings. Designed with rustic character, their utilitarian purpose is expressed with compactness and simplicity.

Campground kiosks, as distinguished from fee kiosks at entrance stations, serve to announce a developed area or a point of contact with park personnel. For example, the kiosk at Camp 4 interfaces with the campers and active climbing community to provide a wide variety of information. Kiosks also provide shelter and a place for signs. NPS kiosks are typically open and have a welcoming aspect, and they may function informally as a meeting place for visitors.

### GUIDELINES

- The siting of small buildings for picnic areas and campgrounds should minimize visual intrusion and blend with the natural setting. Small buildings can be easily sited around natural features such as trees and boulders to minimize their visual impact on the landscape.
- Temporary trailers or modular buildings should be avoided where it is anticipated that there will be an ongoing or permanent need for a building. These structures do not harmonize with the landscape, nor convey appropriate character, nor embody quality construction.
- Design comfort stations and shower houses to be compatible with NPS Rustic design. These include a standard plan, a gable roof, the use of exposed wood framing and siding, and natural colors. They should be

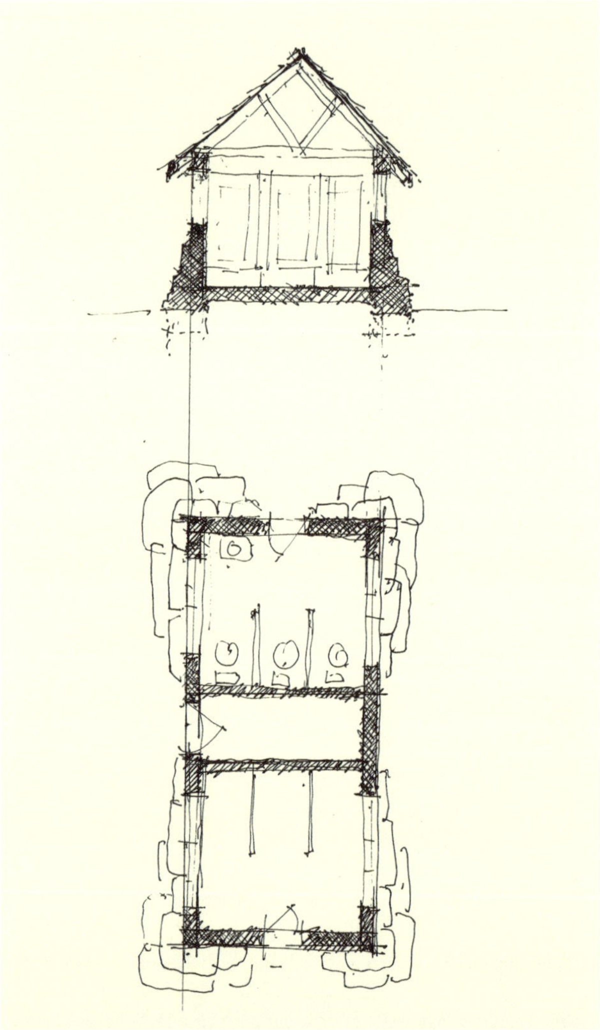

TOP LEFT *Comfort station at the Valley stables (2004) GH* MIDDLE LEFT *Small building at the Valley stables (2004) GH* TOP RIGHT *Comfort station plan and section*
BOTTOM *Comfort station at Union Point (1932) YRL-RA*

simple, one-story, rectangular shapes. Entrances should be at the gable ends. Roof pitches should be at least 5:12, with overhangs to shed rain and snow. Roofing must meet Class A fire requirements.

- Cluster functional and convenience equipment such as public telephones and vending machines in small buildings or integrate with comfort stations. Place equipment within the volume of the structure, sheltered by overhangs or porches or in recessed alcoves.
- Where telephone booths must be freestanding, they should be placed in enclosures with minimal or no lighting. Refer to "Landscape Uses + Structures—Lighting" in this chapter.
- Design facades to be modest in character. They should have a protective base of masonry or board-form concrete. The upper walls should have a single material treatment. Vertical board and batten is a typical siding pattern, using full-size battens and boards of resawn western red cedar with tight knots. Alternative siding treatments may be appropriate depending on site character and that of nearby historic or designated structures and buildings. Refer to "Developed Areas—Building Exteriors" in this chapter.
- A semitransparent stain or paint should be used for all wood elements, including siding and exposed framing members. Apply semitransparent stain where the natural wood grain and color should be seen. Use opaque stain to hide imperfections, if required.
- Doors and window frames should be of the same material as the exterior wall they are set in. Window sashes and doors should be painted with exterior sash and trim paint. Refer to "Developed Areas—Building Exteriors—Color" in this chapter for guidelines on color.
- If new small buildings are needed near or within a Mission 66 complex such as Yosemite Lodge, consider a more functional, contemporary approach that incorporates design and materials that are compatible with the Mission 66 era facility.
- Refer to "Landscape Uses + Structures—Lighting" in this chapter for guidelines on exterior lighting.

## MASONRY STRUCTURES

One of the most durable unifying elements found throughout the park is that of masonry structures. They include dry-laid and mortared retaining and guard walls, fitted riprap and line culverts, building foundations, and base walls. Larger structures include tunnel portals, chimneys, entry pylons, and gate pediments. Many of these structures were built by hand during the CCC era (1933–42). Many have been determined eligible for listing on the National Register of Historic Places. The color and texture of local granite, basalt, or river-washed cobbles blend well with the immediate surroundings. The granite was worked by hand to some degree but seldom gauged, initially because of the lack of refined tools. Early in the 20th century the granite was left deliberately rough to achieve a rustic appearance.

Some of the best examples of rustic granite masonry occur in the vicinity of Hetch Hetchy in the form of guard and retaining walls. Built in conjunction with the dam, they are composed of members ranging from massive, roughly rectangular dry-laid slabs to more evenly dimensioned, lightly worked blocks. Other examples are the mortared guard walls along Big Oak Flat Road, which show great skill in shaping the granite members without compromising the rustic look. The stone work at the historic Geology Hut at Glacier Point is an excellent example of the masterful selection, orientation, and shaping of the partially angular stones of this small building to form a pattern of tightly fitted but nevertheless rustic walls.

IT IS POSSIBLE FOR MARKERS AND RELATED DEVICES TO CAPTURE AND CONVEY IN GREATER DEGREE THAN MOST OTHER PARK STRUCTURES THE SPIRIT OF A PARTICULAR AREA. IT IS THEIR FUNCTION, AND BY NO MEANS A MINOR ONE, TO ACCENT, TO 'HIGHLIGHT,' WHATEVER MIGHT BE TERMED THE ESSENTIAL PERSONALITY OF A PARK. **ALBERT H. GOOD • PARK AND RECREATION STRUCTURES • 1938**

Historically, river-washed cobbles, found in abundance in the streams and rivers that flow down from the High Sierra, were usually available a short distance from construction sites. They soon became important elements of the early Rustic style in the park. At Camp Curry, cobbles were used as foundations for cabins and larger structures. The fireplaces at both the Camp Curry lounge and the Wawona Hotel are fine examples of cobblestone masonry. At the South Entrance Station, the rangers' quarters, the comfort station, and the recently restored ticket office kiosk all use cobbles for the rustic base. Nearby at the Wawona Hotel, cobbles are used on the light standards flanking the main stairs, the large decorative fountain, and the flagpole base with the historic plaque. Nearby, in an area with private inholdings (called "Section 35"), a large chimney has a decorative installation of cobbles that is unique for a residence. The covered bridge at the Pioneer Yosemite History Center has a cobble veneer over the concrete abutment.

**GUIDELINES**

- Design new masonry landscape structures to reference, but not mimic, the quality of hand construction from the era of early park development. This can be achieved through scale of components, finish, and ground-up sequencing, whereby heavier-looking and larger stones are placed at ground level, followed on up by incrementally smaller stones.
- The design for replacement or repair of historic masonry features such as guard walls, fitted riprap, and stone culverts should match the size, scale, shape, texture, materials, color, and joint work of the original features. Do not use faux materials, finishes, or detailing.
- Design new guard walls, culverts, etc., for compatibility with natural surroundings or, if located within a historic property, nearby historic features. Some modern materials such as reinforced concrete may be appropriate. Refer to *The Secretary of the Interior's Standards* where compatibility of new construction within a historic property is required.
- Select stone for masonry structures, whether dry-laid or mortared, to blend with the character of the surroundings. Wall design and finish should be complementary to adjacent elements such as exposed foundations of historic buildings. Local weathered granite should be used when available. Imitation materials should not be used.
- Where mortared masonry is called for, finished jointing patterns should be random with deep-raked mortar joints, as found on most historic structures in the park.

*Recessed steps and retaining wall, Tunnel View, Wawona Road (2009) TP*

*Lower masonry wall of Museum, Yosemite Village (2004) GH*

TOP LEFT *Camp Curry Lounge (2008) GH* TOP RIGHT *Fireplace hearth, Wawona Hotel (2009) GH* MIDDLE LEFT *Dry stacked masonry, Vogelsang High Sierra Camp (2004) RF* MIDDLE RIGHT *Cobble base, South Entrance comfort station (2008) GH* BOTTOM LEFT *Covered bridge and cobble pier, Pioneer Yosemite History Center, Wawona (2009) GH* BOTTOM RIGHT *Masonry detail, Road Crew Camp, Tuolumne Meadows (2007) GH*

Boardwalk in meadow, Yosemite Valley (2004 (TP)

Avoid obvious vertical and horizontal alignment of joints. It is worth noting that historic masonry joints are often smaller than modern ones, and that the new should not always replicate the old.

- Where concrete is exposed on a structure, it should have a rough-sawn, board-formed surface.

## FOOTBRIDGES, CULVERT CROSSINGS, RETAINING WALLS + BOARDWALKS

There is little evidence describing the structure and character of footbridges in Yosemite National Park before the advent of the NPS Rustic style of the 1920s. The 2006 National Register nomination for the Yosemite Valley Historic District refers to the many footbridges that crossed the Merced River and its tributaries over the years, but notes that only the footbridge at Housekeeping Camp and Superintendent's Bridge date to the period of historic significance. Though it has been altered over time, the footbridge that crosses the Tuolumne River near Soda Springs and Parsons Memorial Lodge is historic. A number of historic road bridges, such as the Bridalveil Fall and Ahwahnee bridges, are now used as footbridges.

These Rustic-style stone and timber structures are echoed by smaller footbridges of logs, concrete, and worked-granite boulders scattered throughout the park. These footbridges are detailed and scaled to reinforce their sense of being hand-made with local materials. In the Valley, the walkway of granite-boulder bridges is usually flanked by low stone curb walls. Smaller modern timber bridges and boardwalks have a heavy plank walking surface with either raised timber curbs or handrails. Examples include the main bridge below Lower Yosemite Fall and other bridges that cross branches of Yosemite Creek downstream. Other examples can be seen at Happy Isles and several meadow viewpoints or crossings. The unique bench-bridge near The Ahwahnee is an exception, because it provides an intimate, small-scale place to pause and observe the setting.

Except for those installed in the Mission 66 era, culvert headwalls are built of dry-laid or mortared natural stone that blends easily with the surrounding landscape. Both rough-worked and weathered boulders are used to armor the steep slopes flanking the open ends of culverts throughout the park. The walkway over the larger culverts may be flanked by low boulder curbs. At all of these crossings the boulder size appears to be such that one or two workers could lift them into place, reinforcing the hand-made quality. The Mission 66 era culvert headwalls are not consistent with earlier rustic design.

Although many historic stone walls and other structures exist throughout the park, relatively few are located in the Valley, because most roads and buildings were built on flat terrain and earth-moving capacities in the late 19th and early 20th centuries were limited. Where retention of a slope for a road, building, or outdoor use area was necessary, low dry-laid walls of local stone (or, in some cases, large individual boulders) were used. These walls were mostly constructed for trails. Historic photographs show small-scale dry-laid walls throughout the park, with larger rocks at the base of the wall. The size of the rocks decreases with the height of the wall. Later walls were built of reinforced concrete, some with stone cladding.

Historically, handrail design has varied throughout the park, frequently without reference to the Rustic style. The new bridges at Yosemite Falls are good examples of those incorporating Rustic detailing. The handrails of many bridges in Yosemite Valley consist of stout square posts with square handrails turned 45 degrees. These include the bridges at Yosemite Falls and below Vernal Fall as well as the new pedestrian bridge over Yosemite Creek by Northside Drive.

**GUIDELINES**

***Footbridges and Boardwalks***

- Site new bridges so that the hydrologic processes of rivers, streams, and tributaries are not impeded during high-water periods.
- Design abutments for footbridges using dry-stacked or deep-raked mortared stone. Use stone cladding or rough-sawn, board-formed surface for concrete walls.

*Ahwahnee Bridge, Yosemite Valley (2004) RF*

- Design decking for free-span bridges using heavy, rough-sawn planks. Log substructures should be used where feasible. Weathered steel or concrete girders may be used and should not be overly disguised.
- Design guardrails for nonhistoric bridges using sanded timbers or peeled logs mounted on sturdy supports. The use of natural-weathering steel for components of the structure may be considered.
- Select wood species for their ability to withstand the elements yet be friendly and soft to the touch. Western red cedar, Port Orford cedar, and Alaska yellow cedar are appropriate for handrails, because these species do not produce splinters as they weather.
- Boardwalks for paths or trail crossings may be needed in the vicinity of meadows, wetlands, or other sensitive plant or soil conditions. The standard Yosemite design of heavy cross-planks and rough-sawn timber edging is stylistically appropriate and effective for directing foot traffic. The entire structure is held on piers slightly above native soil level to prevent soil compaction.
- Refer to the "Roads + Entrance Stations" chapter for guidelines on vehicle bridges.

TOP *Wapama Falls footbridge, Hetch Hetchy (2005) RF* BOTTOM *Cascades cabin, 2003 (since removed)*

#### *Small-Scale Culvert Crossings*

- The headwall inlets and outlets of small drainages that are in public view should be designed of dry-laid or mortared stone masonry, boulders, or a single large slab of granite, depending on the specific context.

#### *Landscape Retaining Walls and Riprap Slopes*

- Minimize the need for retaining walls and riprap slopes with careful siting and grading.
- Design retaining walls to reflect the historic, hand-constructed walls found in the park, matching any nearby examples. Where possible, wall ends should die into the adjacent slope. Dry-laid or mortared walls constructed of large, fitted Sierra granite boulders should be used.
- Construct riprap slopes with fitted local stone with flat face exposures.
- Retaining wall heights should be kept to the minimum possible and should not be uncomfortably high in pedestrian areas.

## GRADING + DRAINAGE

Early photographs indicate that most builders used stepped foundations to adapt buildings to the slope rather than changing or flattening the slope. Structures, roads, and trails were sited along contours or on flat or gentle slopes, requiring only minimal grading of the natural landform. This has created a pattern of development in the park that harmonizes and blends with the natural environment.

**GUIDELINES**

- Design all projects so that buildings, roads, and structures are sited to make use of existing landform. Minimize cut and fill to the greatest extent possible.
- Design finished grading to emulate surrounding landforms and natural drainage patterns. Avoid mechanical solutions to manage runoff.
- Design projects to enhance groundwater recharge systems, where soil characteristics permit, using strategies such as porous pavements, run-off retention areas, and specification of appropriate vegetation.
- Avoid grading impacts to streams and drainages, riparian vegetation, and existing trees.

---

## BARRIERS, FENCES + BENCHES

Barriers are defined as any system designed to control or direct the movement of people and protect natural features without blocking or obscuring views from one side of the barrier to the other. Screening, on the other hand, is defined as less-solid fencing intended for privacy or to hide outdoor materials or areas from view. For purposes of yard fencing, trash screening, or control of pets, the park provides prescriptive guidelines for residential spaces.

Barriers may be needed to keep visitors on designated pedestrian pathways and trails and out of sensitive soil areas, plant communities, and habitats. Trampling of vegetation, compaction of soil, and bank erosion are common in Yosemite National Park, a consequence of the great number of visitors to the park each year. A reduction in the number of fence types on a single site, both temporary and permanent, will help unify the landscape.

Solid fencing is often necessary for both private dwellings and visitor services. Lodging units may require screens for privacy and to conceal outdoor storage areas.

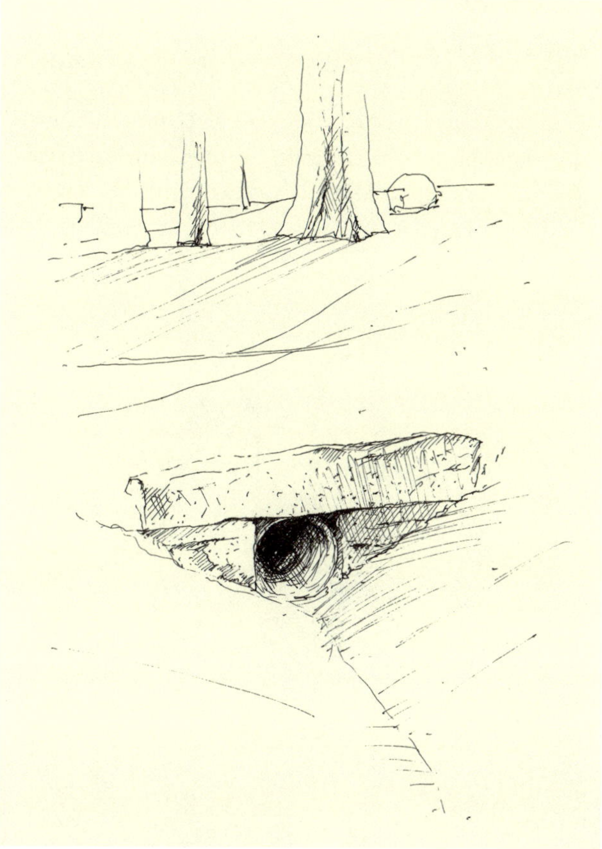

TOP *Footbridge* BOTTOM *Rock-faced culvert*

In addition, such fencing is required to screen the service functions associated with receiving and maintenance activities.

Benches such as those seen in public spaces today were scarce in the late 19th and early 20th centuries, according to photographs of the time. People in outdoor spaces sat either on indoor chairs that were brought outside or on fallen logs, upended log segments, or boulders. Rustic one- and two-sided log benches were shaped from large tree trunks by the Civilian Conservation Corps in the 1930s. These bench forms still exist in some locations and provide a link to the past. They represent a heavy rustic scale and often appear solidly anchored among the surrounding towering trees and massive boulders.

**GUIDELINES**

### Barriers

- Design planted barriers, on either flat or sloping terrain, on grades raised a minimum of 12 inches from the surrounding surface. The edge of the planted barrier should be reinforced with nested and partially buried native cobbles and boulders. Flat-topped boulders, 16 to 20 inches high, may be incorporated into the edge for seating.
- Typical fences in Yosemite include: zigzag fencing, pierced-post fencing, double-post fencing, and post and rope fencing. These emphasize hand-crafted simplicity and the use of park-sourced materials. Cedar, due to its rustic character, longevity, and local abundance, is preferred. (Refer to descriptions in following text.)
- Where temporary barriers are needed, specify a system that can easily be dismantled and relocated, such as a staggered zigzag type.

### Zigzag Fence

Because it requires no posts, zigzag fencing is highly adaptable to level ground. Made of split timbers, this fencing also imparts a rustic, rural, hand-crafted character. It is constructed of several 12-foot-long split-cedar rails, stacked and secured at the joints by a steel reinforcing bar and laid out in a zigzag pattern for stability. The design should be used consistently where impacts to roots or archeological resources is of concern, such as in oak woodlands, sequoia groves, and riparian zones.

*Zigzag fence*

*Pierced-post fence*

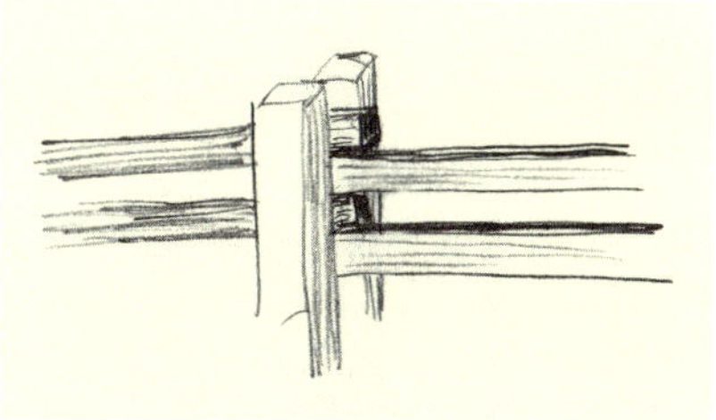

*Double-post fence*

The number of rails can be a reflection of the level of use being managed.

### *Pierced-Post Fence (sometimes called Hetch Hetchy)*

This design uses six-by-eight-inch split and rough-squared cedar posts at normal and low heights, spaced at about eight-foot centers. The posts are secured in compacted, backfilled holes. The fence can have either one or two rails. The rail openings in the posts and the eight-to-ten-foot-long, split-cedar rails imply a degree of woodworking and installation skill. This type of fence may therefore be appropriate for developed areas as well as timbered areas and steep slopes. The low-height version would be appropriate at the edges of newly planted or plant restoration areas and near meadows.

### *Double-Post Fence*

The double-post fence is made of split timbers with a varying number of rails, depending upon the use and level of pedestrian control. Typically, the posts are bolted together to support the rails between the posts. Rails are typically 12 feet in length but vary depending upon site conditions. Often used in conjuction with the zigzag fence, double-posts are needed where tight control of pedestrian flow is critical, such as along raised paths. The height of the fence and the number of rails used is dependent upon the intensity of pedestrian use being managed. Double-post fences are avoided in areas where surface roots (e.g., near sequoia trees) or archeological resources are an issue.

*Cedar-post and rope barricade*

### *Cedar-Post and Rope or Cable Barricade*

This design uses two-to-four-foot-tall split-cedar posts, spaced about 10 feet apart, and buried 12 inches or more in compacted, backfilled post holes. A one-inch diameter hole near the top of the post carries a semi-taut galvanized cable or hemp rope. This design should be used only where a temporary barrier is needed, such as to protect replanted or recovering vegetation. The barricade should be removed when vegetation has grown sufficiently to act as a barrier. Do not use faux materials or plastic-lined cable.

### *Screen Fences*

- Locate or consolidate buildings and associated utility elements so that the need for screening is reduced or eliminated.
- Vegetation should be considered for use in screening before fencing solutions are explored.
- Fence heights should be kept to the minimum possible to provide screening and protect resources, and should not be uncomfortably high in pedestrian areas.
- Screen fencing that is an extension of a structure should be designed as an integral architectural component, using materials of the building where appropriate.
- Design freestanding screen fencing to blend into the natural landscape. Wood, salvaged from NPS vegetation management operations, should be specified when available. Fence-panel infill should present a rough, textured, opaque look, such as that provided by multiple vertical split-cedar grape-stake units or other wood members of a similar scale. Posts may be of peeled logs or rough-sawn timbers. Wood selected should be naturally aged or painted to remain a dark, earth-colored tone such as Wosky brown.

LEFT *Bench with armrest and granite pedestal (2010) RF*
RIGHT *Log bench with armrest (2010) RF*

- Locate and design enclosures for satellite dishes, antennae, and other communications equipment to be as hidden as possible from public view, to blend into the surroundings, and to avoid an industrial appearance. Equipment should be kept lower than the fence-top or sited with a building in the background.

***Benches***

- Design benches to reflect the Rustic style. Timber, salvaged from NPS vegetation management operations, should be used when available. Sierra granite is an appropriate material for use as pads under benches.
- If benches are needed near or within a Mission 66 complex such as Yosemite Lodge, consider a more functional, contemporary approach that incorporates materials and design compatible with the Mission 66 era.
- Design benches for shuttle bus stops from heavy, rough-milled lumber set on granite pads. Incorporate backs and armrests, and design to meet accessibility standards. Cluster groups of benches where site conditions allow. Note: The custom redwood bench in use at shuttle bus stops in the Valley is an appropriate alternative for highly developed areas such as the Yosemite Falls viewing area.
- Design benches for unsheltered settings using unpeeled logs, which contribute a strong rustic character. Three types of log benches are recommended: a three-quarter-round log with seat and back carved out, set on a granite base; a half-round log with no back, set on a granite base; and a complete-round log, partially buried with no base. Include modest pitch to drain water and prolong the life of the bench. Small masonry pedestals or board-form concrete may be appropriate for the base in addition to granite.
- Design individual seats using bucked-up logs at least 24 inches in diameter and about 18 inches tall, set vertically. This type of informal seating may be appropriate around campfires and small amphitheaters.

## SIGN CHARACTER

Signs are found throughout Yosemite National Park, in both densely developed settings like Yosemite Village and on trails deep in the remote Yosemite Wilderness. In these varied locations, signs have considerable differences in frame and support character, including fabrication, size, construction, materials, and function. Some signs use a simple style blending natural brown colors and embossed features appropriate to the area, such as the triangle in the frames of signs at the Indian Village and acorns at Lower Yosemite Fall and other areas. More rustic signs feature stone pedestals or log frames, making them appear to be constructed from surrounding materials.

Sign character reflects the different cultural and natural settings in which they are sited. The Valley is highly developed and has many examples of urban sign forms such as prerusted square tubing supports and

*Log barrier at Crane Flat (2004) GH*

TOP *Civilian Conservation Corps building benches (c. 1930) YRL* BOTTOM *Weathering steel interpretation sign (2009) DN*

frames. In the Wawona/Chinquapin area, white painted buildings contrast dramatically with the dark forest surroundings, suggesting white painted signs with light frames and posts. Semiprimitive, lightly developed areas such as picnic grounds and trailheads have examples of rustic signs constructed of logs and stone. In the NPS Rustic Design era, construction elements were oversized to produce a greater sense of harmony with the massive surrounding landscape of Yosemite.

These guidelines are limited to the visual character of sign frames, coverings, supports, and pedestal materials. Site factors and sign location are also considered. The issues of sign panel design, material typeface, font, lettering, color, and messaging are not dealt with in these guidelines. Refer to the *Yosemite National Park Long Range Interpretive Plan* (NPS 2011f) for more detail on wayside exhibits and other interpretive signs. All signs, regardless of function, should project a National Park Service style and relate to the special qualities of the site. Subgroupings can be related to function, setting, and area.

The basic types of exterior signs include the following:

1. *Informational.* Fees, campground rules, bulletin boards, etc., often including international symbols. The sign elements themselves may include metal panels with white lettering on a brown background, wood panels with white routed lettering, and rustic wooden-roofed bulletin boards. Examples can be found at the Valley Visitor Center, Mariposa Grove, Chinquapin, and at the entrances to several campgrounds.
2. *Wayfinding.* Trail mileage, directions, etc. at trailheads and junctions. Sign elements may include weathered metal panels with incised letters and mileages in the wilderness areas, as well as the park systemwide Meeker sign system: two weathering-steel support legs and removable panels featuring maps and messages about safety, wilderness travel, and natural and cultural resources. In some heavily visited areas or districts such as the Lower Yosemite Fall area and Yosemite Village, a more specialized system of rustic signs using stone, wood, and metal has been designed and installed.
3. *Site Orientation.* Area maps with trail system layouts, descriptions of features and possible destinations, interpretation, and mileages. The standard sign that has developed for site orientation at the entrances of visitor day use areas is the rustic peeled-log orientation sign with two large-diameter logs holding up a horizontal lintel log to frame an information panel. Examples can be found at Happy Isles, Glacier Point, Hetch Hetchy, Lower Yosemite Fall, and The Mariposa, Tuolumne, and Merced Groves of Giant Sequoias. Also, a rustic, roofed, wood bulletin board can accompany the log site-orientation sign to provide additional information.
4. *Interpretation.* Wayside exhibits and sculptural or graphic depictions of view panoramas at roadside turnouts. These signs are typically weathering-steel with inlaid porcelain enamel information panels and a tapered

TOP LEFT *Campground informational sign, Hodgdon Meadow (2008) GH* TOP RIGHT *Trail interpretation sign (2010) RF* MIDDLE LEFT *Granite base for wayfinding sign (2010) RF* MIDDLE RIGHT *Steel plate wayfinding trail marker (2007) RF* BOTTOM *Peeled log site-orientation sign (2010) RF*

weathering-steel support. In some areas the porcelain enamel panel is set into granite blocks (such as at Olmsted Point) in order to minimize the amount of visible metal in the granite-dominated setting. Embossed patterns in the weathering-steel frame add a tactile element. Sculptural wayside exhibits can include bronze topographic depictions of features in the viewshed and can be seen at Glacier Point, Lower Yosemite Fall, Tunnel View, and Half Dome View.

5. *Park Entry Signs and Monuments.* Entry signs, log gates, and stone pylons. These can be more unique, large-scaled, rustic, very visible signs. Examples include the log gates at Tioga Pass, stone pylons with wood signs that announce "Yosemite National Park" at the park boundaries.
6. *Highway and Traffic Related.* Rules and standards related to signs for traffic and highway safety as well as to accessibility are not included in these design guidelines but may be found in applicable state and federal regulations. However, highway and traffic-related signs should be used sparingly, and only when necessary to comply with regulations and meet safety goals.

**GUIDELINES**

- Locate signs to minimize visual clutter; avoid obscuring views of natural, cultural, or historic resources. Wherever possible, consolidate messages within a single sign frame or system with the same supports and frames.
- Locate signs to facilitate maintenance and avoid damage. Signs in snow areas should be placed clear of plow zones and snow storage areas.
- In the design of sign frames, pedestals, or supports, consider providing adequate space for the addition of more information over time.
- In the developed areas of Yosemite Valley, signs should conform to the standards and character developed for Lower Yosemite Fall. Signs in historic properties such

as Yosemite Village or Curry Village should retain the Rustic style or be compatible with the character of adjacent historic structures.

- At Wawona and Chinquapin, signs in the immediate vicinity of historic white-painted buildings should reflect this special character. Signs at the Wawona campground, Wawona trailheads, and other Wawona or Chinquapin facilities that are visually separated from white buildings should be treated the same as wilderness signs. Material such as river-washed cobbles may be appropriate for pedestals when signs are sited close to stream, river, or riparian zones.
- Signs at entrances to wilderness areas should be designed in the Rustic style. Trailhead and view-area signs at Tuolumne and Merced Groves are good examples. These areas call for the use of unrefined, often-oversized, natural materials that are local or give such an appearance. The dominant landscape character of the immediate surroundings should indicate which natural materials are most appropriate. For example, sites in forested areas should make use of rough logs or timbers. Many site-orientation signs already employ a post-and-lintel design consisting of upright log supports bridged by equally heavy horizontal members that frame the sign board. Thick, routed-wood informational or mileage marker signs, on stout, single-log posts, are also appropriate at such sites. The structural system of the logs, timbers, or stones used to construct the frames and supports, as well as the connections (bolts, metal bands, etc.), should be clearly expressed (USDA 2007). In wilderness areas, prefabricated units, such as prerusted steel frames and sign supports, lack a primitive character and should not be used.
- At subalpine or other sites dominated by rock, sign pedestals could make use of that material. Trail distance-marker signs with steel panels and posts and incised lettering are also appropriate at such sites.

TOP LEFT *Wayside exhibit and seating area, Tuolumne Grove (2007) GH* TOP RIGHT *Interpretive sign (2010) RF* BOTTOM *Arch Rock Entrance pylon (2011) RF*

## LIGHTING

One of Yosemite's most profound experiences takes place at night, with the darkness of the mountains and the Valley walls framing an umbrella of stars. Like other natural wonders, the night sky is a diminishing resource that Yosemite and other National Parks seek to manage and preserve. NPS management policies address the protection of the nighttime environment in parks, termed "natural lightscapes." These natural lightscapes are recognized both as an important visitor resource and an integral part of the ecosystem.

But these natural lightscapes are seriously threatened by light pollution, even from within the park. The pressing concerns of safety and security have for several

*Night sky in Yosemite Valley from Glacier Point (2003) NPS-DD*

decades caused a proliferation of electric lighting and a corresponding increase in the ambient light level. Indoor and outdoor lighting design practices common to commercial developments in urban and suburban areas are the principal cause of light pollution in the park. To protect the natural lightscapes, lighting must be designed far more carefully than in the past, with lighting used only when absolutely needed.

Recognizing its responsibility to address lighting issues, Yosemite National Park adopted the *Yosemite National Park Lighting Guidelines* in 2011. This document contains a complete set of standards and guidelines created to prevent new sources of light pollution in the park and mitigate problems of existing lighting, without sacrificing the essential lighting needed to ensure the safety of park visitors and staff. Designers should refer to this document prior to the start of lighting design work. The following is a summary of the lighting guidelines.

**GUIDELINES**

- Employ electric lighting only where needed. Appropriate locations include public walkways, parking lots, and access ramps where normal night use, safety, security, and/or accessibility are essential. Specific locations include building entrances/exits, steps or changes in elevation between buildings and parking lots or major trails, and parking lots adjacent to night-activity centers. Outdoor work areas, such as service or storage yards, should be carefully evaluated for the need for illumination. In general, do not illuminate drives, roads, or streets except for shuttle bus stops or intersections where cross-traffic involving pedestrians is a significant safety concern.
- Avoid landscape lighting and architectural lighting such as building floodlighting. Do not provide any outdoor lighting for wilderness or backcountry locations unless absolutely necessary.
- Design lighting systems that produce an absolute minimum of glare and intrusion on the night. Without exception, use fully shielded lighting gear. Avoid floodlights, lanterns, post-top globes, and any other luminaire that emits light other than downward.
- As a general rule, luminaires should be mounted atop poles no more than 12 feet tall and strategically located to be protected from snow plowing equipment, with a maximum mounting height of 20 feet for parking lots and other areas. Use low-wattage sources with warm-toned lamps. A specific indirect LED luminaire is strongly recommended for most applications.
- Accent lighting, when used, should be aimed downward and be equipped with long "snoot" shields to prevent obtrusive light. Minimize light cast onto building walls, and illuminate steps from directly above as much as possible.

- Uniform illumination is generally not required except for universally accessible areas such as stairs or building entrances. Pathway lighting should consist of a very low-level "pool" of light, if at all.
- Lighting systems should be attractive, consistent with the architecture, and preferably innocuous. Use long-life, naturally-weathering materials or materials designed to minimize degradation, such as composite or Wosky brown powdercoated aluminum poles, granite and concrete bollards, and treated wooden poles. Seek timelessness in style and mounting.
- Locate lighting systems where they will not be damaged. Avoid conventional bollard lights and similar systems that can be easily damaged by people and wildlife. Consider snow and its removal in determining lighting designs and mounting heights.
- Use energy-efficient luminaires with the lowest possible wattage for each application. In general, lighting systems should be LED with permanently installed and heat-sinked 2,700–3,000K sources. Due to the potential for excessive glare, LED luminaires should be indirect or employ a diffusing lens. In some cases, luminaires may employ ceramic metal halide or compact fluorescent lamps.
- Design interior lighting to prevent light from spilling outdoors. Use adaptation compensating controls to reduce interior-light levels at night, which minimizes exterior spill and permits lower exterior-light levels. Aim lights away from windows and skylights.

*Lamp post in Yosemite Village (1928) YRL*

*Mother Curry Bungalow, Curry Village*

- Installing luminaires and feeder lines on trees is not appropriate.
- Internally illuminated vending machines shall not be illuminated at night.
- Signs should not be illuminated.

## Developed Areas

### SITING + BUILDING ORIENTATION

Ideally, buildings in Yosemite are sited to harmonize and blend with the landscape, placed in ways that respect major features, natural open spaces, drainages, trees, and boulders. In addition to visible features, buried archeological sites and other less-apparent, sensitive natural resources must be taken into consideration when siting buildings.

Many major developed areas in Yosemite are organized around a central outdoor space with views of scenic features. Traditionally, the important interior spaces of public buildings are also oriented toward views. Smaller buildings, such as lodgings and residences, are found in informal groupings with generous open space around them, sited to capture views or winter sun exposure where possible.

Each developed area has a unique site layout that influences its architectural character. Curry Village is laid out in a band along the base of a talus slope. The visitor service buildings are organized around a central public space, flanked by tents and cabins carefully integrated with the slopes, boulders, and trees. Yosemite Lodge has a campus layout, with lodging buildings dispersed around the visitor service complex. Yosemite Village began as a group of buildings around a rectangular open space. The open space was later extended into a linear pedestrian precinct to incorporate additional visitor service buildings. The Ahwahnee stands in splendid isolation from other developed areas in the Valley, set on the edge of a meadow against the backdrop of Valley walls. The Wawona Hotel, on a gentle slope above the Wawona Road, offers quiet and solitude for visitors coming to and from the more active Valley. Glacier Point at the Valley rim, some 3,500 feet above the Valley floor, is closely defined at the forest edge as a linear promenade with sweeping vistas of the Valley, Yosemite Wilderness, and Sierra Nevada crest to the east. Tuolumne Meadows, a dramatic subalpine location, is flanked with small areas of development mostly tucked into the forest edge overlooking the meadows.

A unique example of sensitivity to setting was displayed in John Muir's hang-nest—his small, box-like home fastened beneath the gable of James Hutchings' sawmill. Muir wrote, "The hole in the roof is to command a view of the glorious South [Half] Dome...There

*John Muir's sketch of his hang nest at Hutchings' Saw Mill (ca. 1871) from* John Muir in Yosemite *by Shirley Sargent*

*Rangers' Club at the edge of Cook's Meadow, Yosemite Village (2004) GH*

is a corresponding skylight on the side of the roof which commands a full view of the Upper Yosemite Falls, and the window at the end has a view sweeping down the Valley among the pines and cedars and silver firs." He recounted as well the "murmuring hush of the water below" and the window in the roof that allowed him to "look at the stars on calm nights" (Johnston 1971).

The siting and orientation of buildings can take advantage of both silence and the sounds of nature. The sounds of waterfalls and wildlife are key aspects of the visitor experience. In spring and early summer, waterfalls can be heard throughout the Valley, and they can be enjoyed from a private balcony or a dining terrace. With increased visitation and its attendant traffic, human-made noise has disrupted natural silence and sounds. Unnatural noise intrusion can also occur indoors between guest rooms in lodging areas. Attention should be given to the requirements of sound attenuation between lodging units to preserve the opportunity to enjoy natural sounds.

Visual privacy depends on the relationship between indoor and outdoor spaces. Guests should have a degree of separation from people in the adjacent outdoor spaces, and passersby should not feel that they intrude on guests enjoying the view from their rooms or balconies.

**GUIDELINES**

- Designers should provide a pre-design analysis that identifies existing site spatial organization, positive and negative site characteristics, and natural, cultural, and archeological resources and data provided by park staff. Major views, site features, advantageous topography, and opportunities for appropriate solar orientation should be noted for potential incorporation into site

TOP + BOTTOM *Cascades cabins, 2003 (since removed)*

design and building orientation. The pre-design analysis should also note areas such as meadows that may provide view opportunities and natural sounds, such as waterfalls but must not be impacted by development.

- During the schematic design phase, designers should indicate how the location of public- and private-use structures have taken advantage of the site opportunities, avoided negative impacts, and minimized the overall impacts of the planned development.

## ARCHITECTURAL CHARACTER

The architectural character of the older developments—such as Curry Village and Yosemite Village—established rustic design in Yosemite Valley. NPS Rustic style buildings were designed to blend with their natural setting, using materials and colors found in the landscape. The early buildings and structures at Camp Curry, including the welcome sign, the registration building, Mother Curry's bungalow, and the Foster Curry cabin, are distinguished by simple roof forms, wood shingle roofs, and unpeeled logs. Many of the buildings in Yosemite Village make use of local materials found in the landscape and handcrafted construction techniques. The Ahwahnee combines rustic design with contemporary technology. Its facades are composed of granite-clad piers that are joined by concrete infill walls stained and formed to simulate wood. Other rustic elements include low-slope hipped roofs, exposed concrete roof framing elements designed to simulate wood rafters, board-formed concrete simulating wood siding, wood windows arranged in regular patterns, and natural colors.

Buildings in the upper reaches of the park respond to their particular high-altitude remote environment. Important early rustic buildings include the Geology Hut at Glacier Point, Parsons Memorial Lodge, Tioga Pass Entrance Station, and the historic comfort stations designed by NPS landscape architect John Wosky at Tuolumne Meadows. All of these are noteworthy examples of masonry construction and classic alpine architecture.

Later architecture in Yosemite Valley departed dramatically from the Rustic tradition. The buildings at Yosemite Lodge, completed in 1956, were built in the Mission 66 style. The registration building, lounge, cafeteria, restaurant, and souvenir shop buildings are distinguished by steel-frame construction and large expanses of glass. Their goal was sturdy, low-maintenance, permanent structures that could serve the modern-day needs of the traveling public on a large scale (McClelland 1998).

*The Ahwahnee with backdrop of cliff to north (2004) GH*

**GUIDELINES**

- For the design of new structures within a historic property, designers should consult *The Secretary of the Interior's Standards for Treatment of Historic Properties* for guidance to ensure compatibility.

*Rustic porch, Yosemite Village (2008) GH*

- Designers should analyze the architectural character of a developed area and identify the unique response to the natural setting that guided the original development. When building in developed areas, continue the essence of the spatial order, massing, and character using compatible forms, materials, and color.
- Designers should seek inspiration from the rich examples of rustic design that exist in the park, and develop contemporary expressions employing rustic principles. Design buildings to blend in with their natural setting. Employ the colors, texture, and materials found in the surrounding landscape.
- If designing within a Mission 66 complex such as Yosemite Lodge, consider a more functional, contemporary approach that incorporates materials and design compatible with the Mission 66 era facility.
- Designers should specify natural or natural-looking material such as wood, stone, or concrete. Natural weathering of wood is a basic characteristic of rustic

Geology Hut, Glacier Point (2008) RF

architecture making wood a preferred material. Board-formed concrete has historical precedent in Yosemite Valley and is an appropriate construction technique for new buildings. However, avoid imitation of natural materials, such as concrete made to look like stone.

- If composite materials are used, they should be plain-surfaced, not grain-simulated. Stains and paint applications should be carefully selected to blend with the building's natural surroundings.

## BUILDING SHAPE + MASSING

Simple building forms are found throughout Yosemite National Park. These buildings are designed to blend with their natural surroundings and serve as backdrops for park activities. The historic approach to shape and massing for large buildings has been to limit the size of each building and accommodate program requirements in a series of linked structures. Simple rectangular shapes and rustic details help to further reduce the scale of large buildings. Use of building elements that surround portions of a building, such as verandahs, porches, roof dormers, and raised terraces, break down the mass of a large building, for example the Annex at the Wawona Hotel.

Orientation of rooms or major spaces that depart from the overall organization of the plan give emphasis to the importance of the natural world beyond. For example, the axis of the dining room at The Ahwahnee was adjusted from the building's overall plan arrangement to take advantage of views of Upper Yosemite Fall.

In general, buildings within the developed areas of the park have been designed with consistent shape and massing. Features vary within a restrained vocabulary of rustic forms. An example of this can be found in the three early buildings in the Yosemite Village administrative center—the NPS administration building, the museum, and the post office.

Roof detail, comfort station, Tuolumne Meadows Campground (2008) GH

TOP LEFT *Mountain Shop clerestory at Curry Village* BOTTOM LEFT *Museum, Yosemite Village (2004) GH* RIGHT *Small building with jerkinhead roof, near Yosemite Lodge (2004) GH*

**GUIDELINES**

- The size and massing of structures should be designed to reflect and enhance the immediate natural or historic setting. Balance between the functional requirements of the building and the capacity of the site must be maintained. Where a program calls for a large floor area, that area should be broken down into logical elements that fit the site, keeping in mind that too many small outbuildings could detract from the overall massing of buildings.
- Plan shapes should be rectangular, with variations from the basic shape generated by the programmatic requirements.
- The height of new buildings should not be radically different from adjacent, existing structures.

## ROOF FORM + MATERIALS

Although a wide range of roof forms are found throughout Yosemite National Park, each developed area is unified by a predominant roof form, material, and detailing. The most common roof is a simple gable, usually of medium pitch, with moderate overhangs. Steeper roof pitches are sometimes combined with dormers. Less common are hipped roofs, found at The Ahwahnee and Curry Village, and jerkinhead roofs, formerly found at Yosemite Lodge and other areas.

Exposed roof sheathing and framing is seen consistently throughout the park. Rough-sawn framing members and decking weather well, and their use provides architectural consistency in developed areas. Overscaled, wood framing elements were employed during the Rustic period, and these same principles can be used today to establish rustic character.

*Superintendent's House (Residence 1), Yosemite Valley (1942) YRL-RA*

Historically, roofs in the park were clad with wood shingles or shakes, with the exception of The Ahwahnee, which has a slate roof. On historic buildings with wood shingle roofs, wood replacement shingles are used. Asphalt shingles are commonly used on newer structures to satisfy fire protection requirements of a Class A fire-resistant roof.

Metal roofing has little precedent in Yosemite Valley and is not an appropriate replacement material for historic buildings. It has been used to a limited extent in Yosemite Village at the maintenance buildings and the dorms at Lower Tecoya. Metal roofs are found in the remote higher elevations where heavy snowfall and fire are important issues. Metal is less appropriate in Valley locations because of its reflectivity when viewed from a distance, especially from the surrounding cliffs. Weathering metal and durable coatings can address this concern for excess reflectivity. Careful site review of these issues is required.

**GUIDELINES**

- Schematic design of roofs should consider compatibility with existing structures, the use of simple geometry, the incorporation of dormers to break down the scale of a large roof, and provision of usable interior space, sheltering of primary entries, and protection of exterior walkways from roof drainage.
- Roofs should be designed to provide protection and shading for windows. The specification of tinted

glazing is inappropriate due to incompatibility with historic structures and because of the distortion it causes to natural colors in the views.

- Asphalt shingles are an acceptable roof material for new buildings. Asphalt shingles that are complementary to those on existing (and in many cases historic) buildings in terms of color, texture, and thickness of the edge should be specified.
- When circumstances require a metal roof, it should be a standing seam roof treated with a nonreflective coating in an approved color. Refer to the "Huts, Cabins + High Sierra Camps" chapter for guidelines on metal roofs in the high country.
- Roof accessories and structures such as chimneys and mechanical equipment should be combined, where they are less visible, and should be placed to allow snow movement. Recommended details include exposed framing elements with rough-sawn texture.
- Clerestory windows and skylights are useful for letting daylight penetrate interior spaces. Their location and detailing should recognize the hazards of snow and ice accumulation and potential for moisture penetration.

## BUILDING EXTERIORS

The use of natural weathering materials, such as wood and stone, on a building exterior establishes a visual connection between the building and the natural setting. The major components of a building's exterior are the walls, base, windows, entrances, and porches.

Facade design should strive for compatibility with adjacent buildings as well as the natural setting. Many of the historical facade patterns that have been used in the park, including resawn boards, shingles, or shakes, are appropriate for new buildings.

### Walls

Wood used for wall siding, columns (either logs or sawn timbers), and exposed roof framing is common throughout the park. A variety of wood wall siding material is used, including sugar pine shakes, redwood and cedar shingles, vertical board and batten, and horizontal board patterns. Select wood species for their ability to withstand the elements. Siding patterns often change between the first and second floors. Boards are typically rough sawn. Wood with resawn texture creates a rustic surface that blends surface blemishes. The texture can vary from rough-sawn, found in the beginning stages of the milling process, to fine-sawn. Since the 1920s and 1930s, different protective finishes were used for wood siding, including clear oil, clear stains, and paint. While these finishes continue to be used today, pigmented coatings have become the most reliable long-term protection.

*Detail of Administration Building, Yosemite Village*

Granite masonry has often been used as foundation cladding or as a rusticated lower-story wall. At The Ahwahnee, stone was used extensively to clad the massive piers that rise the full height of the building. Parsons Memorial Lodge in Tuolumne Meadows and the Geology Hut at Glacier Point demonstrate how native granite can create a strong visual connection to the boulders and cliffs in the immediate background.

### Base

The protected base or weathering base is an important unifying element for buildings in Yosemite. It is not only a character-defining feature, but also a functional element that extends the life of the lower wall cladding. A base of natural weathered rock similar to that found in the adjacent landscape visually anchors the building to the ground and protects vulnerable upper walls from accumulated snow and wind-driven rain splash.

The protected base has historical precedent in Yosemite Village, Curry Village, and the CCC Mess Hall at Tuolumne Meadows. Contemporary treatments have been used at Yosemite Lodge and Curry Village employee housing.

In Yosemite Village, stone masonry clads the entire ground floor of the museum, the post office, and the administration building. This treatment visually lowers the overall height of the buildings. Concrete formed by rough-sawn boards results in a strong textured surface. This technique has been used extensively at The Ahwahnee and also at the extension of the Mountain Room Restaurant at Yosemite Lodge. At Tuolumne Meadows, the CCC Mess Hall is an excellent example of the masonry protected base.

### Windows, Entrance, and Porches

Window size and design will vary due to functional and architectural requirements. Scale and proportion should be more vertical than horizontal. Lodging and residential buildings require more modestly scaled windows than public buildings. Divided lights are not required but

*Detail of Medical Clinic, Yosemite Village (2004) GH*

*Historic residence, Yosemite Village*

LEFT *Exterior wall of Administration Building, Yosemite Village (2004) GH* RIGHT *Roof framing and wall treatment, CCC Mess Hall, Tuolumne Meadows (2007) GH*

may be appropriate for compatibility in historic properties. Use windows divided into small lights when single glazing is possible. When double glazing is required by energy conservation standards, be careful that the scale of muntins does not become bulky.

The entrances of major public buildings are often identified as important elements of the facade through the use of porches and verandahs. These elements give additional form to the facade, indicate to visitors the location of the entrances, and offer protection from the weather. Smaller buildings frequently incorporate modest porches or shed roofs over entrance doors.

The use of color to blend structures with their natural setting is an important principle. Historically, NPS buildings have been stained or painted a standard brown color, and their roofs have had unpainted wood shingles.

**GUIDELINES**

- Design facades to be compatible both with the prevailing architectural character of the area and with adjacent structures and the natural setting.
- Arrangements of doors and windows should follow regular patterns and also respond to interior requirements. Window proportions and sizes in the commercial buildings should be more generous than those of guest-quarter buildings. Wood windows and glazed wood doors with generous lights are recommended.
- Tinted glazing is inappropriate due to incompatibility with historic structures and because it mutes and distorts colors.
- Building entries must be clearly defined, and easily accessible, and must provide protection from the weather. An entrance accessed through a porch or verandah allows a gracious transition to the outdoors.
- Design buildings with a minimum base of 20 inches above grade of either granite or board-formed concrete to ensure protection from rain splash and snow buildup.
- For new construction, designers should specify granite with the same composition, color, and texture as the granite in the immediate setting. Small quantities of Sierra granite may be available as a result of other projects within the park. When possible, use weathered granite.
- Use granite in places where it will have the most visual impact. It may well be that the most appropriate use will be in interior spaces, such as for fireplaces.
- Exposed framing such as rafters should be sized more generously than for conventionally framed buildings.

## Color

Color used on buildings has an important role in reducing the intrusion of buildings and structures into the natural environment of the park. The NPS architect Albert H. Good was an early advocate of incorporating color that occurs in nature and employing colors dominant in the immediate surroundings of buildings as a basis for their color. Generally, warm browns were recommended for "retiring a wood building in a wooded or partially wooded setting" (McClelland 1998). John Wosky, a NPS landscape architect in the 1930s, advocated the use of a warm brown color for most park service structures in Yosemite. NPS buildings and structures throughout the park soon became unified by their use of "Wosky brown."

Accent color gives relief and detail to an overall subdued rustic character. Typically used are dark black-green, dark umber, warm white, and charcoal grey.

Accent colors applied to sash and doors offer relief to an overall monotone. Stain color on various elements of a building can articulate the overall image; a subtle difference between beams and sheathing can articulate the roof soffit; likewise, columns and frame members may provide contrast to shingles and siding. Consider all elements of the exterior as opportunities to establish an overall palette for the building. These include elements such as masonry, ironwork, and hardware.

Colors found in the park vary from white (warm), dark green, dark burgundy, dark red oxides, and the reliable Wosky brown. The Ahwahnee has a special and distinct color palette that should be reserved for it alone.

The white structures in Wawona, White Wolf, and Chinquapin are in stark contrast to the rustic color palette found throughout the rest of the park. These buildings, located outside of Yosemite Valley, provide a cultural link to the nearby foothill communities with their predominately white buildings. (Refer to the discussion of the Wawona Hotel Complex in the "Wawona" chapter for more details.) Although deliberately temporal, the white canvas tent cabins of the High Sierra Camps and the general store and employee housing at Tuolumne Meadows fit easily with the late summer snow patches and the grey and white granite landscape.

**GUIDELINES**

- Designers must evaluate the building context to establish a color palette for the project in the early stages of work. Identify colors and material textures that will assist in the blending of the structure with the surrounding landscape and development. Palettes should be limited to one or two general colors with additional colors used to designate important project areas. Accent color should be used to provide relief and detail to an overall subdued rustic character. Typically used are dark black-green, dark umber, warm white, and charcoal grey.
- Designers should continue the use of white canvas, as established at the High Sierra Camps and the Tuolumne Meadows store, for any new canvas buildings or cabins. Continue the use of painted doors and framing in the same color as in the established tradition.
- Carefully evaluate the setting for buildings in the High Sierra. Tioga Pass Entrance Station is a good example of building color and texture blending with the natural surroundings. Located in a spare, boulder-strewn position at the edge of the timberline, the station makes generous use of masonry in the sidewalls, establishing a strong connection to the adjacent landscape—the walls seem to emerge from the hillside. The wood framing elements found in the nearby landscape are treated with a warm stain color that is harmonious with the adjacent landscape and the masonry construction.
- In some areas, color has been used to establish an identity for a site. The light green shutters are an unusual application at The Ahwahnee. While variations on color can be pleasing, color should be used with restraint to achieve harmony with the natural setting.

---

*"In these great areas the landscape architect and the architect must approach their problems with humility. In the natural areas the landsape work is done. The landscape architect is in the position of placing intrusions (for human convenience) in the natural picture, knowing full well the landscape will be less perfect when he is through. The architect must subdue his design [so] that the work of man will not attempt to dominate that of nature. Likewise, in historical areas they must endeavor to let the past dominate the present. Their task is a delicate one."* TOM VINT, CHIEF ARCHITECT, NPS WESTERN REGION LANDSCAPE ENGINEERING DIVISION, CA. 1930 (NPS 1989C)

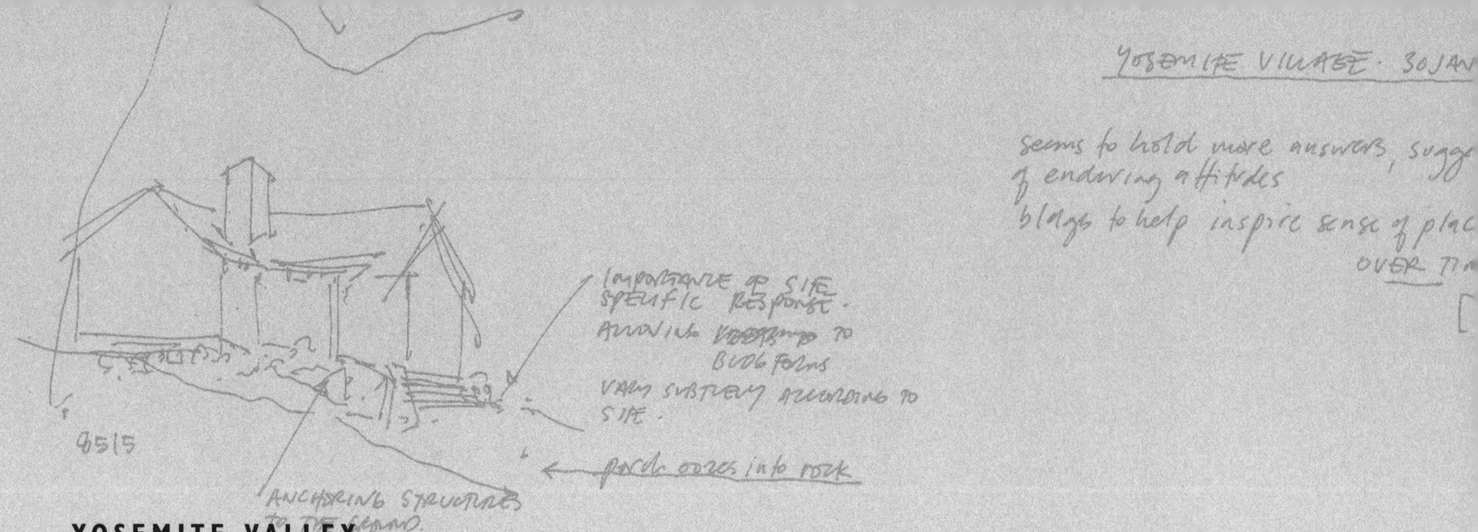


# YOSEMITE VALLEY



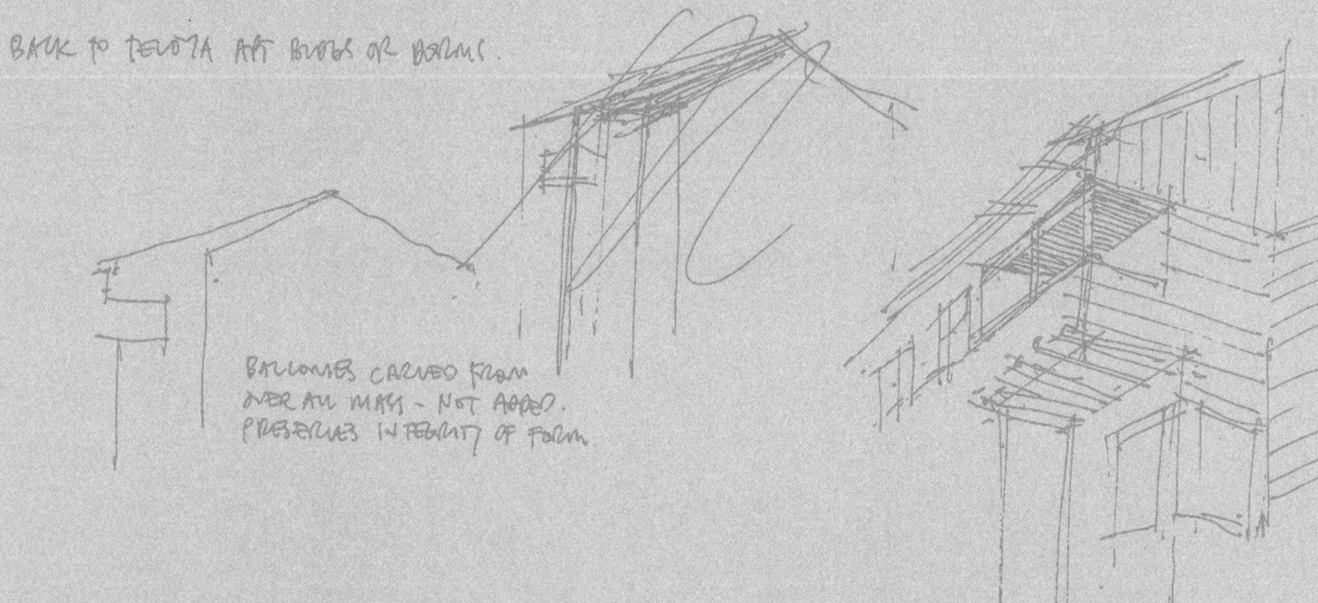


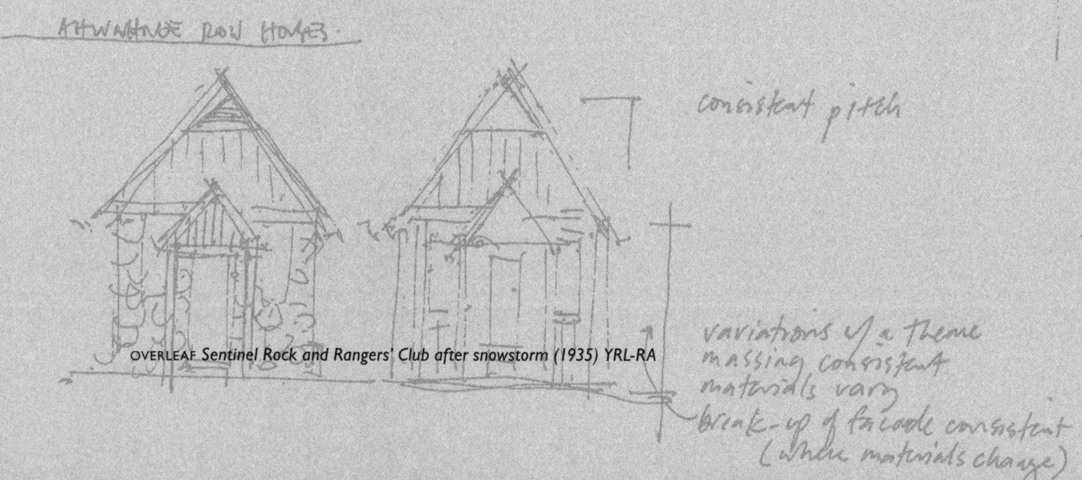


OVERLEAF *Sentinel Rock and Rangers' Club after snowstorm (1935) YRL-RA*

# YOSEMITE VALLEY

THE YOSEMITE VALLEY landscape is the result of a long and complex history of interactions between natural systems and human influences. Today it is the landscape record of one of the most ambitious and historically significant experiments in the preservation of "natural" scenery ever attempted. The Valley floor landscape as a whole is nationally significant in the themes of outdoor recreation, tourism, and conservation. Since 1864, Yosemite has been an archetype for the preservation of scenic places through their development as public parks.

THE CULTURAL PROCESSES OF DEFINING SACRED SPACE, OF TURNING LAND INTO LANDSCAPE, AND OF MAKING A WILD PLACE INTO A PUBLIC PARK, HAVE MADE YOSEMITE VALLEY ONE OF THE MOST CULTURALLY SIGNIFICANT NATURAL PLACES IN AMERICA. THE SIGNIFICANCE OF THE CULTURAL LANDSCAPE OF YOSEMITE CANNOT BE DESCRIBED OR ASSESSED APART FROM ITS SIGNIFICANCE AS A NATURAL LANDSCAPE. THE DISTINCTION BETWEEN WHAT IS NATURAL AND WHAT IS ARTIFICIAL IS RARELY CLEAR IN YOSEMITE VALLEY. THE VALLEY FLOOR LANDSCAPE IS A UNITY THAT COMBINES THE PASTORAL AND THE AWESOME, THE CULTURAL AND THE NATURAL, THE INDIAN AND THE EUROPEAN, THE PAST AND THE PRESENT. **YOSEMITE VALLEY HISTORIC DISTRICT NOMINATION • 2004**

## SETTING

Yosemite Valley is one of the most familiar and scenic places in the American West, and perhaps the most famous glacially carved valley in the world. Within its modest seven square miles are what many consider to be the greatest concentration of natural wonders in the world. Yosemite Valley boasts numerous waterfalls, ranging from the windblown cascade of Bridalveil Fall to thundering Nevada and Vernal falls as they drop more than 900 feet over two gigantic, glacially carved granite steps. The Valley includes many of the highest waterfalls in the world. Yosemite Falls, the highest falls on the continent, descends 2,425 feet. The Valley is bounded by sheer cliffs, spires, domes, and imposing granite monoliths. These monoliths include Half Dome, a massive dome with one side seemingly sheared off, and El Capitan, standing guard at the entrance to the Valley and attracting rock climbers to one of the largest exposed-granite cliff faces in the world.

BUT NO TEMPLE MADE WITH HANDS CAN COMPARE WITH YOSEMITE. EVERY ROCK IN ITS WALLS SEEMS TO GLOW WITH LIFE. SOME LEAN BACK IN MAJESTIC REPOSE; OTHERS, ABSOLUTELY SHEER OR NEARLY SO FOR THOUSANDS OF FEET, ADVANCE BEYOND THEIR COMPANIONS IN THOUGHTFUL ATTITUDES, GIVE WELCOME TO STORMS AND CALMS ALIKE, SEEMINGLY UNAWARE, YET HEEDLESS, OF EVERYTHING GOING ON ABOUT THEM. **JOHN MUIR • THE YOSEMITE • 1912**

The unparalleled drama of these (and many other) features is set on a stage of serene and pastoral beauty. The dazzling juxtaposition of the calm, parklike setting and nearly incomprehensible grandeur has made Yosemite one of the most visited, described, and depicted places in the world. Many have attested that descriptions and photographs are inadequate to fully convey the magnificence of the setting. "I sit in a kind of delicious dream, the scenery unconsciously mingling with my dream," rhapsodizes Joseph LeConte, University of California geology professor, in his Yosemite trip journal during his first trip in 1870."I have heard and read much of this wonderful valley, but I can truly say I have never imagined the grandeur of the reality" (LeConte 1875).

The Valley is set in the south-central portion of Yosemite National Park, which is on the western slope of the central Sierra Nevada Mountains. Oriented in an east–west direction, the Valley is about 7 miles long and 0.5 to 1 mile wide. Elevations along the Valley floor range between 3,800 feet and 4,200 feet above sea level. The exceptionally sheer and nearly vertical walls of Yosemite Valley rise up to 4,000 feet from the almost-level Valley floor. The Valley floor itself is a relatively flat floodplain, through which the Merced River winds, flanked by open meadows and forests of oaks and pines.

Yosemite Valley was formed over a period of millions of years, first by the waters of the ancient Merced River as the Sierra Nevada Mountains were uplifted and then by several advances of glaciers that scraped and carved away the weaker portions of the walls of the upper Merced River canyon. When the climate warmed and the glaciers receded, they left behind a U-shaped Valley with almost vertical sculpted granite walls rising above a shallow Lake Yosemite. This ancient lake eventually filled with sediment to form the flat floodplain seen today.

*Yosemite Falls from Yosemite Lodge*

## VALLEY WALLS

Rising dramatically from the Valley floor are sheer walls of granite. Formed in a distinctive U-shape by three major glacial periods, these cliffs are visible from almost every point in the Valley. Perhaps the most dramatic spatial characteristic of this landscape as a whole is the narrowness of Yosemite Valley in relation to the height of the walls enclosing it. The approximately 1:3 to 2:3 vertical–horizontal ratio creates a highly unusual landscape that has historically influenced the location of development in the Valley.

The often-overwhelming visual impact of the flat Valley floor contrasted with the sheer cliffs (especially the east–west views in the narrow section of the Valley) has for more than a century attracted painters and photographers to capture their effects. This powerful combination imposes a dominant presence from almost any point in the Valley.

The Valley walls provide a powerful context and backdrop for buildings placed on the Valley floor. Many historic buildings, such as The Ahwahnee, were designed

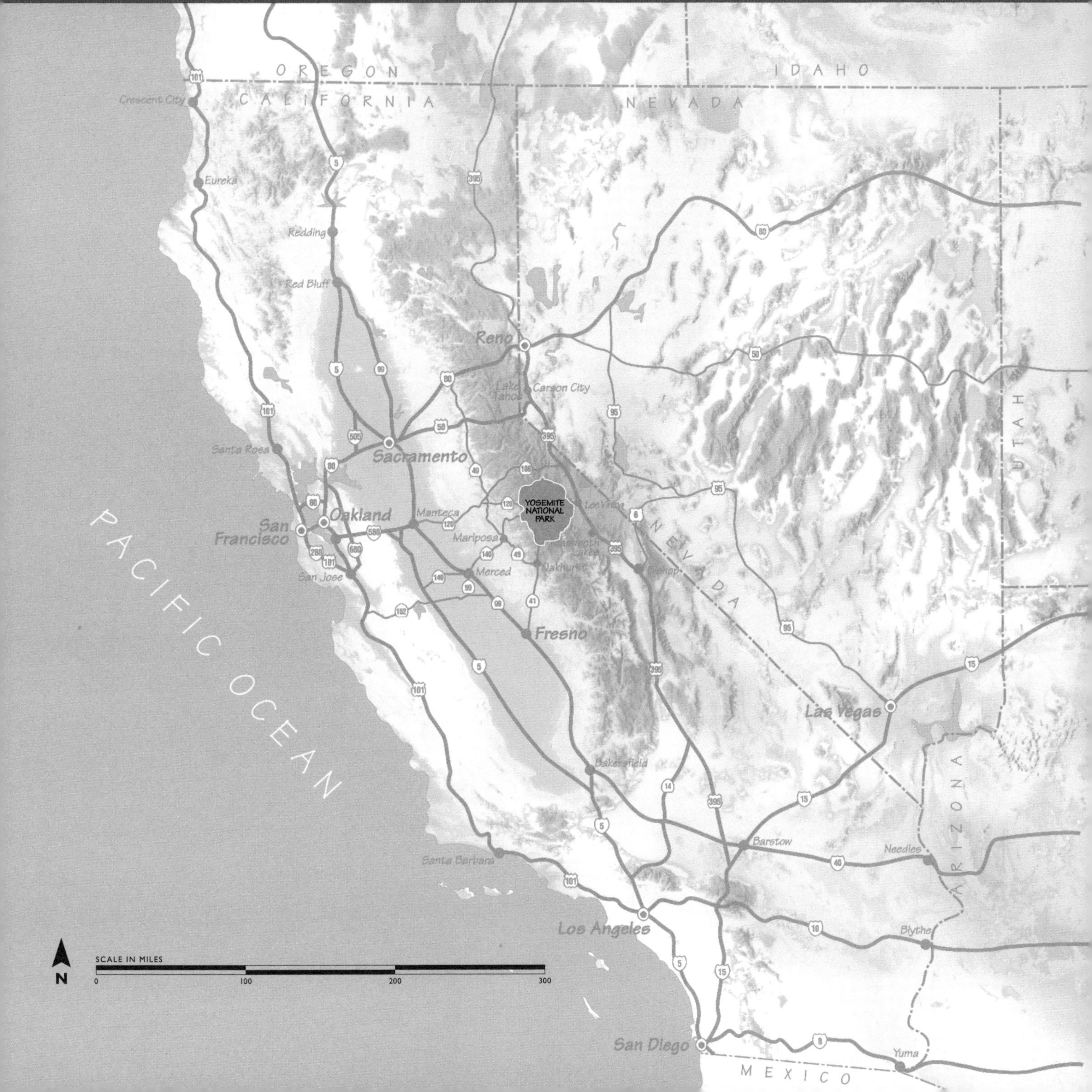
OREGON
IDAHO
CALIFORNIA
NEVADA
UTAH
ARIZONA
MEXICO
PACIFIC OCEAN
Crescent City
Eureka
Redding
Red Bluff
Reno
Lake Tahoe
Carson City
Sacramento
Santa Rosa
Oakland
San Francisco
San Jose
Manteca
Mariposa
Merced
YOSEMITE NATIONAL PARK
Lee Vining
Mammoth Lakes
Oakhurst
Bishop
Fresno
Las Vegas
Bakersfield
Barstow
Needles
Santa Barbara
Los Angeles
Blythe
San Diego
Yuma
SCALE IN MILES
0
100
200
300
N

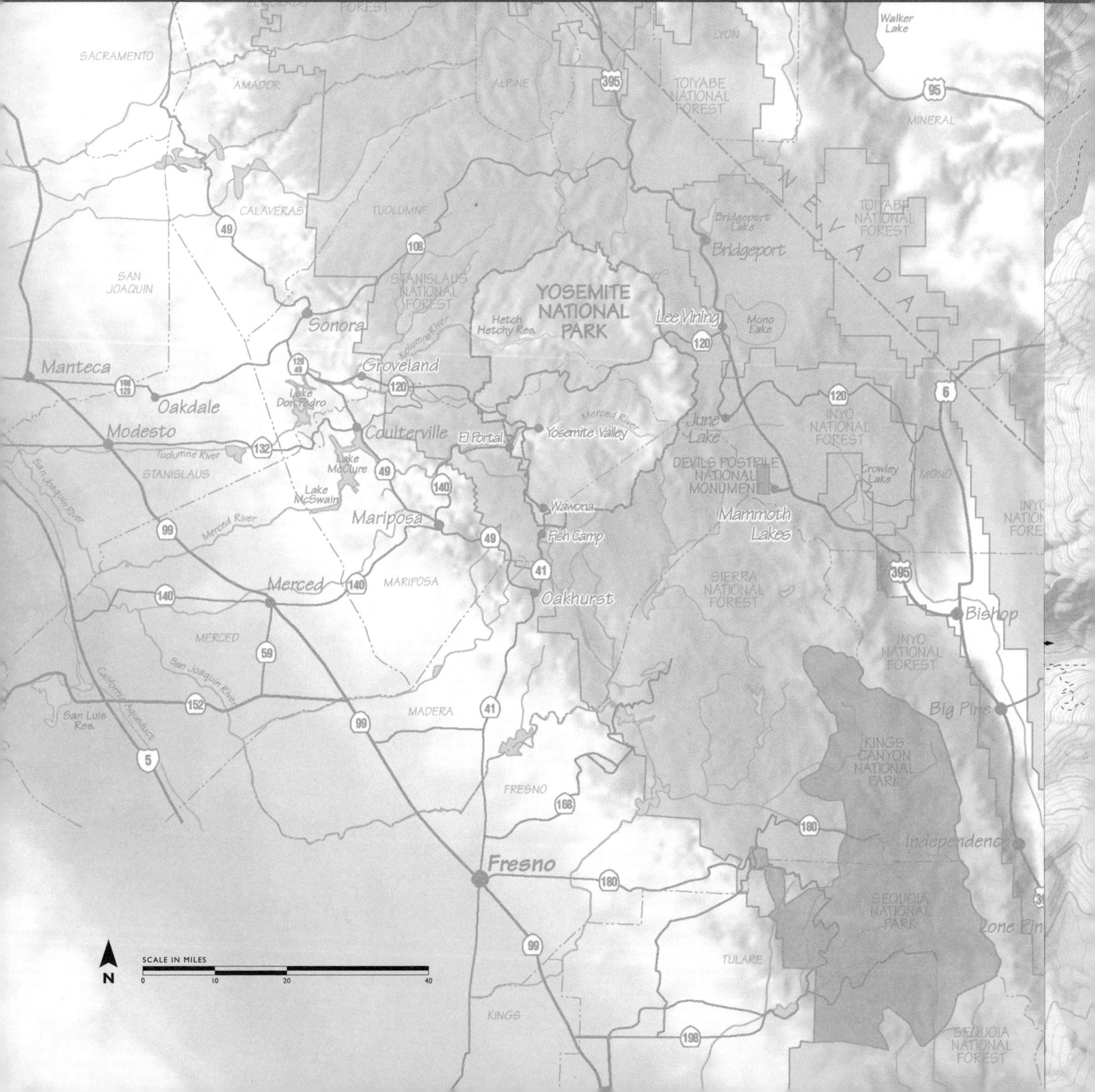
Walker Lake
LYON
SACRAMENTO
AMADOR
ALPINE
TOIYABE NATIONAL FOREST
MINERAL
CALAVERAS
TUOLUMNE
NEVADA
Bridgeport Lake
Bridgeport
SAN JOAQUIN
STANISLAUS NATIONAL FOREST
YOSEMITE NATIONAL PARK
Sonora
Hetch Hetchy Res.
Lee Vining
Mono Lake
Tuolumne River
Manteca
Groveland
Oakdale
Lake Don Pedro
Merced River
June Lake
INYO NATIONAL FOREST
Modesto
Coulterville
El Portal
Yosemite Valley
Tuolumne River
STANISLAUS
Lake McClure
DEVILS POSTPILE NATIONAL MONUMENT
Crowley Lake
MONO
San Joaquin River
Lake McSwain
Wawona
Mammoth Lakes
Mariposa
Merced River
Fish Camp
Merced
MARIPOSA
SIERRA NATIONAL FOREST
Oakhurst
Bishop
MERCED
San Joaquin River
California Aqueduct
San Luis Res.
MADERA
Big Pine
KINGS CANYON NATIONAL PARK
FRESNO
Independence
Fresno
SEQUOIA NATIONAL PARK
TULARE
KINGS
SEQUOIA NATIONAL FOREST
N
SCALE IN MILES
0
10
20
40
395
95
49
108
120
6
132
140
99
41
59
152
5
168
180
198

and sited with the cliffs as a backdrop. Curry Village, by virtue of its small buildings, does not compete with its awesome setting but celebrates the difference in scale.

Because of the geological forces that have shaped the Valley, the surrounding cliffs present a constant and unpredictable danger of rockfall. Periodic rockfall in Yosemite Valley is caused by freeze–thaw periods and earthquakes, among other factors. Rockfall has created steep talus slopes on layers of colluvium in many locations along each side of the Valley.

**GUIDELINES**

- New buildings near or within direct view lines to cliffs in Yosemite Valley should incorporate these views as part of the visual context of the building.
- New buildings near the cliffs should address the issues of building scale and massing in the context of the steep and dramatic cliffs.
- Public gathering spaces, where possible and appropriate, should be oriented to views of the Valley walls as well as the landmark peaks and monolithic forms, such as Half Dome, Sentinel Rock, and Royal Arches.
- New housing or lodging near the rockfall zone must be built in accordance with Yosemite National Park rockfall guidelines.

## WATERFALLS

Yosemite Valley contains a number of magnificent waterfalls that have through time been a major attraction. Each spring, the falls and rapids draw throngs of visitors to Yosemite, Vernal, Nevada, and Bridalveil falls, as well as to smaller waterfalls throughout the Valley.

In Yosemite Valley, developments and buildings have been sited around views of Yosemite Falls. As early as the late 1800s, vegetation was cleared to preserve these views. The plaza in Yosemite Village is oriented toward a view of Upper Yosemite Fall. The Ahwahnee dining room and the Mountain Room at Yosemite Lodge both feature views of Yosemite Falls. Trails provide views of Upper and Lower Yosemite Falls and the Middle Cascades from many different vantage points.

Evening Glow at Yosemite Falls, *Chiura Obata, woodcut print, 1930*

**GUIDELINES**

- Designers should orient buildings, public open spaces, public roadways, pedestrian trails, and gathering places to provide views of the waterfalls, when feasible and appropriate.
- Manage plant communities through prescribed burning, pruning, and removal to maintain views to waterfalls, including important views from main roads. Refer to the *Vegetation Management Plan* (NPS 1997) and vegetation studies for specific areas of Yosemite Valley for more information. Seek guidance from the park's *Scenic Vista Management Plan Environmental Assessment* (NPS 2011d).

*Yosemite Falls from Yosemite Village*

Southeast elevation of The Ahwahnee

- Designers should consider protecting and enhancing winter views of waterfalls when developing landscape and planting plans.
- Refer also to the "Vegetation" and "Scenic View" sections in this chapter.

## VEGETATION

Natural vegetation in Yosemite Valley can be grouped into four major communities: mixed conifer, oak woodlands, riparian, and meadow. Mixed conifer communities border the Valley in higher and drier zones and cover almost half of the Valley floor. Oak woodlands are composed of California black oaks and live oaks. Live oak communities are found on upland areas as well as drier parts of the talus slopes. Riparian vegetation along the Merced River includes willows, black cottonwood, and white alder. At the edge of the meadow, between meadow and forest, lies a zone of mixed-height vegetation, including low shrubs and small trees. The vegetation in this area is dense and varied, and it provides an important habitat for many forms of wildlife.

*Sentinel Rock from Camp 4 with Big Columbine and Little Columbine boulders in the foreground*

As long as people have lived in Yosemite Valley, the meadows have been managed in one form or another. American Indians burned the meadows to make it easier to flush out game and forage for seeds and acorns. Later, the meadows were used by settlers for agriculture and grazing. Nonnative vegetation (trees, shrubs, and grasses) was introduced by early park settlers for orchards and farming. By 1888 the commissioners of Yosemite Valley issued a policy for management of the meadows that would restore the landscape to its 1851 appearance. Fire management was discontinued in the 1850s, which encouraged the encroachment of pines and cedars into the meadows. Through the early 1900s, pasturage was limited in the meadows to ensure that the grasses and flowers had time to seed. Blasting of a glacial moraine in 1879 near El Capitan may have contributed to a drop in groundwater level, causing meadows to become drier, and allowing for the encroachment of conifers, which, in turn, shaded out the black oaks. Today the watering of vegetation in residential areas negatively affects native oak trees.

FROM THE MARGIN OF THESE GLORIOUS FORESTS THE FIRST GENERAL VIEW OF THE VALLEY IS TO BE GAINED—A REVELATION IN LANDSCAPE AFFAIRS THAT ENRICHES ONE'S LIFE FOREVER. ENTERING THE VALLEY, GAZING OVERWHELMED WITH THE MULTITUDE OF GRAND OBJECTS AROUND US, PERHAPS THE FIRST TO FIX OUR ATTENTION WILL BE BRIDAL VEIL, A BEAUTIFUL WATERFALL ON OUR RIGHT. ITS BROW, WHERE IT FIRST LEAPS FREE FROM THE CLIFF, IS ABOUT 900 FEET ABOVE US; AND AS IT SWAYS AND SINGS IN THE WIND, CLAD IN GAUZY, SUN-SIFTED SPRAY, HALF FALLING, HALF FLOATING, IT SEEMS INFINITELY GENTLE AND FINE; BUT THE HYMNS IT SINGS TELL THE SOLEMN FATEFUL POWER HIDDEN BENEATH ITS SOFT CLOTHING. **JOHN MUIR • THE YOSEMITE • 1912**

In the 1930s the Civilian Conservation Corps altered vegetation throughout Yosemite Valley. With the goal of opening up vistas, screening buildings, and improving the appearance of developed areas, CCC crews transplanted, pruned, and removed vegetation. Close to building foundations, they planted a variety of native, nonnative, and non-Valley species.

During the 1970s, there was a significant encroachment of plants—mostly conifers—into the meadows. In some cases, trees have grown large enough to block important scenic views. Although the meadows have been reduced by almost 50% since the 19th century, they remain an important landscape feature, providing crucial foreground for spectacular vistas of surrounding monuments and sanctuary for rodents, animals, reptiles, birds, and insects.

The *Vegetation Management Plan* recognizes that vegetation is "dynamic in form and function," and that the complexity of "plant communities, cultural landscapes, human impacts, development, and management zoning" in the Valley must be taken into consideration. The changing pattern of plants on the Valley floor also reflects the fact that the Merced River has meandered across the width of the Valley for thousands of years.

**GUIDELINES**

- For guidelines regarding Valley vegetation, refer to "Setting—Vegetation" in the "Unifying Elements" chapter.

*Tent cabins at Curry Village*

## Developed Areas

Because of its unique scenic beauty and the attraction it holds for tourists, Yosemite Valley—particularly at the eastern end—has been the focus of most of the development in Yosemite National Park. Six main areas present the highest density of development and range of visitor facilities. These include Yosemite Lodge, Yosemite Village, The Ahwahnee, Housekeeping Camp, Curry Village, and the campground areas.

Yosemite Village is the heart of visitor facilities in the Valley and is at the northernmost edge of the developed valley, between Yosemite Lodge and The Ahwahnee. Northside Drive delineates the area boundary to the south, and the canyon walls bound the area to the north. The Village area is bounded by the Ahwahnee Meadow and the easternmost channel of Yosemite Creek. The concentrated development in Yosemite Village accommodates a constant throng of visitors. The Village contains the main visitor center of the park, a museum, a re-created Indian Village and garden, a historic cemetery, a medical clinic, commercial enterprises, food services, employee housing, recreation facilities, park and concessioner administrative offices, maintenance facilities, and institutional facilities such as an elementary school, a childcare center, a magistrate court, a public garage, and a post office. The western portion of Yosemite Village includes a neighborhood of rustic, mostly single-family units; the park administration building; the museum; the Rangers' Club; the post office; and the Ansel Adams Gallery.

*Cabins at Housekeeping Camp*

To the west of Yosemite Village, within view of Yosemite Falls, is Yosemite Lodge, the Valley's lodging facility with the most modern architectural design, largely built during the Mission 66 period. The Camp 4 walk-in campground and the Lower Yosemite Fall area define much of the northern boundary. Yosemite Creek forms the eastern edge, and to the south are the fluctuating wetlands and floodplain. Developed over many years as a housing, lodging, and administrative center, Yosemite Lodge comprises a number of building clusters set in groves of trees and open meadow areas. These clusters include various lodging developments; a visitor services and recreation complex, containing both indoor and outdoor facilities; and a network of parking and circulation systems geared for pedestrians, vehicles, and bicycles.

Nearby, below the talus slopes of the cliffs to the north, is Camp 4, an informal, walk-in campground that was designated as a national historic site in 2003 for its role in the development of rock climbing. Just west of Camp 4 is the site of the future Indian Cultural Center, which will be at the historic site of the last Indian village in the Valley.

The Ahwahnee is in the northeastern section of Yosemite Valley, east of Yosemite Village. This site is dominated by the 1920s-era hotel building, but it also contains associated 1928 guest bungalows, a dormitory building for concessioner personnel, recreation facilities, and parking and circulation networks related to the facility and adjacent grounds. The hotel is considered the prime example of a Rustic-style grand lodge in a national park, and the hotel has been designated a National Historic Landmark.

Tents at Camp Curry, *Chiura Obata, Sumi on postcard, July 2, 1927*

South of the Merced River are Curry Village and the more seasonal facilities of Housekeeping Camp, Lower and Upper Pines campgrounds, and Happy Isles. Curry Village, historically known as "Camp Curry," is in the southeastern portion of Yosemite Valley, with Southside Drive and Stoneman Meadow bounding it on the north and the steeply sloped base of cliffs and talus below Glacier Point forming the southern edge. Curry Village first provided lodging for park visitors in 1899. Today Curry Village is a densely developed visitor services and lodging facility that incorporates recreation, circulation, and parking, and includes various lodging types, commercial facilities, and services. The predominant feature of the site is a cluster of several hundred tent cabins and simple wood cabins that dot the wooded area at the base of the talus slope. A large visitor services and administrative center containing shops, restaurants, recreational facilities, and an information kiosk is at the center of the complex. The historic significance of the camp includes its philosophy of providing lower-cost lodging for visitors and the Rustic style of architecture used in building construction.

Nearby developments are more seasonal and less dense in character. West of Curry Village, along the south bank of the Merced River, is the more contemporary Housekeeping Camp, which consists of a few core visitor services facilities and multiple open-air structures with tilt-up walls, canvas roofs, and screened and tree-shaded patios. South of Housekeeping Camp is the stone LeConte Memorial Lodge, a National Historic Landmark. Originally built by and still staffed by the Sierra Club, the lodge serves as an interpretive and meeting center open to the general public.

East of Curry Village are all the Valley drive-in campgrounds, which include Upper, Lower, and North Pines campgrounds. They are characterized by open sites under a forest canopy with an intermingling of comfort stations and kiosk structures. Near the entrance to North Pines Campground are the fenced enclosures and rustic structures of the Valley concessioner stable stand. And farther east, where the Merced River tumbles down to the level Valley floor, is Happy Isles, the major trailhead center in the Valley. Located at the start of the 211-mile John Muir Trail, Happy Isles includes a nature center, a comfort station, and a system of pedestrian bridges that provide access to islands set in the rushing river.

Yosemite Valley's primary circulation system features two west–east roads parallel to the Merced River, one on the north and the other on the south, appropriately named Northside and Southside Drives; these drives have branches and loops that provide access to the various developed areas. The roads and pullouts were designed to provide a sequence of ever-changing views as visitors traveled through the Valley. The two roads are connected by a series of vehicle and pedestrian bridges spanning the Merced River from Pohono Bridge at the west to the Happy Isles Bridge at the east end of the Valley. Six of the bridges spanning the Merced River, as well as those spanning Tenaya and Yosemite creeks, are of Rustic design and are listed on the National Register of Historic Places. Portions of the roads to the east have been converted to pedestrian or transit use only.

The Yosemite Valley Historic District features nationally significant examples of architecture, including the Rangers' Club, The Ahwahnee, and the LeConte Memorial Lodge, all of which are National Historic Landmarks. Yosemite Village is a nationally significant example of early NPS "park village" planning. Curry Village is a rare example of a surviving tent cabin complex that was once common in many parks. The bridges and other resources already listed in the National Register of Historic Places are significant examples of park development dating from the late 19th century to 1942.

*Museum with Upper Yosemite Fall, Yosemite Village (1938) YRL*

The Valley's cultural landscape is well documented in the Yosemite Valley Historic District National Register Nomination. The boundaries of the historic district extend from Valley wall to Valley wall, from Pohono Bridge to Mirror Lake and Nevada Fall. By 1942, the Valley landscape had assumed the overall dimensions and character it possesses today; the basic footprint of development has remained relatively constant since the 1940s. Only the Mission 66 era development in the Valley has yet to be fully researched and assessed to establish its significance and integrity. It is in Yosemite Valley that one can find the oldest, fullest, and purest expression of what scenic preservation and park development can achieve on the national scale.

# YOSEMITE VILLAGE

THE PRESENT-DAY YOSEMITE Village originated in the 1920s as a replacement for the outdated, 19th-century Old Village. Increasing numbers of visitors put pressure on the National Park Service to improve and develop new facilities, such as museums, observations stations, checking stations, comfort stations, and administration buildings. The old Yosemite Village, prone to flooding, was moved away from the river and out of the open meadows. Its new site on the sunny north side of the Valley, under the trees and against the Valley walls, was less conspicuous from popular viewpoints above the Valley.

THE YOSEMITE VILLAGE HISTORIC DISTRICT, THROUGH BOTH SITES AND STRUCTURES, REPRESENTS ALMOST THE ENTIRE RANGE OF YOSEMITE HISTORY SINCE 1855, INCLUDING EARLY HOMESTEADING, JOHN MUIR'S EARLY RESIDENCE IN THE PARK, DEVELOPMENT OF THE NATIONAL PARK, THE ARMY'S ROLE IN PARK ADMINISTRATION, AND THE EVOLUTION OF EARLY NATIONAL PARK SERVICE ADMINISTRATION AND INTERPRETATION OF THE RESOURCE OF YOSEMITE. **NATIONAL REGISTER OF HISTORIC PLACES NOMINATION FORM • 1977**



The plan for the new Yosemite Village was devised by Myron Hunt, Daniel Hull, and Thomas Vint, architects and landscape architects for the National Park Service. Drawing from the best of contemporary American and British town planning, three separate areas were created for administrative, residential, and maintenance uses. The plan called for the careful selection of building sites and an adherence to an architectural theme that harmonized construction with the natural environment.

Buildings for the park's administration and concessioner services were to be placed around a central plaza that provided parking. By 1924, with the construction of a new administration building, the new Village center was beginning to take shape. Myron Hunt's administration building was a modest Rustic structure with a lower-story concrete foundation faced with boulders, an upper story of shingled walls, and a broad sloping roof supported on exposed log purlins. This building established the particular mode of harmonious Rustic design to which later buildings in the Village would conform. The construction of a post office and museum followed within two years. The three government buildings and the Rangers' Club of 1921 created the nucleus for the new civic center.

A separate residential subdivision was laid out adjacent to the civic area, with curvilinear streets and Arts and Crafts-style bungalows. A new maintenance area was also planned to the north of the central plaza. Each area of the Village was separated by vegetation, topography, and design to keep each land-use zone independent of the others (NPS 2004h).

By 1925 Yosemite National Park had more visitors and more automobiles than any other park. To accommodate this level of visitation, Yosemite Village continued to grow. Later, during the Mission 66 period, the Village gained a new visitor center, store, restaurant, and other facilities. A few years later, the civic plaza was converted to a pedestrian area, and cars were excluded from the center of the Village.

*Post Office and Upper Yosemite Fall, Yosemite Village (2004) GH*

## Setting

### NATURAL SYSTEMS + FEATURES

Yosemite Village is found on the warm, north side of Yosemite Valley, at the base of a gentle alluvial fan formed over the millennia by debris from Indian Canyon and Lehamite Creek. A year-round creek flows from north to south across the Village and may be a source of wet soils and pavement subsidence just west of the Village Store. The creek bed is obscured and unavailable as an interpretive element throughout most of the Village. Today, the Village site is above the floodplain of the Merced River, though it is within the floodplain of Indian Creek.

The other major natural systems influencing and limiting development in the Village are the nearby cliffs and talus slopes along the northern edge of the Village. This area continues to be subject to periodic rockfall and continues to influence land use and services.

### SCENIC VIEWS

Yosemite Village is set in its current location partly to take advantage of the spectacular view of Upper Yosemite Fall. The main civic plaza of the Village is oriented toward the waterfall, and it is visible from many areas of the central Village. There are also impressive views to such scenic features as Lost Arrow Spire, Indian Canyon, Sentinel Rock, and Royal Arches, some of which are now obscured by the growth of conifers. Historic views to Yosemite Falls remain, although the growth of vegetation within the plaza areas has reduced the number of vantage points and open views that existed historically.

*Historic residences, Yosemite Village (2004) GH*

**YOSEMITE VILLAGE**

A Historic NPS Residential Area
B Visitor Services and Administrative Core
C Maintenance, Service, and Storage
D Upper Tecoya
E Middle Tecoya
F Medical Clinic
G Lower Tecoya
H Village Store and Garage
I Visitor Arrival/Meadow

1 Historic Residences, Garages, and Woodsheds
2 Utility Buildings—Barns, Sheds, Shops
3 Utility Building #527 (Fort Yosemite)
4 Concessioner Warehouse
5 Upper Tecoya Residences
6 Visitor Center
7 Yosemite Medical Clinic
8 Cottages and Garages in Tecoya
9 Tecoya Dormitories
10 Ahwahnee Row Houses and Garages
11 Concessioner's General Offices
12 Village Store
13 Pedestrian Mall
14 Rangers' Club
15 Administration Building
16 Pioneer Cemetery
17 Indian Village
18 Museum
19 Ansel Adams Gallery
20 Post Office
21 Northside Drive
22 Ahwahnee Meadow
23 Degnan's Restaurant
24 Elementary School
25 Village Drive

*California black oak (Quercus kelloggii)*

Key views from the Village include the following: views from the plaza area up to Yosemite Point, Upper Yosemite Fall, Half Dome, and Sentinel Rock, views from the NPS residential area to Yosemite Falls and Yosemite Point, and views from the Lower Tecoya residential area across Ahwahnee Meadow to North Dome, Half Dome, and Glacier Point.

**GUIDELINES**

- Preserve and maintain the documented historic views from the public and residential areas of Yosemite Village.
- Identify and evaluate the feasibility of restoring historic views as part of a new project.
- When siting new or expanded buildings, pathways, and plazas and their related landscape features, orient them to include views of scenic resources.
- Refer to "Setting—Scenic Views" in the "Unifying Elements" chapter for additional guidelines.

*Black oak trees in Yosemite Village NPS historic residential area (2004) TP*

## VEGETATION

The original vegetation in the Yosemite Village area was mostly deciduous oak woodland, interspersed with stands of mixed conifers, primarily ponderosa pines and incense cedars. A primary goal in the original design and development of the Village was to use the site's natural vegetation to screen structures and delineate public spaces.

New planting between 1916 and 1942 emphasized the use of native vegetation (collected and transplanted from nearby areas) arranged in artistic compositions (NPS 2004h). Specimen trees such as sequoias were also planted and identified near the museum and the Rangers' Club for the benefit of visitors. The goal was to mirror natural plant communities by massing plants in groupings commonly found in nature. This approach to planting design became known as landscape naturalization, and was employed in many other national parks during this period. By 1930 it included a specific prescription of non-native plants, for both scientific and aesthetic reasons. Foundation plantings around visitor service buildings were designed to enhance the rustic facades rather than obscure them behind a wall of vegetation.

In the residential area, vegetation was used somewhat differently. Frederick Law Olmsted Jr. recommended siting structures under the canopy of black oaks to screen the visual impacts of the development when seen from Glacier Point and other elevated points. Houses were well set-back on main streets, with significant numbers of black oaks dispersed over the lawn areas. This lent an aesthetic unity and overall character to the area. Vegetation, both natural and planted, was also used to emphasize the divisions between different zones within the Village and to screen the utility areas from public view. Today the condition of many individual oak trees in the residential area has been compromised by excess water, a result of maintaining lawns under trees that are accustomed to dry summers (NPS 2004h).

*Oak Lane in Yosemite Village NPS historic residential area (2004) RF*

Management of vegetation to preserve views from the Village was an important concern in the early years, because the views from the plaza were influential in the selection of the Village site. Today, however, much of the formerly open plaza has been revegetated. As these later plantings mature, they sometimes obscure historic views from the civic plaza area. Vegetation also obscures the early rustic buildings on the plaza, reducing the buildings' ability to define the plaza and imbue it with the presence of the civic administration of the park. As in other parts of the Valley, pine and cedar are slowly crowding out stands of California black oak. Although some vegetation from the historic period survives in the Village (specifically the black oaks and some foundation plantings), much of the vegetation post-dates the period of historical significance (NPS 2004h).

**GUIDELINES**

- Landscape designers should use a naturalistic design approach in developing planting plans, and should develop a plant palette in consultation with park resource staff.
- Refer to "Setting—Vegetation" in the "Unifying Elements" chapter for additional guidelines.

## Landscape Uses + Structures

### LAND USE + SPATIAL ORGANIZATION

The plan of Yosemite Village was based on segregating land-use areas into administrative, residential, and maintenance zones. These zones were arranged to be conveniently near one another but discreetly defined and separated by circulation patterns, topography, vegetation, and cluster siting. Spatial organization within the Village was largely a response to topography and vegetation.

The central administrative zone of Yosemite Village has always accommodated visitor uses of many types. Although there are no overnight accommodations in the Village, there are several restaurants, shops, the main park visitor center, photography studios, the park museum, the Village Post Office, and the park administration building. Central to the design of this area is the open civic plaza, defined by the facades of visitor service buildings and reinforced by foundation planting, as well as natural topography and vegetation (NPS 2004h). The Village plaza created a sense of arrival and place for the entire Yosemite Village. By design, the plaza was a civic zone in which the public administration of the park was symbolically expressed through the architectural facades of important government buildings. These included

*Roadway in historic residential area (2004) GH*

the administration building, the museum, and the post office, all important visitor service buildings. The plaza was used during the early years as the parking area for the Village center.

NPS and concessioner utility areas each have residential zones associated with them, including Upper, Middle, and Lower Tecoya and the historic NPS residential area. The residential areas are separated from the utility yards and the civic plaza but remain within walking distance of both. Although the open character of the plaza encourages views out toward landscape features, the residential areas feature narrow, curvilinear, tree-lined streets that encourage inward views. These more private, intimate spaces enhance the residential character of these zones.

The NPS maintenance area to the north of the civic plaza is located up in the rockfall zone at the base of the talus slope, at the north edge of the Village. The concessioner utility area to the east of the civic plaza was set apart from the central civic zone. This area has since become the main point of automobile arrival into the Village, dominated by a large parking area east of the Village Store that is visible from Glacier Point. This significantly alters the historic design and intent of the Village by routing visitors to a utility area that was not meant to be a primary public space.

In terms of broad patterns and relationships, the overall spatial organization of the Village remains true to the original design. The compactness of the overall plan allows the residential, public, and utility zones to be separate, but within walking distance of each other. The originally designated land-use areas remain the same. Conversion of the central civic plaza from a parking lot to a broad promenade and the modifications to the visitor arrival sequence are the most significant changes to the original concept.

**GUIDELINES**

- The siting of new development should reinforce the historic organization of the Village and its land-use zones.
- New development should be sited to reinforce the sense of a Village edge as well as the importance of a civic plaza for the arrival of visitors to the Valley.
- Redesign of outdoor spaces should continue to provide visitors with opportunities to gather views of the surrounding Valley.

## CIRCULATION

Circulation in Yosemite Village is characterized by a hierarchy of street and path types. Village Drive was a wide road that historically gave access to the open, wide space of the civic plaza. Today a road separates the plaza area from the cemetery and residential subdivision to the west. This road leads directly to the NPS maintenance area, offering direct access for service vehicles without requiring them to pass through the public or residential areas of the Village.

The approach to Yosemite Village was originally from the west, via what is now Village Drive. Currently, the most common approach is from the east. Arriving at the plaza area, visitors are greeted by the facade of the museum, flanked by the administration building to the left. Looking up, they see Yosemite Point and Upper Yosemite Fall directly in view.

Within the gently sloping plaza area, pedestrian zones transition from relatively narrow walkways to broad, irregularly shaped, asphalt areas that obscure a clear circulation hierarchy. The area has retained the feel of a roadway for vehicles rather than a pedestrian area.

In the historic NPS residential area, narrow, curbless streets typically follow a curvilinear grid that generally aligns along the topography. The fronts of houses face the streets, while the backs and garages face service alleys, which are narrower in width and are often cul-de-sacs. Some houses are sited on short cul-de-sacs that branch off main streets.

*Historic residences, Yosemite Village (2004) GH*

In the Lower Tecoya area, the Ahwahnee Row houses face directly onto Ahwahnee Meadow. Between the houses and the meadow is a trail, formerly a narrow street. The houses have a wide alley behind them, which also services a group of larger, dormitory-style residences to the west. Some of these houses are screened by dogwoods and shrubs.

In the NPS maintenance area, and to a degree in the concessioner utility area, the arrangement of larger buildings creates rectangular yards and broad, straight streets with no sidewalks. This pattern is essentially a formalization of the utilitarian nature of early roads and circulation through these areas.

Overall, there is a high degree of integrity related to circulation in Yosemite Village. The elaborate hierarchy of street types is still intact in the residential and utility areas. Modifications to the main entrance to the Village and conversion of the plaza to a pedestrian area are the most significant changes from the historic period (NPS 2004h).

**GUIDELINES**

- New roads should be consistent with historic design patterns and should meet NPS Park Road Standards.
- The arrival sequence and layout of approach roads should allow visitors to see key buildings, or an intermediate marker, from their car, before entering the day-visitor parking area.
- Reinforce the use of a clear hierarchy of street types, including standard-width roads per NPS Park Road Standards, narrower residential streets and alleys, and pedestrian paths.
- Retain the character of roads in the residential areas, using minimal road striping and curbless edge treatments.
- Refer to "Landscape Uses + Structures—Circulation—Parking" in the "Unifying Elements" chapter for more guidelines on circulation and parking.

## Developed Areas

For the purpose of these guidelines, Yosemite Village is divided into distinct use zones: the central Village administrative area; the residential areas; and the maintenance, service, and storage areas. This section provides guidelines for these groups of developed areas that share common architectural and landscape features.

The central Village administrative area incorporates NPS administration and visitor services buildings as well as commercial facilities for the public. It consists of the historic Village center, the Village Store, the concessioner garage facility, and the day-visitor parking area at Camp 6.

The residential areas consist of the Upper, Middle, and Lower Tecoya areas, as well as the historic NPS residential area. The Medical Clinic is discussed in the context of Upper and Middle Tecoya because it has relatively consistent geographical conditions. The Lower Tecoya area consists of distinctly different soil and forest conditions.

The maintenance, service, and storage areas consist of the maintenance yard area north of the central plaza and adjacent buildings.

*Visitors in pedestrian mall in Yosemite Village with the Ansel Adams Gallery on right (2004) RF*

## CENTRAL VILLAGE ADMINISTRATIVE AREA

### Setting

At the heart of the central Village administrative area is the civic plaza, with its mix of historic buildings and contemporary visitor facilities. These buildings are oriented along a pedestrian promenade that widens into gathering spaces at the entrances to buildings. The landscape of the area is characterized by a sense of enclosure, with a mix of tall pines and graceful black oaks.

In the Camp 6 area—currently day-visitor parking—the topography is generally flat and is sporadically covered with ponderosa pine, incense cedar, and black oak. The visitor information and service facilities to the northeast are on the slightly higher, gently sloping Indian Creek alluvial fan.

Several factors affect the prominence of the large mature black oaks, including soil differences toward the western end of the camp. Upslope toward the Indian Creek depositional fan, the oaks are smaller and ponderosa pine and incense cedar are dominant as one approaches the area around the Degnan's complex. Farther to the east, the base-of-talus line angles from the northwest to the southeast. Remnants of a riparian vegetation corridor can be seen in the developed area along Indian Creek.

Ground and surface runoff affect this area in terms of vegetation, flooding, and pollution associated with the day-visitor parking lot in the area. A wet ground zone just west of the Village Store has caused pavement settlement, suggesting a zone of groundwater migration from the Indian Creek alluvial fan through Camp 6 toward the Merced River. Given the topography, soils, and vegetation, much of the southern portion of the area, under undeveloped conditions, acts as a sponge, slowing peak flows in times of flooding. There is potential for flooding in parts of the Yosemite Village main parking area.

*Pedestrian mall, Yosemite Village, looking towards Upper Yosemite Fall (2004) RF*

**GUIDELINES**

- Use of permeable paving (in lieu of impermeable surfaces) is encouraged.
- Layout and design should take into account the possibility of periodic flooding in the vicinity of the lower reaches of Indian Creek and nearby drainages. Avoid placing structures in—or covering over—existing drainages. Designs should address the hydrological and vegetative restoration of any drainage areas impacted by new designs.
- For the design of the new day-visitor parking area, where wet soil, high groundwater, or potential flooding areas exist, the roads and bays should be aligned roughly parallel to contour, allowing for continuous unpaved "green" swales protecting vegetation (especially oak trees and riparian vegetation) and allowing for groundwater recharge.
- Refer to "Landscape Uses + Structures—Circulation—Parking" in the "Unifying Elements" for more guidelines on parking.

### Siting and Building Orientation for the Central Village Administrative Area

In the center of Yosemite Village, the 1920s-era public buildings—the administration building, the post office, the Rangers' Club, and the museum—form two sides of an open civic plaza, with generous open space between. The museum, the visitor center, the Ansel Adams Gallery, the Wilderness Center, and the post office define the north edge of the plaza, roughly parallel to the canyon walls. The administration building is oriented north–south, closing the west end of the plaza. Later buildings such as the Degnan's complex and the Village Store are sited at the eastern end of the plaza. The original plaza continues as a promenade to the Village Store, functioning today as the central spine of the Village center. Canyon walls to the north form the backdrop for buildings on the plaza. The central open space captures expansive views of the north canyon walls and Upper Yosemite Fall.

**GUIDELINES**

- Design should take into account significant elements of the historic civic plaza, such as views of Upper Yosemite Fall. The spatial organization should be respected and reinforced. The edges of major outdoor spaces should be defined by buildings, major vegetation, and viewsheds that are framed within the central Village administrative area.

*Rangers' Club, Yosemite Village*

- Preserve and link the scale and spatial organization of the historic civic plaza area with new buildings that are compatible with the historic architectural elements.

### Architectural Character in the Central Village Administrative Area

Yosemite Village is one of the largest and most significant collections of NPS Rustic-style buildings in the national park system. The basic principle of NPS Rustic style architecture—predominant in the national parks between 1916 and 1942—is that buildings should blend with the landscape. Structures should emphasize a horizontal aspect. Vegetation should enhance the natural appearance of a building and unite it with the landscape. The use of oversized masonry and timbers assures that the image of the building fits and matches its natural setting.

The visual effects of natural materials and colors were fully exploited by early rustic buildings in the park. The upper walls were clad in shingles stained dark brown with special coursing patterns. The rough granite boulders and river-run stones used on walls, foundations, chimneys, steps, and porches harmonized with the towering granite cliffs surrounding the Valley. Stones varied in size and were laid in a rubble bond, weathered side exposed, with a raked mortar joint that emphasized the natural size and shape of individual stones. The use of timber in various forms—thick logs, rough-milled lumber, shingles, and shakes—much of it stained dark brown—harmonized with the bark of ponderosa pine and other conifers of the Yosemite forests. From a distance, the effect is nearly one of camouflage. While it does not eliminate the intrusion of buildings on the natural scene, it measurably reduces the intrusion, which was the intent (NPS 2004h).

Variations in Rustic-style buildings in Yosemite Village include the Rangers' Club, the administration building, the museum, the post office, NPS residential buildings, and a variety of utilitarian buildings and small offices (NPS 2004h). The Rangers' Club is a

*Cornerstone of Museum, Yosemite Village (2004) GH*

two-and-a-half-story wood-frame structure with a granite rubble foundation. Exterior walls are mainly finished with shingles. The building was designated a National Historic Landmark in 1987. The Ansel Adams Gallery (formerly Best's Studio) has an entrance porch with a large masonry chimney and seating overlooking the promenade. Other structures in the Village center depart from the historical precedent and make little contribution to the continuity of historical character in the central space.

**GUIDELINES**

- Consistent with *The Secretary of the Interior's Standards*, new projects should be compatible with the massing, scale, architectural features, and overall character of the historic structures, yet be recognizable as contemporary developments. New development should respect the spirit of historic buildings, without replicating them.
- Incorporate the palette of materials found on adjacent buildings in the historic center into the exterior finishes of new structures.
- Refer to "Developed Areas—Architectural Character" in the "Unifying Elements" chapter for more guidelines.

*Entrance to Museum, Yosemite Village (2004) GH*

### Building Shape and Massing for the Central Village Administrative Area

The present-day Village center is a collection of buildings that are not consistent in shape and massing. However, the three original public buildings at the west end of the civic plaza were constructed in a similar rustic style and have consistent shape and massing, which creates a strong unified presence. The rectangular plan, two-story massing, horizontal emphasis, and robust scale are essential components of these buildings. The museum has an interesting variation at the west end, where the building's mass steps down and is bolstered by a sculptural masonry chimney that flares out to the ground. This flaring motif was employed in early rustic buildings to make a strong connection to the ground.

Nonhistoric buildings built at various times after World War II, such as the Valley Visitor Center, the Degnan's complex, and the Village Store, have little in common with the early rustic buildings or with each other.

**GUIDELINES**

- Consistent with *The Secretary of the Interior's Standards*, new projects should be compatible with the massing, scale, architectural features, and overall character of the historic structures, yet be recognizable as contemporary developments.
- The height of new buildings should be limited to two-and-a-half stories, consistent with the historic structures.
- Use porches and secondary massing elements to reduce the apparent height of a building and make a strong connection to the ground.
- When programs for buildings exceed or are incompatible with the historic settings, reorganize the program so that the building can be broken down into smaller components. Use covered walkways to link functional relationships and emphasize horizontality. This will assist in making the complex subordinate to its setting.

### Roof Form and Materials for the Central Village Administrative Area

The simple gable roof of the administration building, the museum, and the post office is a key element of their character. The administration building has a large entry porch with a gable roof carried on stone piers. The steep roof pitch of the Rangers' Club is a treatment that was not continued in later buildings, but it was used earlier at the LeConte Memorial Lodge. Later noncontributing buildings depart from the historic precedent, resulting in a lack of consistent roof forms throughout the Village center.

**GUIDELINES**

- Use such historical precedents as the administration building, the museum, and the post office as the reference for roof form.
- Designers should consider the use of clerestories and skylights, such as those found in the Mountain Shop at Curry Village and the Yosemite Lodge store, to allow natural light to enter large interior volumes. They can also capture upward views of surrounding landmarks.
- Refer to "Developed Areas—Roof Form and Material" in the "Unifying Elements" chapter for more guidelines.

### Building Exterior for the Central Village Administrative Area

A variety of exterior treatments are used in the Village center, including exposed-wood structural elements, wood siding with natural brown colors and rough textures, and a stone base or rusticated lower wall.

**GUIDELINES**

- The design of new projects should use such precedents as the administration building, the museum, the post office, and historic residential housing as the inspiration for facade design and use of materials.
- Refer to "Developed Areas—Building Exterior" in the "Unifying Elements" chapter for more guidelines.

### Site Furnishings for the Central Village Administrative Area

The central Village administrative area is a major gathering point for visitors to the park. The character of site furnishings, therefore, should be consistent with the Rustic style and must reinforce the historic importance of this area. Signs and educational plaques vary in style and color and are found in various locations. These, as well as pedestrian bollard lights, are unrelated to the Rustic style.

**GUIDELINES**

- New design should emphasize the civic nature of this area by using natural materials that are found in the surrounding setting. These could include generously sized granite boulders, slabs, and cedar logs.
- Bench design is especially important in conveying rustic character in the vicinity of the Valley Visitor Center. Backrests and armrests add comfort and should be included in the design.
- Refer to the "Landscape Uses + Structures" section in the "Unifying Elements" chapter for more guidelines.

## RESIDENTIAL AREAS

There are four residential areas for employees in Yosemite Village: Upper Tecoya, Middle Tecoya, Lower Tecoya, and the historic NPS residential housing area.

#### *Upper, Middle, and Lower Tecoya*

This area stretches from the eastern edge of the maintenance area to the medical clinic, forming an arc along the contour, across the depositional fan of Indian Creek, which divides Middle Tecoya from the medical clinic.

Forest vegetation in the Upper and Middle Tecoya areas consists primarily of black oak, although considerable conifer encroachment is evident. The trees here are more stunted than those on the Valley bottom, presumably due to the thin, rocky soils of the young colluvium formation.

TOP *Western end of Museum, Yosemite Village* BOTTOM *Plaza elevation of Post Office, Yosemite Village*

Clerestory of Yosemite Lodge gift shop, oriented toward Yosemite Falls (2004) GH

Post Office, Yosemite Village (1935) YRL

Conditions in the Lower Tecoya neighborhood are quite different. The Lower Tecoya area is almost totally dominated by tall pine and cedar groves. The southerly portions of this area on the nearly flat Valley floor could be subject to flooding from the Merced River and the lower reaches of Indian Creek.

### Upper Tecoya

Upper Tecoya is a housing complex north and northeast of the administrative center. It contains small one-story and one-and-a-half-story detached, single-family, wood-frame residences; wood dormitory buildings; storage facilities for heavy transportation equipment; and a small parking lot. In addition, an area along the northern boundary of Yosemite Village contains a cluster of single-family and duplex units arranged along a curvilinear roadway. The houses, which were built in the 1960s, have vertical wood siding painted grey, and composition shingle roofs. Most have attached garages.

### Middle Tecoya

Middle Tecoya is situated between the medical complex and a large parking lot. Most of the residences are one-story and one-and-a-half-story wood-frame buildings, painted a tan color. They are smaller than other housing types, more closely spaced, and sited well with the topography. This area has an architectural character that is more contemporary and less formally Rustic than the earlier residential developments in the Village. The design character reflects many features of Bay Area residential design from the post-World War II period, such as rectangular forms, flat roofs, large, single-pane wood windows, and various patterns of wood siding combined in one building. The houses are virtually concealed from public view by skillful siting on the forest slope, which creates the feeling of a separate neighborhood. Several residences and their garages contribute to the historical significance of the Yosemite Valley Historic District.

### Lower Tecoya

Most of the buildings in Lower Tecoya date from the historic period of significance and include the dormitories, apartments and related laundry room, the Ahwahnee Row houses, cottages, and cabins. A series of curvilinear roads connects the housing units.

The Ahwahnee Row houses are a group of structures built in the 1920s on the east side of Lower Tecoya. Many of these one- and two-story residences have enclosed patios and freestanding wood garages. Screen fencing is visually prominent because of the close spacing of the buildings and the narrowness of the street corridor. The row houses form a boundary between a densely developed and coniferous Lower Tecoya area and the open Ahwahnee Meadow.

To the west of the row houses are four dormitory-type, three-story wood buildings and an adjacent kitchen facility. These are more massive than the nearby Ahwahnee Row houses. Half of the dormitories in Lower Tecoya were constructed in the late 1920s and significantly altered in the 1930s, while the other half were constructed in the 1930s and remain unchanged.

The Lower Tecoya dormitories are long, rectangular, three-story volumes with medium-pitch roofs and small shed dormers that articulate the top story. These relatively large buildings are reduced in scale by their roof form and varied siding patterns. The main roof is a simple gable, with the ridge continuing over projecting bays at the ends of the buildings. Main entrances are placed under gables at

Informal seating, log-round (2004) TP

TOP LEFT *Ahwahnee Row Houses* TOP RIGHT *Apartment in historic NPS residential area* MIDDLE RIGHT *End view of apartment* BOTTOM *Houses in historic NPS residential area*

the ends of the buildings. The use of a corrugated metal roof is a unique element in the Village. The slate-green, board and batten exterior walls are a departure from the standard Wosky brown. These features help to unify the group while differentiating the housing area from the nearby maintenance and commercial facilities. The area includes two vehicle bridges and two pedestrian bridges over Indian Creek.

### *The Medical Clinic*

At the east end of Yosemite Village is a medical and dental clinic with related support buildings. The original Rustic-style clinic building was constructed in 1930 as the Lewis Memorial Hospital. A dental facility was added in 1954. The complex contains the medical facility, a parking lot, a dormitory with a two-story garage beneath, and two large, wood-frame residences.

TOP LEFT *Covered entrance to dorm at Lower Tecoya, Yosemite Village (2004) JM* TOP RIGHT *Stepped-down massing on dorm at Lower Tecoya (2004) RF*
BOTTOM LEFT *Roof with shed dormers on dorm at Lower Tecoya (2004) RF* BOTTOM RIGHT *Front porch at Medical Clinic, Yosemite Village (2004) RF*

*Dentist's Residence, Yosemite Village (1932) YRL*

The dormitory and the residences were constructed at the same time as the clinic, in the same Rustic style. The original dentist's residence is one of the finest examples in the Valley of a single-family dwelling designed with Rustic features and details. It is sited to take advantage of its topography and setting at the foot of the talus slope.

**GUIDELINES**

- The design of new projects in the Upper and Middle Tecoya areas should reflect the character of small homes sited among trees and talus blocks on a sloping plane.
- Residential yards and fencing in Middle and Upper Tecoya should be placed behind houses and garages and in locations hidden from public view.
- Trees, shrubs, forbs, and grasses should be limited to species indigenous to Yosemite Valley and appropriate to the Indian Creek depositional fan. They should be allowed sufficient space to grow into their mature forms. See also *Residential Yard Care Policy* (NPS 2001b).
- Facilities such as bear-proof dumpsters and other trash storage, self-storage units, etc., should be clustered and screened behind structures that harmonize with the surrounding architectural character. See the March 2002 *Cultural Landscape Treatment Recommendations Yosemite Village Historic District Housing Area* (NPS 2002) for treatment of such items in historic residential areas.
- New design in these residential areas should be compatible with the scale, massing, and architectural character of the existing structures.
- Refer to "Landscape Uses + Structures" and "Developed Areas—Architectural Character" in the "Unifying Elements" chapter for more guidelines on pedestrian bridges, fences, and lighting.

### NPS Residential Area

The oldest housing development in Yosemite Village is the NPS Residential Area, which is part of the larger Yosemite Valley Historic District. Located northwest of the Village center, it has a neighborhood character, and comprises mainly single-family dwelling units arranged along a series of curvilinear roads. Historically significant elements in the historic district include many of the residences, as well as other structures, clusters of buildings, and circulation routes.

Lying just east of the Lower Yosemite Fall area, this development sits on the level plane of the Valley floor. Located on the warmer north side of the Valley and away from flood and rockfall zones, this site was optimal for residential use. The large, overarching California black oak dominates the landscape in this area, presumably taking advantage of deep soils. The trees impart a gracious, manicured, park-like feeling. Other vegetation in this area consists of understory native trees and shrubs, meadows, manicured lawns, ornamental trees planted in beds, shrubs, and ground covers.

All buildings and structures in the area date from the period of historical significance for Yosemite Valley (1851 to 1942), with the exception of seven residences and the elementary school, which were built in the 1950s. Most of the residences, apartments, dormitories, garages, and woodsheds that contribute to the historic district were constructed during the 1920s and 1930s and have undergone few, if any, exterior alterations. The houses built between 1927 and 1940 reflect the development of Rustic architecture by the Landscape Division of the Western Field Office (based in San Francisco) of the National Park Service. Three army residences, built in 1911 and 1912, were relocated from Yosemite Lodge to this area in 1929. Their character is typical of rural houses of the period that predates the NPS Rustic era, but they are also historically significant.

The Rustic residences are one- and two-story, wood-frame buildings clad with wood siding materials such as coursed shakes, shingles, or lapped boards. Many of the houses from the Rustic period have stone chimneys and stonemasonry cladding at the foundations and porches. Roofs were originally wood shingle, but some are now composition shingle. Most of the one-story residences have simple, rectangular plans and low-pitched gable roofs. Some two-story residences have steeper roofs with dormers. Typical Rustic details include wooden double-hung windows, wood panel doors, exposed roof rafters at eaves, decorative wood brackets, and porches and exterior stairs with wood railings. There are also two apartment buildings that share similar Rustic features and details. They both feature open porches in the center that incorporate recessed stairs.

**GUIDELINES**

- New design should preserve and reinforce the open, park-like setting of historic residences under large, spreading, mature black oaks.
- Limit or avoid gardens and lawn irrigation within the drip lines of black oaks. Refer to *Residential Yard Care Policy* (NPS 2001b) and *Cultural Landscape Treatment Recommendations, Yosemite Village Historic District Housing Area* (NPS 2002).
- New landscape design should be compatible with the pattern established during the period of significance.
- New landscape elements such as fences, screens, and retaining walls that are visible from public streets and pedestrian ways should be consistent with guidance provided in *The Secretary of the Interior's Standards for the Treatment of Historic Properties*. New design should be carefully reviewed to sustain or restore the historically open, park-like character of the neighborhood. See also the *Residential Yard Care Policy* (NPS 2001b) for more detailed guidelines regarding:

    *Trash storage*
    *Shrubs and herbaceous plants*
    *Side and back yards*
    *Self-storage units*
    *Fencing at the schoolhouse*
    *Northern drainage ditch*

TOP *NPS Operations Building (Fort Yosemite), Yosemite Village NPS*
BOTTOM *Historic house porch, residential area*

*Apartment detail, Yosemite Village, NPS residential area*

## MAINTENANCE, SERVICE + STORAGE AREAS

The maintenance, service, and storage areas are found in a talus zone directly below Castle Cliffs, well within the rockfall zone. Although oaks still dominate the thin soils at the base of the cliffs, they are stunted and smaller than those of the deeper soils in the historic NPS residential area.

The park maintenance and concessioner facilities consist of a cluster of buildings with a north–south orientation. Development extends north to the base of the talus slope. More than half of the buildings in the area date from the 1920s and are contributing resources to the Yosemite Valley Historic District. Stable facilities and day corrals are located nearby, in the southwest corner of this area.

The focal point of the complex is a two-story utility building referred to as the NPS operations building (Fort Yosemite), constructed of patterned concrete with large garage bays on the first floor. The building also has a central tower adjacent to the entrance, industrial windows, and a composition shingle roof. The largest structure in the complex is the concessioner warehouse, a modern concrete building with a flat roof. The Village Garage is also an important building, reminiscent of an Arts and Crafts barn (NPS 2004i). Smaller buildings surround the maintenance building, including a stable, barn, warehouses, offices, and a garage. A federal magistrate courthouse is located on the eastern edge of the complex.

### GUIDELINES

- Consistent with *The Secretary of the Interior's Standards for the Treatment of Historic Properties*, new projects in this historic district should be compatible with the massing, scale, architectural features, and overall character of the surrounding historic structures.
- For new projects, architectural character in the maintenance area may reflect a more utilitarian design approach by making use of building materials and details that are suitable for industrial buildings. Metal roofing is appropriate if a muted grey color, and nonreflective finishes are specified.
- New maintenance facilities should include the planting of trees to ensure visual screening, particularly from the vista points along the surrounding cliffs. Where temperature control is a factor in new design, consider the planting of trees that will provide for natural cooling.
- Refer to "Landscape Uses + Structures—Lighting" in the "Unifying Elements" chapter for guidelines on lighting design.

# CURRY VILLAGE

CAMP CURRY WAS established in 1899 by David and Jennie Curry. With its tent cabins and communal dining hall, Camp Curry offered a more affordable lodging experience than other accommodations in Yosemite Valley. As its popularity grew, Camp Curry quickly expanded from a dozen tent cabins to hundreds in a matter of years. By 1905, roads connected Camp Curry to the Old Village to the west, and the Currys had constructed dozens of tent cabin platforms, permanent dining and registration buildings, bathrooms, and tennis and croquet facilities. In 1922 a group of 48

...GOOD BEDS, GOOD MEALS AND COURTEOUS TREATMENT...MY CAMPS ARE DESIGNED FOR THOSE WHO, WHETHER FROM NECESSITY OR INCLINATION, WISH TO MAKE THEIR MONEY GO AS FAR AS IT WILL. **CAMP CURRY PROMOTIONAL BROCHURE • CA. 1900**

wooden bungalows was completed west of the core facility area, providing another level of accommodations separated from the main body of tents. By that time Camp Curry had telephones, evening movies, a pool hall and dance pavilion, a gas station and garage, a soda fountain, and numerous cottages and other residences for employees. The need for increased parking was met in 1927 by allowing parking between the rows of apple trees in the nearby orchard. After a slow period during the Depression and World War II, visitation to Camp Curry increased dramatically. By 1959, the camp operated almost 500 tents and 200 bungalow and cabin rooms. Various other changes occurred in the postwar period. The old dance hall was converted to the Stoneman House and used for lodging; the central dining facility, (1929), burned down and was rebuilt in 1975 at the same site; and a new pool, bathhouse, and skating rink were built. In 2007, employee dormitories were built adjacent to Curry Village's western boundary, and in 2008 several Curry Village cabins were removed due to rockfall hazards.

Since the inception of the camp, the use of Rustic design has been consistent, which helps buildings blend with the natural environment and preserves the primitive character of the development. During the early 20th century, Camp Curry was one of a number of tent camps in the national park system. Today Curry Village, as it is now known, is the largest example of its kind. Because of these attributes, Curry Village was listed on the National Register of Historic Places in 1979 (NPS 1979).

All work in Curry Village should meet compatibility guidance consistent with *The Secretary of the Interior's Standards for the Treatment of Historic Properties* and should also be consistent with treatment recommendations in the *Cultural Landscape Report Camp Curry Historic District* (NPS 2010b).

## Setting

### NATURAL SYSTEMS + FEATURES

Curry Village is south of the Merced River, at the east end of Yosemite Valley. It is located in a cool, shaded portion of the Valley, in the shadow of Glacier Point and the adjacent 4,000-foot-high cliffs. Although the shady climate offers relief from the summer heat, during the winter Curry Village gets little sun and is subject to freezing temperatures and fog. Snow also stays on the ground longer than at the north side of the Valley.

The center of Curry Village was established on the flat Valley floor at the toe of a talus slope. Over time, the camp has expanded to the east and west, along the base of the talus slope, with some structures located quite close to the base of the cliffs. Dozens of tent cabins and wood cabins are scattered among massive talus blocks and smaller boulders in an area now designated a hazardous rockfall zone. Today, the hazard of rockfall precludes any new construction in the delineated rockfall zone.

A seasonal drainage runs through the center of Curry Village. Runoff flows in a northerly direction from the cliffs and talus slope, through the Village's central space, and across the meadow to the Merced River. The water deposits large quantities of rock, gravel, and sand in the Village center, a process that historically has created a variety of problems. Several seasonal tributary creeks and drainages also flow from south to north through developed areas of Curry Village to the Merced River.

*Camp Curry campfire (ca. 1903) YRL*

The Merced River is too far removed to have a strong relationship to most of Curry Village. Views of the river are precluded by distance, vegetation, and Curry Village's flat terrain.

Conifers make it difficult to see views of the waterfalls across the Valley toward the north and northwest when viewed from the central core area of Curry Village. Staircase Falls is seasonally visible to the west, descending from high up the cliffs.

**GUIDELINES**

- Cluster new housing developments in groups around the edges of open spaces to take advantage of natural light and views. Specify deciduous trees in housing areas to increase daylight during the winter.
- Locate and design walkways, parking, pavement, and structures to avoid drainage problems such as ice during winter months and standing water throughout the rest of the year.

### SCENIC VIEWS

Views of surrounding Yosemite Valley natural landmarks inspired the original siting of Camp Curry and helped to determine the internal layout of the developed area.

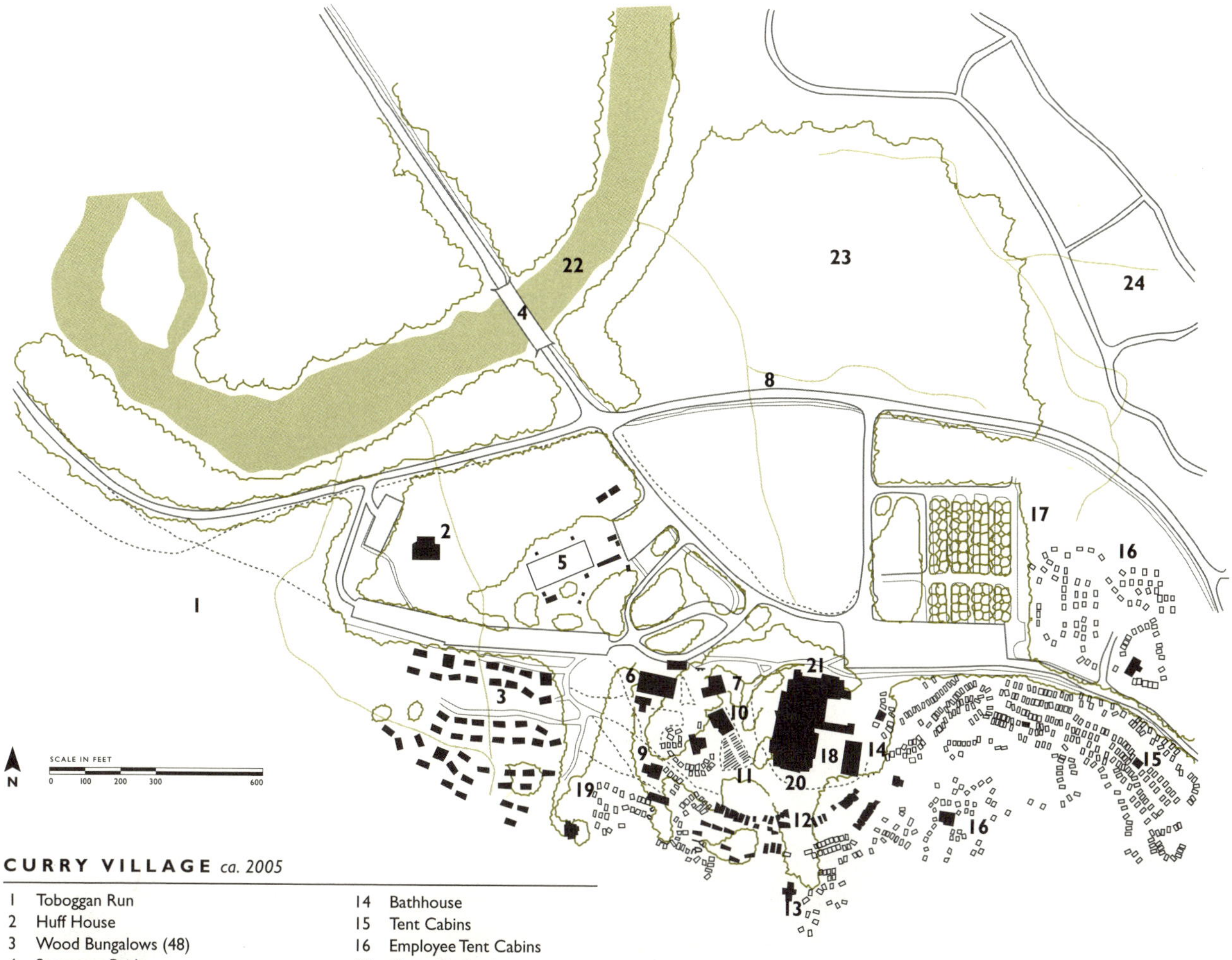


**CURRY VILLAGE** *ca. 2005*

1 Toboggan Run
2 Huff House
3 Wood Bungalows (48)
4 Stoneman Bridge
5 Ice Skating Rink
6 Stoneman Lodge
7 Registration Office
8 Southside Drive
9 Mother Curry's Bungalow
10 Lounge (Historic Registration Office)
11 Amphitheater
12 Wood Cabins
13 Foster Curry Cabin (Tresidder Residence)
14 Bathhouse
15 Tent Cabins
16 Employee Tent Cabins
17 Curry Orchard
18 Swimming Pool
19 LeConte Memorial Lodge (former site)
20 Dining/Retail Building
21 Mountain Shop
22 Merced River
23 Stoneman Meadow
24 Lower Pines Campground

Views from the Curry Village center of Half Dome, Glacier Point, Royal Arches, Washington Column, and North Dome are impressive.

Today, the encroachment of trees makes it difficult to see Yosemite Falls from the Village center. Historically significant views of the Valley's natural landmarks are being encroached upon by naturally regenerating trees within the Curry Village area. Left unchecked, this will profoundly affect the character of Curry Village.

**GUIDELINES**

- Design projects in Curry Village should give consideration to selective removal of trees, particularly those conifers that have seeded into historically open areas and have subsequently blocked views of the historic resources (e.g., the Camp Curry welcome sign and gateway) or the Valley's natural landmarks.
- Orient walkways and gathering areas to optimize views of Half Dome, Glacier Point, Royal Arches, Washington Column, and North Dome.

TOP LEFT *North Dome and Washington Column from Camp Curry* TOP RIGHT *Early toboggan run at Camp Curry (since removed)* BOTTOM *Camp Curry entrance marker (1927) YRL*

- When designing parking for guest arrival do not obscure the view corridors to the north from the center of Curry Village.
- Refer to "Setting—Scenic View" in the "Unifying Elements" chapter for more guidelines on views.

### VEGETATION

In the early years, the Curry family hired professional landscape architects to design and manage naturalistic planting arrangements. Over the years, these professionals removed trees and other vegetation they felt blocked important views, and preserved trees they felt were significant. They also planted shrubs and other vegetation around buildings. Since the 1970s, revegetation of formerly open areas of Curry Village has confused the historic spatial organization.

Vegetation at Curry Village is dominated by mature conifers, especially ponderosa pine and incense cedars. The understory vegetation consists of big leaf maple, California black oak, and dogwood—typical of the shady, moist, south side of Yosemite Valley. There have been historic trends at Curry—as in other areas of the Valley—of increased coniferous forest cover and the incremental destruction of riparian vegetation along annual drainages and creeks.

Stoneman Meadow lies on the flat river plain north of the center of Curry Village. Portions of the meadow lie in the 100-year floodplain of the Merced River. Curry Orchard, originally part of the meadow, was laid out by Frederick Law Olmsted Jr. and planted with fruit trees (primarily apple) for the use of Valley visitors. Parking has subsequently been incorporated under the orchard trees, and many trees have been removed or have died.

**GUIDELINES**

- Evaluate opportunities for selective removal of conifers to allow for additional sunlight and warmth during the winter months.
- Seek opportunities to restore historic views, such as those in and around Stoneman Meadow.
- New design provides an opportunity to consider restoration of the broad swaths of meadow vegetation and California black oak woodlands that have historically defined the arrival experience to Curry Village.
- New construction should attempt to minimize use of hard pavements, restore compacted soils, replace nonhistoric hardened drainage channels with vegetated bio-swales, and restore native vegetation in disturbed areas.
- Native vegetation can be used to screen nonpublic functions from public use areas. For example, native vegetation could enhance screening of new employee housing or facility management structures from public view. This should be informal and based on black oak forest plant communities, as directed by park resources staff.
- Refer to "Setting—Vegetation" in the "Unifying Elements" chapter for more guidelines.

## Landscape Uses + Structures

### LAND USE + SPATIAL ORGANIZATION

The overall layout of Curry Village is linear, with buildings arranged on sloping ground along the base of the cliffs. The Curry Village center contains public gathering, dining, and recreational functions. Guest quarters—in the form of tent cabins and wood cabins—are east and west of the Curry Village center. The cabins are arranged in tiers up to the talus zone at the base of

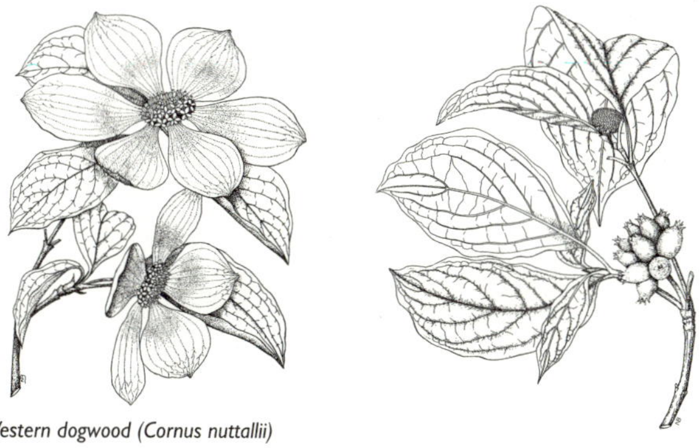

*Western dogwood (Cornus nuttallii)*

Glacier Point, with tent cabins and wood cabins located in separate clusters.

The Curry Village center is defined by commercial service facilities and structures surrounding a central open space, establishing the arrival and public gathering areas for Curry Village. The south edge of the central space is defined by a strong line of cabins with Glacier Point looming dramatically overhead.

The area east of Curry Village center includes hundreds of one-room tent cabins. The small scale of the individual tents, set close together in irregular rows, creates a unique spatial character. The sense of enclosure in this area has a marked contrast to the grandeur experienced in other areas of Yosemite Valley.

Wood cabins with and without baths are grouped together west of the Curry Village center. These cabins are larger than the tent cabins, set with more space between them, and laid out in rows that are straighter and more regular.

**GUIDELINES**

- New construction in the Curry Village center should support and strengthen the spatial organization of the site and enhance opportunities for defining spaces for outdoor activities, socializing, and programs.
- The addition of any new wood or tent cabins should be compatible with the historic spatial organization.
- The selection of sites for new buildings should take advantage of locations with hazard/diseased/downed trees in lieu of locations that would require the removal of healthy mature trees. Refer to existing or ongoing NPS studies of plant community conditions for further guidance.

## CIRCULATION

Curry Village was historically approached by two roads: one from the Old Yosemite Village to the west (aligned with the parking area between Huff House and the Curry Village bungalows), and the other from Stoneman Bridge to the northwest (Curry Village Drive). One parking area was outside the main gate in about the same location as the parking lot today. By 1927, as more visitors were arriving by car, the nearby Curry orchard was converted into a parking area (NPS 2004h).

Today vehicle access is limited mainly to the northwestern approach—Curry Village Drive. The western approach has been converted to a parking area. Circulation is primarily pedestrian in Curry Village, and is characterized by relatively unstructured movement on packed-earth trails. In heavier-use areas, paths of asphalt pavement have been used to delineate pedestrian circulation and to provide universally accessible travel routes.

*Cabins at Curry Village*

**GUIDELINES**

- Design and construction of trails within Curry Village should emulate the character of the compacted-earth paths/trails.
- Pedestrian paths should be designed to take advantage of prominent natural and scenic features and should be primitive in nature.
- Refer to "Landscape Uses + Structures—Entrance Markers" in the "Unifying Elements" chapter for a discussion of the Camp Curry welcome sign and gateway.
- Refer to "Landscape Uses + Structures" in the "Unifying Elements" chapter for more guidelines on circulation and parking.

## GRADING + DRAINAGE

Nestled up against the cliffs, Curry Village lies on a sloping site, with an approximately five-foot drop from north to south across the area. The creek from Staircase Falls is the only significant year-round drainage, running from south to north through the Curry Village center. It crosses several major pedestrian routes and the sloping central open space, depositing sand and gravel wash.

Several smaller drainages impact the area as well. Although seasonal, they carry snowmelt and rainfall run-off from Moran and Glacier points, and they have been substantial enough to require stone-clad culvert crossings. They can also carry considerable loads in heavy winter storms. Rainstorms produce accumulations of sand and gravel wash, especially at the base of the cabins south of the Curry Village center. Additional studies are ongoing to determine the distribution, impact, and future morphological dynamics of these drainages.

**GUIDELINES**

- Planning for the central open space at the Curry Village center should take into account the effects of the slope from south to north on drainage across the area.
- Design must meet accessibility standards on both level and sloping ground.
- Curry Village presents a drainage challenge. New design should carefully evaluate natural drainage patterns and incorporate sufficient grading and drainage structures for mitigation.
- Refer to "Landscape Uses + Structures—Grading and Drainage" in the "Unifying Elements" chapter for more guidelines.

## BARRIERS, FENCES + BENCHES

Much of the fencing and structural screening in Curry Village is associated with historic buildings. Nevertheless, fencing in this shaded side of the Valley shows the wearing effects of longer winters and deeper snow fields.

Many planted areas and areas of natural vegetation are separated from walkways and are edged with barriers of small-diameter logs (and finished lumber in some areas) as well as post-and-rope barriers. Some appear permanent, and others provide temporary protection of planted areas.

Seating in the Curry Village center varies, from horizontal half-round logs and shaped stumps used as benches to the recycled plastic furniture on the deck.

**GUIDELINES**

- In addition to the seating options recommended in the "Unifying Elements" chapter, use of nested flat-top boulders is appropriate within Curry Village and compatible with the talus-sloped nature of the site.
- Specify low, boulder-reinforced grade changes where barriers parallel to contours on sloping areas are needed.
- Areas needing protection from public use should make use of large wooden branches or small-diameter logs. This treatment is unique to Curry Village and is a distinctive and visually appropriate system for the central Curry Village area.
- Refer to "Landscape Uses + Structures—Barriers, Fences + Benches" in the "Unifying Elements" chapter.

### LIGHTING

Lighting of pedestrian ways and public gathering spaces at Curry Village is provided by a limited number of pedestrian standards and soffit lights mounted on the cabins and other buildings. Sparse lighting is particularly appropriate in the tent cabin area, where, because of the presence of large talus blocks and numerous trees, a primitive quality dominates.

Within the limitations of night-sky principles, the canvas tent cabins themselves become a source of light. At night, when lit from the interior, they glow like lanterns, creating an almost magical environment.

**GUIDELINES**

- Because of the primitive nature of the tent cabin area, lighting of pedestrian walks should be minimal while meeting mandated safety standards.
- For more guidance on lighting, refer to the *Yosemite National Park Lighting Guidelines* (NPS 2011g) and "Landscape Uses + Structures—Lighting" in the "Unifying Elements" chapter.

## DEVELOPED AREAS

### VILLAGE CENTER

#### The Entrance Marker

The "Welcome to Camp Curry" sign and gateway stands as the historic entry into the Curry Village center. Characterized by its use of native materials in their natural state, it acts as a wayfinding marker and announces the special, rustic character of the place. The use of unpeeled logs has a thematic link to the early buildings in Curry Village (NPS 1980a). Both the character of the entrance gateway itself and its original function as the gateway to Curry Village are historically significant features.

**GUIDELINES**

- Any redesign of the Curry Village entrance should consider restoring its function as a major pedestrian entrance point. This can be accomplished through improvements to the arrival and circulation patterns at the Curry Village center.

#### Siting + Building Orientation

The Curry Village center is defined by freestanding buildings surrounding a central open space. The lounge and registration buildings sit to the west of the central open space, and visitor service buildings such as the store and cafeteria are located to the east. These buildings, and the spaces between them, provide Curry Village with outdoor gathering points for both organized and informal functions.

Today, the buildings on the east side of the Curry Village center—including the dining hall and the Mountain Shop—have been joined into one linear complex. The buildings on the west side of the center—the lounge and the registration building—are still freestanding. The outdoor amphitheater is connected to the south side of the lounge building by a small platform stage. Enclosing the Curry Village center to the south is a strong line of wood cabins, backed by the massive walls of Glacier Point.

**GUIDELINES**

- New design at the Curry Village center should recognize and be compatible with the established siting and building orientation.
- The Curry Village center is a key social and organizational component of Curry Village. New design and construction should protect the sense of enclosure and minimize infill that might diminish the character of this area.
- Design of service areas should minimize both visual and acoustical impacts to nearby sleeping and public gathering areas.

## Architectural Character

The founders of Camp Curry established a rustic camp with a distinctive atmosphere and primitive style of accommodation. The historically significant elements in this area are the entrance gateway, the lounge, and the registration building. The entrance gateway, with its unpeeled logs and old-fashioned filament light bulbs, is emblematic of the Rustic style of architecture. Especially when lit-up at night, the gateway announces that Curry Village is a special place. The lounge is a one-story wood-frame structure with a rectangular plan and a hipped roof. The roof is covered with wood shingles and has skylights that allow natural light into the interior. An intimately scaled verandah along the front of the building at one time incorporated a large ponderosa pine. The scale of the tree was in sharp contrast to the simple structure of the verandah. The tree's stump has been preserved as a seat.

Buildings in the Curry Village center are one story in height. Those on the east side are contained in a stepped-plan arrangement that turns the corner to the east. This conceals the kitchen and service areas from the dining room. The buildings on the west side are freestanding and have simple plan forms and low profiles.

The Mountain Shop was reconstructed in 1975 following a fire. However, the new building incorporates some of the design characteristics of the original, including massing and spatial organization. The use of a generous clerestory that allows views of Glacier Point gives the space a lively character and brings in natural light. The interesting bay window to the east side had a view of Half Dome that is now obscured by trees.

Although the dining pavilion lacks the spirit of the original building by architect Eldridge T. Spencer, it establishes a compatible character. The decorative approach to detailing and the breaking down of the large facade with a patterning of wall treatments help link it to the older Rustic buildings at Curry Village. Arbors and pergolas used on the historic building were discontinued.

**GUIDELINES**

- Design new projects to be compatible with, and reflect the massing, scale, and form of, existing structures, especially the lounge. Refer to *The Secretary of the Interior's Standards* for guidance to ensure compatibility.
- Additions to the east side of the Curry Village center should not overwhelm the scale of the existing lounge.

## Roof Form and Materials

The buildings in the Curry Village center have medium-pitched roofs with either gable or hip forms. The dining pavilion has a concentric hip roof. The Mountain Shop has gable roof with a clerestory that provides views up to Glacier Point. Eldridge T. Spencer, the architect of the

*Curry Village Entrance, Lounge, and Registration buildings*

original cafeteria, employed a similar clerestory in the store at Yosemite Lodge. Skylights are also found in the lounge. Asphalt shingles have been used to replace wood shingles on most buildings in the Curry Village center.

**GUIDELINES**

- The design of new structures should reflect the massing, scale, and form of existing Curry Village center buildings and should include the use of medium-pitched roofs, either gable or hipped.
- Use dormers, shed or gable, and skylights to bring light into interior spaces.

## Building Exterior

The lounge is a significant example of the historic rustic character found at Curry Village. The exterior walls consist of an applied frame of unpeeled log posts and sawn beams. Strips of cedar bark are used as infill siding in a herringbone pattern. The porch roof is supported on unpeeled log columns. The typical wood casement window is divided into six lights (NPS 1979).

The Mountain Shop is a contemporary building inspired by Rustic design principles. This building features horizontal wood siding, glazed wood doors with a predominant horizontal muntin pattern, and decorative details at rafter ends and wall corners.

**GUIDELINES**

- New buildings should have a protected base of board-formed concrete, granite, or river-rock cladding. (Refer to "Developed Areas—Building Exteriors" in the "Unifying Elements" chapter.)
- Continue the use of Wosky brown as a unifying external treatment.

*Camp Curry Dining Hall (1929) YRL*

- The design details of the trim, roof overhangs, and porches should be compatible with the character of historic structures.
- Generous porches or verandahs that wrap around the public sides of buildings are recommended and should be scaled for seating as well as circulation. Wood-plank floors typical of the early buildings are recommended.
- Arbors and pergolas define outdoor spaces at Curry Village and create pleasant transitions between indoor and outdoor spaces. The scale and character of these structures should be compatible with other examples found in Curry Village.

## CABINS

The guest quarters at Curry Village consist of groups of tent cabins and wood cabins that have a primitive, spare quality. Visitor service buildings such as comfort stations and shower houses are intermingled with the cabins.

### Siting and Building Orientation

Located east of the Curry Village center, the white-canvas, gable-form tent cabins are one of the most distinctive elements of Curry Village, recalling the original Camp Curry. Although they are arranged in rows, the placement of each individual unit responds to the immediate topography and natural features such as trees and boulders. The wood platforms allow the grade to continue around and under the tent cabins without undue grading.

West of the Curry Village center are several wood cabins with baths. These are slightly larger than the tent cabins, and they are laid out in straighter, more regular rows, with their long sides parallel to pathways. The orientation of individual cabins within this arrangement has been adjusted to accommodate trees and boulders. Cabin locations were not sensitive to natural drainage patterns.

The newer wood cabins without baths (known as WOBs) were built between the late 1920s and early 1930s. Due in part to later modernization, these cabins lack the expressive detail and character of the earlier

TOP *Historic view of dining hall at Camp Curry from photo by J.T. Boyston*
BOTTOM *Clerestory of Mountain Shop, Curry Village*

wood cabins (NPS 2004h). They are also grouped more densely and sometimes rotate their long sides perpendicular to the pathways.

**GUIDELINES**

- New cabins should continue the siting and character of the historic cabins and be integrated with natural features like trees and boulders.
- The layout of new pathways should be universally accessible while conforming to existing topography patterns.

TOP LEFT *Mountain Shop window detail* TOP RIGHT *Mountain Shop bay window* BOTTOM *Early view of Camp Curry cafeteria (now the Mountain Shop). The building was notched to accommodate the large conifers. Conifers have since been replaced with a deck. (date unknown) YRL*

### Architectural Character

The tent cabins exemplify the primitive character of Curry Village. Built on wood platforms and made of white canvas stretched over a wood frame, their geometry is simple, with a gable roof and wooden steps leading from the grade to the door. The screened door has a canvas roll-blind, as do the windows.

The original wood cabins, nestled within the forest setting, define the character of the western area of Curry Village. Built between 1918 and 1922, the cabins have a simple and natural character derived from their rectangular plan, gable forms, wood shingle roofs, applied half-log framing, tongue-and-groove diagonal wood siding between frame elements, wood casement windows, and wood paneled doors. Building shape and massing are important character-defining elements of the original wood cabins. These small buildings are one story and low in profile, and they have no projecting bays. Porches without roofs are either flush with the grade or elevated, depending on the slope of the ground. Some of the cabins have river-washed cobble stonemasonry foundations and chimneys. The cabins' dark-brown color blends with the forest setting.

Two historic residences constructed by the Currys inspired the design of the wood cabins: the Foster Curry Cabin (1916) and Mother Curry's Bungalow (1917). These buildings established a rustic theme for Curry Village. They are characterized by unpeeled log pilasters, which simulate a structural frame, and wall panels of unpeeled cedar bark (NPS 1979).

**GUIDELINES**

- The architectural character of new cabins should be compatible with the historic wood cabins without imitating them. Refer to *The Secretary of the Interior's Standards* for guidance to ensure compatibility.
- Provision for winter occupancy will influence the character of new buildings. This may cause them to differ from the historic buildings.
- Refer to "Developed Areas—Building Shape and Massing" in the "Unifying Elements" chapter for more guidelines on winter occupancy.

### Roof Form and Materials

The original wood cabins have gable roofs with medium pitch in the range of 5:12. Their overhangs are well proportioned for the mass of the buildings. Asphalt shingles are typically used on new structures to meet current safety requirements.

**GUIDELINES**

- New cabins should have a gable roof form with medium pitch to be compatible with the historic wood cabins.
- Increased winter use and the need for snow management may influence the design of roofs at entrances. The addition of small gables over entrance doors has altered the original character of many cabins. Entrances on the eave side of the building require protection from rain and snow. Projections from the roof should have structural elements, such as posts and beam supports, that define the entrance and allow the shelter to stand. Alternatively, consider locating entrances to the gable side of the structure.

*Stoneman Lodge, Curry Village (2004) RF*

## Building Exterior

The exterior walls of the original wood cabins consist of simulated half-log frames with infill sheathing of diagonal one-by-four, tongue-and-groove wood siding in a herringbone pattern. Other components include split-log gable ends, foundations of river-washed cobble, wood porches, paneled doors, and casement windows. Wood sash windows with true muntins are a salient characteristic of the building exterior. The cabins are unified by their painted brown color.

**GUIDELINES**

- New cabins should have a base of form-board concrete or concrete with a cobble facing. If cobble is used, it is important to select stone that is of compatible color and size to that found on historic wood cabins.

TOP *Wood cabins without baths, Curry Village* BOTTOM *Tent cabins, Curry Village (2004) JM*

- For one-story buildings, limit wall siding to one material and one pattern.
- Cabin entries should be placed on the gable ends of buildings or under porches with column support as required. Provide protection from snow over the entries.
- Porch railings are optional unless required by code.
- Flush, painted, solid-core doors are recommended. Panel doors, if used, should be of compatible, simple design with a paint finish.
- Use of divided lights in new cabins is not recommended. Window proportion and orientation should reflect those of the original cabins.
- Exposed roof framing of rough-sawn elements is recommended.
- Attic vents of wood are recommended.

TOP *Wood cabin with boulder (2004) RF*
BOTTOM *Trail leading to tent cabins and boulders, Curry Village*

## EMPLOYEE HOUSING

### Siting and Building Orientation

If supplemental housing is considered at Curry Village, it should be located within the existing employee housing area and should be of a character that is compatible with the historic development while blending with the existing, contemporary, employee housing.

The relationship between buildings and the landscape is one of the most distinctive characteristics of Curry Village.

**GUIDELINES**

- Cluster new buildings around natural features.
- Site buildings at the edges of open spaces and into the trees, and use open spaces for natural light, views, and gathering areas. Pedestrian access from parking areas to buildings should weave through these open spaces.

Tent interior, Camp Curry (ca. 1917). Courtesy of the Huntington Library

## Architectural Character

A major issue for new buildings is their compatibility with the existing historic buildings. Curry Village has a distinct architectural character defined by a consistent use of Rustic design principles. It is important that Rustic design principles be observed to achieve harmony with the historic buildings, while blending with the contemporary housing design.

**GUIDELINES**

- New development should share characteristics inspired by and connected to Rustic design while blending with the existing, contemporary, employee housing.
- New buildings should incorporate the shape, mass, and gable roof forms of the historic buildings. Other features and details should be used to distinguish the new buildings as contemporary, consistent with compatibility guidance outlined in *The Secretary of the Interior's Standards for the Treatment of Historic Properties*.

## Building Shape and Massing

The consistent use of rectangular shape and simple mass will help achieve unity between the employee housing and Curry Village. To provide a reasonable transition, buffering, such as vegetation, will be required between new and historic developments.

**GUIDELINES**

- Limit building height to two stories.
- Locate stairs and porches within the main building volume to protect them from the weather.
- Refer to "Developed Areas—Building Shape and Massing" in the "Unifying Elements" chapter for more guidelines.

## Roof Form and Materials

The gable is the dominant roof form throughout the cabin areas.

**GUIDELINES**

- The roof form of new buildings should be a gable with the ridge parallel to the long side of the building.
- Refer to "Developed Areas—Roof Form and Materials" in the "Unifying Elements" chapter for more guidelines.

## Building Exterior

A particular set of exterior features was used consistently in the historic cabins to achieve a rustic character. Key features include a protected base, pilasters to articulate facades, exposed roof framing details, wood sash windows, and a consistent color treatment. Many of

Wood cabin with porch and rustic base, Curry Village (2004) RF

TOP *Bungalow, Camp Curry (1926) YRL* BOTTOM LEFT *Mother Curry's Bungalow* BOTTOM RIGHT *Foster Curry Cabin*

*Back side of entrance sign, Curry Village*

these features remain relevant to the design of new buildings because their use is not limited to a historic time period.

With the advent of year-round use, new entrances and porches are important architectural additions that address snow management.

**GUIDELINES**

- Use board-formed concrete to form a protected base, consistent with recommendations in the "Unifying Elements" chapter.
- For one-story buildings, limit wall siding to one pattern. For two-story buildings, use of one siding pattern is preferred, but no more than two patterns should be used. The historic wood cabins serve as reference for use of wall materials.
- Board and batten siding is recommended for its superior weathering properties and because it would be recognizably different from historic treatments. Other types of wood siding or shingles of various patterns may also be used.
- Entrances should be placed at the gable ends or under porches for protection from the weather. Use of timber columns and beams at entrances and porches may be appropriate to announce the entrance. Service doors should be protected from snow with small roof extensions or porches.
- Arrange windows in an orderly and uniform manner, reflecting the interior furniture layouts. Exterior doors should be sash or solid-core. Windows should be metal-clad. Use windows without divided lights to distinguish new buildings from the historic ones.
- Wood trim elements should be oversized in width and thickness to give character to openings.
- Outlookers are recommended as a detail for supporting roof overhangs at the gable ends.
- The material and texture of exposed framing at eaves should be the same as the exterior siding.
- Use of new colors is acceptable, but the color and hue should be compatible with the traditional Wosky brown.

*Exterior wall detail from historic wood cabin, Curry Village (2004) RF*

# THE AHWAHNEE

DESIGNED BY GILBERT Stanley Underwood, The Ahwahnee is one of the most elaborate lodges ever built in a national park. In its discussion of the specific significance of The Ahwahnee, the 1976 National Register nomination calls the hotel "among the most significant park hotels in the country," in the company of the Old Faithful Inn in Yellowstone National Park and the El Tovar at Grand Canyon National Park.

IT WAS DERIVED FROM THE BEGINNING TO MAKE THE AHWAHNEE ENVIRONMENTAL IN ITS ARCHITECTURE, RATHER THAN TO FOLLOW ANY DEFINITE PERIOD. **FROM A LETTER BY DONALD TRESIDDER, PRESIDENT OF THE YP&CC, TO FREDERICK LAW OLMSTED JR., LANDSCAPE ARCHITECT • 1927**

In spite of the difficulties encountered during the planning and construction of The Ahwahnee, most would agree that Underwood turned this challenging assignment into one of his greatest successes. Skillfully adopting a previously developed architectural vocabulary to a site where proportions had to be carefully considered, he succeeded in creating a new, monumental interpretation of Rustic-style architecture. By echoing the Valley's massive boulders, craggy cliffs, and towering forests, he forged new paths "different from anything previously built in the park," according to publicity bulletins periodically issued during construction by the Yosemite Park and Curry Company. The company called its style "environmental" to stress its departure from established forms of design (Zaitlin 1989).



A few naturalists, who believed that any building in the park should be secondary to the landscape, were critical of the hotel's lavishness. Among them was Ansel Adams, who wrote that "the architect had tried to compete with the environment. He lost." But for those who appreciate the structure's compatibility with the scale of its surroundings, the hotel is a unique and successful blend of Rustic with Art Deco elements. Its design represents a highly individualized interpretation of Rustic architecture (Zaitlin 1989).

Completed in 1927, The Ahwahnee has continued in operation to this day. The one exception occured during World War II, when it was converted to a naval convalescent hospital. Despite this use, The Ahwahnee retains integrity to a period of historical significance ending in 1942. The Ahwahnee was listed in the National Register in 1977, and it was designated a National Historic Landmark for its significant architecture in 1987.

*Porte-cochère, The Ahwahnee (2004) RF*

*The Ahwahnee (1990) DNC-KW*

## Setting

The Ahwahnee has an optimal location in Yosemite Valley, with stunning views, river access, and a mild local climate. The milder climate is due in part to the hotel's elevated location, giving it access to a higher angle of sunlight from the southwest. Attesting to the site's popularity, previous use included an American Indian village, the Kenneyville Stables, J.C. Lamon's homestead, and the Aaron Harris public camping facility.

Sitting as it does, at the northeastern edge of the relatively secluded Ahwahnee Meadow, The Ahwahnee has impressive views of Glacier Point, Royal Arch Cascade, Royal Arches, Yosemite Falls, and Half Dome.

The Merced River winds in a distinctive oxbow bend on the southern edge of the hotel site, creating an effective buffer between the hotel and Curry Village and the maze of campgrounds that occupies the eastern end of the Valley. Elevated above the floodplain, The Ahwahnee was spared during the 1997 flood. While outside the area's designated talus zone, the hotel is within the "shadow line," defined as the probable furthest extent of individual rocks beyond the talus line. A 2009 rockfall damaged several cars in the parking lot north of the hotel, and a few small rocks reached the reflecting pond near the hotel's porte cochère.

*Pair of lanterns at The Ahwahnee*

Management of vegetation at The Ahwahnee has historically focused on attempts to present a natural meadow landscape and native woodlands, as well as to reinforce certain spatial sequences and impressions. To an impressive degree, the original landscape and overall site plan of the area has been maintained. Despite the encroachment of pines and cedars into black oak forests and meadows, vegetation management has successfully preserved most views—both from the building to natural landmarks and of the building in its meadow setting—while still maintaining the area's sense of splendid isolation. These efforts were often based on intuition rather than in-depth horticultural or forestry knowledge, as is evident in the close planting of sequoias to screen buildings and tennis courts. In the 1920s, Frederick Law Olmsted Jr. added more vegetation to discourage deer and create a more varied and lush appearance. He also designed a reflecting pond in front of The Ahwahnee, landscaped with plantings representative of the various ecological zones in the park (Olmsted 1930). Much of this disappeared during World War II due to lack of maintenance.

TOP *The Ahwahnee with Upper Yosemite Fall (2003) GH*
BOTTOM *Ahwahnee bungalow (2004) RF*

The Ahwahnee is accessed by a two-lane entrance road from Village Drive. The road provides access to the parking lots on the north side of the hotel, the porte cochère, and the service entrance to the hotel.

From the parking lot, the hotel is screened by a porte cochère generous enough to accommodate four to six automobiles. Shrubs and trees (including sequoias) planted in the 1920s provide additional screening. The porte cochère connects to a covered walkway, which in turn leads into the registration lobby of the hotel. From this point, access continues to shops, the bar at the Ahwahnee, the elevator lobby, the dining room, the main lounge, and outdoor spaces on the south side of the hotel. The entrance is on the service side of the building, although the service areas and loading docks are completely hidden from view by a heavy board fence.

The entrance as originally conceived by Underwood was to have been on the end of the northeast wing. A portico was built to cover the entrance, but there was a concern that vehicles and arriving guests might create too much noise for the occupants of the guest rooms just above. The present porte cochère and 120-foot covered walkway was hastily built, and the original portico enclosed. Today, the ground floor of the east wing functions as the Ahwahnee Bar, located just off the registration lobby (Zaitlin 1989).

This modification of the entry created a different type of arrival from the one originally designed. Underwood's own watercolor rendering of the hotel before its completion shows that it was his original idea to provide more formal access to the building. A covered walkway made of logs and rough wood made arriving at the entrance lobby a more rustic experience (Zaitlin 1989).

From the south The Ahwahnee makes very different and surprising impressions. Hardly visible from the north side, it emerges as a massive, granite-clad structure that seems both to stand up to its surroundings and acquiesce to them. The building is set in an open meadow with background views of the Royal Arches, Glacier Point, Yosemite Point, and other major formations of the

*Log seat with chevron pattern at The Ahwahnee (2004) RF*

Valley walls. The massive, stone-covered piers and projecting wings of the hotel give it a sculptural quality. The absence of an entrance and the associated traffic enhance this sculptural quality when viewed from the south, east, and west.

The Ahwahnee bungalows, separated from the hotel by Royal Arch Creek, was designed by architect Eldridge T. Spencer and completed in 1928. A unique wooden bridge with built-in Craftsman-style benches leads visitors across the creek to the eight small clapboard and shake buildings. The exclusion of vehicles from this wooded area gives it an intimate, semiprivate feeling distinct from that of the hotel. The bungalows are relatively close to one another, but dense vegetation and the meandering slate pathways prevent the feeling of crowding.

## DEVELOPED AREA

The Ahwahnee is a significant example of Rustic-style architecture in Yosemite Valley. A response to the natural setting informs almost every aspect of the building's design. While the oversized proportions of the building's important elements seek to achieve a scale that relates to the Valley walls, the backdrop of massive granite walls of the Valley seems to diminish the building's massive scale.

The architect of The Ahwahnee, Gilbert Stanley Underwood, created a building that combined contemporary building technology with the use of native materials. The six-story, steel-frame and reinforced concrete structure is clad with stained, textured concrete designed to look like wood, a veneer of weathered granite boulders, and real logs at the porte cochère. Although most of the building materials were far from rustic, their specific treatment and the forms into which they were molded resulted in a building that, despite its rational construction, massive scale, and modern techniques, demonstrates the Rustic-style architecture of rough-hewn logs and rocks reserved for—and that Americans have come to expect of—essential buildings in park settings (Page & Turnbull 1997).

Understanding this sensitive expectation, Underwood created a building that is seemingly just that—logs and rocks. This success is remarkable, given the use of relatively spare amounts of actual rustic materials. The interior design is not Rustic, but rather is a skillful blending of the then-current Art Deco style with Native American decorative motifs. While Underwood was apparently the generator of the Art Deco theme, it was the design team of Ackerman and Pope—with the assistance of interior designer Jeanette Spencer—who succeeded in integrating the Art Deco and Native American decorative arts into the hotel, and it is in fact

*Roof overhang and balcony of concrete, made to simulate wood*

this form of decoration, present in all aspects of the interior, from the furnishings to the decorative paint stencils, fixtures, and fabrics, that is celebrated today (Page & Turnbull 1997).

The building's massing is broken up, creating the sense of a rambling, organic structure that belies the sheer size of the facility. Large wings contain the massive great lounge and a dining room, both of which are extraordinary two-story spaces. The lounge has an ornate, concrete-beamed ceiling, and the dining room features high, exposed timber trusses.

Curry Company president Donald Tresidder and the board of the Yosemite Park and Curry Company instructed Underwood to design the 100-guest-room structure (along with consideration for space for the later cottages) to convey the impression of a large home rather than a hotel. He was told to place the essential commercial elements such as the cashier and telephone booths in an unobtrusive place, preferably in a separate wing. Upon entering the building, guests might take notice of these facilities, but once past them, they would feel they were in a "quiet, luxurious country home" (Zaitlin 1989).

The concept of a large hotel changed many times before the final drawings were completed. As late as January 1926, the plans for the hotel provided for a building no higher than three stories with stone construction on the first floor and wood framing above. Eventually it was decided to build a larger structure, providing 100 guest rooms and several very spacious public areas. The dining room, originally planned for 1,000, was scaled down to accommodate only 350 diners.

Other significant buildings in The Ahwahnee developed area include eight Ahwahnee bungalows and a storage building in the bungalow area. The Ahwahnee dormitory, built as a temporary storage building during the Naval hospital period and converted later to employee housing, is noncontributing.

Eleven significant structures in The Ahwahnee developed area include the entrance road (from gateway to parking lot), gateway piers, main parking lot (west), reflecting pond, bungalow paths, footbridge to bungalow area, footbridge near Merced River, bridle trail ford, drainage ways, tennis courts, and the flagstone terrace (NPS 2004h).

*Large scale glazed opening between porch and lounge at The Ahwahnee*

**GUIDELINES**

- Refer to the *The Ahwahnee Historic Structures Report* (NPS 2011a) and the *The Ahwahnee Cultural Landscape Report* (NPS 2011b) for specific guidelines pertaining to the hotel and its grounds.

# YOSEMITE LODGE

YOSEMITE LODGE IS a 1950s motel-style complex characterized by modern structural forms and modern materials such as glass, concrete, and steel—typical of Mission 66 design. The lodge is located along the base of the north Valley wall, southwest of Yosemite Village, north of the Merced River, and immediately west of Yosemite Creek. The original Yosemite Lodge building (no longer in existence) was constructed in 1915, in response to the advice of Stephen Mather and Franklin Lane. Both believed that there would be an influx of visitors to the park after the completion of

THE GREAT FALL, THE NOBLEST DISPLAY OF FALLING WATER TO BE FOUND IN THE VALLEY, OR PERHAPS IN THE WORLD...THIS NOBLE FALL HAS BY FAR THE RICHEST, AS WELL AS THE MOST POWERFUL, VOICE OF ALL THE FALLS OF THE VALLEY, ITS TONES VARYING FROM THE SHARP HISS AND RUSTLE OF THE WIND IN THE GLOSSY LEAVES OF THE LIVE-OAKS AND THE SOFT, SIFTING, HUSHING TONES OF THE PINES, TO THE LOUDEST RUSH AND ROAR OF STORM WINDS AND THUNDER AMONG THE CRAGS OF THE SUMMIT PEAKS. **JOHN MUIR • THE YOSEMITE • 1912**

the Panama Canal. Increased visitation to Yosemite did occur after World War II, making it necessary to expand the facility. Beginning in 1956, the lodge and associated developments were replaced with several new buildings designed by Eldridge Spencer. Yosemite Lodge today includes the main lodge (registration building), mid-scale motel units, a restaurant, a cafeteria, a bar, a gift and general merchandise store, a specialty gift shop, conference rooms, a bike rental shop, a post office, and a swimming pool. All guest lodging consists of multi-unit-style building construction (NPS 2004i).

In 1996 the visitor service facilities at the lodge were renovated with the extension of the Mountain Room Restaurant, a new Garden Court restaurant, an enlarged and renovated gift shop, and restrooms.

Although Yosemite Lodge is within the Yosemite Valley Historic District, the buildings post-date the period of significance and are noncontributing.

## Setting

### Natural Systems + Features

The Yosemite Lodge complex is on the north side of Yosemite Valley between towering granite cliffs and the Merced River. Yosemite Lodge's location on the edge of Leidig Meadow, just north of the Merced River, and close to Yosemite Falls, gives the complex a dramatic setting. The most prominent natural feature at the lodge is Yosemite Falls to the northeast. Farther up the Valley to the east is Half Dome.

The Yosemite Lodge complex is set on the sunny, warmer side of the Valley. In the winter the lodge gets low-angle direct sunshine, resulting in strong solar radiation that penetrates into areas normally shaded from the summer sun. This effect is more pronounced in areas of deciduous black oaks.

The most dramatic natural feature at Yosemite Lodge is the remarkable tree-framed view of Yosemite Falls to the north. Each year, however, views of the Upper and Lower falls from the lodge are incrementally narrowed or obscured by these tall coniferous trees.

**YOSEMITE LODGE**

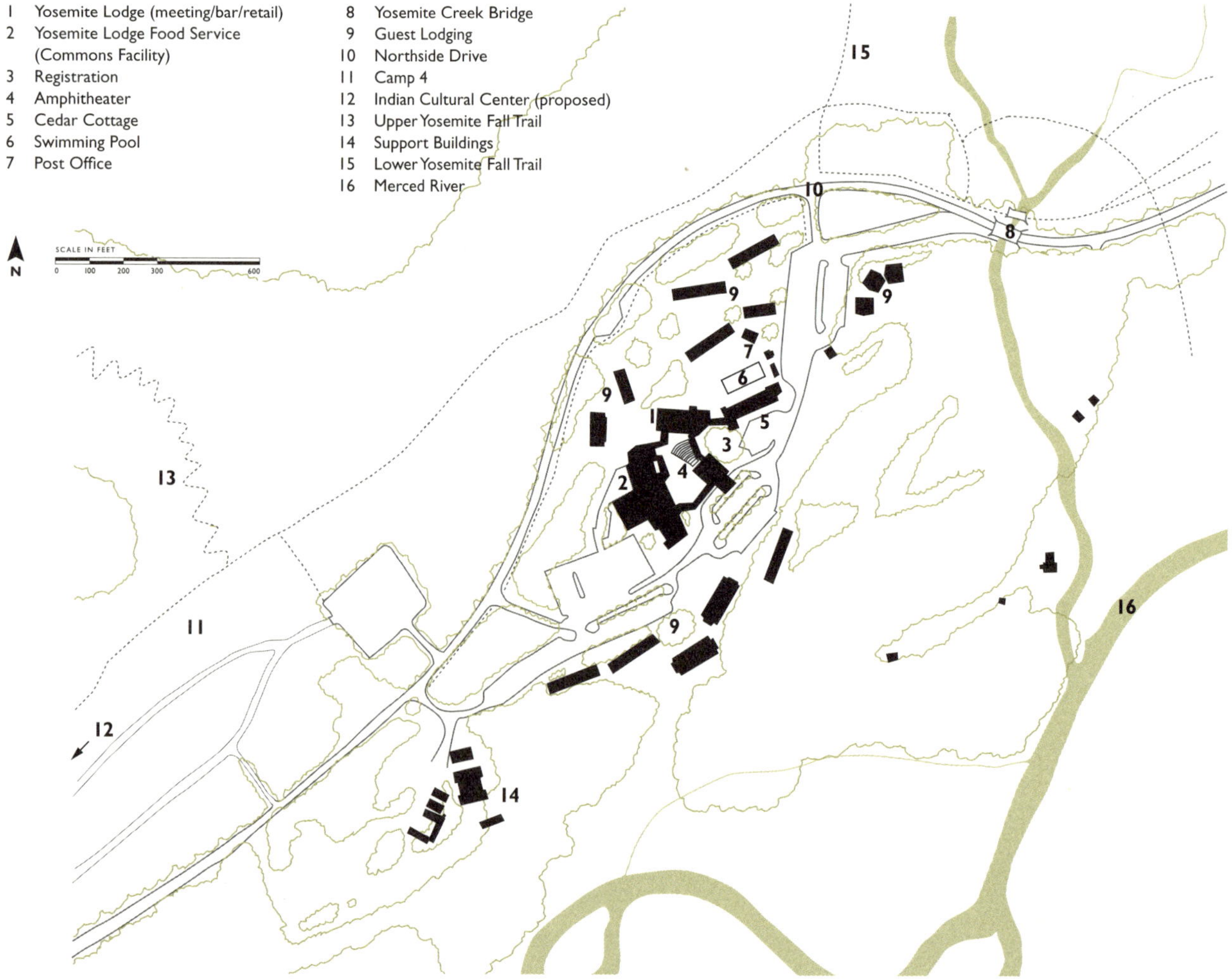

**GUIDELINES**

- New design should enhance the character of black oak and meadow settings through the selection of appropriate plantings.

## SCENIC VIEWS

Yosemite Lodge is situated in one of the most spectacular scenic areas of the park. From Yosemite Lodge one can see a great variety of significant natural features, including Sentinel Rock, Union Point, Half Dome, Washington Column, Lost Arrow Spire, and Yosemite Falls. There are also important views to talus slopes and rock walls at the base of Columbia Rock, Eagle Tower, and Eagle Peak. Views vary seasonally; views that are obscured by spring growth become apparent when leaves are shed in the fall. Distant views become part of an overall composition, with close-up subjects such as trees, talus, and the base of cliffs.

**GUIDELINES**

- New design should include the planting, trimming, or clearing of trees and shrubs as appropriate to frame, emphasize, or open-up views, as consistent with the *Scenic Vista Management Plan for Yosemite National Park* (NPS 2011d).
- Orient new walkways, gathering areas, balconies, and visitor service building windows to optimize views of natural features, such as Yosemite Falls, Lost Arrow Spire, Half Dome, Columbia Rock, Eagle Tower, Eagle Peak, Sentinel Rock, and meadows.
- New design should make use of opportunities to simplify parking at the lodge entrance, enhance views, and restore the open character and view of Leidig Meadow from the Lodge.

*Auto arrival at Yosemite Lodge (ca. 1960) YRL*

## VEGETATION

The character of the vegetation at Yosemite Lodge changes based on location within the site and includes the talus slope, the developed area of the lodge, and the riparian meadow. The talus and developed areas are dominated by a scattered pattern of pines and cedars, with some black oak. Leidig Meadow, which is south of the lodge, is one of the major meadows in the Valley. The meadow and its extension to the west underlie much of the Merced River floodplain. There has been significant encroachment by conifers into some areas of the meadow.

**GUIDELINES**

- Use of native plants for landscape purposes should blend with the natural surroundings in the immediate vicinity. Use of conifers should be carefully evaluated because of their impact on views of the surrounding cliffs and meadows adjacent to the lodge area.
- Specifications for vegetation types and planting should conform to the *Comprehensive Landscape and Revegetation Plan* (Bitterroot 1999).

- Design planted areas in the core of the developed area, near visitor service buildings, to be large and separated from pedestrian areas by grade changes or low stone or timber barriers. This will prevent social trails and will enhance overall maintenance efficiency. Avoid designing planting areas that are too small to support large shrubs and trees or that encourage pedestrians to wander off the paths and into planted areas.

## Landscape Uses + Structures

### LAND USE + SPATIAL ORGANIZATION

Yosemite Lodge consists of multiple building clusters set in groves of trees and open meadow areas. The clusters are organized by function, and are connected by a network of roads, trails, and parking lots. Visitor services and recreational facilities are grouped in the central core of the lodge complex and are flanked by large parking lots. The three primary visitor service buildings in the public core are connected by covered walkways and form an inner courtyard that includes an amphitheater and casual seating. These buildings house the registration office, a restaurant, cafeteria, bar, conference space, and shops. A secondary cluster adjacent to the central core focuses around a swimming pool. Clusters of guest lodging buildings are dispersed around the perimeter of the site and consist of one- and two-story mid-scale motel units.

*View of Washington Column and Half Dome, near Yosemite Lodge*

**GUIDELINES**

- New buildings should be located in disturbed sites outside the floodplain of the Merced River.
- New buildings should be integrated into an existing cluster or should establish new clusters in similar proximity to the existing facilities.

### CIRCULATION + PARKING

Vehicle traffic is concentrated along the paved road and associated parking areas bisecting the developed area. A central paved road runs through the development. Secondary roads connect the central road to parking and service areas. Several large, paved parking lots are located near the registration office and some of the lodging clusters. Less-formal, hard-packed earth roads and small asphalt service roads provide vehicle access to the more remote lodge facilities.

Concrete and asphalt walkways provide pedestrian circulation in the central core area. Hard-packed earthen paths connect the central core to the more remote parts of the lodge complex. Access via parking areas to lodging units is on paved walkways.

**GUIDELINES**

- Vehicle, pedestrian, and bicycle pathways should be separated and clearly delineated for visitor safety.
- Design should minimize the presence of the road as a visual and pedestrian barrier between the lodge and the river.

*Leidig Meadow (1938) YRL*

- New roads in the lodge area should incorporate major natural features into the alignment of the road corridor.
- Parking areas should be designed so that they are screened from the road corridor.
- Locate parking areas out of view from guestrooms and walkways.
- Refer to "Landscape Uses + Structures" in the "Unifying Elements" chapter for more guidelines on circulation.

### STRUCTURES

For guidelines on small buildings, masonry, footbridges, boardwalks, culvert crossings, retaining walls, fences, and benches, refer to the "Unifying Elements" chapter.

## Developed Areas

### VISITOR SERVICE BUILDINGS + COURTYARD

#### Siting and Building Orientation

Guests arrive at Yosemite Lodge by way of Northside Drive, passing through or by the porte cochère in front of the 1956 registration building. Guests park their vehicles in one of several small parking lots and walk back to the registration building.

The visitor service buildings are organized around an informal courtyard and are linked by covered walkways. Yosemite Lodge is the only complex in the Valley where covered walkways connect visitor service buildings. In the center of the courtyard is an amphitheater with views to Yosemite Falls and Sentinel Rock. The registration building faces south. The swimming pool is adjacent to and east of this central area.

**GUIDELINES**

- New visitor service buildings should be sited to take advantage of important views and should have outdoor areas that provide interpretive opportunities. Visitors should be guided toward views of Yosemite Falls or the vistas across the meadow.
- New visitor service facilities should not be placed within the courtyard, in order to preserve the concept of the courtyard space.

TOP *Courtyard from Mountain Room porch, Yosemite Lodge (2004) GH*
BOTTOM *Cafeteria dining terrace, Yosemite Lodge (2004) SA*

- New buildings should enhance the visitor experience of the area around Yosemite Lodge (taking advantage of views, etc.) while meeting the needs of the lodge operation.
- Site new visitor service buildings in and among trees in areas that have been previously developed or disturbed.
- New design should ensure that guests have access to developed spaces adjacent to buildings where they can pause, linger, and enjoy natural surroundings.

## Architectural Character

The architectural character of Yosemite Lodge's 1956-era buildings is the product of the Mission 66 movement, a dramatic departure from earlier NPS Rustic style. The one-story buildings employ a modern architectural vocabulary of exposed steel frames, large expanses of glass, and low-pitch roofs. Within Yosemite Valley, traditional rustic buildings are designed to make strong connections to the natural landscape through their use of natural materials. Although Yosemite Lodge lacks the type of rustic character of Curry Village or The Ahwahnee, the openness and transparency of the lodge buildings allow visitors to connect with the natural setting.

The 1996 rehabilitation and extension of the Mountain Room Restaurant employed contemporary expressions of rustic design—rough-sawn timbers, cedar paneling left in its natural state—combined with modern elements such as large expanses of glass. The success of this project was in its linkage of the Mission 66 style with a more traditional Rustic-style architectural vocabulary.

**GUIDELINES**

- New construction at Yosemite Lodge should be similar in form and scale to the lodge facilities. New additions should build from the openness of the contemporary architectural style while incorporating the natural elements reflective of the site's surroundings.
- Use natural materials and subdued colors that are inspired by the natural setting.

## Building Shape and Massing

The visitor service buildings are one-story structures with low-pitched gable roofs that do not compete with the natural setting. Each space within the complex provides generous interior spaces appropriate to their function. Within their low profile, these structures use roof forms that direct attention upwards toward the surrounding landmarks. For example, the roof of the Mountain Room Restaurant extends in shed elements, creating tall windows facing Yosemite Falls. Other retail spaces use generous clerestories and skylights.

**GUIDELINES**

- New buildings should be based on simple building forms that harmonize with the natural setting as well as the human-made environment. They should not detract from the grandeur of the cliffs and the waterfalls that are the prime backdrop for the lodge.
- New communal gathering areas at the lodge should continue the pattern of spacious, one-story structures with generously glazed exterior walls and exposed structural framing. Variation of building height is recommended to create important interior spaces that make strong connections to the surrounding landscape elements.
- Future planning and design should employ methods that will continue to enhance and foster a sense of unity for the entire complex.

*Courtyard, Yosemite Lodge (2004) GH*

## Roof Form and Materials

The public buildings at Yosemite Lodge have a roof pitch that is considerably lower than many structures in the Valley. This profile gives the buildings a horizontal aspect that does not compete with the landscape. Asphalt cap sheet and asphalt shingles are used as roof coverings throughout the lodge complex.

**GUIDELINES**

- For new buildings, continue the use of roof forms that are compatible with the Mission 66 era buildings at the lodge. However, for major public buildings, dramatic height for interior spaces may be desirable. New roof pitch should not be as steep as that of Cedar Cottage because smaller snow loads (as exist in the Valley) do not warrant steep pitches.

TOP *Lounge, Yosemite Lodge (2004) SA*
BOTTOM *Mountain Room Restaurant, Yosemite Lodge (2004) SA*

- Provide eaves that shed snow and water away from the walls. Prevent snow and rain from dropping and accumulating on pedestrian walkways.
- Use of slightly oversized structural members can be considered in creating a substantial character for important rooms.
- Roof coverings should be nonreflective and dark-colored to harmonize with the natural surroundings. This will minimize reflection when viewed from the trails above the Valley floor.
- Refer to "Developed Areas—Roof Form and Materials" in the "Unifying Elements" chapter for more guidelines.

## Building Exteriors

The exterior treatments at Yosemite Lodge include wood siding, natural colors, large window-walls, over-scaled wood structural elements, covered walkways and porches, and a protected base. The original visitor service buildings are clad in wood siding that is stained brown. Steel columns and windows are painted the same color.

The exterior walls of the Mountain Room addition are resawn cedar boards finished with a clear stain. This treatment recalls early Rustic-style buildings in the Valley that typically had redwood siding with a clear oil finish. Generous window-walls on the original steel-framed buildings allow a strong connection between indoors and outdoors. Glazed doors reinforce this indoor–outdoor connection. The exposed steel columns and beams recall the earlier tradition of exposed structural elements. Additions at the lodge reintroduced the use of over-scaled, resawn timbers for the interior and exterior framing. A concrete base was incorporated into the design of the Mountain Room addition to create a weathering lower-wall treatment.

**GUIDELINES**

- Wood siding with a resawn surface is recommended as the dominant cladding material.
- Appropriate finishes for wood siding include paints or opaque stains in colors consistent with existing structures, semi-transparent stains, or natural weathering sealers.
- Porches and eaves should be of a scale suitable for public assembly. The south loggia at The Ahwahnee is a fine example.
- Moderately overscaled, resawn timbers are recommended for the main structural elements. Logs are not recommended. For reasons of sustainability, glue-laminated members are preferred; however, log framing members may be appropriate in some areas for their special visual or interpretive value.

*Porch of the Mountain Room Restaurant, Yosemite Lodge (2004) GH*

- Exposed timber framing connectors should not be visually distracting. The color of the painted metal connector plates and brackets should be harmonious with the wood framing members.
- Wood detail elements such as trim boards should be sized to have a sturdy character.
- New visitor service buildings should have a defined base that resists deterioration and visually connects the building to the ground. The base should be made of concrete formed with rough-sawn boards. It may be appropriate to use a weathered granite base for important new structures. In this case the granite should be used for adjacent landscape walls to connect the building to the land.

## GUEST LODGING

### Siting and Building Orientation

Traditionally, the setting for guest quarters is quiet and restful, providing guests the opportunity to experience and appreciate the natural surroundings. Guest quarters at Yosemite Lodge are located in clusters at some distance from the visitor service buildings. Approached by pathways from the central public core, the buildings are sited in and among the trees and near the edges of meadows.

Many of the guest quarter buildings are one and two stories in height, long and rectangular in shape, and arranged in an irregular layout, with a general tendency to align parallel with the Valley walls. This east–west orientation allows views of the Valley walls to the north and south.

These buildings have defined front and rear sides, stairs, balconies, entrance doors on the front, and patios and decks on the rear.

**GUIDELINES**

- The clustering of smaller guest quarters has greater flexibility in adapting to landscape elements such as trees and boulders. Informal groupings allow the buildings to fit more naturally into the landscape. It is important to determine the capacity of the site so as to not tax the natural setting.
- New lodging units should avoid removal of mature healthy trees wherever possible.
- Site guest lodgings to take advantage of views, natural light, and solar access (in that order of priority).

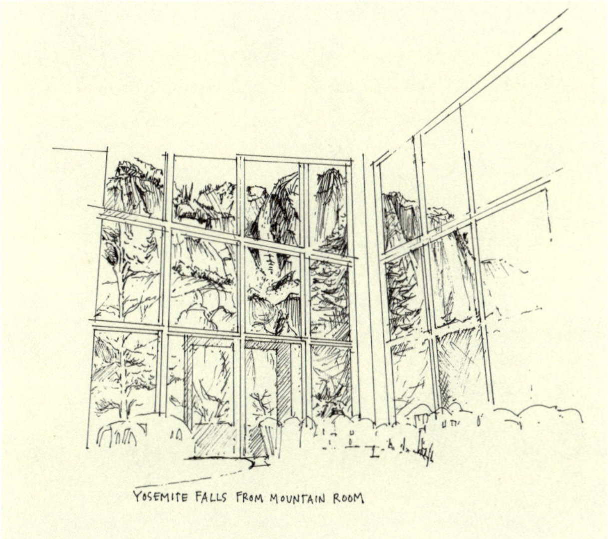


*View of Yosemite Falls from Mountain Room Restaurant*

*Mountain Room Restaurant roof detail from courtyard, Yosemite Lodge*

- Continue the use of rectangular buildings with an east–west orientation as a unifying characteristic for site organization.
- Refer to "Developed Areas—Siting and Building Orientation" in the "Unifying Elements" chapter for more guidelines on building orientation and sound.

### Architectural Character

The overall architectural character of the guest quarters at Yosemite Lodge reflects the Bay Area style of the 1940s to 1960s. This regional modern design style was widely used during the period of the construction of the guest quarters. Like Mission 66 visitor service buildings, the guest quarters departed from the traditional NPS Rustic style. The features that link these buildings to other developments in Yosemite Valley include the use of simple rectangular plan forms with gable roofs, wood siding in simple patterns, and paint and stain colors of dark umber.

New development presents the opportunity to use contemporary materials and techniques that embrace and capture the remarkable setting of the lodge.

**GUIDELINES**

- The architectural character of new guest quarters should be modest, restful, and welcoming to the visitor. The expression of shelter should be enhanced by generous roof overhangs, porches, verandahs, and private outdoor spaces.
- New development should create a sense of identity for the guest quarter buildings by using design themes that are compatible with previous design efforts as well as the physical setting of the site.
- Use of natural materials can contribute rustic character to new guest quarter buildings.

### Building Shape and Massing

Guest quarters at Yosemite Lodge are simple one- and two-story buildings that maintain a consistent scale throughout the development. Most of the buildings have rectangular plans with gable roofs. Each guest room at the lodge provides access to the outdoors by way of a balcony or patio.

Balconies and patios require the proper degree of privacy to make guests comfortable. The Sentinel (since removed) and Wawona hotels provide historic examples of generous two-story balconies providing access to guest rooms, a place to enjoy the outdoors, and a buffer between visitor service and private spaces. Wide enough to accommodate sitting and socializing, the balconies' proportions created a dignified character.

The roof can control the massing of the building by extending beyond the plan, encompassing bays. For instance, the main roof of the Tecoya dorms extends

*View from Lounge toward Mountain Room Restaurant, Yosemite Lodge (2004) GH*

TOP *Porch entry to the Mountain Room Restaurant, Yosemite Lodge (2004) RF*
BOTTOM *Early U.S. Army structures with jerkinhead roofs (since removed) (1926) YRL*

over the projecting bays at the gable ends and thus maintains the overall building form. A simple massing can also be preserved when stairs and elevators are recessed into the main volume and/or covered by the main roof.

The historic Cascades Cabins (since removed) are another reference for new guest-quarter buildings. They had a refined simplicity of shape and massing. Gable roofs defined the main volumes, and the roof slope was kept intact as it descended over the projecting bays.

**GUIDELINES**

- Larger, two-story buildings should use plan forms that generate simple building mass. Use extensions of the main roof to add extensions to the main rectangular plan form. Use sheds on the long sides and gabled bays at the entrances.
- Stairs and elevators should be recessed within the mass of the building to provide weather protection and to maintain the simple overall building mass.
- Guest rooms should have outdoor seating areas such as covered porches, patios, or balconies.
- Where balconies are also used for access to guest rooms, they should be wide enough to accommodate seating as well.
- Edge treatments of patios and balconies should establish visual privacy for both guests in their rooms and passersby. Low walls, built-in benches, and balcony railings should be used to screen furniture and guest clutter. Tall screens should be avoided except where they can help reinforce desirable definition of open space.
- Refer to "Landscape Uses + Structures—Barriers, Fences + Benches" in the "Unifying Elements" chapter for more guidelines.

## Roof Form and Materials

The guest quarter buildings have gable roofs of very low to medium pitch, similar to the roofs of the visitor service buildings in the visitor service core. The roof pitch of Cedar Cottage, however, is steeper and not consistent with the character of other buildings in the lodge complex.

Roof forms at entrances protect visitors from inclement weather. The gable is a traditional form that indicates the entrance to the building while affording protection.

Exposed roof framing is typical at the lodge and throughout the Valley. Roof covering of guest quarter buildings is typically asphalt shingles.

**GUIDELINES**

- Use simple gables as the dominant element, with the ridge parallel to the long axis of the plan.
- Continue use of medium roof pitches in the range of 5:12.
- Gable roof porches over entrances are recommended.
- Shed dormers are recommended rather than gable dormers to minimize snow accumulation on sidewalls.
- Allow at least four feet between the edge of the dormer and the edge of the roof to maintain the plane of a dominant roof.
- Roofs should use relatively dark and nonreflective, colored coverings in order to harmonize with the surroundings, both when viewed from the adjacent ground and from trails above the Valley floor.

TOP *Cedar Cottage, built 1955, with Upper Yosemite Fall, Yosemite Lodge (2004) RF*
BOTTOM *View of Yosemite Lodge Lounge and Meeting Room (ca. 1960) YRL*

- Refer to "Developed Areas–Roof Form and Materials" in the "Unifying Elements" chapter for more guidelines on generous roof overhangs, exposed roof framing and sheathing, and modestly overscaled elements.

## Building Exteriors

Guest quarter buildings are generally more modest than visitor service buildings, serving as quiet backdrops for guests' enjoyment of the park. At the lodge, guest quarters are clad with wood siding with varied patterns and rough textures. The color is predominately dark brown, consistent with colors used throughout the Valley. Cedar Cottage, adjacent to the public center, is an example of recommended treatment for new guest quarter exteriors. It has a simple combination of horizontal and vertical wood siding and is painted a dark raw umber.

Doors and windows are arranged in regular patterns on guest quarter buildings. Porches and balconies complement the facade when they are designed using the same materials and details. Partial screening is advised to obscure the visual clutter sometimes caused by patio furniture and personal effects.

**GUIDELINES**

- Facades of new buildings should be restrained in character, blending with the background and not competing with the natural surroundings.
- Make use of Valley-wide unifying elements such as a protected base, wood siding, windows arranged in simple patterns, overscaled details, and use of color.
- Windows should be generous enough to provide enjoyment of views, let adequate natural light into the interior, and allow natural ventilation. Recessed, metal-clad wood windows are recommended.
- For one-story buildings, a single siding material is recommended. However, varying patterns may be used at gable ends for textural or visual interest.
- For two-story buildings, walls may be designed with different complementary siding patterns at each story. Where materials change, provide a slight offset or a water-table trim.
- Colors and textures should be appropriate to the natural setting. In a large complex of dispersed buildings, color may be used to unify the development and provide a sense of identity. Groups of buildings may be given slight variations from a primary theme. The color scheme of new guest lodging should relate to other buildings in the complex. Refer to "Developed Areas—Building Exterior" in the "Unifying Elements" chapter for more guidelines on color.

# HOUSEKEEPING CAMP

HOUSEKEEPING CAMP WAS originally established as an automobile camp around 1920. It subsequently became Curry Housekeeping Camp and was reserved for housekeeping facilities and equipment rental for those who wished to have a camping experience without bringing all the required gear. The present housekeeping units were designed by Spencer, Lee, and Busse and were built in the early 1960s. Over the years this facility has become a popular visitor facility. Groups return on a yearly basis, vying for riverfront campsites.

Although Housekeeping Camp is within the Yosemite Valley Historic District, it has not been assessed to determine whether it is eligible for listing on the National Register of Historic Places.

ALL THE MERCED STREAMS ARE WONDERFUL SINGERS, AND YOSEMITE IS THE CENTRE WHERE THE MAIN TRIBUTARIES MEET. FROM A POINT ABOUT HALF A MILE FROM OUR CAMP WE CAN SEE INTO THE LOWER END OF THE FAMOUS VALLEY, WITH ITS WONDERFUL CLIFFS AND GROVES, A GRAND PAGE OF MOUNTAIN MANUSCRIPT THAT I WOULD GLADLY GIVE MY LIFE TO BE ABLE TO READ. **JOHN MUIR • 1869**



## SETTING

Housekeeping Camp is the only remaining settlement in Yosemite Valley located on the river's edge, thus offering a unique experience for campers. It lies adjacent to a reverse bend in the Merced River, within the river's 100-year floodplain. The breakaway channels through the second bend in the river suggest that the course of the river will continue to change and will potentially affect the campsite.

Although there are dramatic views from riverbanks and the footbridge, there is dense tree cover in the campground. As in much of the Valley, incense cedar and pine are crowding and shading out the remaining California black oaks and blocking long views. Riparian vegetation along the riverbanks has been severely damaged and in some areas eliminated by the trampling of campers. Dramatic views from the riverbanks are an attraction as are views from Housekeeping Bridge.

TOP *Cabin on the river, Housekeeping Camp (2004) GH*
BOTTOM *Cabin with privacy screen, Housekeeping Camp (2004) GH*

Housekeeping Camp lies between the base of the talus line and the shadow line, which is the furthest extent of individual rocks beyond the talus line.

Southside Drive is adjacent to Housekeeping Camp and serves as the only vehicle access. LeConte Memorial Lodge is nearby, across Southside Drive to the south.

## Developed Area

The visitor service buildings in Housekeeping Camp are clustered at the entrance and are accessed by asphalt walkways. They include the general store, the laundry, the shower facility, and comfort stations. These buildings are all simple forms, varying in size, and finished in a muted brown color, making them relatively inconspicuous. Within the campground, the comfort stations are similar in character.

Cars arriving from Southside Drive park outside the camping area, next to the general store and adjacent to individual campsites. Circulation within Housekeeping Camp is informally defined by crushed granite walkways. The main pedestrian path passes through a small central outdoor space between the general store and the laundry. Housekeeping Bridge provides access to the opposite side of the river, now a restored natural area on the site of the former Lower River Campground.

*Cabins at Housekeeping Camp*

Housekeeping Camp has a consistent character unified by a single type of structure for the campsites, which provide a unique form of accommodation. Neither tent nor cabin, the structures consist of duplex units built back-to-back. The dividing walls and side-walls are tilt-up concrete slabs that are textured using burlap fabric to line the concrete work. The ceiling, front walls, and side walls are made of canvas. Each unit has a sleeping area furnished with beds, chest of drawers, mirror, electric outlet, and light. The patio-kitchen is furnished with a permanently fixed round table, chairs, stove, cooler, cupboards, and workbench. Protected by a nylon fly ceiling and a fence made of saplings, the kitchen is out-of-doors but private. These innovative units were designed to provide more comfort, convenience, and privacy for guests than found in tents or tent cabins. They are also simpler to erect, dismantle, and maintain.

**GUIDELINES**

- New development within Housekeeping Camp should continue the original design intent of providing a camping experience without visitors having to bring their own equipment.
- Design of new visitor service buildings should be compatible with the existing architectural character of Housekeeping Camp.
- Refer to the "Unifying Elements" chapter for more guidelines on architectural character of visitor service buildings, vegetation, circulation, land use, views, bridges, culverts, boardwalks, grading and drainage, benches, fences, screens, barriers, and lighting.

STOP

residences

- MAINTAIN EXISTING CHARACTER W/OUT SLAVISH IMITATION
- ZONES BET NEW + OLD - TRANSITIONS + EDGES
- HIERARCHY OF STRUCTURES
- COMMON ELEMENTS TO EXPRESS COHESIVE CHARACTER + QUALITY

## WAWONA



HELEN HUNT JACKSON IN 1872: OF OLD HUTCHINS HOUSE:

THERE ARE NO SUCH ROOMS IN THE AHWAHNEE AS THE ROOMS ON THE RIVER SIDE OF THIS LITTLE HOUSE. THIS IS THE BACK SIDE; AND THOSE WHO WISH TO SEE THE COMING + GOING OF PEOPLE, THE SETTING-OFF OF SADDLE-TRAINS, THE DRIVING UP AND DOWN OF THE LAUNDRY WAGON, WOULD BETTER TAKE ROOMS ON THE FRONT. BUT HE WHO WOULD LIKE TO OPEN HIS EYES EVERY MORNING ON THE FULL SHINING OF THE GREAT YOSEMITE FALL; TO LIE IN BED, AND FROM HIS VERY PILLOW WATCH IT SWAY TO THE RIGHT + LEFT UNDER MOONLIGHT BEAMS, WHICH SEEM LIKE WANDS ARRESTING OR HASTENING THE MOTION; TO LOOK DOWN INTO THE AMBER + GREEN MERCED, WHICH CARESSES HIS VERY DOOR SILL; TO LISTEN AT ALL HOURS TO THE GRAND VIOLINCELLO TONES OF THE MYSTERIOUS WATERS, -- LET HIM ASK, AS WE DID, FOR BACK ROOMS IN THE COTTAGE BY THE RIVER.

OLD HUTCHINGS HOUSE*
1859

*[UPPER HOTEL]

20 X 60
2 LARGE ROOMS

BUT IF HE IS DISCONCERTED B[Y] THE FACT THAT HIS BEDROOM FL[OOR] IS OF ROUGH PINE BOARDS, + HIS BEDRM WALLS OF THIN LATH, COVERED W/ UNBLEACHED COTTON; THAT HE HAS NEITHER CHAIR, [NOR] TABLE, NOR PITCHER; THAT HIS WASHBOWL IS A SHALLOW TIN PA[N]; THAT ALL THE WATER HE WANTS, [HE] MUST DIP IN A TIN PINT FROM [A] BARREL OUT IN THE HALL; THAT [HIS] BED IS A SACK STUFFED W/ FER[N]; HIS ONE WINDOW HAS NO CURTAIN + HIS DOOR NO KEY; LET HIM LEAVE AHWAHNEE TH[E] NEXT DAY."

1866

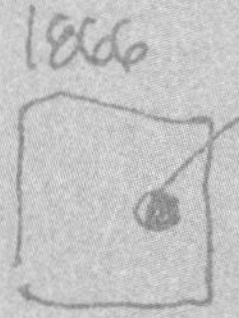

large combo kitchen/sitting room W/ 175' CEDAR TREE ∴ "BIG TREE ROOM"

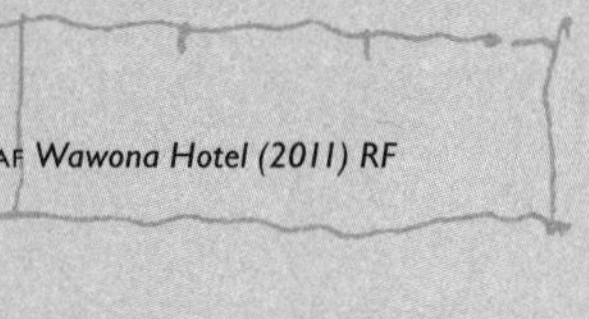

OVERLEAF *Wawona Hotel (2011) RF*

# WAWONA

WAWONA HAS A distinctive local character, far different from other areas of Yosemite. It preserves the relaxed atmosphere of a Victorian-era resort or a small mountain town, in sharp contrast to the bustle often found in Yosemite Valley. This is due in part to the pattern of development prior to acquisition by the National Park Service in 1932.

Wawona was a busy place in the 19th century because it was a natural stopping point for early visitors making their way to Yosemite Valley or the Mariposa Grove. Galen Clark, a man known more for his hospitality than his business acumen, established a homestead in 1856 at the point where the earliest trail to the Valley crossed the South Fork of the Merced River. Clark's home became an inn, which was purchased by Henry Washburn in

NO TESTIMONY TO CALIFORNIA'S NEW ENGLAND HERITAGE IS MORE CONVINCING THAN THE SPREAD OF WHITE-PAINTED, GREEN-SHUTTERED FARM HOUSES OVER THE SAN FRANCISCO DUNES AND THE SIERRA FOOTHILLS. **KIRKER • 1973**

1874 as part of his plan for the Yosemite Stage & Turnpike Company—a toll-road and tour system from the San Joaquin Valley into Yosemite. Washburn's first improvement to the inn was a hotel building called "Long White." Completed in 1876, this building set the pattern for subsequent construction at the hotel and in much of the surrounding area. The white-painted frame structure was meant to convey a sense of civility to visitors who had endured the rough stagecoach ride into the mountains. The main hotel building was completed in 1879, followed by additional lodging units and service buildings in the subsequent decades. During 1917–1918, the Washburn family built a nine-hole golf course at the northwest end of the Wawona Meadow in an attempt to increase the hotel's appeal to visitors who now arrived by automobile. This altered the pastoral character of Wawona while enhancing the resort-like atmosphere.

After the Department of the Interior arranged for U.S. Army troops to patrol the new Yosemite National Park beginning in 1891, Captain A.E. Wood established the first camp a short distance north of the hotel, just inside park lines on the bank of the South Fork of the Merced River. It was a natural choice given the convenience of the location, and that precedent has been followed for other administrative developments in the years since. Two CCC camps were built in the area in the 1930s, one of which has been adapted for reuse as a park maintenance facility. The Mission 66 era saw the creation of the Pioneer Yosemite History Center, a collection of several historic buildings originally located throughout the park that were moved to a new location across the river from the hotel. This development was meant both as an educational opportunity and a means of drawing visitors away from the crowded Valley.

A unique aspect of Wawona is Section 35, an area with a checkerboard of NPS and privately owned lots. In 1932, the Wawona Basin was purchased by matched federal and donated funds and incorporated into Yosemite National Park. At the time, private landowners in Section 35 elected to retain their ownership. However, over the following decades the NPS purchased many of the lots within Section 35. Today, approximately 200 acres, or 30% of the land in Section 35, is privately owned, and the NPS and Mariposa County have jurisdiction over their respective areas. The primarily vacation residential development has generally evolved independent of NPS influence, resulting in a wide range of architectural styles (NPS 1988a).

## Setting

Wawona basin is set at an average elevation of 4,000 feet by the South Fork of the Merced River, on a relatively flat alluvial plain. Wawona Meadow, surrounded by cedar and fir, slopes up gently to the southeast of the river. Surrounded by mixed evergreen forests, the meadow—more than one-and-a-quarter miles in length—roughly parallels the tributary of the South Fork. Its length and breadth were sufficient to accommodate a grassed landing field for early airplane travel. This meadow has also supported grazing and a nine-hole golf course.

The Wawona Hotel complex sits at the edge of a rising shoulder among widely scattered cedars, overlooking the junction of the river and the meadow, safely above the flood zone along the South Fork of the Merced River. The approach from the south parallels Wawona Meadow, which provides a verdant green foreground and

*The arrival at Wawona Hotel, circa 1876. From Sargent (1979)*

*The arrival at Wawona Hotel (2008) GH*

context for the hotel. The approach from the north, however, is compromised by the undistinguished parking area surrounding the store and gas station.

Several different facilities are sited on both sides of the river, some close enough on the flat plain adjacent to the Merced River to be in the floodplain. These include the Pioneer Yosemite History Center, the maintenance yard, and an equestrian campground. Others, including the ranger station and residences, the store and gas station, community center and school, and water and wastewater treatment plants, are on slightly higher ground. The steep slopes north and east of the developed areas are cloaked in dense forest groves of pine and cedar. The Wawona campground, formerly the A.E.

LEFT *U.S. Cavalry Camp A.E. Wood at Wawona Campground (date unknown) YRL*
RIGHT *Shutter detail, Comfort House, Wawona (2007) GH*

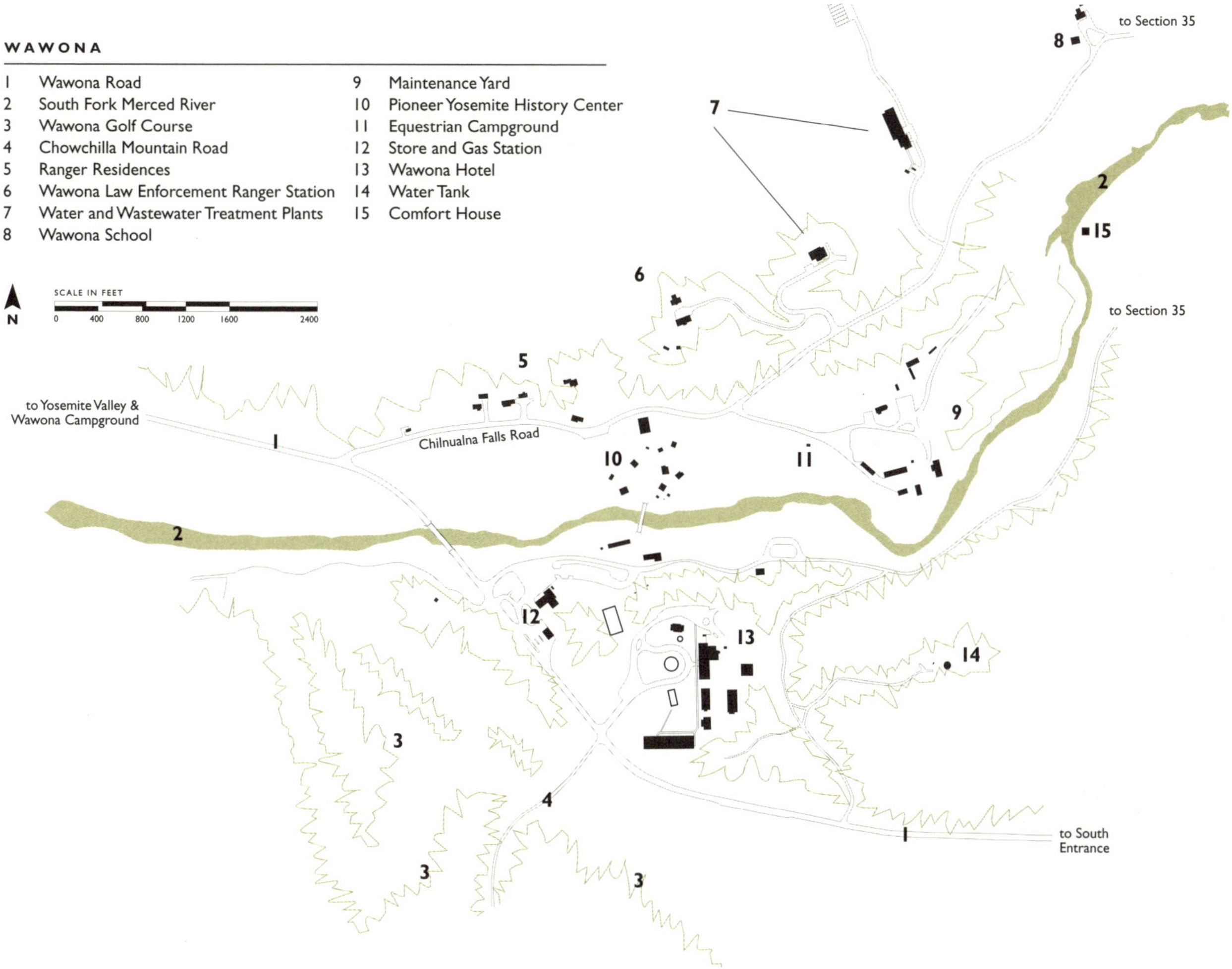

Wood Army Encampment, is sited in a sloping forested strip roughly a mile northwest of the junction of Chilnualna Falls Road and the Wawona Road, between the South Fork of the Merced River and Wawona Road. Here the valley narrows and the steeper gradient of the river gives way to rapids surrounded by a forested mixture of pine, fir, and oak, especially south of the river, in sharp contrast to the openness of the flat valley just upstream.

The contemporary highway bridge over the South Fork (completed in 2006), is the latest of eight bridges, most no longer existing, that have been documented in connection with the Wawona area. This demonstrates Wawona's significance in the development of the park and as an important way station. Of note was the Cavalry Footbridge across the South Fork rapids at Camp A.E. Wood, where African American troops of the 9th Cavalry were stationed at the turn of the 20th century. The footbridge provided access to a unique U.S. Army-initiated arboretum on the south side of the South Fork.

Section 35, the densely settled mixture of NPS and private inholding, is divided topographically into two zones of gently rolling terrain. Relatively small single-family dwellings are distributed in a dark coniferous forest on either side of the South Fork of the Merced River.

*The Annex, Wawona Hotel (2010) RF*

*Incense cedar (Calocedrus decurrens)*

## Developed Areas

### WAWONA HOTEL COMPLEX

The Wawona Hotel complex was included in the NPS Wawona Basin land purchase of August 20, 1932. Thirty buildings, 2,664 acres, a water system, an ice pond, an airport, a truck garden, hay fields, riding stock, a store, 40 milk cows, and a golf course were sold to the United States Government (Sargent 1979). The hotel complex was constructed on the homestead of one of Yosemite's earliest settlers, Galen Clark, who was appointed the first official protector of Yosemite as a state park.

Today the Wawona Hotel stands as a complex of seven structures built on the northern edge of Wawona Meadow at the intersections of Wawona Road and the South Fork of the Merced River. The hotel complex sits on a grassy rise above the historic road alignment and overlooks the meadow. A steep slope of tall, dark conifers parallels the approach, framing and providing contrast to the white building complex. The trees also serve to screen the adjacent gas station and store to the west of the hotel. The sloped driveway to the hotel is a civilized arrival in contrast to the undeveloped, forested Wawona Road. Scattered trees soften the formal arrangement of buildings to the southeast and rear of the hotel complex. This is in contrast to the manicured golf course greens and the sloping open lawns on the approach to the hotel.

The hotel complex buildings have a number of features in common: they are all of wood-frame construction, painted white, with grand verandahs or porches wide enough to allow both comfortable seating and ample space for guest passage. The columns on some of the verandahs are decorated with elaborate scrollwork. All buildings have undergone changes in recent years to improve the quality of the guest services and to make the structures safer for occupancy.

Many of the buildings are examples of balloon-frame construction, which substituted nails for the traditional mortise and tenon joints and used light,

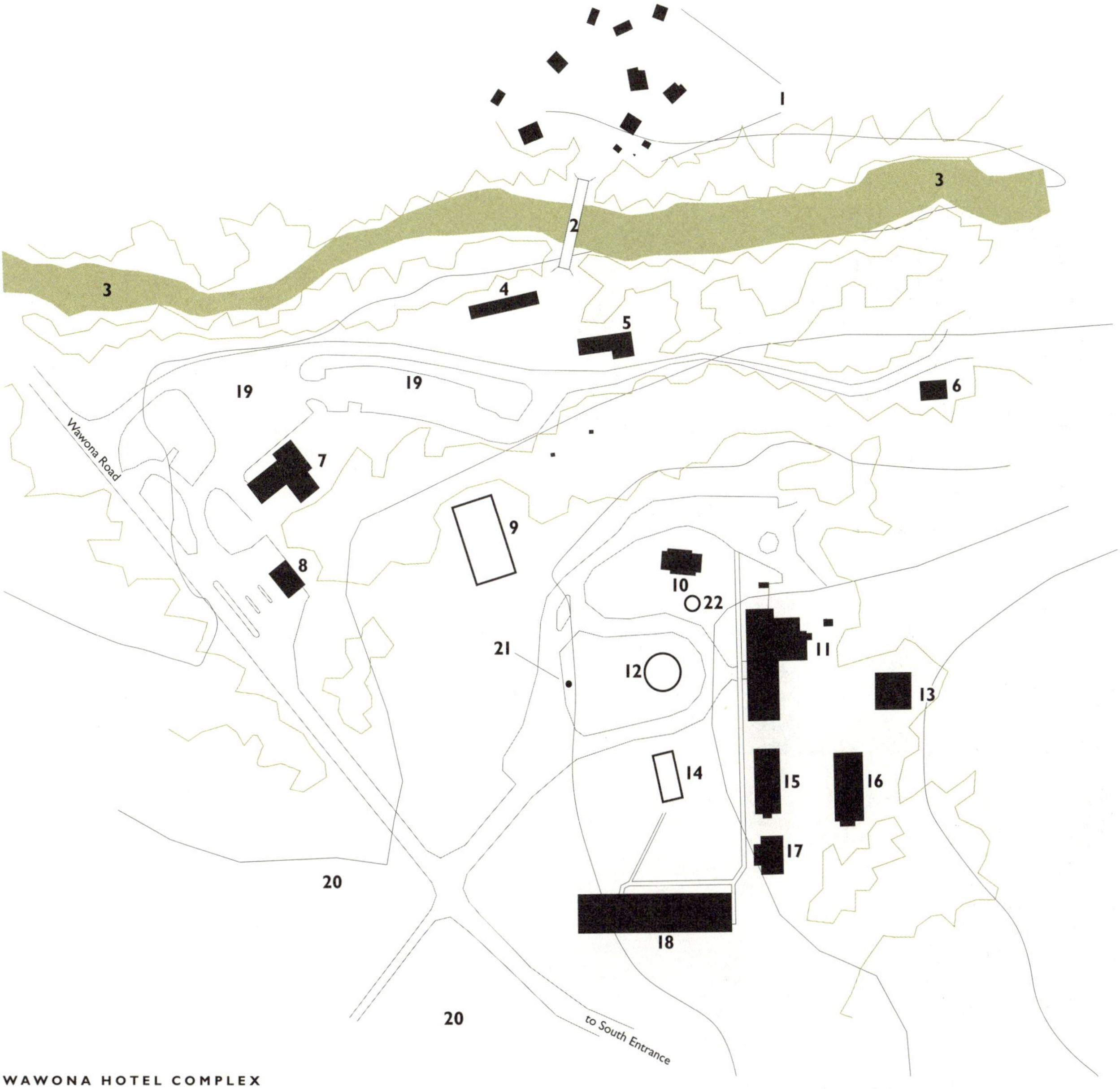


**WAWONA HOTEL COMPLEX**

1 Pioneer Yosemite History Center
2 Wawona Covered Bridge
3 South Fork Merced River
4 Wagon Shelter
5 Grey Barn
6 Carriage Shop
7 General Store
8 Wawona Gas Station
9 Tennis Court
10 Thomas Hill Studio
11 Wawona Hotel
12 Wawona Hotel Fountain
13 Little Brown (Moore Cottage)
14 Swimming Pool
15 Long White (Clark Cottage)
16 Long Brown (Washburn Cottage)
17 Little White (Manager's Cottage)
18 The Annex
19 Store Parking
20 Golf Course
21 Flagpole
22 Thomas Hill Fountain

*Wawona Hotel letterhead*

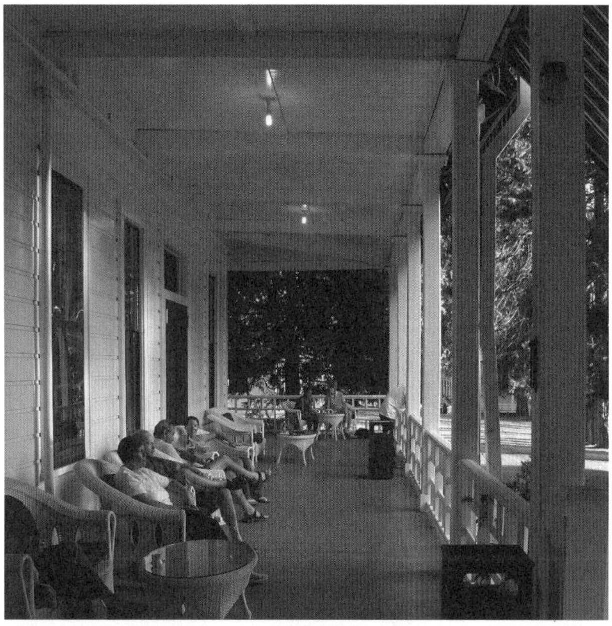

TOP *Verandah, Wawona Hotel (2008) GH* MIDDLE LEFT *Verandah column, Long White, Wawona Hotel (2008) GH* MIDDLE RIGHT *Flagpole base, Wawona Hotel (2009) GH* BOTTOM *Verandahs, Little White and Long White, Wawona Hotel (2009) GH*

two-by-four-inch studs. The technique took its name from the scorn in which it was held by conventional builders, who insisted that such frames would blow away "like balloons in the wind." The finished building, covered with clapboards and roofed with shingles, was similar to the historic New England colonial model. It was widely accepted in California, where a shortage of skilled labor encouraged any practical substitute for costly, heavy-frame, construction (Kirker 1973).

The Wawona Hotel was listed on the National Register in 1975, and it was designated a National Historic Landmark in 1986 for its importance to American architecture as the largest existing Victorian hotel complex within the boundaries of a national park, and one of the few remaining Victorian hotels in the United States with architectural integrity. Nearly all of the buildings' exterior fabric pre-dates World War I. The simple structures and their specific details illustrate a broad spectrum of stylistic concerns present in American architecture from the 1870s through World War I. In particular, there is a strong link to New England.

The Wawona Hotel continues to be popular with travelers seeking a quieter, more subdued atmosphere than that of Yosemite Valley. Arriving from Yosemite Valley to the north, or from the South Entrance and Mariposa Grove, visitors sense that they have entered a special place. The white buildings with their verandahs and white railings establish a serene quality that leaves the tiresome road behind.

Long White (1876), also known as the Clark Cottage, is a balloon-framed structure. The one-and-a-half-story building is rectangular in plan, clad with wood siding. The roof and dormers are finished with wood shakes. The verandah has a skirt roof supported by chamfered posts with curvilinear brackets. The railing and eaves are of a simplified Greek-revival style.

*Dormer and cupola, Little Brown, Wawona Hotel (2008) GH*

The Wawona Hotel (1879) is also a balloon-framed structure. The foundation is stone and wooden piers, screened by latticework covered with vines. Exterior walls are drop-channel siding. A two-story verandah encircles much of the building. The building has a hipped roof, and a secondary roof covers the verandah.

Little White (1884), also known as the Manager's Cottage, is finished with wood shakes. The railing around the verandah is simple and consists of two parallel boards connecting the chamfered posts.

Thomas Hill Studio (circa 1883), to the northwest of the main hotel building, is a one-story building with a cruciform plan. Originally built as a painting studio and sales room for landscape painter Thomas Hill, the building has had a variety of uses since his death in 1908, including that of ice-cream parlor, dance hall, and recreation room. These uses resulted in changes to some of the original building fabric.

The Little Brown (1896), also known as the Moore Cottage, is sited above the main hotel building on a little knoll. It is memorable, with its gingerbread style, cupola, weathervane, and elaborate scrollwork and dormers. Exterior walls are drop-channel siding. A skirting of beaded siding screens the building's foundation.

The Long Brown (1900), also known as the Washburn Cottage, is a large, wood-frame, two-and-a-half-story, rectangular building. The second story and attic were added in 1914, and the hipped-roof addition at the south was built sometime between 1914 and 1932. The exterior is clad with drop-channel siding edged with corner boards. The foundation is screened by a vented skirting of horizontal siding. A staircase was added to the north end of the building in 1951 to act as a fire escape.

TOP *Little White and Long White, Wawona Hotel (2008) GH*
BOTTOM *Long White, Wawona Hotel (2008) GH*

The Annex, constructed in 1917–18, is a two-and-a-half-story building with a partial basement at the west end. The large, wood-frame structure is rectangular in plan and surrounded by a two-story verandah. The roof is finished with wood shakes. Exterior walls are finished with wood shingles painted white. The foundation is screened by a latticework on the north and central portions of the building. The large room at the west end is a communal space with a large stone fireplace, wood paneling, and decorative ceiling moldings. The building has changed little since its initial construction.

The Wawona Golf Course was built in 1918—the first mountain golf course in California. It was designed for the Wawona Hotel by San Francisco architect Walter G. Fovague and is located on the Wawona Meadow, south of Wawona Road. In 1924 the course was expanded with a back nine set of tees. The vintage course, an integral part of the Wawona Hotel complex, remains almost unchanged. The description that follows is taken from the June 1990 issue of *Golf Journal* (the official publication of the United States Golf Association before 2003):

> *"Its nine holes measure 3,017 yards from the back tees, and the par-35 course rambles along a meadow and deep into dense forest. Deer graze fearlessly on its fairways, and a bobcat may trot along minding its own business. Female black bears favor a secluded cedar and fir grove behind the sixth tee to birth their cubs, and a horse trail roams throughout the layout. Sun dappled brooks draped with willow, and golf ball carrying creeks add to challenges. The South Fork of the Merced River flows*

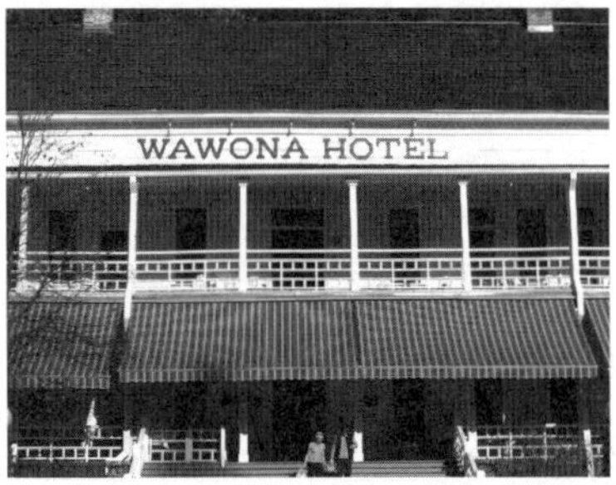

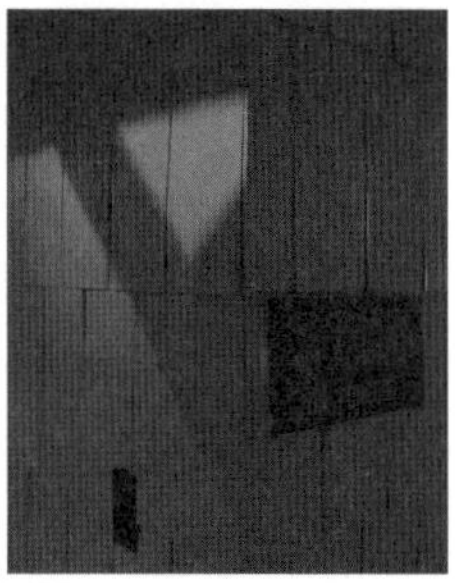

TOP LEFT *Thomas Hill Studio, Wawona Hotel (2010) RF* TOP RIGHT *Little White, Wawona Hotel (2008) GH* BOTTOM FAR LEFT *Wawona Hotel (2009) RF* BOTTOM CENTER LEFT *Railing, Long Brown, Wawona Hotel (2008) GH* BOTTOM CENTER RIGHT *Verandah, Long White, Wawona Hotel (2008) GH* BOTTOM FAR RIGHT *Whitewashed shakes, the Annex verandah, Wawona Hotel (2009) GH*

AN ENGLISH GENTLEMAN TRAVELING THE WEST IN THE EARLY 1900'S TOLD MY GRANDMOTHER, "YOUR WAWONA IS LIKE A BRIGHT GREEN EMERALD SET BETWEEN THE SPARKLING DIAMONDS OF YOSEMITE VALLEY'S WATERFALLS AND THE RED RUBIES OF THE SEQUOIAS IN THE MARIPOSA GROVE." **WAWONA WASHBURN HARTWIG • 1979**

*Long Brown, Wawona Hotel (2009) GH*

*The Annex from the verandah of Little White, Wawona Hotel (2008) GH*

*around the eighth green, and the Chowchilla Mountain Road, the original stage road into Wawona, interrupts the third fairway...."*

A slaughterhouse, built in 1929 at the end of the golf course and later turned into a tool shed, processed the hotel's cattle, sheep, and hogs. The slaughterhouse still stands and is currently used as storage for the groundskeeper (NPS 1987b).

**GUIDELINES**

- For new design within the Wawona Hotel Complex, designers should consult the Wawona Hotel Complex Historic Structures Report and Cultural Landscape Report (NPS 2011c). For National Historic Landmarks, the preferred treatment is "preservation," in accordance with *The Secretary of the Interior's Standards for the Treatment of Historic Properties.*
- New projects should use wide verandahs for circulation and seating. Detailing exterior framing, porches, and balcony railings to reflect existing details and proportions. Avoid blocking views for seated guests with new porch or balcony railings.
- The white exterior color should be used on new buildings, unless historic color schemes are restored based on paint analysis.
- When designing universally accessible routes between the main building and neighboring outbuildings, lay out routes to avoid slopes greater than 4.75%, thus avoiding the need for visually disruptive curbs and handrails. Use stabilized granular paving, such as resin-based decomposed granite where snow clearance is not required. Where curbs and handrails are required, they should be detailed in a manner compatible with the detailing and design vocabulary of the surrounding historic structures.
- Refer to "Landscape Uses + Structures—Masonry Structures" in the "Unifying Elements" chapter for guidelines on the use of river-washed cobbles.
- Refer to "Landscape Uses + Structures—Lighting" in the "Unifying Elements" chapter for exterior lighting.

*Wawona Golf Course (1935) YRL*

## GAS STATION + STORE

In 1923 the Shell Oil Company established the original service station at Wawona near the covered bridge. This gas station also included a garage and repair shop, which enabled the complex to better provide full service to the touring public.

Today the gas station and general store are sited at the intersection of Wawona Road and Forest Drive, surrounded on the approach side by broad asphalt parking areas. A dark band of coniferous forest backs the white structures on the slope behind the buildings.

The general store at Wawona is in the tradition of rural roadside commercial buildings typical of the early development of foothill communities. The porch is the focus for the entrance and a gathering place for travelers. The low functional form of the store with a porch for shelter and for locating community notices, vending machines, benches, and the post office, make it a focus for local activities. The white picket fence, unique in this instance, is a clear demarcation of the porch and adjacent parking—an essential element similar to the hitching post of earlier days. This form, derived from local and regional influences, becomes a vernacular structure that is adaptable for many uses. The traditional sign located above the porch provides identity in a direct and appropriate manner. Additions to the building can easily be made as part of its linear character. The simple shape of the gas station, placed adjacent to the store but related to the road, has a functional character that contemporary motorists find familiar. The gas pumps are the recognizable forms that identify the function of the structure. Large overhead doors to the repair shop complete the ensemble. This building recalls the gas station buildings at Tuolumne Meadows and Crane Flat. All functions are packed into a simple gable form reminiscent of nearby barns. Painted white, the structure identifies with the Wawona design character.

### GUIDELINES

- New site-design projects should clarify and simplify vehicle circulation and minimize paving at entries and turnouts.
- New buildings should employ a similar palette of materials consistent with the historic pattern and shape of windows, doors, and porches.
- New structures should continue the white theme established by the adjacent hotel complex.
- New signs should be designed for compatibility with the established scale of signs and graphic style.

*Gas station, Wawona (2008) GH*

*General store, Wawona (2010) RF*

*Ranger residences, Wawona (2007) GH*

*Wawona ranger station (2008) GH*

- All exterior lighting should be shielded, recognizing the nearby historic hotel complex. Conform to park standards, and observe night-sky recommendations. Refer to "Landscape Uses + Structures—Lighting" in the "Unifying Elements" chapter.
- Mechanical equipment (on roofs or adjacent to buildings) should be screened and/or painted to blend with immediate surroundings.

## ADMINISTRATION AREA

A number of National Park Service administrative facilities are accessed from the Chilnualna Falls Road, which runs parallel to the South Fork of the Merced River. This narrow road is in a natural setting, with Sierra mixed conifer forest bordering the northern edge and the South Fork of the Merced River just to the south. Development along the road is sparse for the first mile. The most prominent structures are the rangers' residences, the district ranger offices and maintenance area, the Pioneer Yosemite History Center, the water treatment plant, the wastewater treatment plant, and the county-owned Wawona School. Beyond these facilities, the road enters the Section 35 area—a more densely configured mixture of privately owned cabins and National Park Service employee housing tucked within the forest.

### Rangers' Residences

The rangers' residences consist of four historic white buildings (originally two garages and two residences), set well back along the north edge of the alluvial plain on the slightly sloping ground parallel to Chilnualna Falls Road. Visible from the Wawona Road, they are excellent examples of buildings designed by the National Park Service to be compatible with the Wawona Hotel complex and the nearby Chinquapin ranger station. Built by the Civilian Conservation Corps between 1934 and 1939, they contain elements of early Californian and Colonial Revival styles. Painted white, they identify strongly with the Wawona Hotel community.

Simple, narrow, unpretentious pathways flanked by plain grass areas lead directly from the road edge to the front porch steps of the buildings. Forest vegetation is concentrated largely on the slopes behind the buildings, giving the foreground area a feeling of generous openness. Garages are farther back with simple driveway approaches directly from the road. One ranger residence (formerly a CCC Mess Hall), set on

*Masonry detail, Wawona Ranger Office (2008) GH*

steeper ground on the forested slope several hundred feet to the east, is not visible from the road and is reached by a curving driveway. The nearby modern telephone and pump house buildings do not reflect this historic siting pattern.

**GUIDELINES**

- For new buildings in this area, refer to *The Secretary of the Interior's Standards for the Treatment of Historic Properties* for guidance to ensure compatibility.
- Site new structures so that both the foreground and background spaces around existing buildings fronting on Chilnualna Falls Road are preserved.
- New structures should retain the existing site pattern (i.e., parallel to and set back from the road), with spacing between buildings similar to the existing buildings.
- Landscape treatment of foreground and intervening space for new buildings should match the character at existing historic structures, including narrow, direct pathways to entries and mowed grasses as the dominant planting fronting the buildings. Any landscape improvements should be compatible with the simple design of CCC-era works.
- New parking areas should be placed away from the foreground space and screened with existing or planted forest vegetation matching the surrounding indigenous species types and distribution.
- New buildings should continue use of the white and green palette that is characteristic of this group of buildings.

*Ranger residences, Wawona (2008) GH*

## Pioneer Yosemite History Center

During the Mission 66 era of development in the park, Yosemite staff realized that a number of historic buildings would be lost unless they could be moved to a location where they would receive proper care. Several buildings stood in areas due to be restored to natural conditions; others, in isolated places that had become susceptible to vandalism. The park conceived of moving those buildings to Wawona, which already contained structures of historical interest such as the old covered bridge, an old wagon shop, and the hotel. At Wawona, the park developed an interpretive center concentrating on the history of the area with the intent of lessening visitor pressure on Yosemite Valley.

*Porch detail, ranger residence, Wawona (2008) GH*

Workers brought in historic structures from various areas of the park and reassembled them. Each one represented a phase of Yosemite's history: pioneering, homesteading, early transportation, visitor accommodations, army administration, ranger services, and pioneer artists. Machinery from the Tioga Mine illustrated the story of mining in the Sierra Nevada. Each structure was furnished to its period and in accordance with its original use, and interpreted to visitors (NPS 1987b).

The Pioneer Yosemite History Center buildings flank the South Fork of the Merced River and are connected by a historic covered bridge. On the south side, the old wagon shop, the grey barn, and the vernacular shed protecting various antique wagons and utilitarian machines sit among trees on the slightly elevated riverbank ridge. The main grouping of historic buildings is on the north side, approached via the covered bridge. These structures are located on lower ground with generous spacing, sometimes separated by clusters of mature conifers. The broad, unpaved areas of pedestrian and wagon circulation connect to a more open meadow area and a functioning corral and barn to the north.

The Yosemite Transportation Company Office (Wells Fargo Building), located on the north side of the bridge, is an exceptional and rare example of rustic architecture as it first developed in the Yosemite region. Characteristic of the style is the use of cedar-bark strips applied in decorative patterns as exterior sheathing material on the wood-frame building. Structures that are similar in design include the Yosemite Valley Railroad Station at El Portal (destroyed by fire in 1949) and four still-standing Yosemite Valley buildings: the

TOP *Grey Barn, Pioneer Yosemite History Center (2008) GH*
MIDDLE *Wells Fargo Building, Pioneer Yosemite History Center (2007) GH*
BOTTOM *Log structure, Pioneer Yosemite History Center (2007) GH*

Curry Cabin, the Tresidder Cabin, the original Camp Curry Registration Office, and the Pohono Studio, all nominated on the National Register of Historic Places. These rustic structures represent an effort to design facilities that are not intrusive or incompatible with the natural environment (NPS 1977d). It is not anticipated that additional structures will be added to the Pioneer Yosemite History Center, but if additions are warranted, restraint should be exercised.

**GUIDELINES**

- For new design in this area, refer to *The Secretary of the Interior's Standards for the Treatment of Historic Properties* for guidance to ensure compatibility.
- Any new additions should retain the informal character and generous spacing between individual buildings that suggests the widely dispersed locations in the park where the buildings were originally found.
- Provide adequate space around new additions that will allow them to be viewed from all sides, or as many sides as were visible when they were located in their original setting.
- New fences should continue to use split-log fencings (either double-post or zigzag) to define routes, protect vegetation, and retain a primitive, rural appearance.
- New visitor parking should be kept distant from, and screened by appropriate forest vegetation from, the Pioneer Yosemite History Center, Chilnualna Falls Road, Forest Drive, and Wawona Road.
- Refer to "Landscape Uses + Structures—Circulation—Parking" in the "Unifying Elements" chapter.

TOP LEFT *Covered bridge, Pioneer Yosemite History Center (2009) GH* BOTTOM LEFT *Covered bridge detail, Pioneer Yosemite History Center (2007) GH*
TOP RIGHT *Stable (2007) GH* MIDDLE RIGHT *Wells Fargo Building, Pioneer Yosemite History Center (2007) GH* BOTTOM RIGHT *Stable (2008) RF*

*Maintenance yard, Wawona (2008) GH*

*Section 35 cabins, Wawona (2011) RF*

## Maintenance Yard

All major maintenance and administrative functions for the south part of the park are based out of Wawona. The former repair garage for the Civilian Conservation Corps is the largest structure in the complex. This simple building forms one edge of the maintenance yard. Other structures are clustered around an informal quad in the yard. The exterior finishes are metal roofing and wood siding in various patterns, primarily board and batten.

**GUIDELINES**

- New buildings and developed areas should be located out of view from the main highway to maintain the rural character of the area.
- New development should not impact historic views/ vistas from within the surrounding historic properties.
- New development is not permitted in meadow areas; it should be integrated into previously disturbed forested areas, if available.
- New construction should use simple, basic building-plan shapes, with uncomplicated roofs of gable and shed porches that follow existing patterns.
- New buildings should continue using the dark-brown color for structures that blend the complex into the landscape.
- New communication structures, solar collectors, and satellite dishes should be in the darker ranges of color and be nonreflective.
- Site new material and equipment storage or temporary structures so they are not visible from Chilnualna Falls Road, the Pioneer Yosemite History Center, or other visitor areas. If siting alone is insufficient, screen with vegetation or fencing.
- Retain the natural pattern of meadows or meadows/ pine groves that screen the maintenance yard.

## Utility Buildings

The water treatment plant is a modest concrete structure composed of conventional architectural elements that achieve a calm image well-suited to the building's purpose. Natural concrete walls with a darker-toned base and a simple roof form make the plant an appropriate structure for its remote location.

The wastewater treatment plant is a contemporary concrete structure that extends far into the uphill site. The treatment plant is broken down into functional elements that adapt to the hillside. Several large concrete tanks in the forest are well-screened from the access road. Concrete surface treatments of the structures vary, giving texture and scale to the walls.

These two contemporary NPS utility buildings are relatively hidden at the ends of long driveways off Chilnualna Falls Road adjacent to Section 35. They are located on south-facing slopes, surrounded by mixed coniferous vegetation.

## Section 35

Section 35 contains a small, privately owned store, an elementary school, a church-owned summer camp for children, privately owned lodging for visitors, and low-density single family homes and cabins of various size, design, and age. The NPS owns approximately 70 of the more than 250 homes. Most of these NPS homes were originally built by private landowners to be used as vacation cabins; they were purchased by the NPS and are currently used as NPS, concessioner, and park partner housing.

In the Mariposa County General Plan, Section 35 is characterized as having "mountain residential character." The county-owned roads are narrow and without sidewalks or curbing; they serve as circulation for both vehicles and pedestrians. Private and NPS-owned lots are approximately 6,000 square feet, and cabins are generally less than 2,000 square feet. These cabins are typically no more than two stories tall and have generous setbacks from roads. Most of Section 35 is covered in mature Sierra mixed conifer forest interspersed with small or modestly sized cabins.

TOP *Water treatment plant, Wawona (2011) RF*
BOTTOM *Cobblestone chimney, Section 35, Wawona (2008) GH*

## Wawona School

The schoolhouse is sited in a clearing that captures sunlight in this heavily wooded site. The building's color and proportions establish a welcome and cheerful character that is most appropriate for its use. The massing of the building is composed of a series of shed roofs oriented to the north to capture daylight for the classrooms.

*Wawona School (2008) GH*

**GUIDELINES FOR NPS-OWNED FACILITIES**

- New buildings should be compatible with the rural character and setting, terrain, and vegetation.
- New buildings should be compatible with massing, height, scale, setbacks, and materials of existing, smaller scale cabins.
- If new buildings are built on slopes, they should be designed to match the natural contours and topography in order to blend with the natural environment. The use of cut and fill should be avoided.
- Existing mature native vegetation should be retained.
- New vegetation planted at new buildings should be native and reflect natural vegetation patterns in the area.
- Future utility buildings or additions to existing complexes should be sited at a distance from roads, and screened by topography or existing vegetation to avoid impacting the natural character along Chilnualna Falls Road.

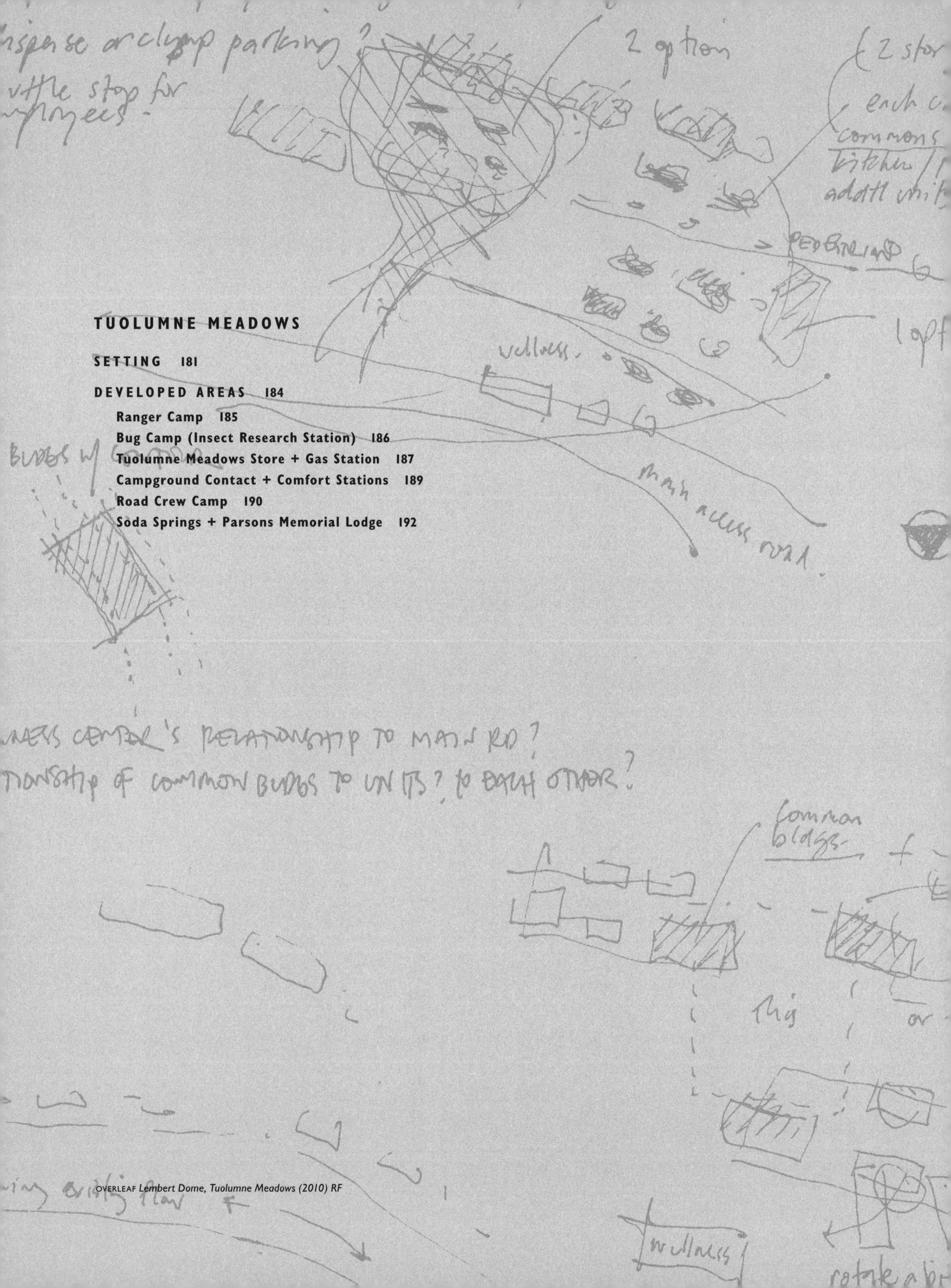

## TUOLUMNE MEADOWS



OVERLEAF *Lembert Dome, Tuolumne Meadows (2010) RF*

# TUOLUMNE MEADOWS

One of the most easily accessible subalpine meadows in the Sierra Nevada, Tuolumne Meadows has supported a wide range of human use for centuries. While it serves visitors and backcountry adventurers today, its past is characterized by layers of history. For millennia it has served as a seasonal camping and trading site for American Indian groups from the western and eastern sides of the mountains.

Nonindigenous people were initially drawn to the Tuolumne region by the discovery of precious metals in the eastern Sierra. Although the first miners simply passed through the area, the discovery in 1860 of silver at Tioga Hill brought more attention to the meadows themselves. Greater access came through construction of the Great Sierra Wagon Road from the western side of the mountains in 1882. To supply the Tioga mining district, sheepherders brought their flocks to the high pastureland. Among the herders was John Muir, who spent his first summer in the Sierra tending sheep and pondering the mountains' natural processes. The original route of the Great Sierra Wagon Road and the ruins of several log enclosures along the trail to Mono Pass remain from this era.

THOUSANDS OF TIRED, NERVE-SHAKEN, OVER-CIVILIZED PEOPLE ARE BEGINNING TO FIND OUT THAT GOING TO THE MOUNTAINS IS GOING HOME; THAT WILDNESS IS A NECESSITY.... **JOHN MUIR • 1898**

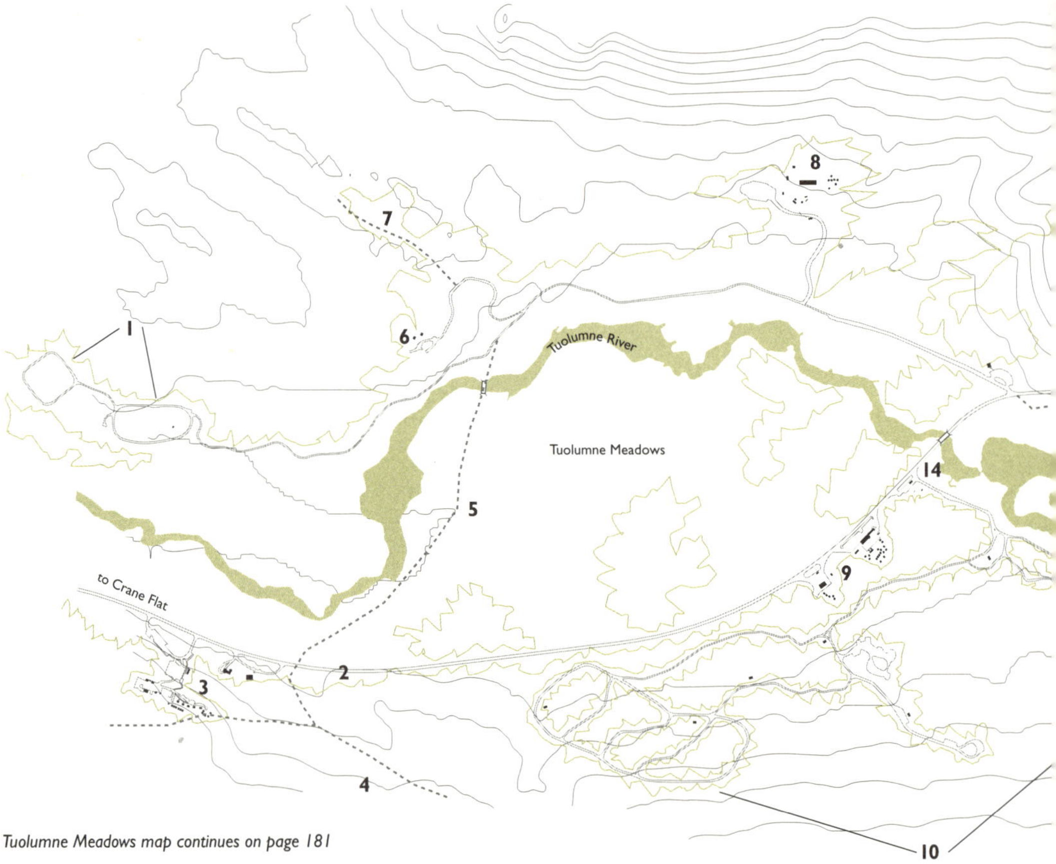


*Tuolumne Meadows map continues on page 181*

John Baptiste Lembert established a homestead in 1885 near Soda Springs in Tuolumne Meadows, which he surrounded with a log enclosure to keep out grazing animals. The McCauley family, who operated the Glacier Point Hotel, acquired the property in 1896 to graze their livestock and built a cabin that still stands. After the creation of Yosemite National Park in 1890, the United States Army maintained a patrol post at the same location until 1913. The Sierra Club acquired the McCauley property in 1912 and set about developing a lodge as a base of operations for its annual wilderness outings. Parsons Memorial Lodge, completed in 1915 and designed by the Maybeck and White office, was an important forerunner of the Rustic style later adopted by the National Park Service. During the same year, with the help of the Sierra Club, the old Great Sierra Wagon Road was opened to motorists as the Tioga Road.

*Tuolumne Meadows (1915) YRL*

The Tioga Road provided access to a new category of visitor—the auto-tourist—in ever-increasing numbers. To accommodate them, the precursor of the present Tuolumne Meadows Lodge opened in 1916. By 1923 it also served as the base for Yosemite's new High Sierra Camp loop. The area's popularity prompted the NPS to begin construction of a rustic administrative center (Ranger Camp) in 1924 along the eastern edge of the meadow. A parkwide master plan, adopted in 1929, guided successive development. Central to this plan was a campground intended to minimize damage caused by unregulated camping, together with a water treatment and sewer system. Additional facilities included the 1934 Road Camp, the post-war Insect Research Station (Bug Camp), the Mission 66 era gas station and store complex, and Mission 66 era alterations to Tioga Road and the Tuolumne Meadows Campground.

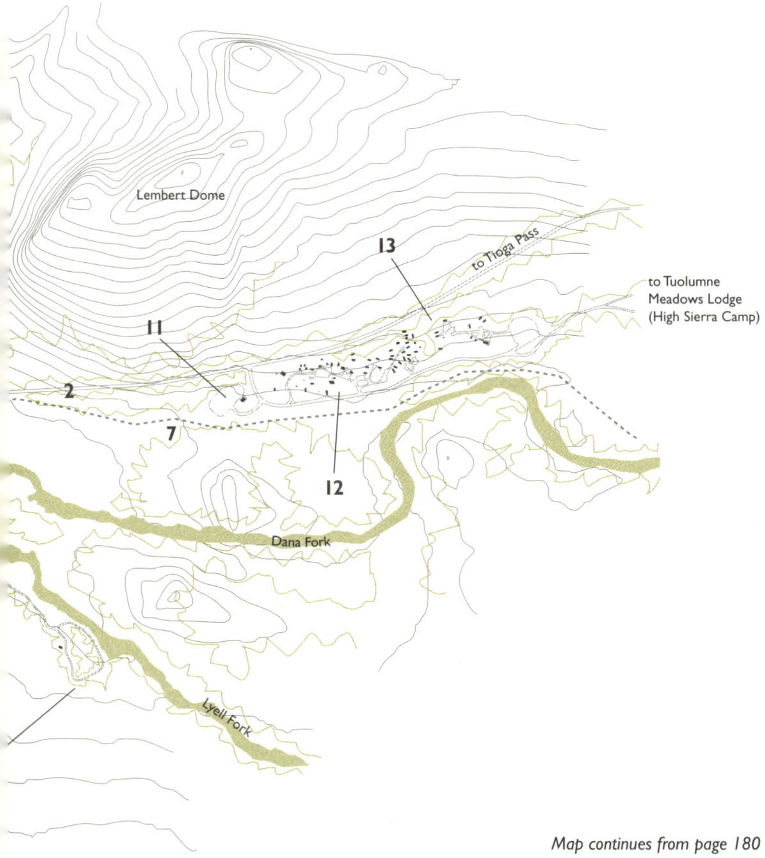


**TUOLUMNE MEADOWS**

1 Water Treatment Settling Ponds
2 Tioga Road
3 CCC Mess Hall/Road Crew Camp
4 John Muir Trail
5 Trail to Soda Springs
6 Soda Springs/Parsons Memorial Lodge
7 Pacific Crest Trail
8 Concessioner Stable
9 Store, Grill, and Gas Station
10 Tuolumne Meadows Campground
11 Wilderness Permit Office
12 Ranger Camp
13 Bug Camp (Insect Research Station)
14 Campground Reservation Building

N

SCALE IN FEET

0 600 1200 1800 2400 3000

*Map continues from page 180*

In 2007 Tuolumne Meadows was determined eligible for listing on the National Register of Historic Places as a historic district. The district encompasses all of the developed areas including Tuolumne Meadows Lodge, Bug Camp, Ranger Camp, the Tuolumne Meadows Campground, the gas station and store area, Road Camp, Soda Springs, Parsons Memorial Lodge, Tioga Road, and the adjacent natural resources of the broad meadow flanking the river to the west of its junction with the Dana and Lyell forks. To the east it includes the drier, more broken terrain between the Dana Fork and the Tuolumne Lodge. The northern and southern limits are defined by the Yosemite Wilderness boundaries (NPS 2007f).

## SETTING

Tuolumne Meadows is one of the largest subalpine meadows in the Sierra Nevada. At an elevation of 8,600 feet and surrounded on all sides by stunning mountain peaks, Tuolumne Meadows offers visitors a unique high-country experience vastly different from Yosemite Valley. It is an unparalleled landscape, dominated by natural scenery and soundscapes.

*North elevation, Parsons Memorial Lodge (2010) RF*

JOHN MUIR ONCE DESCRIBED TUOLUMNE MEADOWS AS THE FINEST CAMP GROUND IN THE WHOLE HIGH SIERRA. **SIERRA CLUB RESOLUTION • DECEMBER 16, 1911**

The Tuolumne River flows through a string of meadows roughly half a mile wide and twelve miles long. In 1984 Congress designated the Tuolumne as a Wild and Scenic River because of its largely primitive condition, extensive undeveloped banks, and lack of impoundments or road access. The river is supplied by the Lyell and Dana forks, which stem from two of the three glaciers within the park. The Tuolumne and its tributaries are subject to periodic seasonal flooding in some areas, as well as active channel migration and riverbank erosion (NPS 2010c).

The Yosemite Wilderness surrounds Tuolumne Meadows, making Tuolumne a primary staging area for backpackers, day hikers, and "through-hikers"—those hardy visitors who are hiking the Pacific Crest Trail or the John Muir Trail.

The meadows and riparian corridors are replete with a remarkable diversity of meadow and river species, both flora and fauna. The predominant vegetation communities are a subalpine meadow type of grassland composed of sedges and grasses, and willows in the riparian corridors. The depth of alluvial fill, high groundwater, and periodic flooding from the river give this subalpine meadow high ecological, scientific, and educational value. At the edge of the meadow, vegetation changes to a

TOP *View of Tuolumne Meadows from Pothole Dome (2008) DV* LEFT *River, Tuolumne Meadows (2009) RF* RIGHT *Tuolumne Meadows and Lembert Dome (2010) RF*

*Tuolumne River (2010) RF*

predominantly lodgepole pine forest, scattered with Jeffrey, western white, and white-bark pines. Above this forest rise the vast and often snow-covered granite peaks, ridges, and domes that ring the meadow.

There are numerous breathtaking views from roads, trails, and developed areas in Tuolumne Meadows. This is due to the low topography of the expansive grasslands, the proximity of the river to viewpoints, and the clear meadow edges framed by the glacially carved domes and rugged mountain slopes. Views from Tioga Road are particularly important for the many visitors who drive through without stopping, as this is their only contact with a High Sierra meadow.

The surrounding peaks offer evidence of the complex geomorphologic processes that formed the meadows. These include upwelling, volcanism, subsidence, erosion, and glaciation. The area displays some of the country's finest examples of glacial polish, glacial erratics, moraines, roche mountonnées, striations, and hanging valleys (NPS 2007f).

The meadow's flat topography, high elevation, and subdued artificial light allow for night-sky observation that is among the best in Yosemite's frontcountry. Visitors need only walk a relatively short distance from the road and developed areas at night to experience an unimpaired celestial display with a natural soundscape.

Tuolumne Meadows is a jumping-off point for several important trails to wilderness destinations along the Sierra crest and the high country. These include the Pacific Crest Trail and the John Muir Trail, both of which cross the meadows. In the winter, Tioga Road is closed to cars, allowing Tuolumne Meadows to provide a solitary wilderness experience for cross-country skiers and snowshoers, including rangers and snow survey crews who access remote areas and cabins.

*Pothole Dome, Tuolumne Meadows (2008) GH*

## Developed Areas

Despite the presence of a built environment, the stunning, expansive, and dramatic natural landscape at Tuolumne Meadows rightfully dominates the scene. Over the last several decades, permanent and semi-permanent structures arose in relatively small clusters tucked into the lodgepole forest at the edge of the meadows. Building character in the Tuolumne Meadows Historic District ranges from large, boulder-faced historic NPS Rustic architecture to seasonal, light, canvas-roofed structures. Relatively simple and understated wood-frame structures make up most of the buildings throughout the district. Most of these buildings are rustic and meant to blend unobtrusively into their natural settings, but they lack the careful craftsmanship and architectural detailing of the typical NPS Rustic style (NPS 2007f).

A number of buildings in the Tuolumne Meadows Historic District are significant examples of the historic NPS Rustic style. Designed by NPS staff to minimize the visual impact of constructed development, these include the old visitor contact station, the three original campground comfort stations, and the original Road Crew Camp complex. Another example is Parsons Memorial Lodge—a National Historic Landmark—designed by the Maybeck and White office for the Sierra Club in 1915 (NPS 2007f). All of these sites or structures are either individually listed on the National Register of Historic Places or are contributing features of the Tuolumne Meadows Historic District.

The Civilian Conservation Corps built some of the most distinctive and architecturally significant structures in Tuolumne Meadows, often using materials from the site. The Rustic style employed was perfectly suited for the patient handiwork of the corps and benefited from such labor being readily available during the Depression. Many of the finest examples of the NPS Rustic style in Tuolumne Meadows would be difficult to replicate under modern conditions. These buildings thus reflect a unique moment in time as much as they embody this distinctive architectural style.

Much of the early history of the meadows is related to pioneering conservation activism in the late 19th and early 20th centuries, including that of the Sierra Club. The predominance of the NPS Rustic style of architecture, the concentration of development in limited areas, and the absence of modern improvements attest to the intense concern for and love of the meadows maintained by the conservation community over the decades.

**GENERAL GUIDELINES**

- For new development within the Tuolumne Meadows Historic District, designers should consult *The Secretary of the Interior's Standards for the Treatment of Historic Properties* for guidance to ensure compatibility.
- The character of new structures should be compatible with the architectural vocabulary of the rustic structures at Tuolumne Meadows. They should, in addition, be of a scale, form, massing, and color that blends with the immediate natural surroundings.

*Lodgepole pine (Pinus contorta)*

- New development (including parking) should be located in adjacent forested areas or in areas that are naturally screened along the meadow perimeter. New development should avoid visual impacts to the setting from the broader meadow and from the peaks and domes that surround Tuolumne Meadows.
- New roadside parking should use naturalistic barriers such as rocks, berms, granite curbing, and grading to delineate parking while blending with the natural environment.
- For guidelines on Tuolumne Meadows Lodge, refer to the "Huts, Cabins + High Sierra Camps" chapter.
- For guidelines on Tuolumne Meadows Campground, refer to the "Campgrounds" chapter.

## RANGER CAMP (ADMINISTRATIVE AREA)

Ranger Camp is between the Old Tioga Road and the modern Tioga Road at the eastern end of Tuolumne Meadows. Ranger Camp was constructed to provide maintenance and administrative services for the Tuolumne Meadows area. Historically known as the Government Administrative Area, or simply the Administrative Area, it has since become more commonly known as Ranger Camp (NPS 2007f).

Cabins and hard-sided tent cabins sit in a randomly scattered pattern among sparse pine and occasional boulder and granite outcroppings. This results in a random, character reminiscent of the small-scale encampments found in the foothills and other parts of the Sierra.

TOP LEFT *Stable, Ranger Camp (2008) GH* TOP RIGHT *Tuolumne Meadows Ranger Station, Ranger Camp (2007) GH*
BOTTOM LEFT *Cabin, Ranger Camp (2008) GH* BOTTOM RIGHT *Parsons Memorial Lodge (2007) GH*

*Detail of masonry at CCC Mess Hall, Road Crew Camp (2008) GH*

Each unit thus has a unique sense of location within the overall site that would seem to enhance long-term occupancy. Ranger Camp's contributing structures to the Tuolumne Meadows Historic District include the five original buildings built in 1924: ranger station, naturalist cabin, patrol cabin, barn, and shower house. Over the years, other buildings and structures have been added, including tent cabins for park employee housing. The ranger station, NPS stable, and small, two-person, seasonally occupied cabins define the architectural character of the western end of the area.

The ranger station was erected in 1924 and served as the original park entrance and ranger station on the Tioga Road. The 525-square-foot, single-story building has an exposed peeled-log frame structure with vertical plank infilling and a gable roof with log framing and brackets. The roofing material is corrugated metal. The building is painted Wosky brown, a color named for landscape architect John Wosky in the 1930s and used widely throughout the park.

During the winter, three buildings are in use in Ranger Camp: the ranger's cabin, the snow survey cabin, and the ranger station. The canvas for the tent cabins is removed at the end of the summer season, contributing to the camp's seasonal character.

The only other Tuolumne Meadows building that remains open in the winter is the campground reservation building, used by cross-country skiers as an overnight shelter. This building is west of Ranger Camp, at the entrance to the Tuolumne Meadows campground.

**GUIDELINES**

- New or replacement structures should maintain the general spacing, scale, and color of the existing structures.
- New structures should be constructed of materials that are compatible with the temporary, seasonal, minimal style currently and historically found here.
- New structures should be laid out in a way consistent with historic patterns, which were based on proximity to natural features such as boulders or tree groupings.
- Minimize visual impacts of new parking areas on the housing.
- New design should include measures to ensure protection of existing vegetation. Use appropriate barriers to prevent trampling of such areas.
- New design should not impact the current utilitarian character of the area.
- Refer to the "Unifying Elements" chapter for guidelines on circulation, parking, vegetative screening, barriers, and utility structures such as repeater towers.

## BUG CAMP (INSECT RESEARCH STATION)

Bug Camp was constructed in response to a needle miner infestation that occurred during the 1950s. The camp is located to the east of Ranger Camp. Aside from a slightly steeper south-facing slope, the terrain and subalpine forest of the Bug Camp area is similar to that of Ranger Camp. Small, two-person, seasonally occupied tent cabins and other 1950s structures are tightly clustered among pines and boulders and are accessed through a paved parking lot off the Old Tioga Road. Of the original camp, the mess hall, comfort station, and research shed are considered historic and date back to the period of significance

*Residences at Bug Camp (2008) GH*

(NPS 2007f). During the winter, none of the buildings are used. Similar to Ranger Camp, the white canvas for the tent cabins is removed at the end of the summer season, contributing to the camp's seasonal character.

The typical tent cabin (at Bug and Ranger Camps) measures 12 feet by 14 feet. It is constructed by stretching heavy duck canvas over an open framework of wood or metal to create a simple shelter with an entrance on the gable end. All of the cabins have small stoves that vent through the sidewall thimble to the metal flue.

**GUIDELINES**

- New or replacement structures should maintain the general spacing, scale, and color of the existing structures.
- New structures should be constructed of materials that are compatible with the temporary, seasonal, minimal style currently and historically found here.
- Minimize visual impacts of new parking areas on the housing. Refer to the "Unifying Elements" chapter for guidelines on parking and vegetative screening.
- New design should include measures to ensure protection of existing vegetation. Use appropriate barriers to prevent trampling of such areas.

## TUOLUMNE MEADOWS STORE + GAS STATION

The Tuolumne Meadows Store and Gas Station are west of the historic campground reservation building. Surrounded by lodgepole pine forest, the buildings are accessed directly off the Tioga Road by way of adjacent asphalt parking areas. The southern portion of the store/grill area periodically floods during spring runoff. A cluster of employee tent cabins sits on an abrupt rise behind the store. Immediately to the north across the Tioga Road is a grand, uninterrupted view of the meadows. A narrow strip separates the gas station and store parking lot from the main road.

TOP *Tuolumne Meadows Store and Grill (2008) GH* MIDDLE *Canvas roof removed for winter, Tuolumne Meadows Store and Grill (2010) RF* BOTTOM *Tuolumne Meadows Gas Station (2008) GH*

The store is a wood-frame structure that measures approximately 50 feet by 80 feet, with a white canvas roof and plywood sidewalls covered with canvas. A simple canvas-roofed porch protects the doors to the general store, post office, and the Tuolumne Meadows Grill. The structural frame is painted white to match the canvas roof, in the same manner as for the Tuolumne Meadows Lodge. (Refer to the "Huts, Cabins + High Sierra Camps" chapter.) The translucent canvas roof provides a pleasant, warm, filtered light. At the end of the summer season—generally around mid-October, prior to the closing of Tioga Road—the canvas roofs are removed, allowing snow to fall into the structure. The following spring, when the winter snow melts, the canvas roof is reinstalled for the summer season.

The gas station, a compact structure at the rear of the site, faces Tioga Road. In contrast to the tent structures nearby, the building contains equipment and inventory that remain at the site at the close of the season. In addition to the attendant's office, it contains a small repair shop, restrooms, and a sales area for sundries related to mountaineering. The fuel pumps are arranged in front of the station on the Tioga Road side. Stained a warm umber, in contrast to the white store to the east, the wood structure recedes visually into the wooded background. The wood shingle roof has a modest pitch with overhanging eaves. The hipped roof form has small louvered gables at each end for attic ventilation. The architectural character of the structure is similar to the Crane Flat and Wawona gas stations.

**GUIDELINES**

- New parking areas should minimize negative visual impacts from Tioga Road, the meadow, and surrounding peaks and domes. See also the "Unifying Elements" chapter regarding parking areas.
- Where pedestrian barriers are needed in the open meadows, use low fencing, as described in the "Unifying Elements" chapter, and low mounds planted with low subalpine vegetation that incorporate boulder clusters, so that vegetation is allowed to reestablish.
- Ensure that new picnic areas are buffered from parking areas with appropriate subalpine zone shrubs, grasses, boulder clusters, and planted berms, if compatible with the topography. Refer to "Landscape Uses + Structures—Circulation—Parking" in the "Unifying Elements" chapter.
- For new buildings and structures: At an elevation of 8,600 feet, the gable roof form is appropriate in Tuolumne Meadows. It offers protected areas at the gable ends that are snow-free, allowing easier egress. The roof slope used at the CCC Mess Hall at Road Crew Camp, the bunk houses, and the historic comfort stations by Wosky are appropriate references for the Tuolumne Meadows area. If year-round buildings are to be added to this area, consider a traditional building shape with gable ends and a shed porch at the eave side to accommodate entrance, signs, and receptacles.
- New food preparation facilities should have efficient air-exhaust systems to ensure a pleasant interior environment. In addition to mechanical ventilation, generous openings in exterior walls provide natural ventilation and allow good visual contact with the natural environment. Install openings that conform to good bear-aware practice.
- When designing porches as architectural elements of structures such as stores, porch length should be sufficient to generously provide shelter for patrons of the store, bulletin boards, miscellaneous receptacles, and vending machines.

- Utility areas, such as receiving areas, should be screened from public view with rustic boards or quarter-round log segments, placed vertically, similar to what is found elsewhere in the area. The finish should be natural, with no stain, and allowed to weather.
- The exteriors of new all-season buildings and structures should be wood and should recede into the background. New roofs should be black or brown, and of similar form and character to the adjacent structures. (For example, new structures in the gas station area should be the same material and color.)
- Minimize the addition of new commercial signs that distract from the natural environment. At the gas station garage, new commercial signs should be carefully controlled and not be visible from the road. The gas pumps are sufficient to identify the station. At the store, confine new signs to the porch area, similar to the Wawona store.
- Refer to "Landscape Uses + Structures—Lighting" in the "Unifying Elements" chapter.
- Refer to the "Unifying Elements" chapter and the "Huts, Cabins + High Sierra Camps" chapter for additional guidance on roof design.

*Campground Reservation Building, Tuolumne Meadows (2008) GH*

*Porch and chimney detail, Campground Reservation Building, Tuolumne Meadows (2008) GH*

## CAMPGROUND CONTACT + COMFORT STATIONS

The campground reservation building, previously used as a visitor contact station, stands near the entrance to the Tuolumne Meadows Campground on the south side of the current Tioga Road. Built in 1936 as a replacement for the older ranger station in the administrative area, it remains open in the winter, providing accommodations for cross-country skiers. The manner in which the generous porch and chimney are joined lends a strength and sense of shelter to the overall image of the building. Masonry elements of a warm brown and rust color are an interesting contrast to the granite that emerges and surrounds Tuolumne Meadows. It is worth noting that the contact station and the nearby comfort stations were constructed during the same period as the Tioga Pass Entrance Station (1934). Designed by NPS

Comfort station, Tuolumne Meadows Campground (2008) GH

landscape architect John Wosky, they are classic examples of NPS Rustic architecture. The natural color and heavy texture of the native stone and wood used in their construction are in harmony with the surrounding natural landscape (NPS 2007f).

> *"Responding to the alpine environment and to the nearby Tioga Pass station erected several years previously, Wosky chose a heavy masonry design for the facilities. Adapting a plan used two years earlier at another site in the park, Wosky gave maximum emphasis to the horizontal nature of the massive granite buildings. Jerkinhead roofs and battered walls added to the almost geological character of the structures. Viewed from a short distance, each comfort station appeared similar in color and shape to the alpine skyline of Sierra peaks."* NPS 1977B

John Wosky, NPS Landscape Architect (date unknown) YRL

## ROAD CREW CAMP

Road Crew Camp is an enclave 400 feet south of Tioga Road at the western end of the Tuolumne Meadows Historic District. Built in 1934 by the Civilian Conservation Corps to provide maintenance and administrative facilities for the higher elevations of Yosemite, the development cluster still retains its six original structures. These include the CCC Mess Hall, the shower house, and four bunkhouses.

The CCC Mess Hall (currently the visitor center) is on a lightly forested ridge, surrounded by lodgepole pines. If not for the presence of parked cars, the slight incline of the parking area would provide a centered foreground for viewing the handsome rustic building. The CCC Mess Hall is an excellent example of 1930s NPS Rustic architecture. This wood-frame structure measures roughly 33 feet by 60 feet. The foundation, main fireplace chimney, and front porch floor and steps were constructed of rubble stonemasonry. The roof is 8:12 pitch and is sheathed in wood shingles. The lower portion of the walls has horizontal bevel siding, and the upper portion has vertical redwood board siding, originally finished with a coat of clear linseed oil (NPS 2007f).

The mess hall originally served as the kitchen, dining room, and social hub for the Road Crew Camp. It was listed on the National Register of Historic Places in 1978. In 1980 it was converted to a visitor center.

Bunkhouses, Road Crew Camp (2007) GH

*CCC Mess Hall, Road Crew Camp (date unknown) YRL*

*Entrance, CCC Mess Hall, Road Crew Camp (2008) GH*

Four identical bunkhouses and a shower house are clustered in the trees to the east of the CCC Mess Hall. These were the first structures to be built in the Road Crew Camp area and are fine examples of NPS Rustic architecture. Built during the CCC era, all are wood-frame structures with rubble masonry foundations and redwood board and batten siding. A large rubble masonry chimney distinguishes the shower house. The bunkhouses are still in use as NPS housing and retain most of their original materials and details of workmanship. These structures were all listed on the National Register in 1978.

**GUIDELINES**

- The character of new structures should be compatible with the architectural vocabulary of the rustic structures at Tuolumne Meadows. They should, in addition, be of a scale, form, massing, and color that blends with the immediate natural surroundings.
- Cluster new parking in small groups, screened with native vegetation.
- New design should include measures to ensure protection of existing vegetation. Use appropriate barriers to prevent trampling of such areas.
- Maintain the pattern and spacing of the CCC Mess Hall with the other buildings and structures on the moderate forested slope, regardless of future use. Do not allow temporary or permanent structures to encroach into the spaces surrounding the buildings, in particular the foreground when viewed from the parking lot and the pedestrian approach routes to the immediate north. Refer to the "Unifying Elements" chapter for guidelines on parking and vegetative screening.

TOP *Eave detail at entrance, CCC Mess Hall, Road Crew Camp (2008) GH*
BOTTOM *Plaque at CCC Mess Hall (2008) GH*

LEFT *Shower House, Road Crew Camp (2007) GH* RIGHT *CCC Mess Hall, Road Crew Camp (2008) GH*

- The openness of the approach to the CCC Mess Hall is a character-defining aspect of the site, and new construction should not occur within this area.
- Any new construction, including alterations to the wastewater treatment buildings and surroundings, should be done in a manner that is obscured from trails, roads, and public view, and acoustically buffered. Lighting should be limited (refer to Yosemite Lighting Guidelines) to avoid polluting the dark night sky.
- Refer to "Developed Areas—Building Shape + Massing" and "Developed Areas—Architectural Character" in the "Unifying Elements" chapter.

## SODA SPRINGS + PARSONS MEMORIAL LODGE

Soda Springs is nested within the larger Tuolumne Meadows Historic District. It comprises 140 acres at the northern edge of Tuolumne Meadows (NPS 2007d). Soda Springs takes its name from a group of natural mineral carbonated springs on the site. The Soda Springs area comprises several distinct habitat types: riparian, open grassland, upland pine forest, and wetlands around the springs.

Development in this area was sited along the natural ecotone where subalpine meadow transitions into a coniferous forest. This location allowed Soda Springs' early inhabitants to be near the meadow and mineral springs while enjoying privacy and protection from the wind and sun on the edge of the lodgepole pine forest (NPS 2007d).

Adjacent to the springs, a sunny, south-facing, upland plateau presents an ideal location for camping and building. Four structures—Parsons Memorial Lodge, McCauley Cabin, Bruin Baffle, and the Soda Springs enclosure—are sited along natural contours on a granite

*Parsons Memorial Lodge and McCauley Cabin (2007) GH*

bench overlooking the Tuolumne River. The enclave is connected to the meadow by a footbridge. Their wide spacing permitted features such as trees and boulders to remain interspersed among the constructed elements. The impact of development was minimized by locating buildings outside the meadow within a grove of lodgepole pine. The buildings were designed in a manner that minimized their visibility by harmonizing their appearance with the surrounding natural environment (NPS 2007f).

Although some portions of historic wagon routes and trails have been obliterated, the Soda Springs Trail, the road to Parsons Memorial Lodge, the Great Sierra Wagon Road, the Glen Aulin Trail, and the Pacific Crest Trail all traverse Tuolumne Meadows. This highlights Soda Springs' important location as a natural crossroads through Tuolumne Meadows at Soda Springs (NPS 2007d).

Because of the compaction of roots and possible damage to the fragile subalpine vegetation, a campground initially established by the Sierra Club was discontinued after it was acquired by the National Park Service in 1976. By 2007, more than 30 years later, faint circulation routes of that campground still endured within the landscape (NPS 2007f). This demonstrates the fragility of the vegetation and soil at this altitude.

Two of the buildings—Parsons Memorial Lodge and McCauley Cabin—are of national architectural significance and are individually listed on the National Register of Historic Places. Parsons Memorial Lodge has received further recognition and was designated a National Historic Landmark in 1987.

Parsons Memorial Lodge, built in 1915, is one of the earliest stone rustic buildings in a national park. It was built as a memorial to one of the early directors of the Sierra Club, Edward Taylor Parsons, and received contributions from the mountaineering community, including the famous British alpinist Edward Whymper. Situated at an elevation of 8,640 feet at the northern edge of Tuolumne Meadows, Parsons Memorial Lodge was designed by the office of renowned Berkeley architect Bernard Maybeck, who with Mark White produced a building with a thorough understanding of the harsh environmental conditions encountered at this altitude. It is a small but robust building of approximately 1,040

*Parsons Memorial Lodge (2007) GH*

*Parsons Memorial Lodge (date unknown) YRL*

RIGHT *Bruin Baffle (2008) GH* LEFT *Log enclosure, Soda Springs (date unknown) YRL*

square feet. The masonry walls are made with locally gathered pink feldspar and grey granite stones with a reinforced concrete core. Deeply raked mortar joints accentuate the stonework. Walls are battered, approximately three feet thick at the bottom and two feet thick at the top. A Roman arch frames the wood door at the south-facing entrance. The exterior of the door is covered with galvanized metal. The interior of the door reveals heavy plank construction with heavy wrought-iron strap hinges. The voussoirs and keystone are dressed, as are lintel and jamb stones throughout the building. The low-pitched gable roof is finished with galvanized corrugated metal. The building has undergone a few minor changes over the years, but none mars its integrity.

The use of natural materials, a hallmark of the Rustic style, was indicative of the Bay Area tradition as developed in the work of Bernard Maybeck and others. In subsequent years, Rustic-style architecture became emblematic of the National Park Service. Parsons Memorial Lodge is a most important forerunner of that design ethic (NPS 1987a).

In 1973, the National Park Service acquired the building from the Sierra Club. Parsons Memorial Lodge continues to function as a high-country nature center, open to the public.

McCauley Cabin is a one-story, one-room, log building measuring approximately 18 feet by 21 feet. The peeled logs that make up the walls of the structure are round on the exterior and hand-hewn to a flush surface on the interior. The original chinking of mud and grass has been replaced with mortar. The cabin was used by the Sierra Club as a caretaker's residence. McCauley Cabin was listed in the National Register in 1977 (NPS 1977a).

The Soda Springs enclosure, constructed between 1885 and 1889, is a small, 12-foot-by-nine-foot log structure with V-notched corner details and no windows or floor. Several of the springs are located inside the enclosure walls. Originally, the log walls were erected for the purpose of protecting the springs from livestock. Although it once had a corrugated metal roof, the enclosure has been open on top for an unknown number of years. The structure was listed on the National Register in 1979 (NPS 2007d).

Bruin Baffle is a two-story, stand-alone structure built by the Sierra Club in 1937. As its name suggests, the building was designed to prevent bears from accessing stored food. The exterior walls are clad with corrugated galvanized steel. The east facade has a small porch, and a ladder provides access to the upper floor, known by local campers as the Coo-coo's Loft (NPS 2007d).

A footbridge crosses the Tuolumne River on the meadow floor directly south of Parsons Memorial Lodge. The original footbridge, built in the summer of 1915 at the same time as the lodge, had a simple triangular truss structure with a center pier and masonry abutments of recessed mortar joints, similar to the masonry of the lodge. Log girders have been replaced with steel, with thick wood-plank decking. The center pier continues to rest on a large boulder mid-stream. The abutments and pier are historic (NPS 2007d).

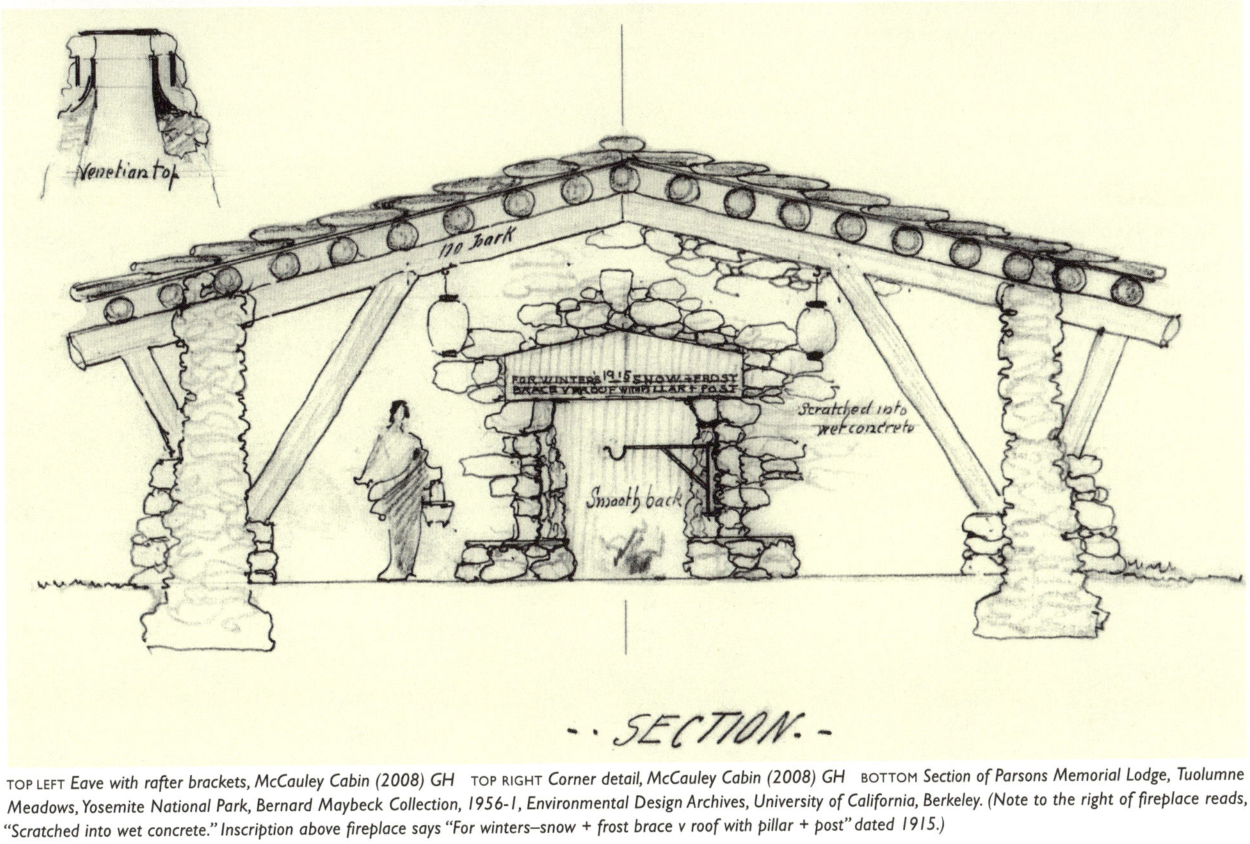


TOP LEFT *Eave with rafter brackets, McCauley Cabin (2008) GH* TOP RIGHT *Corner detail, McCauley Cabin (2008) GH* BOTTOM *Section of Parsons Memorial Lodge, Tuolumne Meadows, Yosemite National Park, Bernard Maybeck Collection, 1956-1, Environmental Design Archives, University of California, Berkeley. (Note to the right of fireplace reads, "Scratched into wet concrete." Inscription above fireplace says "For winters–snow + frost brace v roof with pillar + post" dated 1915.)*

Footbridge over Tuolumne River, near Soda Springs (2008) GH

Small-scale features such as cooking grills, a trash vault, stone retaining walls, interpretive signs, and a picnic table were constructed from locally found materials that blend with the landscape.

**GUIDELINES**

- Any new construction in the Soda Springs, Parsons Memorial Lodge and adjacent wastewater ponds area should be done in a manner that is ecologically compatible and hidden from public view along the road and trails.

*Life in the meadows was not all sheepmen-and-soldiers or surveyors-and-peaks. Artists came also, to add their visual images to the words of writers extolling and protecting high places. One of these was William Keith....*

*In the autumn of 1872 while John Muir was working in Yosemite Valley, Keith arrived with two artist friends and a letter of introduction....*

*Keith was looking for a scene to paint, something which would seem to him more of a picture than the massive undifferentiated Sierra he had seen so far.*

*'Yes,' said Muir, 'I saw it only yesterday. The crown of the Sierra is a picture hung on the sky, and mind you, it needs none of your selection or composition. I'll take you there tomorrow.'*

*...They rode up the Lyell Fork to the point where they could see the glacier-hung presence of Mount Lyell rising majestically above them. Dismounting, they enjoyed a moment of silent awe, and then Keith dashed forward waving his arms and shouting.*

*'It was the grandest thing I ever saw,' [Keith] wrote.*

*—From O'Neill,* Meadow in the Sky, *69 (1993)*

Mount Lyell, California Sierra, *William Keith, oil on canvas, 1874. Courtesy Hearst Art Gallery, Saint Mary's College of California*

# HUTS, CABINS + HIGH SIERRA CAMPS



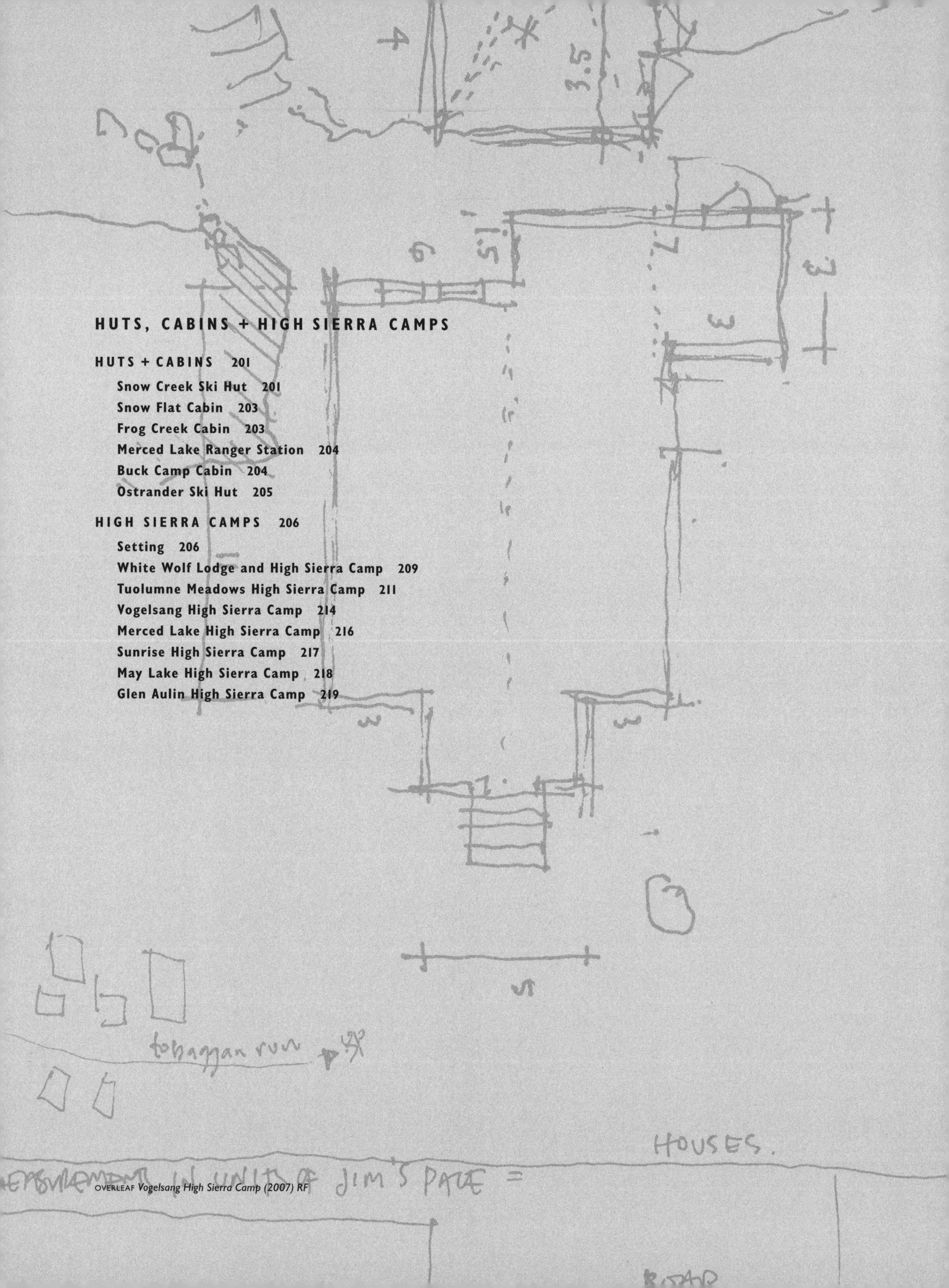


OVERLEAF *Vogelsang High Sierra Camp (2007) RF*

# HUTS, CABINS + HIGH SIERRA CAMPS

FROM RECREATIONAL, EDUCATIONAL, and experiential perspectives, one of the greatest assets offered by Yosemite National Park is its vast undeveloped wilderness. At 1,100 square miles, with thousands of lakes and 1,600 miles of streams and rivers, Yosemite Wilderness is, ecologically speaking, one of the largest and least fragmented habitat blocks in the Sierra Nevada. The vast majority of lands in Yosemite—over 95% of the park's 747,956 acres—are designated wilderness and protected from development.

NATURE'S PEACE WILL FLOW INTO YOU AS THE SUNSHINE INTO TREES. THE WINDS WILL BLOW THEIR FRESHNESS INTO YOU, AND THE STORMS THEIR ENERGY, WHILE CARES WILL DROP OFF YOU AS AUTUMN LEAVES.... IN GOD'S WILDNESS LIES THE HOPE OF THE WORLD—THE GREAT FRESH, UNBLIGHTED, UNREDEEMED WILDERNESS. **JOHN MUIR • 1890**

The protection and perpetuation of use of Yosemite Wilderness is a primary goal of the National Park Service. The sense of remoteness is conveyed by the absence of obvious development, distance from other individuals, views of vast, rugged landscapes, and the near-absence of human-generated sound.

*Vogelsang High Sierra Camp (2009) LH*

The construction of the first "mountain chalet" camps in 1916 marked a significant change in the use of Yosemite's backcountry areas. In earlier decades, travel in such areas required either an expensive pack outfit or long days of hiking with heavy gear. Forerunners of the present High Sierra Camps, the mountain chalet camps made it possible for people of more modest means and ability to venture out of the developed areas of the park and experience first-hand the grandeur of the backcountry. This was an idea dear to Stephen Mather, the first director of the National Park Service, who believed it was essential to build public support for the national parks through improved access and education. The camps also served as a way to draw visitors out of Yosemite Valley and thus reduce impact to its increasingly popular natural resources.

The earliest of the current High Sierra Camps were established in 1916 on sites identified by park naturalist Carl P. Russell for their scenic beauty and availability of water, as well as the park's desire to have the camps be one day's hike apart. High Sierra Camps located in the backcountry include Merced Lake, Vogelsang, Glen Aulin, May Lake, and Sunrise. Two camps—Tuolumne Meadows Lodge and White Wolf Lodge—are sited in the frontcountry.

White Wolf Lodge was added to the camp system in 1953, but has a unique history. It was established as a homestead by John Meyer in 1884 and converted to a lodge by his son and daughter-in-law in 1927. The family operated it as a private inholding until 1951, when Meyer's grandson sold the property to the National Park Service. Where the other camps employ the Rustic style for their permanent structures, White Wolf has white, wood-frame buildings similar to those seen at Wawona and Chinquapin.

In addition to the High Sierra Camps, there are a number of individual cabins scattered throughout the Yosemite Wilderness. Some were built for visitor use, while others were intended for administrative or scientific duties. Lake Vernon, Miguel Meadow, Snow Flat, and Buck Camp cabins were constructed near areas of prior pioneer settlement. About half of the wilderness cabins have associated corrals and fenced pasture meadows (fences are taken down in the winter) for stock support for park staff who use the cabins. The historic Miguel Meadow Cabin has a late-1800s crib barn that contributes to its historic character. Ostrander Ski Hut (1940) and Snow Creek Ski Hut (1928–1930) were developed as part of an unfulfilled effort to establish a European-style

*Ostrander Ski Hut (date unknown) YRL*

*Pack train (2008) DV*

ski touring circuit. Cabins at Lake Vernon, Sachse Springs, Snow Flat, and Merced Lake were all constructed through agreements with the state of California and the city of San Francisco to provide shelters for winter snow survey crews. In the summer, some function as patrol cabins for wilderness rangers. Frog Creek cabin was used for patrols, but originally housed workers collecting trout eggs for the former fish hatchery at Happy Isles. Most of these cabins are variations on the vernacular log cabin, but the Ostrander Ski Hut, constructed of native granite, was one of the last structures built in Yosemite during the NPS Rustic period of design.

## HUTS + CABINS

Located in isolated areas, the wilderness cabins are important historic resources for the park. Equally important, they have a long and continuing history of functioning as shelters for snow surveyors and NPS rangers in both summer and winter—aiding in wilderness patrol, trail crew operations, visitor assistance, and search-and-rescue activities.

The cabins are maintained with as little intrusion on natural resources as possible. Their simple Rustic architectural style enables them to blend in with their surroundings and remain unobtrusive.

Since these backcountry huts and cabins were constructed, the vast area in which they reside was officially designated as wilderness, forever restricting new construction. These historic wilderness structures are eligible or are in the process of being evaluated for listing on the National Register of Historic Places and are subject to *The Secretary of the Interior's Standards for the Treatment of Historic Properties*. There are three distinct types of backcountry cabins: log structures, frame structures, and masonry structures. The following are descriptions of some of the cabins in Yosemite Wilderness.

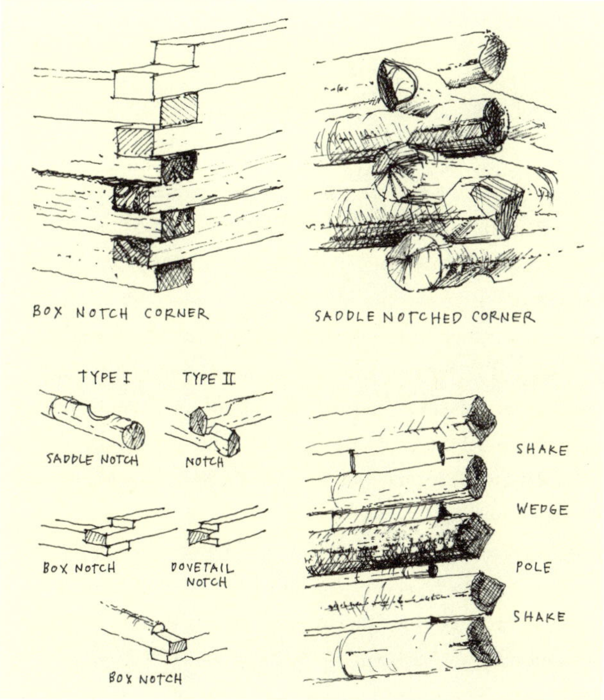

TOP *Log framing details* BOTTOM *Snow Creek Ski Hut*

### Snow Creek Ski Hut (Frame Structure)

The Snow Creek Ski Hut was constructed in 1929 as the initial phase of a proposed system of ski and mountaineering huts in the Yosemite high country. The plan was devised by Donald Tresidder of the Yosemite Park and Curry Company, and would be the first implementation of organized backcountry ski-touring with overnight accommodations offered in the United States. The trail system included the construction of Snow Creek Ski

Hut, temporary winter usage of several Park Service ranger stations Tenaya Lake and Tuolumne Meadows, and the rehabilitation of Glacier Point Mountain House for winter use.

Architectural plans for the hut were prepared by Eldridge T. Spencer of San Francisco, with Tresidder making suggestions inspired by a book of illustrations and plans of Swiss mountain huts. The hut is a hybrid of NPS Rustic style, with elements of the architecture of the Swiss Alps. The Swiss influence complemented the NPS Rustic style by emphasizing the use of natural wood materials for both structural and decorative elements. Years later in 1935 at the Badger Pass Ski Lodge, Spencer continued the tradition of the distinctive NPS Rustic style with elements of Swiss and Austrian Tyrol architecture. The Snow Creek Ski Hut was completed in 1929 and received some modifications the following year (NPS 2004d).

The hut is a two-story building constructed predominately with local, natural materials. The overall massing of the building is a gable roof with extended porches. Exterior walls are finished with double-course shakes and peeled logs. The windows have shutters that are painted in a green and white chevron pattern, attesting to the influence of the Swiss Alps. The modest foundation is comprised of local granite rubble with a recessed mortar bed. The building consists of a living room, kitchen, small bedroom, mudroom, storage area, and two loft bedrooms. The use of materials within the interior spaces—exposed log beams, wallboard panels with battens, naturally finished tongue-and-groove flooring, quarter-round log stairs—continues the rustic character that harmonizes with the exterior treatment.

The Yosemite Winter Club, established in 1928 to promote winter use in Yosemite, used the Snow Creek Ski Hut frequently throughout the winters of 1930–1934 as the first layover during instructed ski-touring expeditions. Famed photographer Ansel Adams also frequented the ski hut along his route to the high country to photograph skiers and the winter landscape. Although Tresidder had grand plans of promoting ski-touring throughout Yosemite, his dream never gained the momentum it needed and was not carried forward.

From 1939–1947, the ski hut was used by NPS personnel during snow survey trips to Gin Flat and Tioga Pass. The building went into disrepair and was only minimally used until extensive restoration work was completed in 2003 and 2006. The Snow Creek Ski Hut continues to serve its historic function as a backcountry accommodation during summer and winter months with public access.

*Snow Creek Ski Hut (date unknown) CW*

*Dossen Hut, Swiss Alps (ca. 1931), from* Club Alpin Suisse Cabanes

*Snow Flat Cabin (date unknown) YRL*

## Snow Flat Cabin

The Snow Flat cabin was built in 1947 by the California Division of Water Resources to be used for snow surveyors. Originally constructed for winter service in connection with the acquisition of hydrologic data along the Tuolumne and Merced River's watersheds within Yosemite National Park, these cabins served as shelters for personnel and as bases of operation for employees patrolling snow courses and for equipment maintenance. Today, the cabin continues to be used by rangers and snow surveyors in the winter. Its basic shape is a simple rectangle of approximately 22 feet by 14 feet, with a gable roof that includes a generous two-story, south-facing porch. The attic access in the upper part of the porch serves as the winter entrance. The interior contains a cook stove, three double-deck bunks, a table, and chairs. The original roofing material was probably shakes (NPS 2004e). The roof was recently stabilized and rehabilitated.

## Frog Creek Cabin (Frame Structure)

The Frog Creek Cabin was constructed in 1936 by the Civilian Conservation Corps. The building housed seasonal workers at the nearby Frog Creek Egg-Collecting Station who harvested rainbow trout eggs for the Happy Isles Hatchery in Yosemite Valley. The Frog Creek Egg-Collecting Station was in full operation between 1934 and 1956. In 1956, the park began using aerial drops for fish stocking, making the Happy Isles Hatchery and facilities at Frog Creek obsolete. Today the cabin is maintained by the National Park Service as an outlying patrol post.

Building plans for the operation were produced by the regional National Park Service Branch of Plans in the NPS Rustic style that emphasized function and soon became vernacular for backcountry buildings. At the time of construction, the surrounding areas of Lake Eleanor and Miguel Meadow had already become a hub for development in conjunction with the building of the O'Shaughnessy Dam in Hetch Hetchy Valley and structures relating to other natural resource management activities.

*Frog Creek Cabin*

The Frog Creek Cabin is a vernacular, single-story frame cabin intended for utilitarian purposes. The plan of the cabin is rectangular, approximately 14 feet by 28 feet, with a small screened porch extending from the west facade. The main portion of the building is clad in stained lap-board siding, while the porch has stained board and batten half-walls and upper screened panels. A wide, overhanging gable roof and a rubble granite foundation wall serve to visually anchor the cabin to the surrounding landscape. The roof is clad in sugar pine shingles and has a rubble granite chimney on the west slope. The floor plan consists of a single bunk room, kitchen, and enclosed screened porch. The cabin is in good condition and has had very minimal alteration since its construction.

*Merced Lake Ranger Station (2009) LH*

*Buck Camp Cabin*

## Merced Lake Ranger Station (Log Structure)

The three-room Merced Lake Ranger Station, constructed in 1927, is nestled in a forested area three quarters of a mile east of Merced Lake, at the junction of the trail from Yosemite Valley and trails leading to the Clark Range and Tuolumne Meadows. This is one of the first structures built by the NPS in Yosemite's backcountry. The cabin was funded by the Merced Irrigation District and was designed in the NPS Rustic style, which served as a model for other Yosemite backcountry cabins. The cabin is used primarily in the summer by wilderness patrol rangers.

With an irregular floor plan of 21 feet by 25 feet, the building is constructed of lodgepole pine logs chinked with jute and cement grout over nails to make the structure weatherproof. Granite rubble is used for the foundation and the fireplace chimney. The shallow pitched roof has a generous gable form to shelter the entrance, which is covered with sugar pine shakes (NPS 1986b).

## Buck Camp Cabin (Log Structure)

The Buck Camp Cabin was originally constructed in 1931 as a snow survey shelter. Today it is used by wilderness patrol rangers in the summer. The cabin was planned for and built under a cooperative agreement between the NPS and the Merced Irrigation District. The Irrigation District funded this cabin, along with the construction of the Merced Lake Ranger Station in 1927 and the rehabilitation of the Deer Camp Cabin in 1931 (since destroyed).

The Buck Camp Cabin, designed by John Wosky, landscape architect for the National Park Service, was constructed in the Rustic style to harmonize with its surrounding environment and relate to the log structures built in the Yosemite region by homesteaders in the 1800s. The cabin is a log structure constructed of vertical logs (rather than the traditional horizontal construction technique) resting on a stone and wood pier foundation. The vertical logs are load-bearing, supporting the roof structure. The inside surface is sheathed with one-by-six-inch rough-cut boards, and the roof is covered with sugar pine shake. Overall dimensions are 14 feet by 29 feet, with the major axis running north–south (NPS 2004a).

### Ostrander Ski Hut (Masonry Structure)

The gable roof of Ostrander Ski Hut is a welcome sight for cross-country skiers who have just traversed the 10 miles from the Badger Pass Ski Lodge. The hut was designed as a ski-touring shelter and built in seven weeks by the Civilian Conservation Corps in 1940. It was the last building the CCC built in Yosemite and is considered one of the finest examples of late NPS Rustic architecture.

Ostrander Ski Hut was no doubt influenced by the mountain huts and refuges of the Swiss and Austrian Alps that Donald and Mary Curry Tresidder had seen when they were sent abroad by the directors of the Yosemite Park and Curry Company in 1936 to study winter alpine resorts. Ostrander Ski Hut was intended to be part of a network for winter sports starting at the Badger Pass Ski Lodge. Like its European counterparts, Ostrander was intended to have accommodations more austere and communal than those at Yosemite's High Sierra Camps. Today, Ostrander continues to provide accommodations that are spare, providing bunks downstairs and bedframes attached to the roof framing upstairs. A long table and wood stove continue to be the center for communal dining in the evening after the day's events. There are separate quarters for the winter caretaker. The floor plan of 20 feet by 50 feet has a north–south alignment for the major axis, sited on a downslope toward Ostrander Lake. The ground falls 6–10 feet below the entrance on the south end. When snowfall overcomes the entrance level, the balcony, overlooking the lake, serves as the alternate access for the hut.

The use of local rock, timber, and a weathered grey metal roof enable Ostrander hut to be compatible with its surroundings regardless of season. "Unlike the use of stone for facades in many Valley buildings of the Rustic architecture period, the use of stone in the Ostrander Hut was structural, clearly affecting the building's character" (NPS 2004c).

**GUIDELINES**

- For historic huts and cabins, follow *The Secretary of the Interior's Standards for the Treatment of Historic Properties.*
- New structures intended only for park administrative functions should be sited as discreetly as possible to minimize visibility from trails and to discourage unauthorized entry.
- New backcountry buildings should be visually non-intrusive and should harmonize with the surrounding landscape. The NPS Rustic style achieved this by the use of local materials, battered masonry foundations and chimneys, horizontal emphasis, exposed structural members, and wide, overhanging eaves.
- Any new structures should also be sensitive to existing structures in the vicinity. New structures should be

*Views of Ostrander Ski Hut, winter (left) and summer (right) (dates unknown) YRL*

*Ostrander Ski Hut (date unknown) YRL*

influenced by, but not mimic, the historic structures in order to create a cohesive built environment.

- The simple gable and shed roof shapes are well-suited for alpine settings where snowfall reaches extreme depths, because they can shed snow and protect the entrance. Metal roofing with a steep roof pitch allows free fall of snow clear of sidewalls and has historic precedent. Wood shingled roofing blends well with the natural environment.
- Masonry walls are appropriate for remote areas because they are fire resistant and low maintenance, and visually relate the structures to their settings.
- Upper-level entrances should be included because ground-level exits can become blocked by snow.
- Use nonreflective exterior materials such as metal, wood, and stone to match the existing structure. Select colors and stains to blend into the site conditions.
- Refer to "General Guidelines for High Sierra Camps" in this chapter.
- Refer to "Developed Areas—Architectural Character" in the "Unifying Elements" chapter.

# HIGH SIERRA CAMPS

## Setting

Appropriately, all seven High Sierra Camps are found at elevations exceeding 7,000 feet. The lower camps—Merced at 7,150 feet, White Wolf at 8,000 feet, and Glen Aulin at 8,300 feet—are set in the red fir or upper montane belt. The highest is Vogelsang at 10,300 feet, followed by May Lake at 9,300 feet, Sunrise at 9,200 feet, and Tuolumne Meadows at 8,600 feet. These camps are in the subalpine belt dominated by mountain hemlock, whitebark pine, and lodgepole pine. There is less vegetation at the higher levels because of a significantly harsher climate, thinner soils, and shorter growing season. These factors make it difficult to restore vegetation once it is damaged or removed. These camps have been located in fragile landscapes. All of the backcountry High Sierra Camps are in officially designated "Potential Wilderness Additions" that are tightly and permanently confined by the surrounding Yosemite Wilderness boundaries—and therefore cannot spread beyond their current footprints.

The arrangement of tent cabins and service buildings varies from camp to camp. Some tent cabins are scattered at the forest-meadow interface, laid out in a dispersed, uneven fashion near major boulders or clusters of mature trees, such as at Vogelsang, May Lake, and Sunrise. Others are laid out in regimented linear patterns, such as at Merced Lake and, to a lesser extent, at Glen Aulin (NPS 1965). At Merced Lake the evenly spaced tents create three sides of a central rectangular space, resembling a military layout.

The concept of building separated masonry structures in the backcountry to protect against the threat of fire has roots in Bernard Maybeck's 1921 resort at Glen Alpine Springs, near Fallen Leaf Lake in the Lake Tahoe basin. Large-scale structures were destroyed by fire the year before, and Maybeck replaced them with a connected group of small, separate, low-lying pavilions. This project broke new ground in Rustic design through its use of

Red fir (Abies magnifica)

contemporary building materials and its advances in the use of stone. Maybeck's use of natural materials produced an efficient, fire-resistant structure that blended with its setting in the High Sierra. His design incorporated battered piers and walls of heavy stonemasonry, heavy timber roof framing, industrial steel sash, and corrugated iron roofing. The concept of separation and masonry construction is found today at many High Sierra Camps (McClelland 1998).

**GENERAL GUIDELINES**

- For new development within the High Sierra Camps (all of which have been determined eligible for listing in the National Register of Historic Places), designers should consult *The Secretary of the Interior's Standards for the Treatment of Historic Properties* for guidance to ensure compatibility.
- New stonemasonry should be compatible with existing examples in terms of stone size and color, mortar joints, and raking.
- Because most of the camps are located in "Potential Wilderness Additions," renovations and new construction must comply with Yosemite Wilderness policies.
- The sense of remoteness and the qualities of undeveloped and apparent unspoiled wilderness should underlie the location, siting, and design of built structures in the backcountry. Continue the tradition of the seasonal character of tent cabins.

Glen Alpine Springs Resort, B. Maybeck, Fallen Leaf Lake, near Lake Tahoe (2007) GH

- The landscape character of the High Sierra Camps derives largely from the scale and spacing of tents, cook houses, and other structures in relation to each other and to the natural features of the site and its surroundings. In the case of replacements or additions, every effort should be made to preserve the unique character of each camp.
- In backcountry settings, the siting of new buildings should not negatively impact historic views or vistas.
- High Sierra Camps should have a healthy and natural mix of vegetation, from ground-cover to overstory. Delineate pathways to protect vegetation. Refer to "Landscape Uses + Structures—Barriers, Fences + Benches" in the "Unifying Elements" chapter.

Storage shed, Glen Aulin High Sierra Camp (2004) RF

Dining tent, Vogelsang High Sierra Camp (2009) LH

*Dry-stack masonry, Vogelsang High Sierra Camp (2007) RF*

- New paths should fit within the existing site hierarchy and retain traditional edging of cobbles of local rock. Refer to the "Unifying Elements" chapter for guidelines on circulation.
- New tent cabins and structures should be designed with material and siting similar to existing historic structures.
- For frontcountry High Sierra Camps, provide vegetative screening for parking areas to protect views from tent cabins.
- In case of repair, replacement, or fabrication of small-scale features such as fences, signs, and retaining walls, maintain a sense of the wilderness by using materials and designs that are rustic and unfinished in character and that would appear consistent with materials found on-site.
- New utility structures—including toilet structures—should be modest in size, unobtrusive, constructed of materials and colors that blend with the immediate surroundings, and compatible with the historic character of the buildings at each camp.
- Provide vegetative or rustic fence-screening for outdoor dumpsters and storage units and/or locate them so that they are screened from visitor use areas and trails.
- If service areas cannot be screened using natural topography or vegetation, use rough boards or quarter-log sections with bark, set vertically on foundations of stone or concrete to avoid direct contact with the soil.
- New tent cabin entrances with more than three risers require handrails that withstand heavy snow loads. Consider masonry steps with removable pipe railings set in sleeves.
- Wood left in its natural state is subject to accelerated decomposition and weathering at most elevations. In the high country, such weathering is severe; preserve exterior wood with clear or semitransparent stain to allow natural weathering to proceed without the uneven shedding of surface pigments found on weathered painted surfaces. Use stains and paints that have additives to reduce the effects of ultraviolet degradation.
- The use of color on buildings in backcountry or wilderness areas should be considered carefully. Wosky brown or dark green should be the first choices. Most colors, when exposed to the ultraviolet light of direct sunshine, will fade in intensity. For painted finish, use exterior sash and trim paint in gloss finish, which can provide additional protection. The sheen will diminish quickly when exposed to the weather.
- The color of metal should be restricted to natural weathering material, dark grey or prefinished in dark green or Wosky brown.
- Use of log-plank sections for the roof covering, such as at Vogelsang and May Lake High Sierra Camps, is recommended. However, if metal roofing is used, the metal should be restricted to natural weathering material or prefinished in dark grey, or Wosky brown.

*McCauley Cabin, Tuolumne Meadows (2008) GH*

- Exterior wall cladding for wood structures should be natural weathering material—rough-sawn boards, cedar, or redwood—with a minimal thickness of ⅞-inch.
- Locate vent piping below the ridgeline of the roof so it will not be seen in profile. Paint using approved colors, or use natural weathering metals.
- Solar collectors should be in frames of dark, non-reflective metals and should be integrated with the structure.
- To be compatible with backcountry design character, if prefabricated buildings are used, they should sit on foundations with continuous skirting to enclose sub-floor space. Use the same guidelines for roof and walls as stated above, or screen structures as called for in service areas.
- Refer to "Landscape Uses + Structures—Small Buildings" in the "Unifying Elements" chapter.

## White Wolf Lodge and High Sierra Camp

White Wolf Lodge is located on a segment of the Old Tioga Road approximately one mile north of the current alignment of the Tioga Road, near McSwain Meadows. A small parking area fronts the lodge. The lodge/dining building is the organizing element for circulation at the center of two loops of white tent cabins that are linked by the bathhouse. The loop directly behind the lodge is arranged in a rough semicircle around a low, broad granitic outcrop and knoll, in a sunny open space at the edge of a lodgepole pine forest. The second loop to the north is immersed in a shaded forest on an incline that slopes down and away from the open space. The tent camp and nearby campground are adjacent to the wilderness boundary, precluding any expansion. Trail connections include Harden Lake and the Grand Canyon of the Tuolumne River. Across the road is the White Wolf Campground.

Though originally a homestead founded in 1884, White Wolf was converted to a lodge in 1927, when improvement to the Old Tioga Road brought increased traffic to the park. The owners added cabins and tent cabins, a power plant, and a small gas pump and soda fountain across the road. When it was acquired by the National Park Service in 1953, White Wolf was added to the High Sierra Camp system, becoming the second frontcountry High Sierra Camp.

*White Wolf Lodge and gas station*

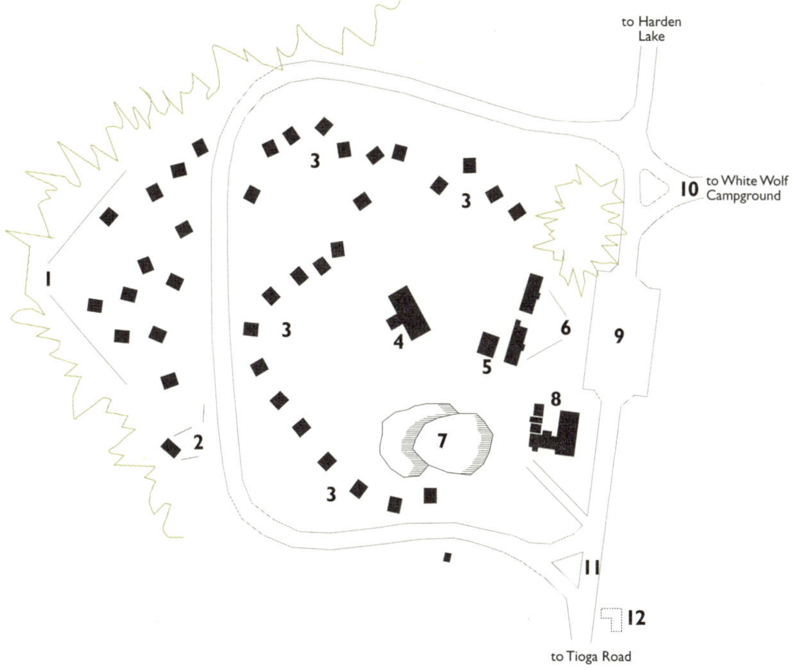


**WHITE WOLF LODGE AND HIGH SIERRA CAMP**

1 Employee Tent Cabins
2 Stables
3 Guest Tent Cabins
4 Bathhouse
5 Storage
6 Guest Cabins
7 Rock Outcropping
8 White Wolf Lodge
9 Parking Area
10 Road to White Wolf Campground
11 Road to Tioga Road
12 Service Station (razed)

N

SCALE IN FEET
0 25 50 75 100 200

During the harsh winter of 1968–69, heavy snow caused the collapse of the lodge and cabin roof-structures, leading to their removal. Because plans to update the lodge structure had not been approved, the lodge was rebuilt without any changes to the earlier design. Architecturally, White Wolf Lodge stands apart from the other High Sierra Camps. While the other camps are rustic in their design, with dry-stacked masonry and weathered wood, White Wolf Lodge relates more to the white-painted buildings at Chinquapin and Wawona. The lodge drew inspiration from the early California Territorial style found at the former Sentinel Hotel in Yosemite Valley (1876) and at the Wawona Hotel (1879).

The structures at White Wolf have wood shingle roofs, light wood-frame construction, and vertical board and batten siding. All the buildings are painted white, with windows and doors painted dark green. The lodge porch has a light timber framework that is covered with canvas during the summer season. The porch has a light picket railing and lattice enclosing the underfloor spaces, painted dark green similar to that of the Wawona Hotel buildings.

At the end of the summer season, the canvas of the tent cabins is removed and stored. The framework is taken down and stacked on the concrete floor for the winter season, awaiting reassembly the following spring.

*White Wolf Lodge (2008) RF*

*Framing for tent cabins, White Wolf Lodge (2008) GH*

**GUIDELINES**

*Porch detail, White Wolf Lodge (2008) GH*

- For new development within White Wolf, designers should consult *The Secretary of the Interior's Standards for the Treatment of Historic Properties* for guidance to ensure compatibility.
- Refer to the *White Wolf Lodge Main Building and Duplex Cabins Historic Structures Report* (NPS 2011e).
- New utility, storage, and service areas should be minimally visible from public use areas. If needed, screen with native vegetation or use fencing that matches the color and detailing of the lodge.
- New structures and additions should continue the treatment of board and batten siding, painted white.
- New porches should use materials that match existing in size and profile.
- Refer to "General Guidelines for High Sierra Camps" in this chapter.

## Tuolumne Meadows High Sierra Camp (Tuolumne Meadows Lodge)

Tuolumne Meadows High Sierra Camp (1916) is at an elevation of 8,600 feet on the north bank of Miller Rapids on the Dana Fork of the Tuolumne River. It consists of a tent reception/dining room, kitchen, bathhouse, storage buildings, and tent cabins.

Tuolumne Meadows is one of two High Sierra Camps accessible by auto (the other being White Wolf). The narrow drive passes through a dense lodgepole pine forest. The natural landscape sets a peaceful tone, allowing visitors to decompress from the long drive as they approach the lodge. This is an important component of the sense of arrival.

The large paved parking area west of the dining hall and downslope of the tent cabin area is expansive and highly visible from the tent cabins: its size overwhelms the setting and the arrival experience. To the east, tent cabins are dispersed on an uneven upslope among boulders, granite outcrops, and lodgepole pines. A group of exposed, highly visible propane tanks, along with other supplies, is clustered adjacent to the bathhouse. Intensive foot traffic has obliterated most pathways, leaving extensive areas of unvegetated and, in some areas, eroding, barren soils.

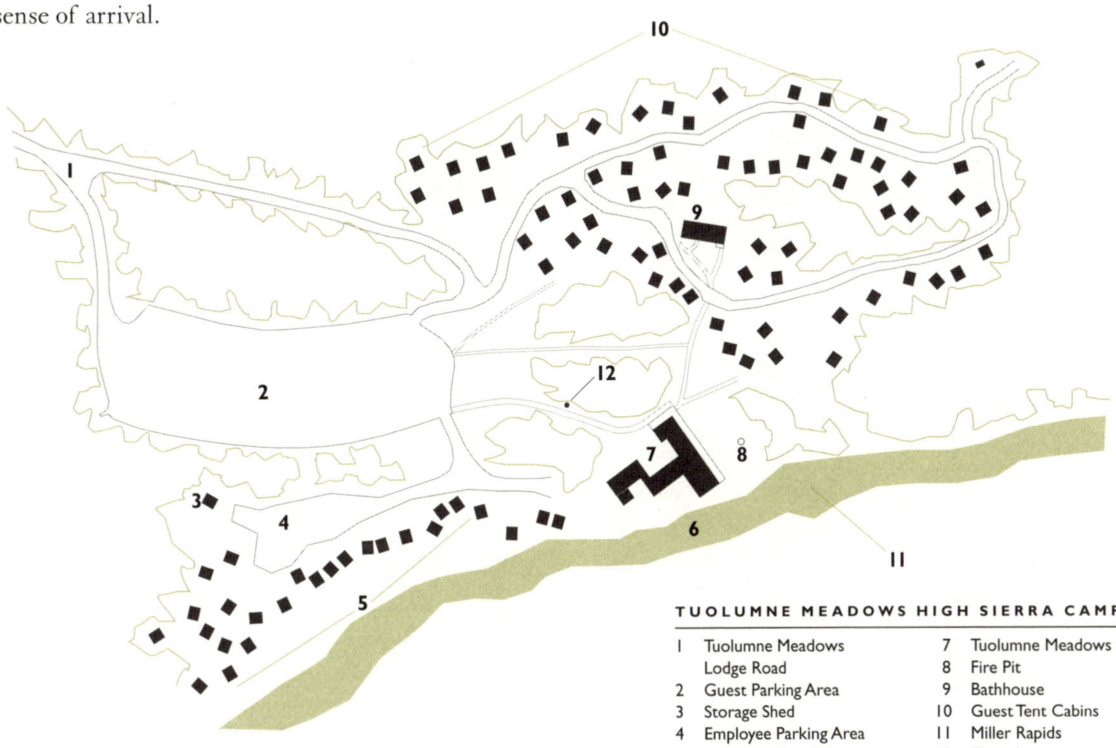


TUOLUMNE MEADOWS HIGH SIERRA CAMP

1 Tuolumne Meadows Lodge Road
2 Guest Parking Area
3 Storage Shed
4 Employee Parking Area
5 Employee Tent Cabins
6 Dana Fork of the Tuolumne River
7 Tuolumne Meadows Lodge
8 Fire Pit
9 Bathhouse
10 Guest Tent Cabins
11 Miller Rapids
12 Flagpole

N

SCALE IN FEET
0 50 100 150 200 300

Employee tent cabins, permanent service buildings, and the canvas-roofed reception and dining hall are aligned in a row facing the river. Beyond these buildings to the south is a popular view of Miller Rapids, where intensive foot traffic has all but eliminated riparian bank vegetation.

Buildings and structures are simple, in the tradition of the High Sierra Camps. Except for kitchen, storage, and bathhouse structures, most are roofed with white canvas stretched over permanent wood or metal frames.

The reception/dining room structure has a timber frame with canvas walls and roof, set upon a slightly elevated concrete slab. The framing members are painted white to blend with the canvas. Double-hung windows provide ventilation. On the east side, a canvas awning extends from the structure to provide a protected seating area adjacent to a fire pit. At the end of the summer season, canvas roofs, walls, and windows are removed, leaving the concrete floor and framing exposed to the elements in winter, when the camp is closed.

Adjacent to the tent dining area, permanent kitchen and storage structures are built of conventional wood-frame construction. The exterior of the kitchen is sheathed in board and batten siding and painted brown.

The typical tent cabin measures 12 feet by 14 feet, constructed by stretching heavy duck canvas over an open framework of wood or metal to create a simple

LEFT *Tuolumne Meadows Lodge (2008) DV* TOP RIGHT *Tuolumne Meadows Lodge (2008) GH* BOTTOM RIGHT *Interior, Tuolumne Meadows Lodge (date unknown) YRL*

Pack mule (2008) DV

shelter with an entrance on the gable end. All of the cabins have small iron stoves that vent through the sidewall thimble with a metal flue. Tent cabins are for seasonal occupancy and are disassembled at the end of summer.

**GUIDELINES**

- For new development at the Tuolumne Meadows Lodge, designers should consult *The Secretary of the Interior's Standards for the Treatment of Historic Properties* for guidance to ensure compatibility.
- New structures should be sited and spaced in a manner consistent with historic patterns, which were based on proximity to natural features such as boulders or tree groupings.
- New structures along the arrival road should maintain the general spacing, scale, and color of the existing tent cabins at Tuolumne Meadows Lodge.
- New structures in this location should enhance the sense of arrival to this historic lodge, not detract.
- New structures should be constructed of materials that are compatible with the temporary, seasonal, and minimal style of the tent cabins currently and historically found here.
- In the new employee housing area, the pedestrian pathway network should be well-delineated to protect vegetation. Use appropriate naturalistic barriers, such as partially buried boulders or lodgepole pine logs, to prevent trampling of such areas.
- New parking should be clustered in small groups and screened with native vegetation or natural features.
- New exterior storage areas, service areas, and equipment should be out of public view. If this is not feasible, then these areas should be screened with vegetation and/or fencing to ensure that the historic and natural scenes are minimally impacted. This guideline applies to the arrival experience along the road leading up to the lodge as well as within the lodge area itself. Refer to "Landscape Uses + Structures—Barriers, Fences + Benches" in the "Unifying Elements" chapter.
- Refer to "General Guidelines for High Sierra Camps" in this chapter.

TOP *Tent cabins, Tuolumne Meadows Lodge (2006) GH* BOTTOM *Dana Fork, Tuolumne River (2008) DV*

RIGHT *Incinerator, Vogelsang High Sierra Camp (2007) RF*
FAR RIGHT *Roof detail, Vogelsang High Sierra Camp (2007) RF*

## Vogelsang High Sierra Camp

At 10,100 feet, Vogelsang (1940) is the highest High Sierra Camp in the park, accessible only by foot or on horseback. More than seven miles from Tuolumne Meadows Lodge via the Rafferty Creek Trail, Vogelsang embodies the essential character of a remote High Sierra wilderness retreat. The camp is set at the base of Fletcher Peak, near Fletcher Lake, at the end of a windswept, treeless, boulder-strewn plateau. The site is starkly open and typical of the subalpine vegetation zone, with alternating rock outcrops and areas of sandy, decomposed granite. Tent cabins are scattered along a central main pathway at a bend in Fletcher Creek. The dining tent, stonemasonry cookhouse, and a variety of small wood-and-metal-clad structures are clustered on the gently sloping rock exposure. Severe weather conditions and prolonged use have resulted in the need for increased maintenance and, in some cases, replacement of utilities.

The core buildings have walls of dry-stacked masonry and natural shingles. Log slabs over corrugated metal and wood shingles form the roof coverings. These natural roof materials allow the structures to be visually compatible within their setting. Prefabricated metal structures, some painted with warm tones, are less visually compatible, standing as objects apart from the landscape. The roof of the central bathhouse–storage structure has flat solar collectors and vent pipes at the roof ridge. Nearby, a two-level bath structure, standing at the edge of the treeline, disturbs the sweeping vista of the surrounding basin. In the center of the compound, the masonry chimney and weathered cast-iron fire-box and door add a rustic charm.

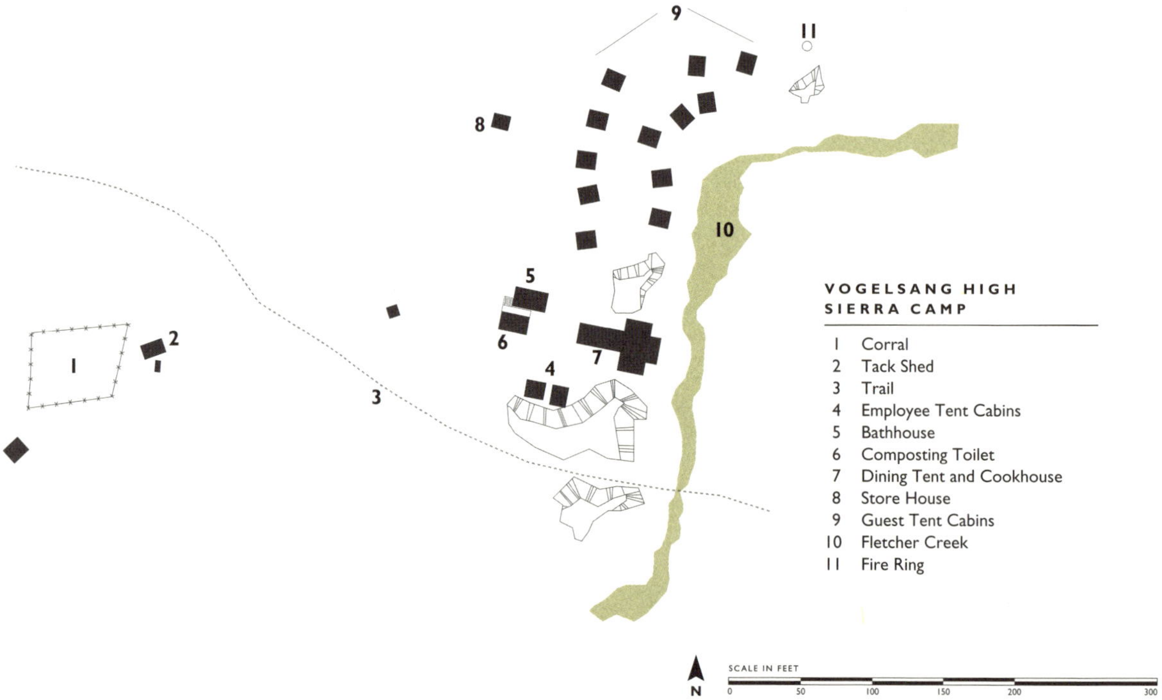

TOP LEFT *Kitchen, dining tent, tent cabins, Vogelsang High Sierra Camp (2007) RF* TOP RIGHT *Dining tent, Vogelsang High Sierra Camp (2004) RF* BOTTOM *Kitchen and showerhouse, Vogelsang High Sierra Camp (2007) RF*

## Merced Lake High Sierra Camp

Backed up against a massive north-facing slope, the Merced Lake High Sierra Camp (1916) is the most remote in the High Sierra Camp loop, being the farthest in distance from the nearest road. A strenuous 12.9 miles from Tenaya Lake and 13 miles from Happy Isles, it is accessed only by foot or on horseback. Set back from the lake but adjacent to the river, Merced Lake Camp offers 19 tent cabins arranged in three rows, defining a large central rectangular meadow with neat, cobble-lined pathways. At 7,200 feet, the lake and dense surrounding mixed-conifer forest form a more serene and placid environment than is associated with the harsh climatic conditions of the higher camps. The cookhouse, dining room, baths, and storerooms, along with the log cabin, corral, and barn, suggest a ranchlike setting.

*Merced Lake High Sierra Camp (date unknown) HJ*

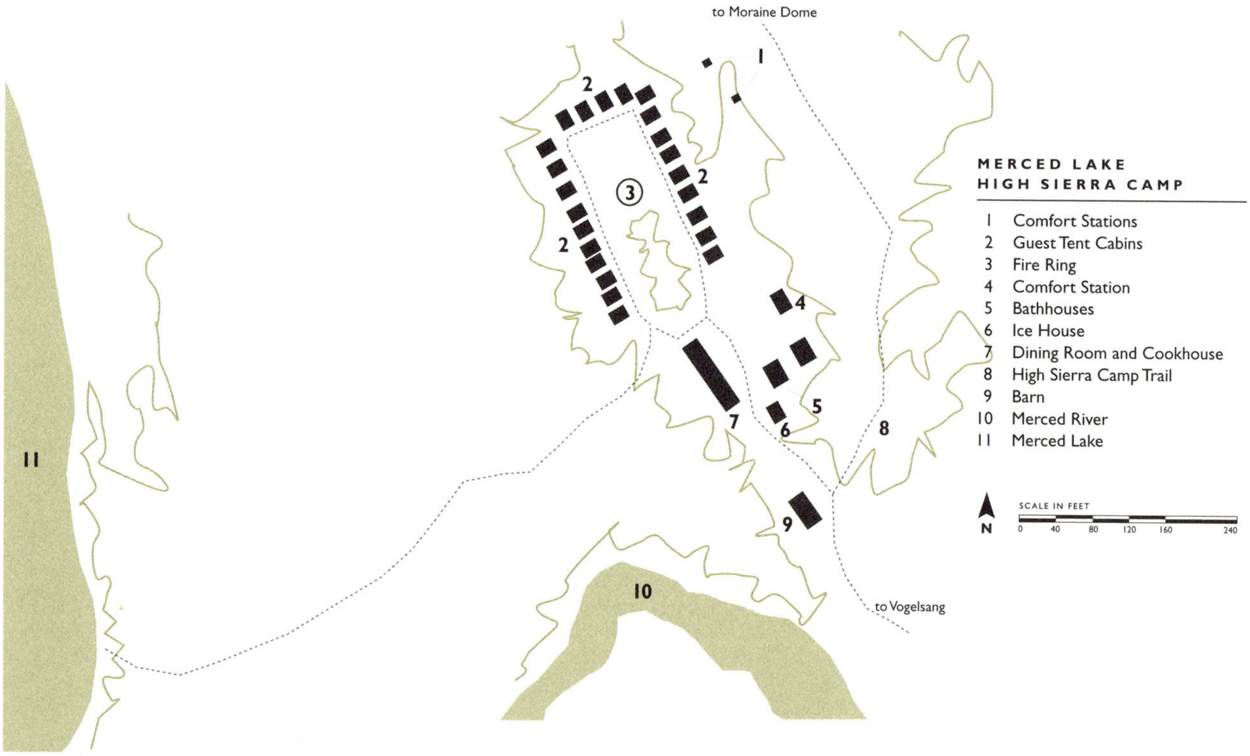

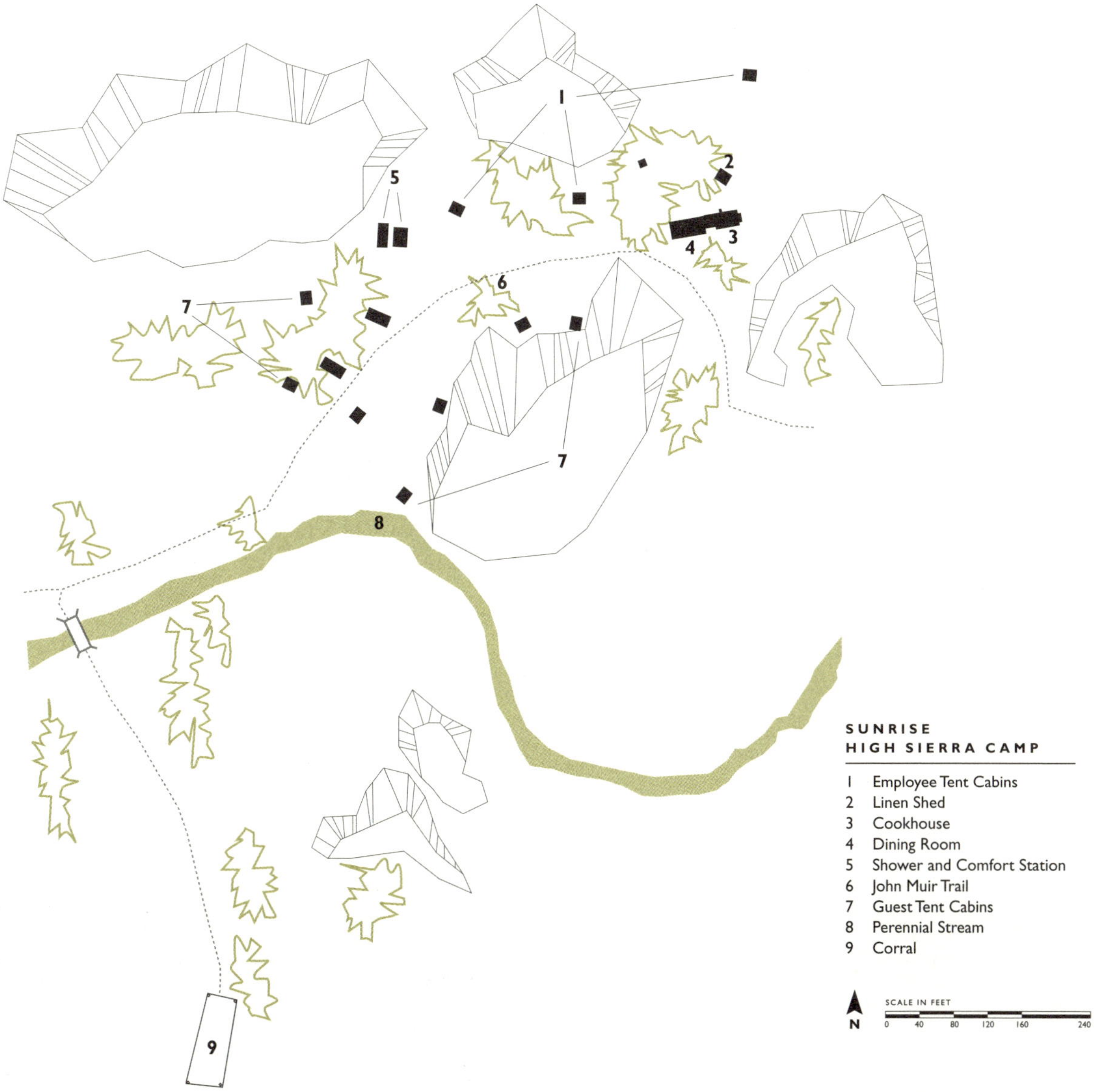


## Sunrise High Sierra Camp

Sunrise High Sierra Camp (1961) is near the southern end of Long Meadow at an elevation of 9,400 feet. It sits in a zone of sparse subalpine vegetation just west of the John Muir Trail. With only a dozen tent cabins, it is among the smallest of the High Sierra Camps, along with May Lake and Glen Aulin. A stonemasonry building houses the kitchen and pantry functions. Dining takes place in a canvas tent. The building and the tent platforms are tucked in an irregular pattern among conifers and boulders that surround most of the camp. This was a favorite place of Mary Curry Tresidder. "The Sunrise Camp," she wrote, "was a long time dream of mine, as I felt that the Sunrise Trail ran through such a beautiful region that it should be made more accessible to people" (Sargent 1997). A plaque, embedded in granite, explains Tresidder's role in the camp's founding.

*Sunrise High Sierra Camp (date unknown). From Sargent,* Yosemite and Its Innkeepers

## May Lake High Sierra Camp

One of the smaller camps, May Lake High Sierra Camp (1938) is located a short distance north of the end of May Lake service road at an elevation of 9,300 feet. Because it is only 1.3 miles from the trailhead, it is easily accessible to dayhikers. The flanks of Mount Hoffman (elevation 10,850) loom directly to the west of the camp—an added draw for dayhikers. May Lake's tent cabins are scattered in an irregular pattern in an open, subalpine, lodgepole pine forest between the east shore of the lake and the trail connecting Glen Aulin with Yosemite Valley. Several of the tent cabins are located on the lake's sloping shore, a short distance from the water. The stonemasonry cookhouse and tent dining structure are at the south end of the cluster. A corral is located nearby along the trail to the south.

**MAY LAKE HIGH SIERRA CAMP**

1 Employee Tent Cabins
2 Guest Tent Cabins
3 Bathhouse
4 Dry Storage
5 Stone Cookhouse
6 Dining Room
7 Fire Ring
8 May Lake
9 High Sierra Camp Trail
10 Corral

N — SCALE IN FEET 0 40 80 120 160 240

TOP *May Lake and Mount Hoffman (2008) RF* CENTER *Dining room tent, May Lake High Sierra Camp (2008) RF* BOTTOM *View of May Lake from dining room (2008) RF*

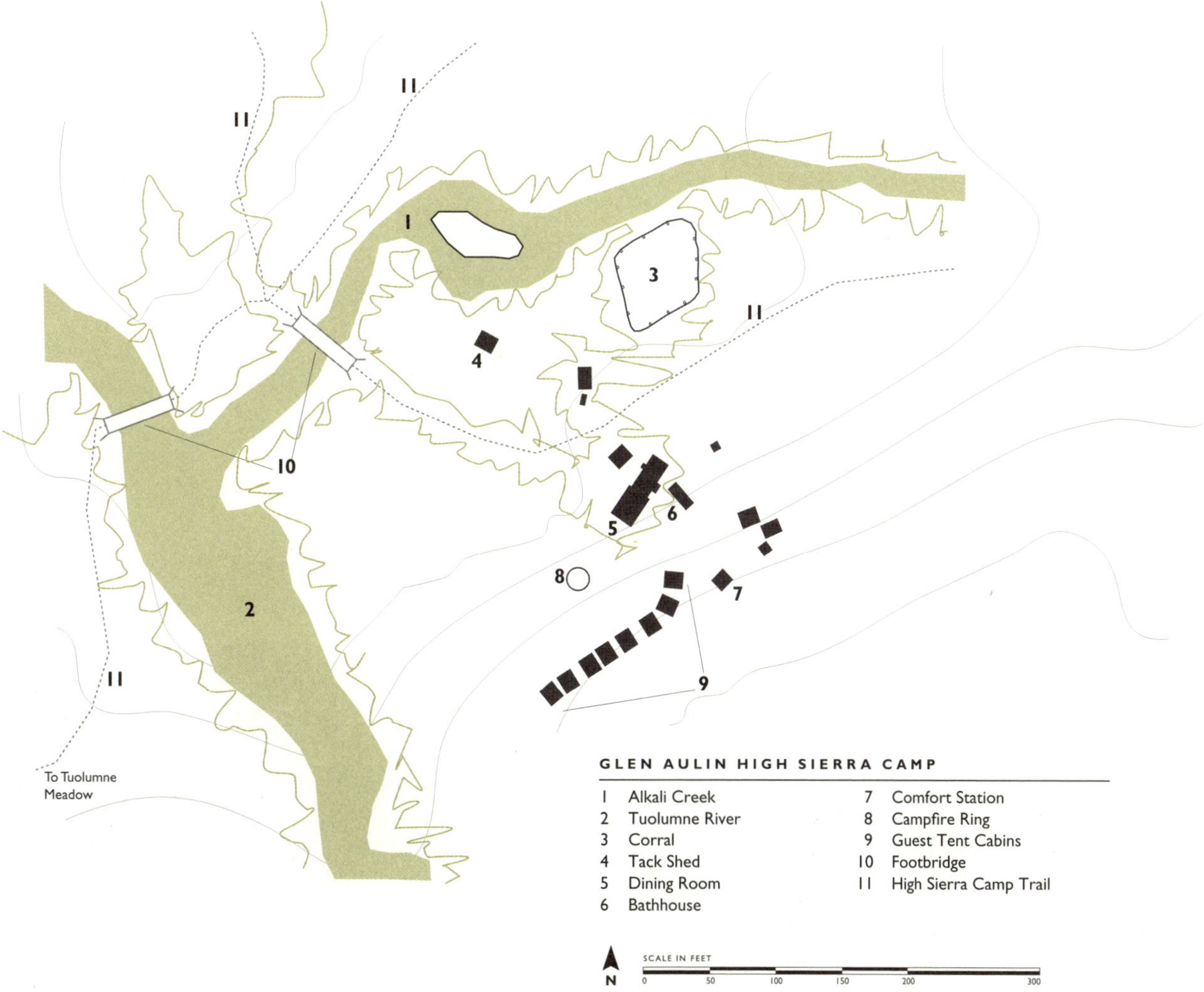


## Glen Aulin High Sierra Camp

Sited along the banks of the Tuolumne River at the confluence of Alkali Creek, Glen Aulin High Sierra Camp (1927) is at an elevation of 7,800 feet. The camp is immediately adjacent to the base of the spectacular White Cascade on the Tuolumne River. It can be reached relatively easily by foot and by pack train from Tuolumne Meadows. Tent cabins, bathhouse, and dining room are all neatly aligned in an arc, facing southwest and focused on the juncture of Alkali Creek with the Tuolumne River. A corral is sited on a gentle slope a short distance from Conness Creek. Despite heavy traffic on the Glen Aulin and Pacific Crest trails, the rushing water, massive granite slopes, bald sunny

*Guest tent cabins, Glen Aulin High Sierra Camp (2004) RF*

shoulders, and ridges interspersed with dark, forested ravines make a stay at this camp a special backcountry experience, both visually and audibly. Glen Aulin also provides access to a series of cascades and falls along the Tuolumne River, including the famous Waterwheel Falls.

**GUIDELINES**

- For new development at Glen Aulin High Sierra Camp, designers should consult *The Secretary of the Interior's Standards for the Treatment of Historic Properties* for guidance to ensure compatibility.
- Glen Aulin High Sierra Camp falls within the boundaries of the Tuolumne Wild and Scenic River corridor. Buildings, structures, use policies, preservation/restoration of historic vistas, vegetation, and trails will be governed by the Tuolumne Wild and Scenic River Comprehensive Management Plan.
- If the replacement of historic structures is necessary, maintain their distribution pattern and relation to the open space at the junction of the creek and river.
- Refer to "General Guidelines for High Sierra Camps" in this chapter.

TOP *White Cascades on the Tuolumne River at Glen Aulin High Sierra Camp (date unknown) YRL* BOTTOM *Glen Aulin High Sierra Camp (2004) RF*

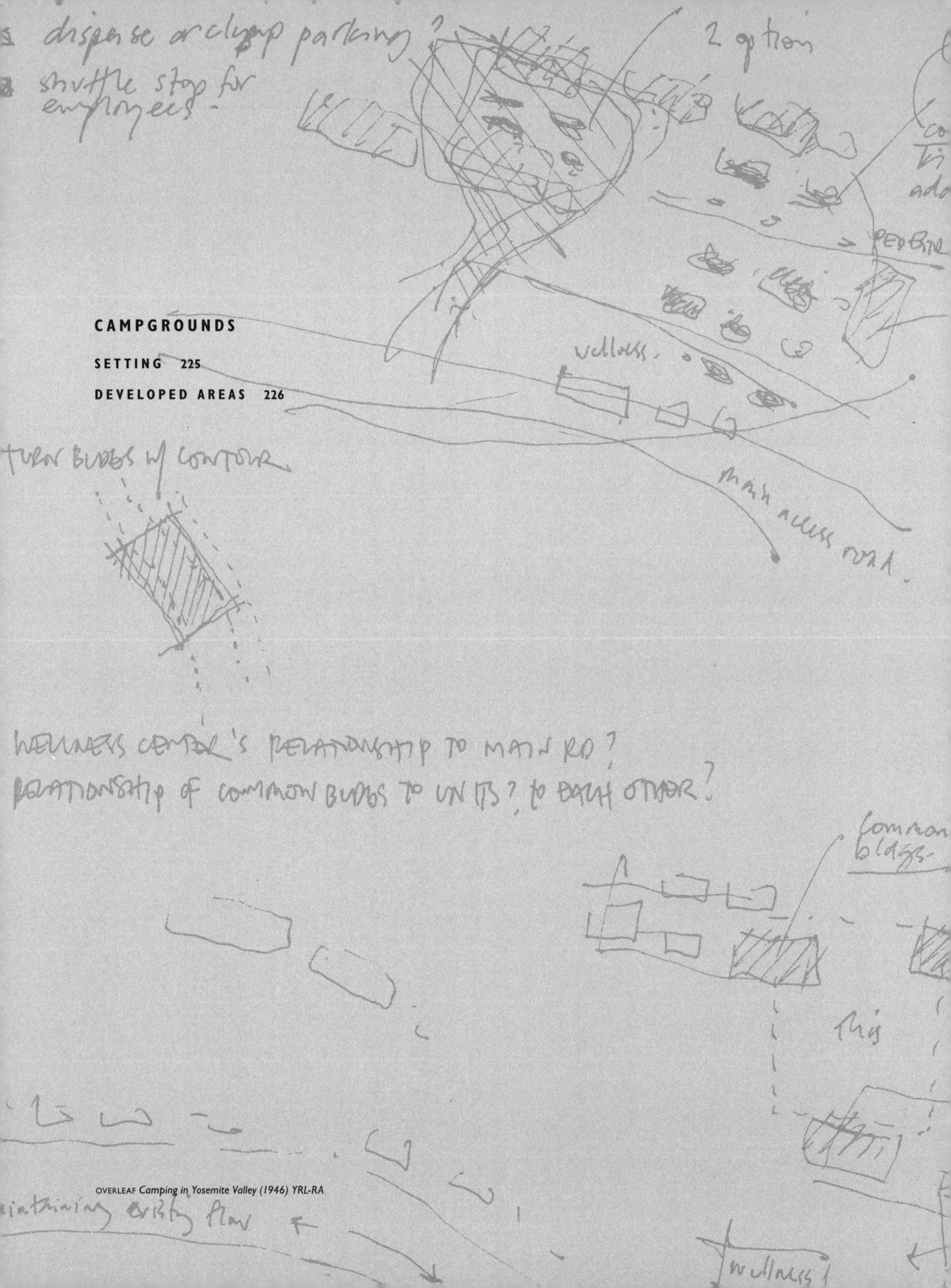


# CAMPGROUNDS



OVERLEAF *Camping in Yosemite Valley (1946) YRL-RA*

# CAMPGROUNDS

YOSEMITE CAMPGROUNDS PROVIDE visitors with opportunities for a more rustic outdoor experience than other types of lodging. These relatively less-expensive accommodations are generally located in quiet, forested settings, and some are close to rivers or streams. Campsites in the park are among the most popular in the entire national park system, with reservations for sites filling up months in advance for the warmer season. Many families return year after year to the same campground, perpetuating a cherished tradition. The enactment of typical camping activities produces

(IT WAS) BULLY! I'VE HAD THE TIME OF MY LIFE...JUST THINK OF WHERE I WAS LAST NIGHT. UP THERE AMID THE PINES AND SILVER FIRS, IN THE SIERRAN SOLITUDE, AND WITHOUT A TENT, I PASSED ONE OF THE MOST PLEASANT NIGHTS OF MY LIFE. **THEODORE ROOSEVELT ON HIS EXPERIENCE IN YOSEMITE WITH JOHN MUIR • 1903**

fond memories such as learning how to start a wood fire, cooking a meal outdoors, swimming or wading in the nearby river, toasting marshmallows and telling stories over the campfire, making new friends with campground neighbors, attending an evening campfire program, and stargazing.

Campsite types can vary from simple walk-in sites for tents to larger, pull-through sites that accommodate long recreational vehicles. Campsite occupants represent a range of users and might include backpackers sleeping for one night before the start of a long hike, rock climbers using the site

*Tuolumne Meadows Campground (2008) GH*

as a base camp for daily climbs, or an extended family in a trailer or motorhome staying in one site for an entire week to relax and enjoy a leisurely respite in Yosemite.

Vehicle traffic, parking, and heavy pedestrian use in camp areas have resulted in a notable loss of grass and shrubs and a ground plane barren of duff, branches, and twigs. Parking is allowed at most individual campsites, which means that vehicles—both small and large, and many with trailers—have access over unpaved ground.

Yosemite's standard for closely spaced campsites was initiated in the 1920s, when planners for Tuolumne Meadows decided to concentrate impacts rather than allow them to spread over a wider, less manageable area (NPS 2007f). Nevertheless, in the early 1930s, as the overall condition of camping areas in public forests and parks had deteriorated because of overuse, the National Park Service hired the eminent plant pathologist Emilio P. Meinecke, who had advised on many problems in Yosemite and other national parks. He formulated a theory of camp planning and reconstruction that has continued to influence the design of picnic areas, campgrounds, and waysides in national parks, state parks, and forests (McClelland 1997). Among the ideas he recommended were "revolutionary changes" such as the selection of new campsite locations based on soil type, length of seasonal use, type of vegetation, and type of camper. One of his important innovations was the "garage spur," an open space for vehicle parking adjacent to the campsite, cleared of vegetation and marked by heavy rocks or posts. Neutral zones provided privacy between campsites and protected the sites from road dust and noise (McClelland 1997). He recommended a

*Lower Pines Campground (2004) RF*

*Wawona Campground, South Fork of the Merced River (2010) RF*

system of campsite rotation whereby new grounds were opened and older ones closed until affected vegetation could recover by natural processes or planting. He also assumed that proper campground design involved an intensive knowledge of the area to be developed as well as detailed planning, pointing out that "no two camping areas are alike. Each has to be planned and arranged on its own merits" (McClelland 1997). Meinecke's ideas and recommendations completely changed camping in the national parks and influenced the design of the many campgrounds built by the Civilian Conservation Corps in the 1930s.

Several building types support visitor functions in campgrounds. These include entrance kiosks, comfort stations, shower houses, and sheds for storage, lockers, vending, and other uses. Site elements include a vehicle access road, parking areas, pathways, individual campsites, and site equipment such as picnic tables, bear-proof food lockers, fire pits, grills, and trash receptacles.

## SETTING

Campgrounds in Yosemite Valley provide the basic level of overnight accommodation for visitors. These campgrounds are also convenient to scenic landmarks and are linked by shuttle bus and walkways to day-use destinations and visitor services. Sites include Lower Pines, Upper Pines, and North Pines and its adjacent Backpackers Campground. Camp 4 is treated separately in this chapter.

In Yosemite Valley, the Upper, Lower, and North Pines campgrounds all lie on the flat, forested Valley floor north of Curry Village and Glacier Point. Although there are views of some surrounding walls and peaks from Upper Pines (e.g., to Half Dome), those from other campgrounds (many of them documented in the past by artists and photographers) may be limited or obscured by forest vegetation. Portions of Lower and North Pines are within the Merced River's 100-year flood zone, and some parts of Upper and Lower Pines were inundated by flood waters in

*Wawona Campground (2008) GH*

1997. Local views to the Merced River from sections of the Lower and North Pines campgrounds are very attractive, drawing significant numbers of campers to the water's edge. This has resulted in the damage or elimination of substantial reaches of riparian vegetation.

Camp 4 is a historic site listed on the National Register of Historic Places for its significant association with the growth of rock climbing in Yosemite Valley during the golden years of pioneer mountaineering, (1947–1970). Campgrounds and base camps at important climbing locations provide more than just the provision of overnight accommodation. They serve as a vital meeting ground for climbers to train, plan ascents, and share information and equipment. Camp 4 provides a place where the camaraderie and sense of community that defined the early days and history of the mountaineering movement carries on into the present (NPS 2001a).

Camp 4 is located at the base of a talus slope on the sunny north side of Yosemite Valley near Yosemite Falls. Located at the base of Eagle Peak, the site lies on young colluvium between the vertical cliffs to the north and Northside Drive to the south.

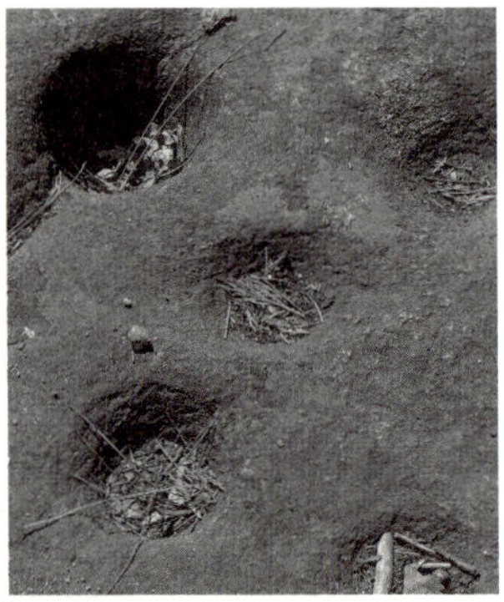

Bedrock milling feature at a campground (2008) DV

Because of thin soils, Camp 4 is only sparsely vegetated, and many trees are stunted compared to those on the rest of the Valley floor. To the south, one looks out toward a thin cover of scattered pines and cedars, with some black oak. Prominent natural features on-site include large talus boulders and significant seasonal drainages currently denuded of riparian vegetation. Views across the Valley to Sentinel Rock provide a connection to the majesty of the Valley walls.

As a walk-in campground, Camp 4 is different from vehicle-accessed sites. Camp 4 campsites have an austere, natural setting, and the parking area has visual impact when viewed from Northside Drive, Camp 4, and other visitor-use areas such as the Valley Loop Trail.

Within and at the north edge of Camp 4, large scattered talus blocks and boulders—providing ready access for climbers—are evidence of the rockfall hazard. Some of these blocks are associated with the historic significance of the site, because they were named and used for "bouldering" during the growth of the sport of climbing in the United States. These natural features have an integral relationship with the site and with the climbing community.

Outside Yosemite Valley there are more than 1,000 individual campsites distributed throughout the park in 10 variously sized campgrounds. Most are within a short distance of one of the park's main roads and are accessible by vehicle or shuttle bus. These campsites are a mix of vehicle-accessed and walk-in sites. The largest campgrounds are at Tuolumne Meadows (304 sites), Crane Flat (166 sites), Bridalveil Creek (110 sites), Hodgdon Meadow (105 sites), and Wawona (93 sites). The campsites are at widely varying elevations. The lowest is Wawona (4,000 feet), which sits in a mixture of riverbank riparian and sparse coniferous vegetation. The highest is Tuolumne Meadows (8,600 feet), set within a subalpine lodgepole forest at the edge of the meadow. The smallest is the Backpackers' Campground (19 sites), overlooking the Hetch Hetchy Reservoir, the O'Shaughnessy Dam, and the pines and oaks of the rugged Tuolumne River Canyon. Tamarack Flat, White Wolf, Yosemite Creek, and Porcupine Flat campgrounds range from 52 to more than 80 campsites.

## Developed Areas

Small buildings and support structures collectively define the architectural character of a campground. Entrance kiosks, comfort stations, shelters, and other structures can share a set of typical features and details, presenting a consistent character. They are traditionally designed to blend with their surroundings and embody a rustic character.

The entrance kiosk is the first building a visitor sees upon entering a campground. It serves as a symbolic marker, welcoming the visitor. The kiosk also serves as a contact point for guests by providing camping and park information.

Several comfort stations were constructed in campgrounds in Yosemite during the 1920s and 1930s. These are simple, rustic, wood-frame buildings with shake-covered gable roofs. In the Valley these comfort stations are the only campground structures that contribute to the Yosemite Valley Historic District (NPS 2004i).

Albert Good's *Park and Recreation Structures* provides relevant historical examples of small buildings such as shelters, as well as landscape structures such as picnic tables, that may serve as references for campground design (Good 1938). It is recommended that new construction has a contemporary character that makes use of NPS Rustic design principles.

The relationship of campground elements to the natural setting is a primary factor in establishing a sense of place. Special care must be taken when organizing the various elements: entrance road, entrance kiosk, parking, access roads, campsites, pathways, and common facilities. Small buildings, such as entrance kiosks, comfort stations, shower houses, shelters, vending machine structures, and storage sheds, should be rustic in character. Individual campsites should be arranged to provide for both privacy and views where possible.

In many Yosemite campgrounds, heavy use has eliminated all but a few fragments of shrub and ground-cover vegetation. Considerable damage to bankside riparian vegetation has occurred as well. There is virtually no screening vegetation between campsites in many of Yosemite's campgrounds. In some campgrounds, pedestrian zones and pathways are largely indistinguishable from vehicle circulation routes.

Desirable conditions within and surrounding the campgrounds include: the design and siting of human-made features so that natural sounds, vegetation, and scenery predominate; a hierarchy of roads and trails that is easily understood by users and distinguishes those areas where the public is allowed to drive and park; the concentration of uses within well-delineated campsites and pedestrian paths; and visual separation between campsites, provided by natural vegetation, topography, boulders, etc.

**GUIDELINES**

### *Siting and Building Orientation*

- Locate and orient buildings, gathering spaces, and interpretive points to benefit from views of the park's natural features.
- Service/storage facilities, trash bins, and telephone booths should be consolidated and located in screened areas adjacent to other structures or in integral small buildings such as bathhouses and comfort stations. Refer to "Landscape Uses + Structures—Small Buildings" in the "Unifying Elements" chapter.
- At walk-in campgrounds, take advantage of site topography and existing vegetation to provide a natural screen from parking areas. If additional screening is necessary, plant native vegetation in such a way that plantings blend into the surroundings and their overall appearance does not appear designed.

*Tuolumne Meadows Campground sign (2008) GH*

*Wawona Campground sign (2008) GH*

### Comfort Stations

- Campground comfort stations should be designed to be rustic in appearance.
- Use NPS Rustic-era comfort stations, located throughout Yosemite's campgrounds, as inspiration for layout, design, and character. The Yosemite Falls comfort station is a good contemporary example, designed with a rusticated base and side walls of board and batten.
- Roof coverings for new comfort stations should be noncombustible.
- Design of new structures should ensure that long-term maintenance needs are addressed, such as the use of a plumbing chase and space for storage of equipment and supplies.

### Cooking Shelters

- Cooking shelters should be open, rectangular, timber structures, with log columns, roof framing members of saw-sized lumber, and low masonry walls.
- Light fixtures should be shielded with a sharp cut-off to confine the light within the structure. Electrical conduit should be concealed in the roof assembly to the extent possible. Refer to "Landscape Uses + Structures—Lighting" in the "Unifying Elements" chapter.
- Fireplaces should be constructed with masonry facing. Grill and sink areas should have concrete countertops with masonry sidewalls. The shelter floor should be concrete. Concrete colorants should be used to ensure that the flooring blends with the natural surroundings.

*Lyell Fork of the Tuolumne River near Tuolumne Meadows Campground (2008) GH*

### Picnic Tables

- Use stoutly constructed, timber picnic tables that can withstand snow loads and are in keeping with classic NPS Rustic style.

### Vegetation

- Refer to "Landscape Uses + Structures—Circulation," "Setting—Vegetation," and "Landscape Uses + Structures—Barriers, Fences + Benches" in the "Unifying Elements" chapter.

### Campsites

- Campsites should be located on sites sloping less than 10%, or where vegetation and soil conditions plus foot traffic will not lead to erosion and permanent vegetation loss.
- Campsites near creeks, rivers, or other bodies of water need to include design setbacks based on potential water-quality impacts. Bioswales and/or oil/water separators may be needed to collect and filter runoff from roads, spurs, and other developed areas.
- Campsite design should take advantage of natural topography and other features, such as vegetation, to screen campsites from one another. If screening is needed, consider using vegetation to ensure privacy and visually buffer large RVs and trailers from adjacent campsites. Vegetation should be planted, maintained, or restored as necessary to provide adequate screening. When possible, campgrounds should be screened from roads and trails.
- Define edges of individual campsites with natural materials such as logs and granite boulders. A clear definition of use areas helps to reduce uncontrolled expansion of the site, reduces soil impacts, and encourages growth of screening vegetation, providing a greater sense of privacy between campsites.
- Use of materials like native vegetation and granite boulders should integrate with the surrounding natural patterns.

TOP *Detail, comfort station, Tuolumne Meadows Campground (2008) GH*
BOTTOM *U.S. Calvary Camp A.E. Wood, which became Wawona Campground (ca. late 1800s) YRL*

LEFT *Typical campsite at Tuolumne Meadows Campground (2008) GH* RIGHT *Typical firepit with grill, Yosemite Creek Campground (2010) GS*

- Tent pads should be designed to blend with the natural environment in texture and color.
- New campgrounds should be located on previously impacted areas whenever possible.
- Establishment of walk-in and/or "tent only" camping areas, separate from RV and car camping areas, is appropriate for a more rustic camping experience (in lieu of all mixed-use camping).
- Bear boxes should be accessible but sited to not dominate natural settings, and should be kept out of identified view corridors or vistas. Refer to "Landscape Uses + Structures—Small Buildings" in the "Unifying Elements" chapter.

## Campground Roads

- New roads in campgrounds (both primary and secondary) should have widths, crowns, and paving similar to historic campground roads while allowing for large vehicles (such as RVs) and two-way circulation (designed for low-speed travel) where appropriate. See NPS Park Road Standards (1984) for guidance.
- New roads should have a curvilinear alignment designed to lay lightly upon the topography, and should avoid crossing unstable or steep slopes.
- Where the control of parking along roads is needed, define the road shoulder edge using natural features such as partially buried granite boulders or logs to discourage parking.

## DAY-USE AREAS



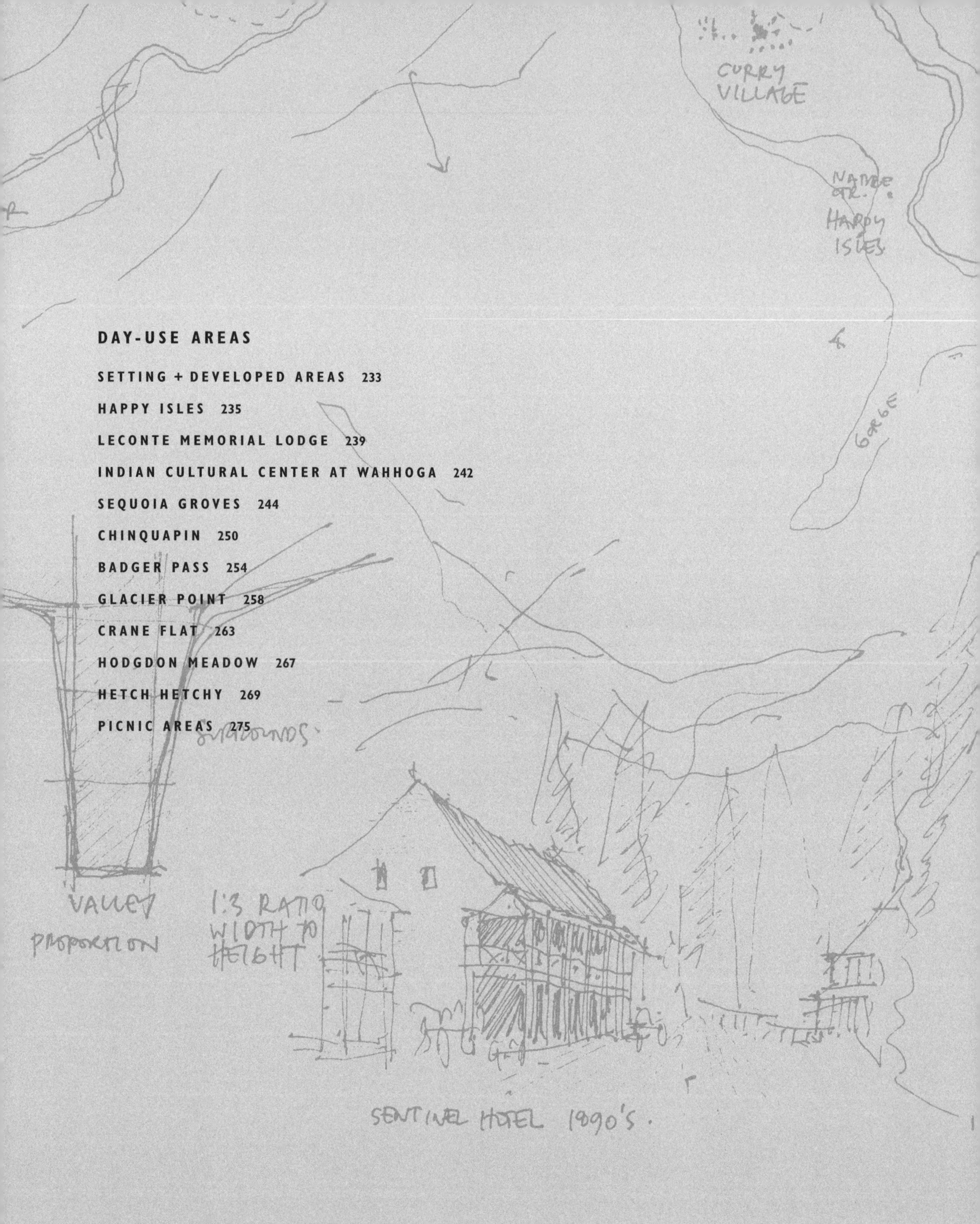


OVERLEAF *Mariposa Grove Museum and giant sequoias (2011) RF*

# DAY-USE AREAS

DAY-USE AREAS SERVE the largest numbers of visitors to Yosemite. During peak visitation, the majority (approximately two-thirds) of visitors to Yosemite National Park are day users, compared to the approximately one-third of visitors staying overnight. These visitors spend the day hiking, sightseeing, picnicking, swimming, skiing, and auto-touring—arriving in the morning and leaving in the evening. Large numbers of these visitors make their way to several popular day-use destinations.

Day use occurs in a variety of places such as scenic viewpoints, picnic areas, beaches, sequoia groves, and trailheads. These areas support short-term or occasional-visitor use with small buildings and landscape structures such as picnic tables, benches, trails, boardwalks, or interpretive wayside exhibits.

TALK OF IMMORTALITY AFTER A WHOLE DAY IN THE WOODS, WE ARE ALREADY IMMORTAL. WHEN IS THE END OF SUCH A DAY? **JOHN MUIR • 1875**

The following is a list of day-use areas addressed in this chapter:

- Badger Pass
- Chinquapin
- Crane Flat
- Glacier Point
- Happy Isles
- Hetch Hetchy
- Hodgdon Meadow
- Indian Cultural Center at Wahhoga
- LeConte Memorial Lodge
- The Mariposa, Tuolumne, and Merced Groves of Giant Sequoias
- Picnic Areas

## SETTING + DEVELOPED AREAS

Day-use areas are typically located in or near a natural setting such as a meadow, riverbank, or scenic view where visitors are tempted to explore the immediate surroundings. This can have an impact on vegetation and other natural elements where pathways are not provided. In many locations, some form of barrier is needed to define or limit the extent of the pathways and activity spaces within the day-use area.

Because day-use areas are often at the edge of undeveloped areas, it is particularly important that human-made structures blend with the landscape. This can be achieved through sensitive site design and by minimizing interventions. Overall consistency of character is also desirable.

Many day-use areas provide parking. These parking areas are adjacent to main roads and are therefore highly visible. In some cases, the parking area is immediately adjacent to the point of interest, creating a distraction with its expanse of paving and road noise. In others, a pathway leads to a more remote location and may help establish character for a site.

Facilities such as picnic areas often offer visitors an opportunity to enjoy scenic vistas. The specific character of the day-use site and the accommodations provided affect the visitor's decision to stop and use the site. Some visitors seek picnic sites with conveniently located restrooms and tables, while others prefer a quiet retreat in natural surroundings.

Many day-use areas in Yosemite Valley—including picnic areas at Sentinel and Cathedral beaches—are on the flat Valley floor, well within the 100-year floodplain. Often dominated by conifers, these sites are close to meadows that provide views of the Valley walls and waterfalls. Other areas—including the base of Lower Yosemite Fall or trailheads leading to the high country—sit at the edges of the Valley floor, at the toe of rockslides or stream depositions. Many of these are within the talus and shadow lines. Large boulders, talus blocks, and adjacent Valley walls provide evidence of the dynamic geologic processes at work in Yosemite Valley. The vegetation mosaic is patchier in these areas.

*Vernal Fall*

*Yosemite Valley Chapel*

At the Lower Yosemite Fall day-use area, great care was taken to design a natural visitor experience around features such as the waterfall, large boulders, trees, and drainages. The area was designed to separate pedestrians from vehicle traffic, disperse visitors throughout the site, and provide adequate viewing space at popular areas. Special attention was paid to wayfinding, interpretive displays, and seating areas.

The character and settings of day-use areas outside the Valley vary considerably from site to site, reflecting wide-ranging differences in elevation, forest type, and topography. Varied experiences include picnicking on Tenaya Lake's broad, sandy beaches, hiking through the cool shelter of sequoia groves, or experiencing breathtaking views of Half Dome and Yosemite Valley from Glacier Point.

### GENERAL GUIDELINES

- Design should ensure minimal impacts to the natural setting to the fullest extent possible.
- Use consistent, rustic-style elements throughout the park's day-use areas to minimize visual impacts and unify character.
- Refer to the "Unifying Elements" chapter for guidelines on vegetation, circulation, parking, views, entrance markers, small buildings, bridges, culvert crossings, boardwalks, retaining walls, grading and drainage, benches, fences and screens, barriers, pathways, and lighting.

## HAPPY ISLES

Happy Isles is southeast of Curry Village on a braided and dynamic portion of the Merced River in an ecologically diverse community. The Nature Center at Happy Isles is a kid-friendly facility that features natural history exhibits with an emphasis on wildlife, interactive displays, and a bookstore. Nearby are short trails focusing on the area's four different environments: forest, river, talus, and fen. There is also substantial evidence of the July 1996 rockfall from the Glacier Point cliff far above the Nature Center. This catastrophic rockfall caused a great air-blast that leveled hundreds of trees and damaged buildings.

*Merced River at Happy Isles, Yosemite Valley (2004) GH*

I HAVE NAMED THEM HAPPY ISLES FOR NO ONE CAN VISIT THEM WITHOUT FOR A WHILE FORGETTING THE GRINDING STRIFE OF HIS WORLD AND BEING HAPPY.

**WALTER DENNISON, GUARDIAN OF YOSEMITE • OCTOBER 1885**

A power station was built by the state of California in 1902 in the Happy Isles area. It was removed in 1919, the same year that the California Fish and Game Commission installed a fish hatchery. A permanent hatchery building and two residences were subsequently built in 1927. The new hatchery made an important connection with the educational work carried out by the National Park Service. At that time, the park instituted nature-guide, or interpretive, services at Happy Isles.

The hatchery building, built of local rock and heavy timber, contained dozens of troughs for hatching and rearing trout. A smaller room held four 250-gallon aquariums. The structure also held displays explaining the fishery program in Yosemite.

In 1956 the state abandoned the hatchery and ceded the facilities to the National Park Service. The fish hatchery was converted to the Nature Center at Happy Isles in 1957. While the building's use changed substantially, its appearance did not, as renovations to the structure were primarily to the interior.

The Nature Center at Happy Isles is a contributing building within the Yosemite Valley Historic District.

## Setting

Distinct from the Valley floor, Happy Isles is sited in a narrow, geologically and hydrologically active area. Here the turbulent Merced River, joined by waters from Illilouette Creek, enters the flat Valley floor. It descends noisily and rapidly on a sloping plane from the south, bringing rock and sand debris and creating deposition areas such as the south and north islands—the Happy Isles.

Happy Isles provides one of the best opportunities to observe the dynamic geology of Yosemite Valley. Stream deposition provides evidence of periodic flash flooding in the area. Downed trees and scree resulted from the catastrophic rockfall in 1996. The air blast from the rockfall flattened 11 acres of forest in its path. The damaged forest, the light-colored scar on the nearby granite wall, and the scree cone at its base are evidence of the power of the event. The concrete footbridge at Happy Isles was damaged by the 1997 flood and was subsequently removed.

The fen, a unique wetland just west of the Nature Center (fed by high groundwater from the river), is part of the setting. Pines and cedar dominate the forest area not damaged by the rockslide. Riparian communities exist along the braided channels of the river.

There are three pedestrian routes from the shuttle bus stop to the Nature Center: a service road, the primary trail, and a paved but deteriorating asphalt trail parallel to the river. A variety of paving treatments are used, including asphalt, packed decomposed granite, and a boardwalk through the fen. The Happy Isles Bridge (the road bridge, not to be confused with the former footbridge mentioned above) is a historic structure.

Happy Isles contains one of the park's major trailheads in Yosemite Valley: the famous 211-mile John Muir Trail begins here. Visitors embark from here, both for short day hikes to Vernal and Nevada falls and for longer treks to Half Dome, Merced Lake High Sierra Camp, and other destinations in the park's extensive wilderness.

## Developed Areas

The natural landscape is the primary character-defining element at Happy Isles. Structures are disbursed around the site and include the 1927 Nature Center, a comfort station, a small snack stand, a shuttle bus stop shelter, and a system of pedestrian bridges providing access to islands set in the rushing river. A historic stream-flow gauging station sits on the opposite side of the river from the Nature Center. It is the oldest continuously operating U.S. Geological Survey station in the western United States.

Trails and walkways run parallel to the river from the shuttle bus stop to the Nature Center. At the end of

*Historic stream gauging station and bridge abutment, Happy Isles (2004) JM*

**HAPPY ISLES**

1 Fen
2 Nature Center
3 Blast Zone
4 South Island
5 Mist Trail
6 John Muir Trail
7 Historic Stream Gauging Station
8 Merced River
9 Happy Isles Bridge
10 Shuttle Bus Stop
11 Restrooms
12 North Island

a pathway lies the Nature Center, close to the riverbank and set against the backdrop of a narrowing canyon.

The former fish hatchery, with its high ceiling and masonry walls, provides good adaptable space for the exhibition and education functions of the Nature Center. The exterior of the building, with a 12:12 roof slope, clipped eaves, and rake, is starker in appearance than the rustic character of nearby buildings. However, the log entry porches give some contrast to this severity. Here, the use of local rock for walls, the warm color of the shingle roof, nearby tree massing, and the dynamic Merced River all contribute to the success of this facility.

**GUIDELINES**

- New designs should be compatible with the architectural character of the historic Nature Center. Scale and massing of any new structures should be subservient to the Nature Center. Refer to *The Secretary of the Interior's Standards for the Treatment of Historic Properties* for guidance to ensure compatibility.
- The layout and design of all structures (buildings, bridges, kiosks, pedestrian routes, etc.) need to recognize the location and the structural implications of building in this narrow, geologically active, flood-prone canyon.

TOP LEFT *Happy Isles Nature Center (2004) GH* TOP RIGHT *Evidence of 1996 rockslide at Happy Isles (2004) GH* BOTTOM *Happy Isles Nature Center (2004) GH*

*Traditional wood sign for the John Muir Trailhead, Happy Isles (2004) RF*

- Trails and walkways should be sufficiently spread-out, screened, and aligned to sustain the sense of isolation and maintain the visitor's connection to the landscape.
- Pathway paving should reflect the strong backcountry character of this area, making use of compacted, stabilized, decomposed granite paving where feasible and integrated sand-topped asphalt paving where necessary. Use boardwalk construction within the fen to minimize impacts to natural hydrology.
- Because of the backcountry character, lighting should be limited to the shuttle stop and the comfort station.
- New buildings and structures should be designed in a way that helps to sustain the sense of isolation at Happy Isles.
- Refer to the "Unifying Elements" chapter for guidelines on vegetation, entrance markers, small buildings, bridges, culvert crossings, boardwalks, retaining walls, grading and drainage, benches, fences and screens, barriers, and lighting.

## LeConte Memorial Lodge

LeConte Memorial Lodge was built in 1903 in memory of Joseph LeConte, co-founder of the Sierra Club, original member of the University of California faculty, and noted geologist. The lodge also served as a historical and scientific museum. Today, LeConte Memorial Lodge, the oldest of the Sierra Club lodges, is open to the general public, which finds in its quiet atmosphere a small mountaineering library, historic and educational collections of pictures, and a source of information on conservation, the national parks, and the High Sierra. At one point in time, LeConte Memorial Lodge was the northern terminus of the John Muir Trail (Gill 1967).

The Sierra Club originally constructed the building at the base of Glacier Point, adjacent to Camp Curry. About 15 years later, Mary Curry moved the structure, at her own expense, so that she could expand her camp operation. Gutleben Brothers Construction Company, hired to move the building, dismantled the roof and as much of the original stonework as they could. The lodge was rebuilt according to the original plans on a new site a short distance west of its original location. The building reopened in 1919.

In 1987 the LeConte Memorial Lodge was designated a National Historic Landmark. The lodge is "a unique building for a national park. It is a transitional structure of strong European roots combined with the revolutionary way that Bay Area environmental designers used building materials" (NPS 1985).

*LeConte Memorial Lodge (2004) GH*

## Setting

LeConte Memorial Lodge is located on the cooler, forested side of Yosemite Valley, within the shadow line of the steep southern cliffs. The lodge is directly south of Housekeeping Camp, across Southside Drive. At the northern edge of the talus line and surrounded by large, dispersed boulders, the stone building fits well into the sloping terrain. The scale and spacing of trees, allowing for dappled sunlight, and the lack of substantial understory give the setting the sense of a managed, parklike estate. The building's generous distance from Southside Drive and the multiuse path also contributes to the serene setting of this memorial structure.

**LECONTE MEMORIAL LODGE**

1 Meeting Lodge
2 Porch
3 Walkway
4 Parking

N
SCALE IN FEET
0 10 20

*Entrance to LeConte Memorial Lodge (2004) GH*

## DEVELOPED AREAS

LeConte Memorial Lodge is an example of the Tudor Revival style of architecture that has been slightly modified to make it appear more rustic and thereby appropriate to its Valley setting. Built of granite masonry with a high timber roof, the building is attributed to John White, brother-in-law and business partner of architect Bernard Maybeck.

The timber roof, exposed in the interior, is a structural expression characteristic of many San Francisco Bay Area buildings of the period. Extreme verticality and multiple members create a rich layering of structure that gives the interior space a mood of lofty serenity. The tall fireplace, set on the main axis and kept well within the central area, dominates the space, allowing the chimney to be an important element for the interior.

The Sierra Club currently operates LeConte Memorial Lodge as a visitor center, a reference library for conservation affairs, and a site for interpretive programs. The lodge provides a space that can be used for quiet research or the exchange of ideas in a setting evocative of rustic character.

*LeConte Memorial Lodge with North Dome (2004) GH*

*East facade of LeConte Memorial Lodge (2004) GH*

**GUIDELINES**

- LeConte Memorial Lodge is a National Historic Landmark and contributing resource within the Yosemite Valley Historic District. Refer to *The Secretary of the Interior's Standards for Treatment of Historic Properties* for guidance to ensure compatibility.
- Changes should not significantly alter any historically character-defining features of the site or building.
- Ongoing changes such as forest succession should be managed in accordance with park resource guidelines for management of the building's historic setting.
- Because the LeConte Memorial Lodge is a freestanding building on a relatively undeveloped site, any new structures will have a significant impact on the setting. New buildings or structures should be located a sufficient distance away from the lodge so that the historical relationship between the lodge and the landscape is preserved.

## INDIAN CULTURAL CENTER AT WAHHOGA

The park's Indian Cultural Center was being established at the time of publication at the site of the last occupied Indian village in Yosemite Valley. The center, west of Camp 4, will provide a location for culturally associated Indian people to conduct traditional ceremonies and to practice and teach techniques of traditional lifeways. Although the center will be open to the public, access may be limited during special ceremonies. Some public interpretation will occur, but this cultural center will not replace the primary educational function of the current Indian Village of Ahwahnee at Yosemite Village.

### Setting

The Indian Cultural Center sits at the base of a talus slope below Middle Brother Peak on the north side of Yosemite Valley. Leidig Meadow is nearby, to the south across Northside Drive. Part of the area is within the rockfall zone, and several of the center's important components (roundhouse, sweat lodge, and bark houses) will be sited in relation to massive boulders (Royston et. al. 2002).

The gently sloping site supports an open forest of relatively even-aged pines and cedars that appear to be shading out the site's few remaining California black oak trees. Although undergrowth is very limited, there are no views to prominent scenic features. A significant swale at the east edge of the area, separating it from the cluster of search-and-rescue tent cabins in Camp 4, suggests significant seasonal drainage. The cluster of search-and-rescue tent cabins in Camp 4 is being relocated farther east to provide a wider buffer zone.

## Developed Areas

Facilities at the Indian Cultural Center are clustered into two groups: traditional village structures and modern facilities. The traditional structures, which are being built by tribal members, include a large, partly subterranean ceremonial roundhouse, a smaller sweat lodge, and approximately 15 cedar bark umachas (conical shelters). Plants important for food, basketry, and medicinal uses may be grown in the vicinity of the traditional structures.

Additional facilities will include the Wilson cabin, a community center, and three shade structures. The Wilson Cabin, formerly the home of Westly and Alice Wilson, is the last remaining structure from the original Indian village. It is currently located in Yosemite Village and is being used as an NPS office. It will be moved back to the Indian Cultural Center site and adaptively reused. The community center will be a new structure, with a large meeting room for community events. A large kitchen will provide a working area for food preparation and scullery functions. Extensive bathrooms and dressing rooms will serve both for ceremonial functions and for visitors. A manager's office and storage structure will complete the building program. Utilities, including water, sewer, propane, unimproved road access, and electrical service, will be provided to the site. Screening will be established where necessary to visually separate the cultural center and Northside Drive, Yosemite Lodge, Camp 4, and the Valley Loop Trail. Only limited parking will be available at this location.

Umachas

**GUIDELINES**

### *Site Design*

- Locate new structures on the relatively flat site locations, away from the drainage swale, to minimize the amount of grading and ground disturbance.
- The health and remaining lifespan of oaks in the area should be assessed when making site decisions.
- Utilitarian structures such as trash enclosures and propane tanks, while accessible by service vehicles, should be screened from the arrival sequence, the Valley Loop Trail, and public gathering areas.
- Roads within this area should meander, should not dominate the space, and should relate to topography, trees, and boulders.
- Refer to "Landscape Uses + Structures—Parking" in the "Unifying Elements" chapter.

### *Landscape Elements*

- Use evergreen scrub oaks to create year-round screens of roads and utilitarian structures and to visually separate adjacent areas such as Camp 4.
- Refer to the "Unifying Elements" chapter for more guidelines on vegetation, views, grading, and drainage.

TOP *Lucy Telles with basket (1933) YRL* BOTTOM *Wilson Cabin, proposed for adaptive use at Indian Cultural Center*

***Buildings***

- Because of the history, association, and close proximity of the Wilson Cabin to the Indian Cultural Center, new buildings and structures should be compatible with the design and character of that historic building. Character-defining features include its roof and rustic base/foundation. Refer to "Developed Areas—Building Exteriors" in the "Unifying Elements" chapter.
- Exterior lighting should be minimal and shielded. Refer to "Landscape Uses + Structures—Lighting" in the "Unifying Elements" chapter.

## SEQUOIA GROVES

Three distinct sequoia groves are located within the park. The Mariposa Grove of Giant Sequoias provided one of the earliest motivations for the protection of natural wonders in the Yosemite region. Since the creation of the Yosemite Grant in 1864, the Mariposa Grove, together with the Merced and Tuolumne Groves, has remained among the park's most popular sites and has driven new policies for resource protection.

Local American Indian groups had long been aware of the giant trees, and early American explorers made passing references to them in the 1830s. The first definitive written account of the Mariposa Grove, however, came from prospectors in 1852. Within five years it was being promoted as a tourist destination, giving rise to fears of overexploitation that led to the grove being included in the Yosemite Grant—the federal action to preserve the Mariposa Grove and Yosemite Valley. The less-accessible Tuolumne Grove was encountered by a group of sightseers in 1858, and the Merced Grove came to the attention of surveyors laying out the Coulterville Road in 1872.

Early development in the groves was primarily limited to roads and the creation of tunnel trees. Between 1878 and 1895, tour promoters had fire scars enlarged in the Dead Giant of the Tuolumne Grove and the Wawona and California trees in the Mariposa Grove to create stagecoach-sized tunnels as novelties for visitors. The Old Coulterville Road was specifically routed through the Merced Grove to take advantage of the scenery, leading to the establishment of a ranger/patrol cabin in 1915, which was replaced by the current building in 1934.

The Mariposa Grove's proximity to the Wawona Hotel made it the focus for both development and protection. Galen Clark, the first guardian of the Yosemite Grant, built a small cabin in the grove by 1864, which the state of California either modified or replaced in 1881. After visiting the Mariposa Grove with John Muir, President Theodore Roosevelt wrote, "We lay in the open, the enormous cinnamon-colored trunks rising above us like columns of a vaster and more beautiful cathedral than was ever conceived by any human architect" (Fox 1986). The small cabin, in turn, was replaced by the present Mariposa Grove Museum in 1930, with the nearby comfort station added in 1931. In 1932 the park completed Wawona Point, a scenic overlook above the grove. Additional work in 1932 produced the Big Trees Lodge, a 12-room hotel in the upper grove designed by Eldridge T. Spencer. This replaced an earlier tent cabin complex that featured a cafeteria built around the base of the Montana Tree. The Big Trees Lodge closed in 1972 and was ultimately demolished.

*Museum and historic log comfort station, Mariposa Grove (2007) GH*

*Ranger station, Merced Grove (date unknown) YRL*

As early as 1911 it was apparent that visitor traffic posed a threat to the health of the giant sequoias. At various times roads were relocated away from the trees, but studies showed that vehicles still caused excessive soil compaction. Soil compaction is an issue because Sequoia have a shallow root system that can spread to an acre. As a result, the present tram system was introduced at the Mariposa Grove in 1970, and the Merced and Tuolumne Groves are open to pedestrian use only. Efforts continue to further reduce human impacts by concentrating visitor facilities on the periphery.

*Detail, Mariposa Grove Museum (2011) RF*

## Setting

### The Mariposa Grove of Giant Sequoias

The giant sequoias of the well-known and popular Mariposa Grove near the southernmost boundary of the park are distributed over a wide area, between 6,000 feet and 6,500 feet in elevation. A west-facing slope divides the area into upper and lower groves. The upper grove lies in a gentle, broad bowl and the lower grove is in a smaller, somewhat more linear depression. In spite of a limited understory of pines and fir, the giant sequoias are the overwhelmingly dominant landscape feature. Their massive, deeply furrowed, cinnamon-colored trunks contrast with the dull grey trunks of intermixed pine and fir. Wet soils, seepages, and seasonal drainages through the center of each bowl are the reasons for the survival of the grove at this location. These water sources also support small, grassy wetlands that provide bright-green color-contrast in pockets of sun (Thomas 1991).

At the lower grove, visitors arrive at a large parking area with multiple vault toilets, a cluster of photovoltaic panels, a snack shop, and several footpaths or tram options. A paved tram route and footpaths connect this area to the upper grove, where visitors find a self-guided nature trail, historic museum, and comfort station. The road extends to Wawona Point but is closed to private vehicles except for those displaying NPS disabled placards following the tram. Several pedestrian pathways to many famous, named giant sequoias crisscross the slopes and connect to trails leading to the more distant Wawona and Mount Raymond areas.

Because of its distance from the lower-grove parking area, the upper grove is quieter, except for the occasional noise associated with the tram. Attentive visitors can hear the whispering branches as breezes blow through the exceptionally tall conifers. They can also hear birdsong, including that of owls whose call, according to one version, inspired the American Indian name for Wawona.

In 1863 Frederick Law Olmsted visited the Mariposa Grove. The immense sequoias seemed like "distinguished strangers" that "have come down to us from another world," he wrote his wife, who was preparing to join him in California. His fascination with the Yosemite region had begun. "One or two annual trips to it," he told her, "are the highest gratifications peculiar to the country that you have to look forward to" (Olmsted 1865).

LEFT *Chimney detail, Mariposa Grove Museum (2008) DV* MIDDLE *Mariposa Grove Museum (2007) GH* RIGHT *Mariposa Grove and Museum (2004) RF*

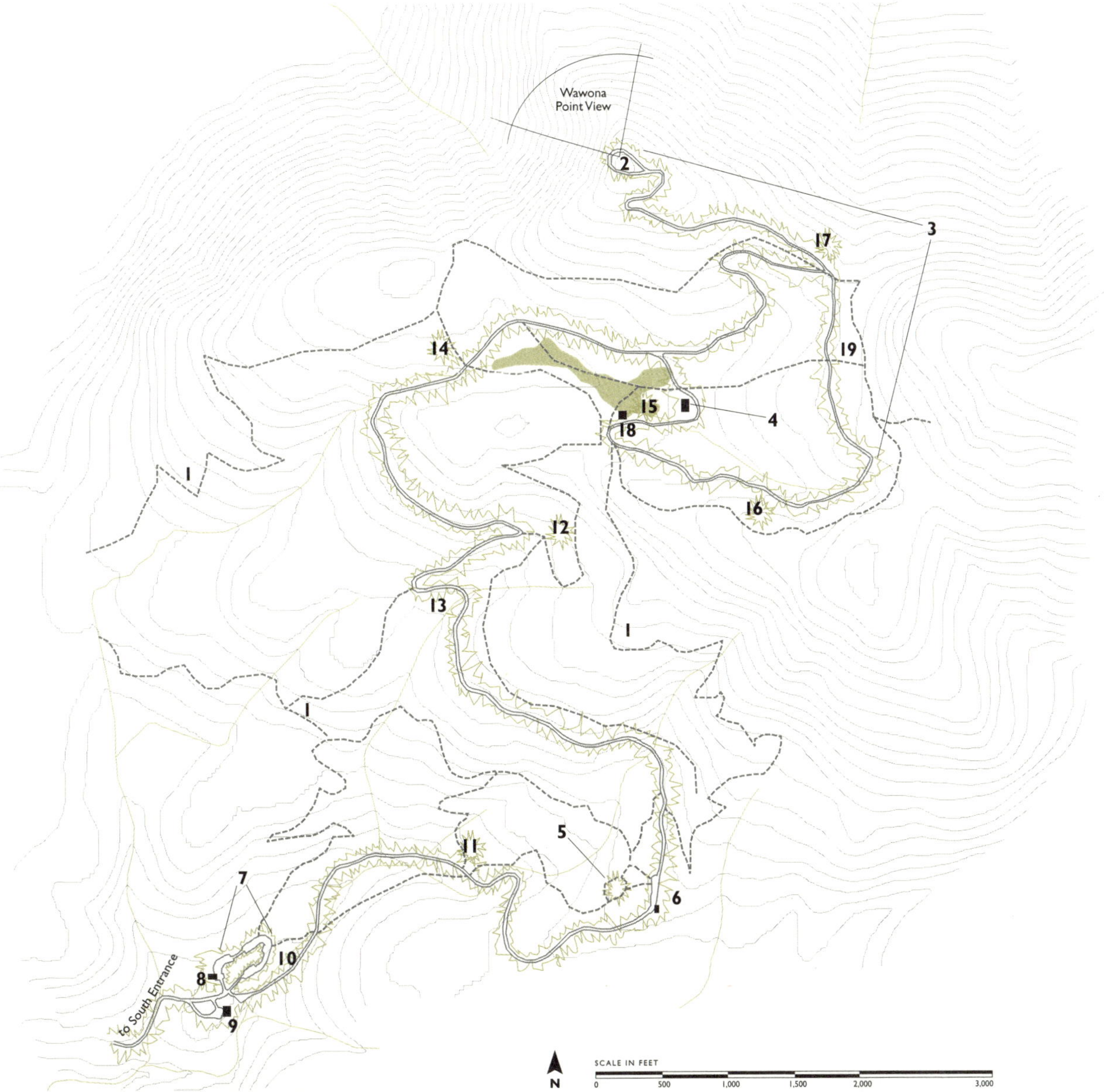


**MARIPOSA GROVE**

1 Trails
2 Wawona Point
3 Loop Road
4 Museum
5 Grizzly Giant
6 Grizzly Giant Parking and Toilet
7 Parking Area
8 Vault Toilets
9 Gift Shop
10 Fallen Monarch
11 Bachelor and Three Graces
12 Clothespin Tree
13 Faithful Couple
14 Mariposa Tree
15 Columbia Tree
16 Telescope Tree
17 Galen Clark Tree
18 Historic Log Comfort Station
19 Fallen Wawona Tunnel Tree

*Historic log comfort station, Mariposa Grove (2007) GH*

*Giant sequoia*
*(Sequoiadendron giganteum)*

*Mariposa Grove in winter (2008) RF*

## The Tuolumne and Merced Groves of Giant Sequoias

Because they are near the northern limits of the range for giant sequoias, the trees of the Tuolumne and Merced Groves are relatively small compared to trees in the Mariposa Grove. Both are far from busy roads, and neither grove is open to unofficial vehicles or trams. This makes the natural range of forest sounds a valuable addition to the historic, visual, and educational values afforded those willing and able to reach these groves on foot. Neither is very developed—there are no significant manmade structures in the Tuolumne Grove, for example—which significantly enhances the sense of remoteness.

The entrance to the Tuolumne Grove, with its large parking area, is adjacent to Tioga Road at an elevation of 6,200 feet. At the head of the trail leading to the grove is an educational interpretive exhibit and a comfort station. A CCC-era ranger station is located nearby. The grove is accessed by a tree-shaded, one-mile downhill walk along the historic Old Big Oak Flat Road through an extensive old-growth forest. Trail connections in the grove provide access to the Big Oak Flat Entrance Station and Hodgdon Meadow.

*Giant sequoia (2008) DV*

The Merced Grove, at 5,300 feet, is two miles from the Big Oak Flat Road. In comparison with the Tuolumne Grove, this grove provides a greater sense of solitude and remoteness, where the sequoias "convey the silent majesty that has characterized them for thousands of years" (Medley 2002). The 20-acre area surrounding the grove was logged in the early 20th century and has fewer trees than the forest surrounding the Tuolumne Grove. The spacing of the sequoias, the surrounding conifers, and the contrasting patterns of shade and sun are similar to that of the Mariposa Grove. Trail connections in the Merced Grove lead south to the Stanislaus National Forest. The Merced Grove Ranger Station, built in 1934, is listed on the National Register of Historic Places.

**GUIDELINES**

- New buildings in the vicinity should be compatible with the Rustic style, consistent with guidance in *The Secretary of the Interior's Standards for the Treatment of Historic Properties.*
- Refer to "Landscape Uses + Structures—Small Buildings" in the "Unifying Elements" chapter.
- Ensure clarity of wayfinding by providing a hierarchy of circulation and an adequate amount of trail delineation that relates to the design character at the grove. Refer to the "Unifying Elements" chapter for further guidance on circulation.
- Any new design in the Mariposa Grove should be sited away from the core of historic trees in both the lower and upper groves.
- Refer to "Landscape Uses + Structures—Masonry Structures" in the "Unifying Elements" chapter.
- Design for new uses within all of the sequoia groves should consider protection of the subtle natural acoustical environment.
- Split-timber, double-post and zigzag barriers are the standard within the grove for directing pedestrian traffic and protecting sensitive soils, vegetation, and wetlands. Refer to "Landscape Uses + Structures—Barriers, Fences, and Benches" in the "Unifying Elements" chapter.

TOP LEFT *Ranger station, Merced Grove (date unknown) YRL* RIGHT *Tuolumne Grove, Dead Giant (2011) ML* BOTTOM LEFT *Sequoia cone on forest floor (2008) DV*

- Signs and associated structures should be uniform throughout the giant sequoia groves, and should blend with the surrounding landscape. Refer to "Landscape Uses + Structures—Sign Character" in the "Unifying Elements" chapter.
- Grading, runoff diversion, and impervious pavements in the vicinity of the sequoia groves should be minimized to prevent concentrations of surface runoff. Natural hydrology should be restored where feasible. Refer to "Landscape Uses + Structures—Grading and Drainage" in the "Unifying Elements" chapter.
- Protect the shallow root zone in the groves by minimizing disruption to the greatest extent possible.
- The colors of painted or stained structures and signs should be compatible with, but not mimic, the ambient color of the natural grove landscape, dominated as it is by the cinnamon-colored trunks of the sequoias. Complementary earth tones of a darker hue such as Wosky brown should be considered.

UNLIKE MOST PRACTITIONERS TODAY, [ARCHITECTS] HAD A GOOD FUND OF GENERAL CULTURE, AND WERE BROADLY EDUCATED IN LITERATURE AND HISTORY AS WELL AS THE ARTS. THEY CREATED BUILDINGS CAREFULLY. SCALE AND PROPORTION, MASSING AND TEXTURE, SYMBOLIC FORM AND NOBILITY ALL WERE INGREDIENTS OF THEIR WORK. **TEMKO 1987**

## CHINQUAPIN

Chinquapin, at the intersection of the Wawona and Glacier Point roads, is an example of NPS design projects constructed during the New Deal era of the 1930s that coordinated road construction, building construction, and landscape architecture. The Chinquapin Historic District was determined eligible for listing on the National Register of Historic Places in 2004. Park officials had decided to place an administrative unit at the intersection—previously a stage stop on the Old Wawona Road—to address increasing visitor traffic in the area. Plans called for a ranger station, comfort station, and a gas station with refreshment stand, all built in a style that would echo buildings in both Yosemite Valley and the Wawona area. The comprehensive design also included details of road construction, curbing, walkways, and a complete vegetation scheme for landscape naturalization. Together with erosion control work directed by ecologist Frederic E. Clements of the Carnegie Institution, this project made the Wawona Road the most closely studied development in the park system to that point (McClelland 1998).

The use of frame structures with white-painted lap siding represented a deliberate and unique departure from the NPS Rustic style of architecture. Rather than following the Rustic ethic of blending with the natural landscape, the development was meant to blend with Yosemite's historic past. The park had acquired the Wawona basin and its historic hotel in 1932, one year before work was completed at Chinquapin.

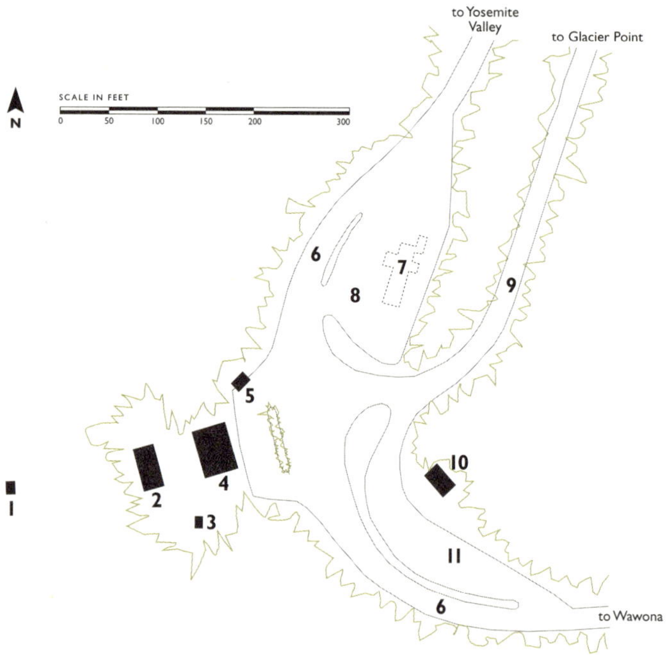


**CHINQUAPIN**

1 Barn
2 Garage
3 Pump House
4 Ranger Residence
5 Gas and Oil House
6 Wawona Road
7 Gas Station/Lunchroom (Razed)
8 Staging and NPS Parking Area
9 Glacier Point Road
10 Comfort Station
11 Visitor Parking Area

*Comfort station, Chinquapin (2008) GH*

The wood-framed Wawona Hotel, a relatively short drive away from Chinquapin, represented a style of architecture common in 19th century California. This building style recalled a more adventurous era of travel at the park. By adapting this style to contemporary uses, NPS designers hoped to emphasize the cultural link between the oldest and newest sections of Yosemite, while providing visitors with needed services along the way (NPS 1991b).

Changes to Chinquapin since 1933 have eliminated much of the visual cohesiveness that once distinguished the intersection. The most notable changes have been the demolition of the gas station and lunchroom due to a leaking fuel tank, together with the associated traffic islands that defined the northern end of the complex. The former ranger station has been converted into park employee housing, restricting visitor use at Chinquapin to just the comfort station. In 2009–2010, the Glacier Point Road and Wawona Road rehabilitation projects altered portions of the intersection alignment and turnouts. Stone-faced guard walls and granite curbing were installed, and the water fountain and comfort station were rehabilitated.

*Verandahs, Wawona Hotel Complex (2009) GH*

*Chinquapin intersection at Wawona and Glacier Point Roads (lunchroom and gas station in foreground, since removed, ranger residence in background) (date unknown) YRL*

*Chinquapin (Chrysolepis sempervirens)*

## Setting

Chinquapin is at the intersection of the Wawona and Glacier Point Roads at an elevation of 6,040 feet. It is surrounded by a landscape of dense, mixed-conifer forest. Against this background of dark green, the pale-green leaf masses of bush chinquapin, after which the site is named, stand out in nearby open areas. The white ranger station, garage, and comfort station provide a bright contrast to the dark conifer background.

A broad curving swath of roadway paving at the center of the district accommodates winter chain-up activities. The geometry of the intersection—the sweeping curve of the Wawona Road and the beginning curve of the Glacier Point Road—is notable. The latter road wraps around the back, uphill side of the former gas station site. The visual cohesiveness of the original intersection of interlocking curves, reinforced and triangulated by three pristine white buildings of the same architectural vocabulary, should serve as a model for future improvements to this historic property.

The site has always been an important wayside rest area for visitors traveling the long route between Wawona and Yosemite Valley. It sits at the alignment of the historic wagon road. The complex originally included a plaza surrounded by landscaped areas connecting the Glacier Point and Wawona roads.

## Developed Areas

The simple, white-painted frame buildings with gable roofs, verandahs, and bevel siding are typical of the architectural style of many buildings in 19th century California, particularly hotel structures. The white cottage form had its origins in the East, but locally became a generic form with regional variations.

The significance of this complex was noted by Allan Temko, San Francisco Chronicle architecture critic, who in 1987 stated that the two gas stations at Yosemite (one in Yosemite Valley, the other at Chinquapin) prepared in the office of Eldridge T. Spencer reveal the "forward movement": a period when designers had more freedom to be imaginative when confronted by perplexing architectural problems. The buildings at Chinquapin, Temko said, are important because they were executed at a time when architects

*Chinquapin ranger residence (date unknown) YRL*

*Santa Cruz residence ca. 1928. Designed by William Wurster (2008) GH*

could still practice their "high calling" and were not yet "reduced to servitude to fast-buck promoters and prepackaged structures."

During the same period, other examples of this style were designed by William Wurster in California during the first half of the 1930s. The architectural idiom that evolved was unostentatious in style; simple in construction technique, color (white), and materials; respondent to climate; ideally suited to California living; and reflective of client taste (Treib 1996).

The principal building at the Chinquapin intersection is the ranger residence, on the west side of Wawona Road. Facing the road is a generous porch that runs the full length of the structure. Its essential character is defined by the roof shape, white-painted bevel siding, and masonry foundation. To the rear on a gentle downslope is the garage, whose simple plan shape forms a service yard with the ranger station. This site plan screens the maintenance activity from the road and from motorists at the intersection.

Across the road to the east stands the comfort station. Set into the hillside, it is of the same construction and finish as the ranger station. A handsome dressed stone wall retains the slope to allow for end entrances into the building. A small plaza in front of the comfort station contains a rustic cobblestone drinking fountain.

*Comfort station, Chinquapin (2007) GH*

**GUIDELINES**

- New design should consider the character of the original buildings at this important intersection and would need to meet compatibility guidelines in *The Secretary of the Interior's Standards for the Treatment of Historic Properties*.
- If new structures are added to the site, they should be inconspicuously located well back from the intersection behind mature trees and should take advantage of topography. Use color that will allow the structures to blend and recede with their setting. Reserve white only for the original structures at the intersection.
- New buildings should not be located in front of the comfort and ranger stations to maintain the historically open character of this area.
- Pathways and parking areas should be designed to prevent encroachment on vegetation. Refer to "Landscape Uses + Structures—Barriers, Fences + Benches" in the "Unifying Elements" chapter.
- Locate trash, recycle bins, and bear boxes so they do not impact views from roads or public/residential areas.

*Comfort station, Chinquapin (2008) GH*

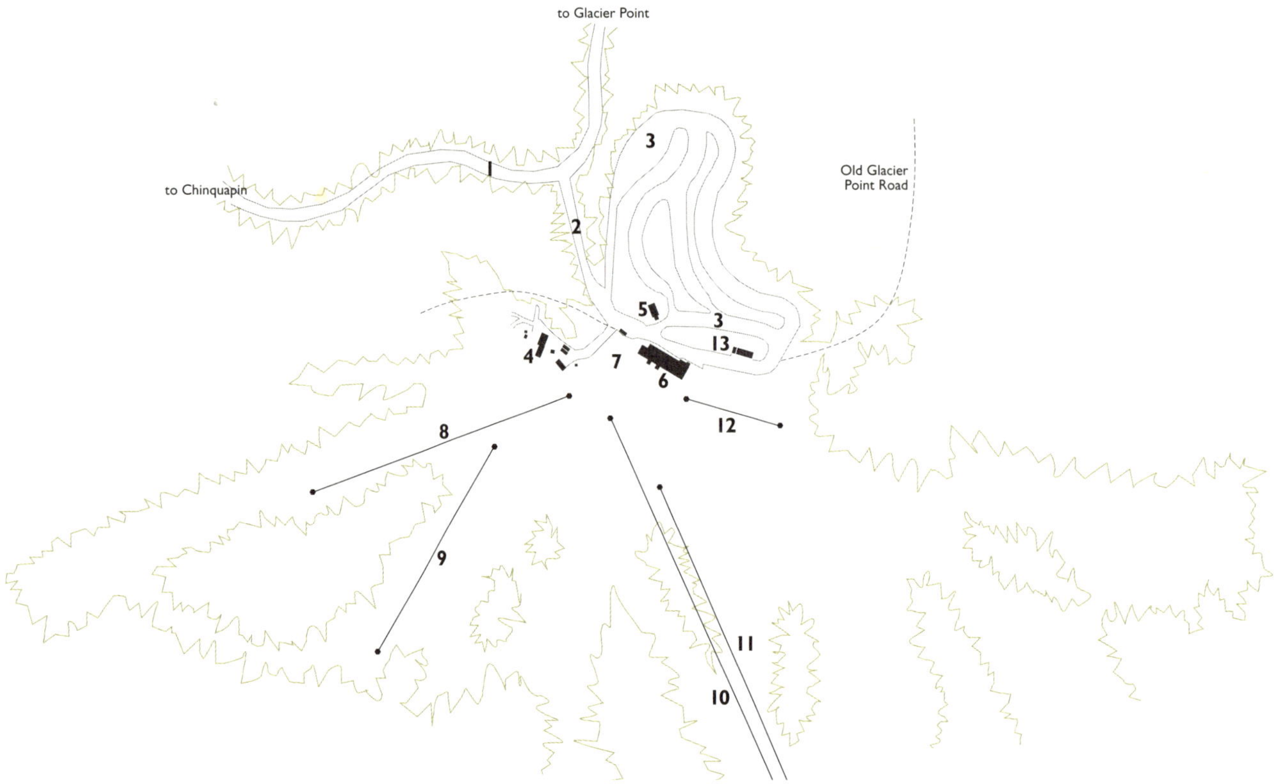


**BADGER PASS**

| | | | |
|---|---|---|---|
| 1 | Glacier Point Road | 8 | Bruin Ski Lift |
| 2 | Badger Pass Road | 9 | Badger Ski Lift |
| 3 | Parking Loop | 10 | Eagle Ski Lift |
| 4 | Maintenance Garage | 11 | Red Fox Ski Lift |
| 5 | Historic Ranger Station | 12 | Turtle Rope Tow |
| 6 | Badger Pass Ski Lodge | 13 | Cross Country Ski Rental |
| 7 | Monroe Meadow | | |

N

SCALE IN FEET
0 250 500 750 1000 1500

*Badger Pass Lodge and "Queen Mary" sledge*

## BADGER PASS

The Badger Pass ski area was developed largely at the instigation of Donald Tresidder, president of the Yosemite Park and Curry Company. In cooperation with NPS managers, Tresidder sought to develop winter sports in Yosemite in hopes of making the park more of a year-round destination. Early efforts had focused on sites in and around Yosemite Valley, including the glacial medial moraine between the Merced River and Tenaya Creek. After the completion of the Wawona Road and tunnel in 1933, skiers increasingly made use of better slopes near Chinquapin and especially at Badger Pass, known earlier as Monroe Meadows (NPS 1987b).

The park and the concessioner responded to visitor demand. The lodge, or Badger Pass Ski Lodge, was designed in a Tyrol style by San Francisco architect Eldridge T. Spencer. It opened in the middle of the 1935 season to immediate success. Among the growing ranks of skiers was Walt Disney, who saw enough potential in

*View from parking area, Badger Pass Lodge (date unknown) YRL*

the sport to help establish a new resort—Sugar Bowl—near Lake Tahoe in 1938 (McHugh 2003). During this same period the Civilian Conservation Corps built several ranger cabins at Badger Pass for winter use. The ski lodge was significantly expanded in 1954 with a large, modernistic extension that housed ski rentals, repair facilities, and employee quarters. Since then, modest additions have occurred.

Badger Pass (determined eligible for listing on the National Register of Historic Places in 2009) is one of the first downhill ski areas in the West, and it was the first to be developed within a national park. Because of its small scale and proximity to the San Francisco Bay Area, Badger Pass has become a largely family-oriented resort. Increasing winter visitation to the park has ensured its popularity.

## SETTING

The gently sloping bowl and wetland meadow of the Badger Pass ski area sit at an elevation of approximately 7,400 feet. Upper montane coniferous trees—red fir, lodgepole and western white pine, western juniper, and quaking aspen—form a deep green belt surrounding and interspersed with the ski runs. The soils are relatively deep, as evidenced by their dark color, the consistent vegetated cover, and the lack of major rock clusters or ridges. The Clark Range and Quartzite Peak can be seen from the top of Eagle Run—the highest point at the ski area.

The lodge and the ranger station sit at the north edge of the meadow. The meadow's grassy wetland

*Badger Pass Lodge (2008) GH*

and saturated soils abut the south-facing lodge deck, although the meadow is obscured and protected from skiers by winter snows.

After pulling off Glacier Point Road, drivers turn north of the lodge where parking is accommodated in a series of large terraces. Between this parking area and the lodge entrance is a broad, undefined, paved area used for service, drop-off, and parking. This paved area is on the historic alignment of the Glacier Point Wagon Road, reconstructed from a saddle trail by the Washburn family in 1882 (NPS 2007a).

## Developed Areas

In the early 1930s the National Park Service approved Eldridge T. Spencer's plans for the Badger Pass Ski Lodge, noting that the project was "not overly injurious to the scenic values of the area" (ARG 1995). Spencer and his wife, Jeanette Dyer Spencer, were active in the design of many Yosemite buildings, including the "new" cafeteria and dining room at Camp Curry (1928–29), Yosemite Lodge (1956), Big Trees Lodge in Mariposa

TOP LEFT *South elevation, Badger Pass Lodge; from Park and Recreation Structures (1938)* TOP RIGHT *South facade before addition, ranger station, Badger Pass (date unknown) YRL*
BOTTOM LEFT *Early photograph of Badger Pass Lodge with bark roof and wall treatment (date unknown) YRL* BOTTOM RIGHT *Badger Pass Lodge (2009) RF*

*Detail of wood carving by Robert Boardman Howard, originally on Badger Pass Lodge, south facade (see lodge photo on p. 256); from* Park and Recreation Structures *(1938)*

Grove (since removed), the cottages at The Ahwahnee, and Housekeeping Camp in the Valley. Jeanette Spencer also designed the leaded glass windows in the lounge at The Ahwahnee. The Badger Pass Ski Lodge was dedicated in January 1936.

Badger Pass Ski Lodge derives much of its character from the ridgeline of the roof, which is placed off-center of the axis of the main facade. The long roof-slope to the east, with a pitch of 4:12, ties the structure down to the ground and lends a strong sense of shelter. This alpine motif has roots in the Austrian Tyrol. It establishes a strong character for the lodge and, perhaps more importantly, provides a snow-free assembly area on the south side of the building, where guests may bask in the sun in full view of the ski slopes.

The original structure was clad in a unique pattern of log planks with bark, recalling early Rustic buildings in the Valley. Rustic in appearance, this treatment was used not only for the sidewalls but also for the roof. The same treatment can be found at Vogelsang High Sierra Camp. The unique roof was eventually replaced with asphalt shingles.

Much of the original interior of the lodge was finished with knotty sugar-pine paneling. The ceiling of the lounge retains elements of the structural truss system for the roof. The fireplace has been removed. The handsome cast-iron bas-relief of skiers now resides on the lounge fireplace at the Yosemite Lodge in the Valley.

Spencer endowed the lodge with a special and appropriate architectural character. Over the years this character has all but disappeared as a result of many awkward alterations to its original form. Every effort should be taken to restore the character-defining elements of the original building.

**GUIDELINES**

- For new development at Badger Pass, designers should consult *The Secretary of the Interior's Standards for the Treatment of Historic Properties* for guidance on compatibility.
- Refer to the *Badger Pass Historic Structures Report* and the *Badger Pass Cultural Landscape Report* (NPS 2010a) for treatment recommendations concerning buildings and the setting.
- The design of small-scale landscape features such as barriers, fences, bear boxes, trash containers, lighting fixtures, etc., should be based on and integrated with the design of the historic ski lodge. Refer to "Landscape Uses + Structures—Small Buildings" in the "Unifying Elements" chapter.

*Fireplace treatment with bas-relief, since removed, lounge, Badger Pass Lodge; from* Park and Recreation Structures *(1938)*

## GLACIER POINT

Glacier Point is one of Yosemite's iconic destinations, and it was a focal point of early park development. Visitors originally had to approach it from above the Valley, until local entrepreneur James McCauley commissioned John Conway in 1871 to build the Four-Mile Trail from the floor of Yosemite Valley. Shortly after the trail was completed, McCauley, either by design or by accident, created the first firefall—a spectacular cascade of glowing embers pushed over the edge of the cliff to entertain visitors in the Valley below. The memory of the firefall remains linked with Glacier Point long after the National Park Service discontinued the practice in 1968.

McCauley charged a toll for the use of his trail, and he eventually concluded he could increase his business by providing food and lodging at the upper end. The Glacier Point Mountain House (1878) was a modest, wood-framed hotel that made up for its lack of size by offering expansive views of Half Dome and Little Yosemite Valley. Direct road access became possible after John Conway built a stage route from Chinquapin Station in 1882, the same year the state of California purchased the Four-Mile Trail and eliminated the toll.

Ever-increasing visitation at Glacier Point prompted park managers to authorize the construction of a new hotel by the Desmond Park Service Company. Opened in

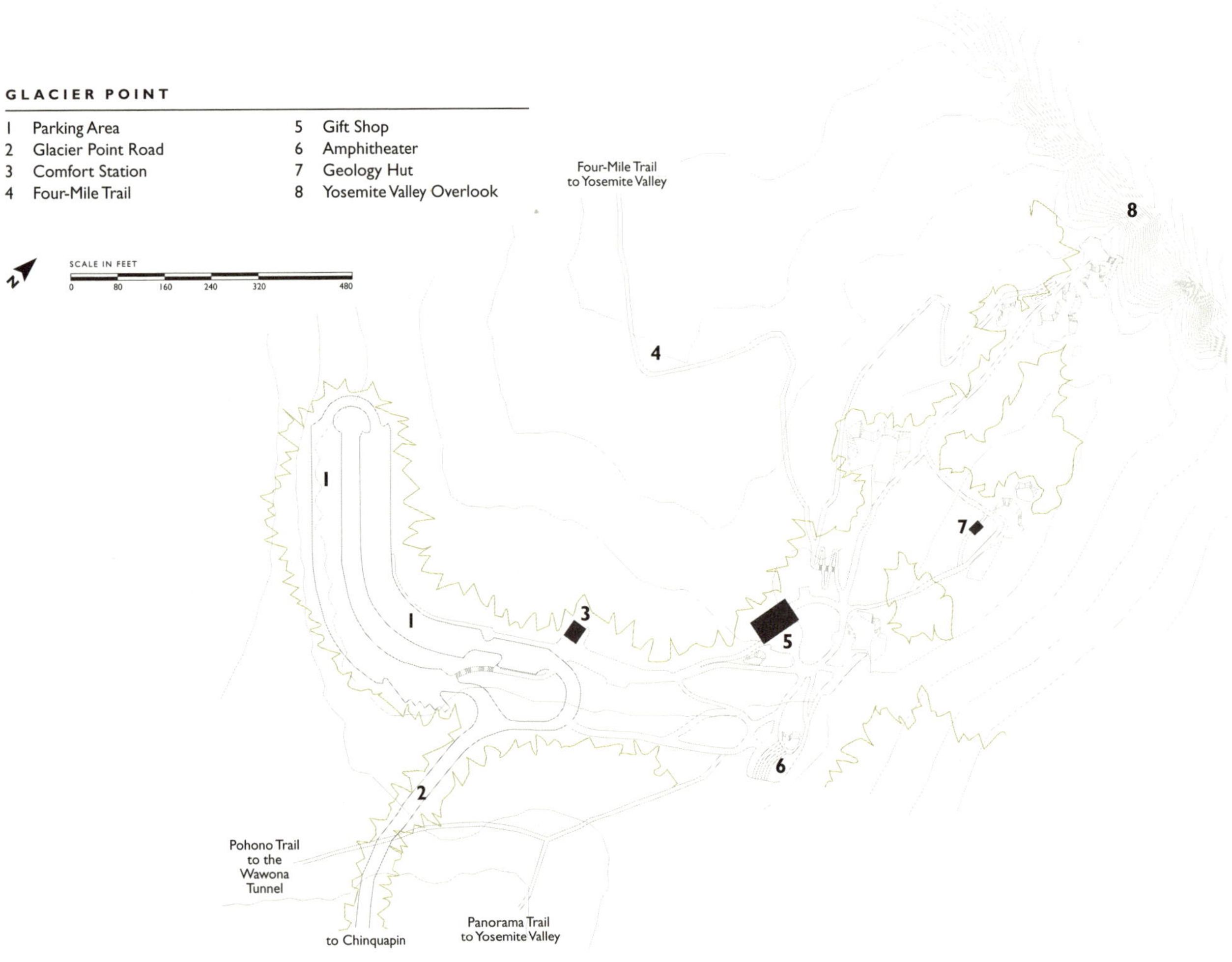

TOP LEFT *Overlook, Glacier Point (2004) RF* TOP RIGHT *Geology Hut, Glacier Point (date unknown)* BOTTOM LEFT *Arrival, Glacier Point (2004) RF*
BOTTOM RIGHT *Glacier Point Hotel, since destroyed; from* Yosemite's Yesterdays, *by Hank Johnston (1878)*

1917, the Glacier Point Hotel was an elaborate, shingle-covered building featuring a long verandah facing east toward Half Dome. The Mountain House was remodeled to serve as the hotel's cafeteria. A stable was maintained for guest use, and there was also a small campground south of the complex.

The views available from Glacier Point made it a natural point of interest when the National Park Service began to develop an organized interpretive program. The first trailside museum (referred to as the Geology Hut) was created under this effort. This lookout was designed in 1924 by architect Herbert Maier and NPS chief naturalist Ansel Hall, and was sited on a prominent granite high-point with stunning views toward Half Dome, Little Yosemite Valley, and Tenaya Canyon. The rustic granite structure appeared to have grown out of the surrounding rock, and it provided a location for ranger–naturalists to explain the park's geology. Construction in the subsequent decade added comfort stations, an expanded parking lot, and two ranger cabins that were designed to be easily relocated if needed.

In 1968 fire destroyed the entire Glacier Point Hotel complex. The hotel was not rebuilt but was replaced by temporary concession buildings and a comfort station. In 1997 the Glacier Point complex underwent redesign. The temporary buildings were replaced by permanent buildings, an outdoor amphitheater was constructed, new viewing areas were added, and the site underwent extensive ecological restoration. The area now largely represents a contemporary interpretation of traditional Rustic design principles.

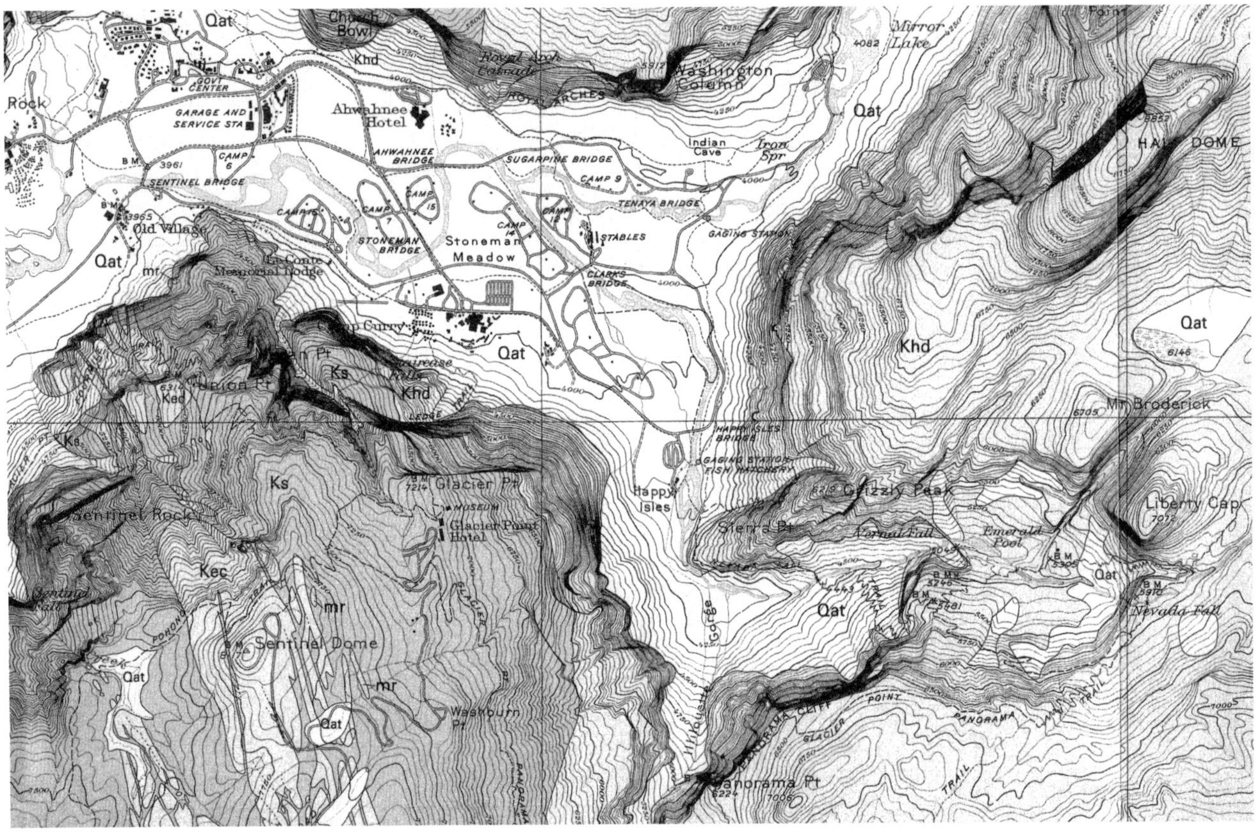


*Portion of Bedrock Geology Map of Yosemite Valley, 1949 USGS*

## Setting

Glacier Point, at an elevation of 7,214 feet, is one of the most spectacular overlooks in the park and one of the most frequently visited. The Glacier Point Road from Chinquapin winds for 15.5 miles through red fir forest and then breaks into a vast open and stunning view of Yosemite Valley and the Sierra crest. The Pohono, Panorama, and Four-Mile trails converge on this point.

The developed area is strung along a rim of cliffs 3,200 feet above Yosemite Valley and is configured in two loops. The southern loop is devoted largely to a two-level parking area divided by a stone-clad retaining wall. In a partially forested setting of red fir, it accommodates close to 200 private autos and at least five buses. The northern loop is dedicated to pedestrian use. Trails and stairs wind through huge boulders and granite shoulders to breathtaking views of Yosemite Valley over the edge of the granite walls. The viewing areas are well-distributed in a linear fashion, accommodating substantial numbers of people at one time.

Located prominently along a trail, the Geology Hut is nested atop a rounded granite outcrop. The small stone structure, with battered walls of rough-dressed granite and approach steps carved into the granite slope, is a fine example of the skillful blending of handcrafted masonry with the natural setting. The materials were most likely found or quarried in the immediate vicinity (NPS 1976b). It is one of the best sites in the park for a self-guided introduction to the impressive geology and geomorphology of Yosemite Valley. The amphitheater, composed of granite blocks, serves a variety of more passive uses when not in use for ranger talks, including resting, picnicking, and scenery viewing, all possible because it is set back from the active viewing areas at the rim. Structures such as the gift shop and restroom buildings are set sufficiently back from the rim's edge so that they are hidden from lower trails and the Valley.

Low-pierced post timber rails define some pathways, while galvanized and elaborate pre-rusted steel handrails flank modern concrete stairways. In some places adjacent to the Geology Hut and elsewhere, simple CCC-era iron handrails, sagging at some points from decades of heavy winters, have been polished to a satin sheen by thousands of hands over the years. Heavy pedestrian use requires clear delineation of boundaries to ensure the survival of understory vegetation. The style of small-scale landscape features varies throughout the site.

*Masonry wall of viewing terrace, Geology Hut, Glacier Point (2007) GH*

**GUIDELINES**

- Any redesign of the pedestrian circulation and viewing areas at Glacier Point should encourage an even distribution of visitors.
- New stonemasonry projects should specify stone that matches as closely as possible the color and grain of boulders and outcrops of the site. Stone coursing should start below settled ground-level and should be installed horizontally if the face stones are of uneven or random dimension. The rough-worked, rectangular granite members of the Glacier Point Road guard walls (built in 1934 by the Civilian Conservation Corps) provide a good model to follow. Refer to "Landscape Uses + Structures—Masonry Structures" in the "Unifying Elements" chapter.
- The finish of new handrails should be patterned after the existing handrails at the Geology Hut.

## Developed Areas

Three small wood structures dating to 1931 remain from the early development at Glacier Point. Modest and in the Rustic tradition, with exposed timber wall framing, horizontal siding and shake infill, and exposed roof construction, they are quiet reminders of the earlier structures at this important site, overlooking the Valley and the imposing Sierra crest beyond.

The Geology Hut, skillfully sited on the trail to the popular Valley overlook, was constructed in 1924 and can be described as one of the high achievements of the Rustic period in Yosemite. It was listed on the National Register of Historic Places in 1978. True masonry construction, with segmented arch openings, exposed on the interior as well, give this modest building its extraordinary character. Exposed roof framing, with its direct

*Geology Hut, with masonry showing incised steps into granite, Glacier Point (2008) RF*

*Glacier Point Naturalist Cabin. From Greene, Historic Resource Study Vol. 2 (1984). Photograph by Trovert C. Pavlik*

and honest presentation of construction, adds to the rustic charm of this shelter. The combination of wood shingles and granite are in the true Rustic tradition. The engagement of the granite forms into the terrace walls demonstrates architect Herbert Maier's skill in joining the pavilion to its site.

The newer buildings at Glacier Point were added in 1997 as part of the Glacier Point Restoration Project. They are clad with vertical board siding, with stone veneer at the lower wall as the rustic base. Heavy log framing supports the roof, which has a weathering metal covering with a strong rust hue. The buildings are set well back from the viewing edge, and lower floors are adjusted downslope so the building appears to be one story at the plaza level. To the rear of the parking area are pre-cast concrete comfort stations, cast in wood forms, with a painted finish.

**GUIDELINES**

- For new development at Glacier Point, designers should consult *The Secretary of the Interior's Standards for the Treatment of Historic Properties* for guidance on compatibility.
- New structures should conform to the setbacks established by the 1997 buildings. New buildings should be sited away from the viewing edge as defined by the network of trails and the edge of the tree line.
- Limit building heights to the adjacent tree mass immediately adjacent to the specific site.

LEFT *View to the southeast from Geology Hut, Glacier Point (2007) GH* TOP RIGHT *Amphitheater, Glacier Point (2008) DN* BOTTOM RIGHT *Looking north from amphitheater, Glacier Point (2011) RF*

- Exterior finishes should include wood walls and shakes, Wosky brown color, and masonry style as found at the Geology Hut. The roof color should be dark grey if buildings are located in visible areas.
- Refer to "Landscape Uses + Structures—Lighting" in the "Unifying Elements" chapter for night-sky recommendations to avoid light spillage from buildings.
- Refer to "Developed Areas—Architectural Character" in the "Unifying Elements" chapter and to the "Huts, Cabins + High Sierra Camps" chapter.
- Refer to "Landscape Uses + Structures—Sign Character" in the "Unifying Elements" chapter.

TOP LEFT *Geology Hut masonry detail, Glacier Point (2008) GH* TOP RIGHT *Handrail detail, Glacier Point (2008) GH* BOTTOM *Comfort station, Glacier Point (2008) GH*

## CRANE FLAT

According to archeological investigations, Crane Flat has seen thousands of years of American Indian occupation. In the modern era, it primarily served as an administrative post and a place for a brief pause on a longer journey. The area received its present name in 1856, when Lafayette Bunnell and George Coulter observed a large flock of "cranes" (possibly great blue herons) there while laying out the Coulterville Free Trail. This route, together with the Old Big Oak Flat Road, established Crane Flat as a natural stopping point on the way to Yosemite Valley from the west. By the 1870s Louis Gobin's summer ranch developed into an important stage stop and hotel, while Billy Hurst's saloon catered to the additional needs of visitors and local residents. Both ceased operation during the 1890s.

Crane Flat's administrative role began in 1905 when Captain Harry Benson selected it as the location of a patrol outpost for cavalry troops guarding the park. The army's tents were replaced by a permanent log cabin in 1915, after the Department of the Interior began direct management of the park. Yosemite's first fire lookout tower was built on a height above Crane Flat in 1931, as an element of a new fire management plan. It was designed in the Rustic style by the National Park Service's Landscape Division, while resident landscape architect John Wosky ensured its harmony with the surroundings. The Civilian Conservation Corps constructed a pair of camps in 1933, and realignments of both the Tioga Road and the Big Oak Flat Road included a checking station and a new ranger duplex in 1940.

After World War II, in 1946, park managers established a camp for the control of the white pine blister rust fungus at Crane Flat. Blister rust was accidentally introduced into the United States around 1908 from Europe, and by the 1930s it had spread west to California, sparking concern that the fungus could damage the state's sugar pine timber industry. The National Park

*Meadow, Crane Flat (2009) TP*

*Gas station, Crane Flat (2010) RF*

Service cooperated with the U.S. Forest Service to develop a control strategy that centered on clearing currant and gooseberry bushes that acted as hosts for the fungus.

After World War II, the National Park Service inherited a number of temporary wooden buildings that the U.S. Navy had installed on the grounds of The Ahwahnee when it functioned as the Naval Special Hospital. Park managers took the opportunity to use these in the blister rust program, relocating the buildings to a location on Tioga Road near the old CCC camp in Crane Flat, and to a new camp at Carl Inn (Carlon). The camps were closed after a reevaluation of blister rust in the mid-1960s concluded that the danger to sugar pines was less than previously believed.

*CCC structure, Crane Flat (2008) GH*

Crane Flat's location away from Yosemite Valley, combined with its ease of access, brought it to the attention of Mission 66 planners attempting to reduce crowding in the park's more heavily visited areas. This led to the creation of a 160-site campground south of the Big Oak Flat Road in 1965, and a service station at the Tioga Road–Big Oak Flat Road intersection.

In 1973 the Yosemite Institute (now known as NatureBridge) acquired a special use permit to operate the blister rust facility for its environmental education program. NatureBridge has since made use of the site for a longer period than originally envisioned. At the time of publication of this document, plans were being finalized to relocate the environmental education center to Henness Ridge (near Chinquapin) and completely restore the Crane Flat blister rust facility area to natural conditions.

## Setting

Although the remaining physical evidence is limited and fragmentary, the concentration of historic trails, wagon routes, and waystation sites found at Crane Flat is remarkable. The 1874 Big Oak Flat Road, the American Indian Mono Trail, Big Oak Flat Trail, the Mann Brothers Coulterville Free Trail, and Lower (Coulterville) Trail all converged in this area. The waystation elements—Gobin Hotel and Billy Hurst's Saloon—were clustered on either side of the wagon road. Early photos indicate typically unadorned utilitarian structures and, with the exception of fencing, a site free of small-scale landscape structures.

The modern Tioga Road was built through the meadow, around which the early structures had been clustered. A small portion of the meadow extends north of the road. It is surrounded by mixed conifers that are encroaching along its edges.

The heart of the Crane Flat area is a short distance northeast of the entrance road to The Tuolumne Grove of Giant Sequoias at the former blister rust camp. At 6,250 feet, Crane Flat is set at the head of a gentle swale leading to Crane Creek. An unscreened parking area serves the camp and is directly adjacent to and west of a major bend in the Tioga Road.

In the 1930s cabins for the Civilian Conservation Corps, and later the blister rust camp, were arranged in hierarchal fashion on the slopes overlooking the meadow—sleeping quarters at the top and service buildings below. Although the hierarchical arrangement has been compromised by many changes in the last decades, a straightforward arrival sequence from the Tioga Road to parking, administration, dining hall buildings, and cabins remains evident. The administration building and dining hall at the center of the facility are close to the western edge of the parking area, at the head of the swale. Small cabins are scattered among fir and pine trees on adjacent slopes to the southwest. Although there is little or no substory vegetation, the dark-painted structures blend in well with the dark tree trunks and dark sloping soils. The views of the sunlit meadow through the open forest and the quiet soundscape of this relatively protected site suggest the calm quality of the pre-internal-combustion-engine era.

At the Big Oak Flat Road and Tioga Road junction, a gas station and store serve motorists who have traveled long distances. The gas station is screened from Big Oak Flat Road by a narrow slope of vegetation.

*Billy Hurst Saloon and Gobin's Hotel (since removed)*

*Ranger residence, Crane Flat (date unknown) YRL*

## Developed Areas

During each stage of development, the buildings on the meadow at Crane Flat were built employing the typical construction methods of the period. Log cabins, frame structures, and prefabricated buildings were all adapted to the function and use of their occupants. These structures served their purpose well, and were useful into the next phase of occupancy.

The earliest buildings and structures at Crane Flat were the cluster of buildings—including the Gobin Hotel and Hurst Saloon—located along the historical alignment of Big Oak Flat Road near the junction with Tioga Road. They were small-scale frame and log structures with gable roofs. Porches and verandahs afforded protection from the extreme weather at this elevation. Entrance doorways and verandahs for sitting and daily use required shelter from the elements. These structures no longer exist.

The ranger patrol cabin (1915) is a four-room log cabin with shake roof, approximately 32 feet by 25 feet square with a stone fireplace in the living room. It functioned as an outpost checking station for autos entering the park and civilian rangers employed to protect the park after the removal of the U.S. Army troops. The cabin also had a 12-by-20-foot shed of match poles and shakers (NPS 1987b). The cabin was dismantled in 1960 and moved to the Pioneer History Center at Wawona.

The rangers' quarters that still exist at the Tuolumne Grove entrance at Crane Flat employ the same plan as the rangers' quarters at South Entrance. The ranger residence is a wood-frame structure, approximately 36 feet by 68 feet, with two separate living quarters. The exterior steps and the foundation of the structure are made of rubble masonry. Originally, the gable roof was covered with shingles that were hand-brushed with a green creosote shingle stain. Today it is a standard cedar shingle, weathered a dark grey. A porch is at each end of the structure. The asymmetrical gable on the south elevation is worth noting. A garage was also constructed at this time, sited uphill at the end of a narrow drive to the rear of the residence. The garage structure also has a stone foundation and a gable roof, with the ridge running the long axis of the structure. Both the house and the garage are clad with bevel siding.

**GUIDELINES**

- Refer to "Major Road Corridors—Big Oak Flat Road" in the "Roads + Entrance Stations" chapter.
- New structures should be sited well back and screened from Tioga Road.
- Small-scale landscape structures should be kept to a minimum, and should be compatible with the Rustic style.
- Incorporate important elements of earlier construction—such as porches, verandahs, and gable roofs—into the architecture of new buildings, as appropriate.
- Building height should not exceed one-and-a-half stories. Locate larger structures in close relation to tree massing to mitigate the appearance of excessive bulk.
- The form and shape of new structures must be responsive to the climate extremes at this altitude. Roof design should recognize the principles of proper snow management. The gable and shed roof form should continue to be the dominant roof form. The pitch should match that of the historic buildings.
- Continue the use of wood as the dominant material for exterior treatment. Examples of different treatments are found on the site, such as large-scale siding patterns. Split-log siding can be found on some structures.
- Colors and finishes should be nonreflective and in the warm range when visible from the road.
- Refer to the "Unifying Elements" chapter for further guidance.
- Carefully observe night-sky recommendations and conform to park lighting guidelines.

*Shining willow*
*(Salix lasiandra)*

## HODGDON MEADOW

### SETTING

The Hodgdon Meadows maintenance station and employee housing area is accessed by and directly adjacent to Old Big Oak Flat Road. The road is now a hiking route and NPS service road leading to The Tuolumne Grove of Giant Sequoias. The complex sits at the edge of a narrow but lush meadow and wetland at an elevation of 4,700 feet. The developed area is downslope but screened from the Hodgdon Meadows campground by a forest of mixed conifers. Surrounded by cedars and pines, the area drains to a tributary of North Crane Creek. The two uses for this area are maintenance and employee housing.

The maintenance area is close to the road and includes functional sand and material storage surrounded by a mixture of storage units, parked cars, and trailers adjacent to a large warehouse and utility area. Next to this are six units of trailer housing.

Employee housing, a short distance downhill, consists of numerous residential structures farther away from Old Big Oak Flat Road. Two of the units are Mission 66 duplexes.

**GUIDELINES**

- To retain the natural, less-developed character of this area, new construction should be located out of view from the historic Old Big Oak Flat Road.
- New design should take advantage of opportunities to enhance historic views of the meadow from Old Big Oak Flat Road and trail, including appropriate vegetation thinning or removal of succeeding conifers.

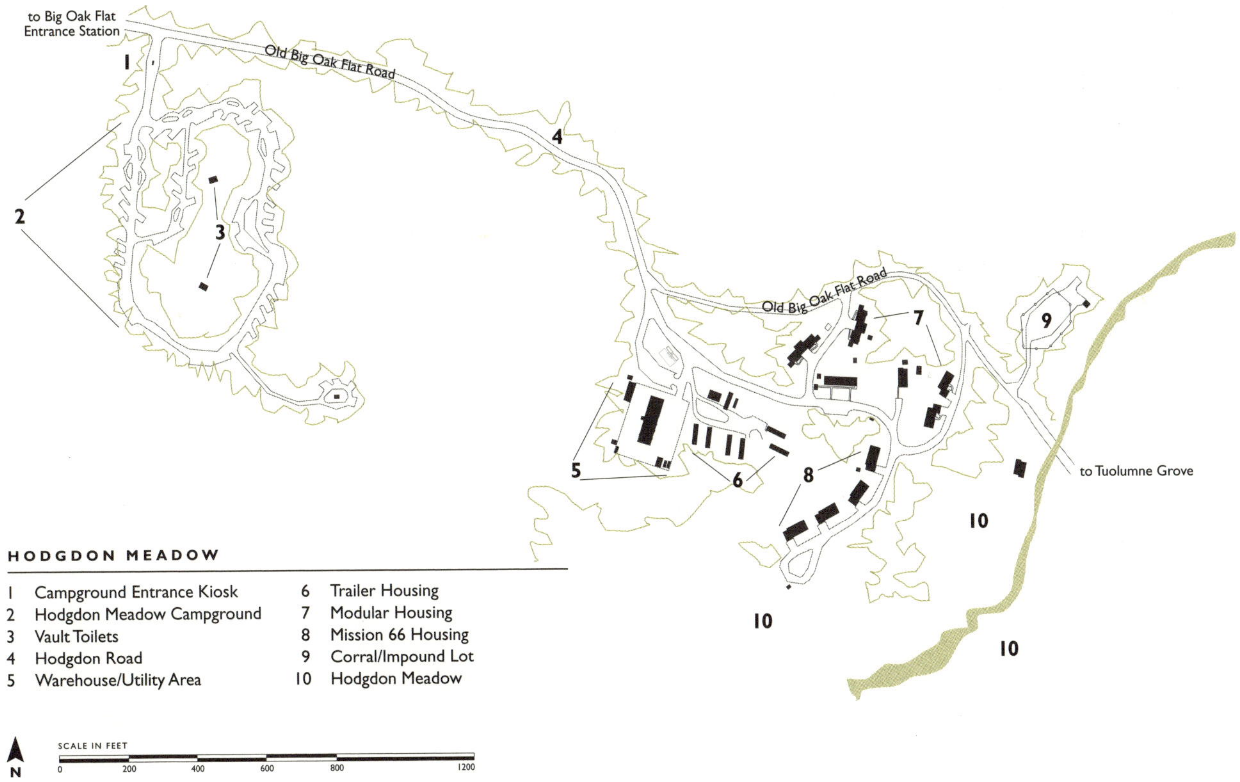

LEFT *Campground sign, Hodgdon Meadow (2008) GH* TOP MIDDLE *Maintenance area, Hodgdon Meadow (2008) GH* TOP RIGHT *Hodgdon Meadow (2008) TP*
BOTTOM *Residential area, Hodgdon Meadow (2008) GH*

## Developed Areas

Hodgdon Meadow is part of a remote setting, well away from the busy Big Oak Flat Entrance. The residential quarters are useful references for new housing. Appropriate architectural character and privacy for the occupants are issues that appear to be lacking at the site. Refer to "Developed Areas—Architectural Character" in the "Unifying Elements" chapter.

**GUIDELINES**

- When joining new buildings, such as duplex units, common walls should be offset to relieve long expanses of walls and provide identity for the individual units.
- Provide protection from the weather at entrances and other openings that are integral to the design and avoid a "tacked-on" appearance. Porches and small verandahs are effective for this purpose.
- Establishing outdoor areas for housing units is appropriate. Where such areas face the street or need additional privacy, use of natural landforms or native vegetation for screening is preferred.
- Roof form should be gable or shed, with 5:12 minimum slope for positive flow. Provide extra-wide valley flashing when using standing seam configuration to allow snow and tree duff to flow easily.
- Provide garages or screened carports for vehicles.
- Refer to the "Developed Areas" section in the "Unifying Elements" chapter for guidance on architectural character and color.

## HETCH HETCHY

In 1869, California State Geologist Josiah D. Whitney commented on a recently mapped area of the High Sierra, called the Hetch Hetchy Valley:

> *It is not on quite so grand scale as [Yosemite Valley], but if there were no Yosemite, the Hetch-Hetchy would be fairly entitled to a worldwide fame; and, in spite of the superior attractions of the Yosemite, a visit to its counterpart may be recommended, if it be only to see how curiously nature has repeated herself. (Whitney 1871)*

John Muir first visited Hetch Hetchy in 1871 and was likewise impressed, terming it "one of Nature's rarest and most precious mountain temples." Some three decades later, word leaked out that the city of San Francisco was planning a reservoir in the valley to create a badly needed municipal water supply. This touched off a nationwide debate, not just over Hetch Hetchy but over the best use of public land in general. Muir and his fellow Sierra Club members organized a grassroots campaign—likely the first of its kind—hoping to sway Congress in favor of scenic preservation. Though unsuccessful, the campaign was a landmark in America's natural preservation movement. The passage of the Raker Act in 1913 that authorized the reservoir quickly transformed Hetch Hetchy into a major engineering site, including not just a growing dam but also a concrete plant, sawmill, railroad lines, huge overhead conveyor systems, quarries,

*View of Hetch Hetchy Valley before inundation (date unknown) YRL. Photograph by J.N. LeConte*

*Las Pulgas Water Temple, Crystal Springs Reservoir, Woodside, California (2009) GH*

and a construction camp. The many Rustic masonry structures adjacent to the dam were built with rock from these quarries.

The monumental Hetch Hetchy enterprise came into being out of a heroic struggle between two sides that both asserted they represented the highest use of Hetch Hetchy Valley. John Muir was the iconic leader of the natural preservationists, while Michael M. O'Shaughnessy, the design engineer for the city and county of San Francisco, symbolized the advocates for the reservoir. Muir died at the age of 76 in 1914, the year the first contract for the construction road from Hog Ranch (now Camp Mather) to the dam site was awarded to the Utah Construction Company. Twenty years later, O'Shaughnessy died at the age of 72, just days before the Hetch Hetchy aqueduct was completed in 1934. San Francisco celebrated the completion of the Hetch Hetchy system at the Las Pulgas Water Temple, which marked the western terminus of the Hetch Hetchy aqueduct at Crystal Springs Reservoir in Woodside, California. The Greco-Roman style temple was designed by San Francisco architect William Gladstone Merchant to commemorate the completion of Hetch Hetchy.

San Francisco removed much of its heavy infrastructure from Hetch Hetchy after the first stage of the O'Shaughnessy Dam was completed in 1923. The city turned over most of the construction camp to the National Park Service, while retaining the caretaker's building and guest cottage. Park managers were particularly interested in a barn, bunkhouse, mess house, and an office, but removed a number of other structures to reduce the visual clutter. Advocates of the reservoir project had originally promoted the idea of a major resort at the site, but concerns over water quality prevented extensive development. Visitor use was limited to viewing the dam itself or passing over it to gain access to the newly established hiking trails north of the reservoir.

In 1934 an earlier restroom building was replaced by an NPS Rustic comfort station, built by the Civilian Conservation Corps, which set the architectural tone for further work at the site. This included the city of San

*O'Shaughnessy Dam (2011) RF*

*Tueeulala and Lower Wapama Falls, Hetch Hetchy (2005) RF*

*Hetch Hetchy Reservoir (2011) RF*

Francisco's new chalet, completed in 1938, the same year that work to raise the height of the O'Shaughnessy Dam was finished. The chalet is along the north side of the old wagon road to Hetch Hetchy Valley, approximately 400 feet east of Hetch Hetchy Road, perched on the edge of the reservoir. The Rustic-style chalet was constructed by the city and county of San Francisco as a guest cottage for official city visitors; Eleanor Roosevelt was one of the more notable guests. Since then, the guest list has grown to include senators, members of Congress, and former presidents.

Also in 1938, the city turned two cottages over to the National Park Service—the older guest cottage and a duplex unit. In anticipation of the transfer, the two buildings were designed and constructed to NPS standards and were thought of as permanent fixtures, as opposed to the temporary structures characteristic of the construction camp.

## SETTING

The pre-reservoir valley, called Tuolumne Valley by the early settlers, was carved by glaciers only 15,000–20,000 years ago. It is relatively young compared to Yosemite Valley, where glaciation took place 750,000 years ago. The steep cliffs and domes surrounding Hetch Hetchy reservoir are evidence of a still-active geologic landscape (NPS 2007b). The bright white streak of Wapama Falls contrasts with the steep surrounding granite. The grey cliffs and walls of Hetch Hetchy Dome seem to demonstrate the cutting power of glaciation and active year-round creeks.

Evidence of prehistoric and 19th century settlers includes American Indian settlements, wagon tracks, and fence lines below the reservoir waters (NPS 2007b).

O'Shaughnessy Dam, constructed between 1914 and 1938, impounds the Tuolumne River at the mouth of the Tuolumne Gorge, creating the Hetch Hetchy

Reservoir, an eight-mile-long body of water (NPS 1987b). Downstream from the dam is the Poopenaut Valley, a set of verdant meadows located in the narrow Tuolumne River canyon. The massive, arch-shaped, cyclopean masonry dam measures 325 feet in height, 910 feet in length, and 289 feet in width at the base. The dam was constructed in two phases. The first phase, from 1914 to 1923, included the initial construction of the dam to a height of 226 feet and the construction of ancillary structures such as the spillway. During the second phase of construction, which lasted from 1933 to 1938, a number of additions were made to the water system, including increasing the height of the dam.

For the backpacker or day visitor, the Hetch Hetchy area offers striking scenery and a special soundscape. O'Shaughnessy Dam is a major backpacker's gateway to the High Sierra, with trails leading west, north, and east into the remote Yosemite Wilderness. The artifacts of early 20th century engineering, along with the powerful cliffs and domes of this rugged mountain setting, make visits here a unique experience.

*Outfall below the dam, Hetch Hetchy (2007) GH*

**HETCH HETCHY**

1 Hetch Hetchy Trail
2 O'Shaughnessy Dam
3 Hetch Hetchy Reservoir
4 Hetch Hetchy Loop Road
5 Spillway
6 Tuolumne River
7 Chalet
8 Comfort Station
9 Dormitory and Cookhouse
10 Office/Guest House
11 Dam Keeper's Cottage
12 NPS Bunkhouse
13 Corral
14 Water Tank
15 Backpackers' Campground
16 Hetch Hetchy Road
17 Drum Gates

N
SCALE IN FEET
0 125 250 375 500 750

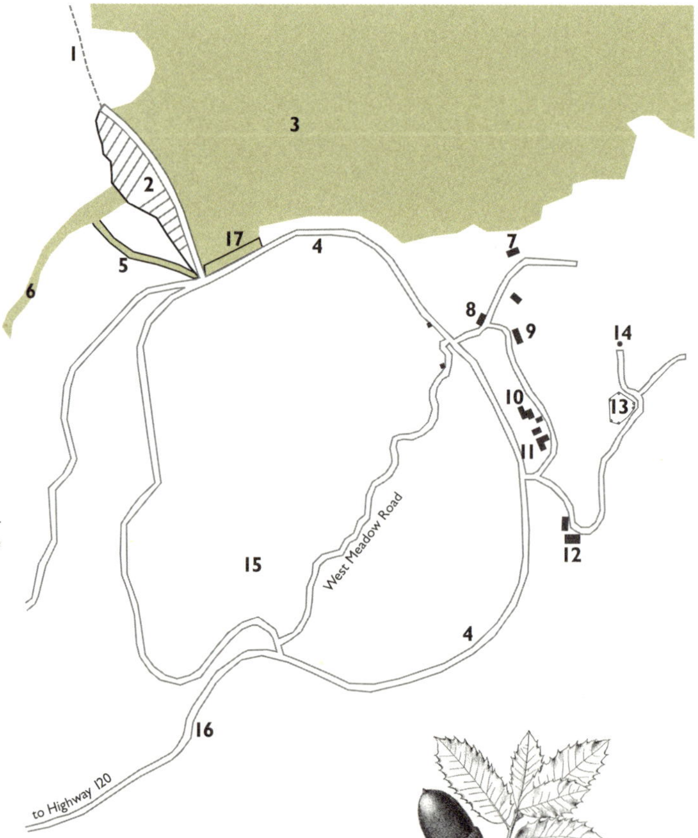

*Canyon live oak (Quercus chrysolepis)*

*Residences, Hetch Hetchy (2007) RF*

*Residence with screened porch, Hetch Hetchy (2007) GH*

**GUIDELINES**

- For new development at Hetch Hetchy, designers should consult *The Secretary of the Interior's Standards for the Treatment of Historic Properties* for guidance on compatibility.
- Major utility structures should be carefully designed and located to minimize visual disruption of the surrounding wilderness. For example, power lines and microwave or repeater towers should be sited to blend with a background of a forested slope when seen from major or special viewpoints like the dam, Hetch Hetchy Road, visitor parking, major trailheads, trails, etc. Keep such utilities from being silhouetted against the sky. They should be of nonreflective materials and of a color blending to the greatest extent possible with colors and light values of the natural surroundings.
- Locate walk-in camping in wooded sites at Backpackers' Camp to minimize visual impacts. Refer to the "Campgrounds" chapter.
- Refer to "Landscape Uses + Structures—Masonry Structures" in the "Unifying Elements" chapter.
- Refer to "Setting—Scenic Views" in the "Unifying Elements" chapter.

## Developed Areas

The buildings and structures found at Hetch Hetchy convey how the landscape developed through its many phases, from early settlement, to dam construction, to recreation. The largest cluster of historic buildings occurs along the eastern loop of Hetch Hetchy Road. An office, guest cottage, dam keeper's cottage, assistant dam keeper's cottage, and ancillary buildings are at the center of the cluster.

Associated with the 1916 O'Shaughnessy work camp, these buildings are the oldest examples of Vernacular Rustic style in the region. At the north end of the cluster is a distinct series of Rustic-style buildings: the Hetch Hetchy Comfort Station (circa 1934) and garage (circa 1935), and, farther to the east, off the old wagon road to Hetch Hetchy Valley, is the chalet (1938).

Sources indicate that the park constructed only one building in this region, the Rustic-style 1934 comfort station. The city and county of San Francisco constructed all the other buildings (NPS 2007b), including:

- Dam Keeper's Cottage (1916): Part of the original O'Shaughnessy work camp, this cottage is the most elaborate of the San Francisco-built Rustic-style cottages, and it is currently used as the city and county of San Francisco's water keeper's office.
- Assistant Dam Keeper's Cottage (1916): Constructed as a part of the first O'Shaughnessy Dam work camp, this cottage was originally for the assistant dam keeper, and it is currently being used as a park ranger's residence.
- Official Guest House (1916): Constructed as part of the first O'Shaughnessy Dam work camp, this house was originally constructed as the office for the dam's project engineer and later enlarged for use as a guesthouse.
- Hetch Hetchy Comfort Station No. 1 (1934): This comfort station is a classic example of the NPS Rustic style. It is one of three identical comfort stations built during the 1930s; the other two are located at Tuolumne Meadows Campground.

*Kolana Rock, Hetch Hetchy (2011) RF*

Comfort station, Hetch Hetchy (2007) GH

**GUIDELINES**

- For new structures at Hetch Hetchy, designers should consult *The Secretary of the Interior's Standards for the Treatment of Historic Properties* for guidance on compatibility.
- New structures should reflect the character, height, and massing of these early vernacular structures. Refer to "Developed Areas—Yosemite Village—Developed Areas—Central Village Administrative Area—Residential Areas—NPS Residential Area" in the "Yosemite Valley" chapter for a discussion of distinguished examples of vernacular architecture.
- New buildings should continue the combinations of gable and hip roof found on nearby historic and vernacular structures. Continue the roof pitch used on the dam keeper's and assistant dam keeper's cottages. Shed roof appendages are used for entrances and additions. In particular, note the use of screened porches.
- Exterior materials and color treatment as discussed in other areas of these guidelines apply here. The basic principles of "background" and blending with the environment apply here.
- Refer to "Landscape Uses + Structures—Small Buildings" in the "Unifying Elements" chapter for guidelines.

Chalet, Hetch Hetchy (2007) GH

Picnic area, Lower Yosemite Fall (2005) RF

## PICNIC AREAS

The visitor's relation to and perception of the natural environment should be considered an important element in the location and design of picnic areas. Issues of natural resource protection and interpretation are intertwined with the desire to place picnic sites in scenic locations. In Yosemite, picnic areas are frequently found in sylvan settings, placed under or among trees, oriented to a special or unusual scenic view, or often close to a stream, river, or lake. Parking is usually nearby, allowing reasonable access for persons with disabilities and for transporting picnic supplies. A picnic unit typically consists of a table and grill. The units may occur separately or clustered in combination with a number of other units to form a picnic area. Most picnic areas, but not all, are furnished with potable water, recycling and trash containers, restrooms, and accessible paths to parking. Most furnishings are commercially available off-the-shelf items. At some sites, particularly those close to water, soils and vegetation are fragile and easily damaged because of high groundwater tables.

One of the great innovators in the design of picnic areas was Emilio P. Meinecke, the plant pathologist engaged by the National Park Service in the early 1930s

TOP *West end of Tenaya Lake (2007) GH* BOTTOM *Forest Service picnic table (2010) RF*

to investigate and advise on the deteriorating conditions at campgrounds and picnic areas in Yosemite and other national parks. A proponent of early ecological principles, Meinecke suggested that picnic area placement be based on soil and vegetation capacities, and he urged that picnic areas be separated from campgrounds.

## GUIDELINES

### *Location*

- Site new picnic areas away from roadways to mitigate road noise and take advantage of natural topography to shield picnic areas for the same effect.
- At sites where the likelihood of impacts to vegetation is high, furnishings (tables, trash containers, bear boxes, braziers, etc.) as well as portable toilet or storage structures should be moveable for relocation to alternate sites. Refer to the "Unifying Elements" chapter for guidelines on pathway design and small buildings.

### *Layout*

- Size roadside turnouts and parking areas that serve picnic areas to a minimum dimension to accommodate safe vehicle ingress and egress. Parked vehicles should be partially screened with vegetation and/or topography to minimize their view from the road and picnic area. Cluster trash bins, bear boxes, and vault toilets at the parking areas for ease of maintenance in areas with minor visual impact to the surroundings and picnic area. Where needed, screen with vegetation and mounding that is well-integrated into the surrounding topography. Refer to the "Roads + Entrance Stations" chapter for guidelines on turnouts, and to the "Unifying Elements" chapter for guidelines on parking areas.
- Proximity of picnic area components (parking, table clusters, comfort stations, dumpsters, etc.) to one another will vary. Service access will need to

be reasonably close to the main road, but should be screened with natural topography or native vegetation to the greatest degree possible. The location, size, and extent of picnic areas should be determined by the visual and ecological conditions of the site, including such factors as soil type, vegetation conditions, and rock outcrops. Where possible, anchor picnic areas visually by arranging them in relation to major rock outcrops, distinctive groves of trees, and the like.

- Site individual tables or clusters of tables using tree clusters, rock outcrops, etc., as natural spacers to provide greater distance between tables for privacy. At sites lacking natural topographic or vegetation spacers, add screening with native plant materials for greater privacy, as needed.
- When paving is necessary, use a universally accessible, porous, granular type, of a color and texture that blends with the surrounding soil or leaf litter color.
- Protect adjacent vegetation areas, wetlands, or water bodies by providing clearly defined pedestrian paths, partially buried cobbles where appropriate, or other low barriers. Refer to the "Unifying Elements" chapter for guidelines on pathway design and barriers.

*Picnic area, Lower Yosemite Fall (2005) RF*

***Furnishings***

- Furnishings should be compatible with the character of NPS Rustic design. Primary characteristics include oversized, stout components with the use of Wosky brown for painted elements and the avoidance of reflective surfaces and bright, shiny metals. Trash containers, bear boxes, dumpsters, and the like should be painted Wosky brown.
- Furnishings for permanent picnic areas (those not planned for rotation) may employ masonry (local or matching) for table and grill supports as well as rough, board-formed concrete of generous proportions, with thick planks of western red cedar for the table top.
- Where picnic furnishings may be seasonally shifted, anchor equipment to the ground in a manner that allows for relocation and installation at alternate sites.
- Avoid reflective, light-colored, industrial-looking materials such as galvanized metal tubing for table supports. Frames of stout, prerusted tubing are acceptable.

TOP *Stone seating area at Lower Yosemite Fall (2010) RF* BOTTOM *Heavy timber picnic table (2008) GH*

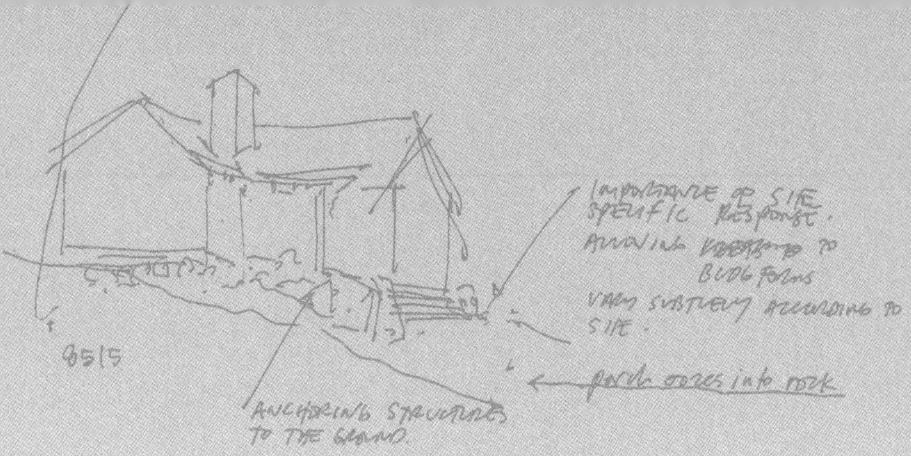


seems to hold more answers, sug
of enduring attitudes
bldgs to help inspire sense of pl
OVER T

## ROADS + ENTRANCE STATIONS

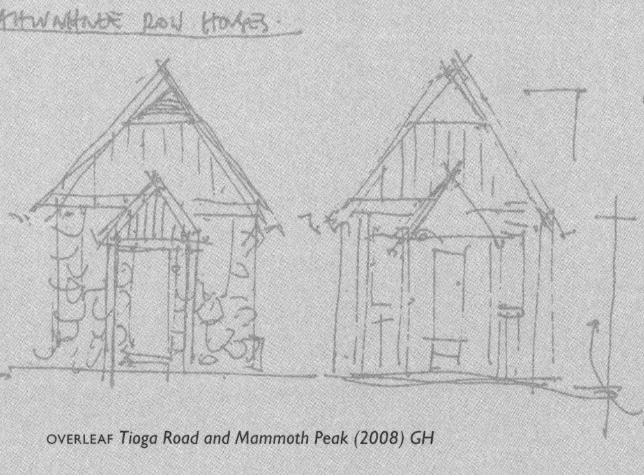


OVERLEAF *Tioga Road and Mammoth Peak (2008) GH*

# ROADS + ENTRANCE STATIONS

YOSEMITE'S ROAD SYSTEM is integral to the visitor experience and plays a major role in how the park is perceived. For many visitors, Yosemite is what they see from a car or tour bus. The park's road system was deliberately designed with turnouts and larger parking areas that provide views of the natural landscape, reflecting the philosophy of early NPS officials such as Stephen Mather and Horace Albright, who sought to popularize the parks through improved automobile access while preserving the essence of their natural landscapes (Carr 1998). Park roads are more than a means to a destination: the journey itself along the roads becomes part of the overall park visitor experience.

IN MOST PARKS, THE BASIC MEANS OF PROVIDING FOR VISITOR ACCESS IS THE PARK ROAD SYSTEM. IT IS BOTH A MEANS AND AN END. IT ENABLES ONE VISITOR TO REACH HIS GOAL; FOR ANOTHER, IT IS THE GOAL. **NPS PARK ROAD STANDARDS • 1984**

Five road corridors are introduced by the park entrance stations, which are located near the edges of the park where the visitor crosses the threshold into the unique realm of Yosemite. Park visitors find way-finding information at entrance stations where they are welcomed by uniformed staff before they begin their exploration of Yosemite along one of the road corridors.

## MAJOR ROAD CORRIDORS

Early access to Yosemite was on horseback or by stagecoach, which limited the number of people entering the park. The trip was arduous and expensive, and it tended to discourage casual visitors or those of modest means. Travel to the park increased with the opening of the Yosemite Valley Railroad line to El Portal in 1907, but most visitors continued the earlier pattern of staying in hotels for weeks or even months to justify the time and cost of the trip. However, starting in 1913, the rise of automobile tourism brought not only more visitors to the park, but a new class of visitor as well. Working-class families who had never before had the time or disposable income for an extended vacation were now able to make the trip to Yosemite. Their cars often served as both transportation and lodging (Rothman 1998). Stephen Mather, the founding director of the National Park Service, was an early advocate of auto tourism, and he strongly favored development that would make the parks more accessible to these new visitors (Shaffer 2001). Mather thought it essential that the large parks should have a major road into their scenic backcountries, and in 1915 he formed a group to purchase the Great Sierra Wagon Road to serve as a model (Sellars 1997).

Most importantly, auto tourism changed the fundamental nature of the visitor experience at Yosemite and became a dominant factor in future development. The new breed of tourists not only wanted to drive *to* Yosemite, they wanted to drive *in* Yosemite and see the sights from their cars (Louter 2001). A new road-building program, initiated in 1924 after much delay, was among the most significant of the responses to auto tourism because it produced a series of structures that came to be identified as essential elements of Yosemite's landscape. The tunnels and bridges of the Big Oak Flat Road, together with the Wawona Road and its Tunnel View overlook, were carefully planned to give visitors views of some of the park's most spectacular features. Where possible, the roads incorporated turnouts to give

**MAJOR ROAD CORRIDORS**

- Existing Road
- B Big Oak Flat Road
- E El Portal Road
- G Glacier Point Road
- H Hetch Hetchy Road
- T Tioga Road
- V Valley Loop Road
- W Wawona Road
- Historic Road Alignment
- S Great Sierra Wagon Road
- M Mariposa Grove Road
- O Old Big Oak Flat Road
- P Old Glacier Point Road

*See also page 14 for detailed park map*

*Many visitors view Yosemite's landscape from their vehicles (2007) TP*

motorists further opportunities to take in the vistas. The central portion of Tioga Road, from White Wolf to the point just west of Tuolumne Meadows, was the site of extensive and controversial realignment between 1957 and 1961 as a part of the NPS Mission 66 program of facility modernization. Park officials saw the work as necessary to ease congestion and improve views, and thus draw visitors away from the crowded Yosemite Valley. Environmental advocates believed that the earlier, more primitive road would better preserve the park's wilderness and high country by limiting the number of people willing to venture into it (Carr 2007).

The design of the roads and their associated features advanced the blending of art, architecture, and landscape design that is characteristic of the National Park Service's development programs, while serving as a model for future work both in the park and in other units in the system. This design approach was honored in 1996, when the Tioga Road and the Big Oak Flat Road jointly received the Federal Highway Administration's designation as a National Scenic Byway. This designation recognized that the trans-Sierra route was among the nation's most exceptional roads, possessing "distinctive cultural, historic, natural or other qualities unique among neighboring states" (USDOT 2007). Winter conditions in Yosemite require the annual closure of Tioga Road between Crane Flat and Lee Vining Canyon, and of the Glacier Point Road beyond Badger Pass.

NPS landscape architects during the 1920s and 1930s expended considerable time and effort on road design to ensure that each visitor was given the opportunity to discover Yosemite's vistas from the most spectacular angles. Alignment and design improvements were based on the idea that modern, high-quality roads would be less likely to distract visitor attention from the scenery than roads that were too rough or winding. Other techniques used to improve the visitor experience included naturalistic rock cutting, drill-hole removal, the planting of vegetation, and the use of local building materials, including native stone and logs, to help the road blend with its surroundings and appear to be lying lightly on the land. The new Glacier Point Road, re-built in the 1930s, is an example of aesthetic road alignment. Another example of such alignment is that of the El Portal Road. Many of the masonry improvements in the 1930s along that road were based on principles of naturalistic design and use of native materials.

## Setting

Six of the park's major road corridors are discussed in this document—Tioga, Big Oak Flat, El Portal, Wawona, Hetch Hetchy, and Glacier Point—and cover more than 135 miles, making up the bulk of Yosemite's circulation system. Five are clustered near or along the western border of the park. The exception is Tioga Road, a trans-Sierra route that stretches from Crane Flat to the Tioga Pass Entrance Station at the eastern boundary of the park. These roads wind through a wide range of altitudes and forest communities, offering breathtaking views of the unique and rugged Yosemite landscape. They differ markedly in character from the picturesque roads of the flat Yosemite Valley floor.

*Yosemite's complex geology is revealed in road cuts, Tioga Road (2008) GH*

TOP *The view from the road is influenced by surrounding forest conditions and topography, Tioga Road (2008) GH* BOTTOM *The travel experience along major roads is accentuated by significant landscape features such as cliffs, Big Oak Flat Road (2008) GH*

Elements that define the character of a road fall into one of two groups. The first involves the road's alignment, width, gradient, depth of shoulders, and color of pavement, among others. The second includes all the elements and spaces adjacent to or through which the road is placed. These include views, surrounding topography, vegetation, bedrock color, and soil.

The color of the adjacent soil and bedrock also affects the character of the road. Color varies substantially throughout the park, from dark-brown soils at lower altitudes to light-grey, granitic soils higher up.

Throughout the park and along each of the road corridors there are many impressive views—some of vast landscapes and others of foreground forest, meadow, or lake settings. The park maintains many important and historic views through vegetation management, allowing views to be experienced from moving vehicles or at one of many turnouts. Much of the geology visible from the road is a result of the ancient interaction between glaciers and the underlying rocks (NPS 2004h). Areas of polished granite are a prominent example. Landslides, rockfalls, and avalanches are common in Yosemite, leaving evidence in the form of boulders, talus, and cleared vegetation.

The park is replete with beautiful, functional, and historic roadside features. These include handmade, native-stone guard and retaining walls, fitted riprap, stone curbs, swales and culverts, and small bridges. The stone, mostly local granite, has been rough-cut or simply left natural, and skillfully laid among similar stones. These features vary slightly from road to road and add to the visitor's visual experience.

TEN DAYS IS THE MINIMUM A TRAVELER SHOULD ALLOW FOR THE JOURNEY FROM SAN FRANCISCO, AND OF THIS THREE DAYS COULD BE SPENT IN THE VALLEY, ONE IN THE BIG TREES, THE REMAINING SIX IN TRANSIT. **EARLY VISITOR TO YOSEMITE VALLEY • YOSEMITE ROADS AND BRIDGES • NPS HISTORIC AMERICAN ENGINEERING RECORD • 1991**

Many informal turnouts are inadequate in terms of circulation and safety. In addition, along roadsides without barriers, motorists frequently park on shoulders, damaging adjacent vegetation and blocking the views to the surrounding landscape for passing motorists. This happens often along Tioga Road, in Tuolumne Meadows, at Tenaya Lake, and in Yosemite Valley. Reconfiguration of turnouts, usually on the downslope side of the road, can have negative impacts on vegetation, especially in the subalpine belt, where growth and recovery can be slow. Snow management, including plowing and storage, is a constant maintenance and design issue. Curbs, particularly asphalt curbs, are subject to plowing damage at high-elevation turnouts and parking areas.

All of these natural and human-made features contribute significantly to the character of the park's roads and therefore strongly influence the visitor experience of Yosemite. How they are maintained, modified, or added to is directly relevant to the interpretive and experiential goals of introducing the public to the park's wilderness areas.

**GENERAL GUIDELINES**

These guidelines refer to all human-made structures associated with Yosemite's roads, including the roadbed, shoulders, and adjacent natural features, such as soil and vegetation, that are impacted by the location of the road. The guidelines are focused on the character of features attendant to the major road corridors (guard walls, bridges, turnouts, view management, etc.) and do not address areas of roadway safety and alignment, sectional or structural design, or geometrics. Refer to Director's Order 87A for park road standards (NPS 1984b) and all current applicable standards related to road design and safety.

### Road Design

- Road design, alignment, and paving width and material, as well as road hierarchy within Yosemite National Park, should be consistent with the *NPS Park Road Standards*, including intentional traffic calming provided by narrow, curving roads (NPS 1984b). The current alignment and width of many roads promotes slower driving, as do the exaggerated turns of historic roads, all enhancing scenic touring opportunities.

*Snow clearance along Tioga Road in the 1950s YRL*

*Site-sourced, worked-granite guard walls, Hetch Hetchy Road (2008) GH*

*Overview of Olmsted Point, Tioga Road (2008) DV*

- Redesign of a road corridor should employ improvements that are natural in appearance and restore native vegetation.
- The design of roads and turnouts should include provision for snow management. This includes no-impact snow storage areas and plow-resistant structures such as drainage swales, culverts, barrier walls, gently sloping concrete flanges that are pitched upward from the pavement, and boulders. In areas where plowing is necessary, vertical face curbs should be limited.
- Continue to design hardscape and vegetation as a transition from road edge to wilderness. There should be an imperceptible transition from the constructed road edge to the wilderness beyond.
- To maintain the seamless transition from road edge to wilderness, introduction of curbs should be minimized where shoulder parking is not an issue.

## Vista Management

- New design should take advantage of developing views and vistas along the travel corridor. The resultant changes in clearing of vegetation for views should take advantage of gaps created by fill slopes, and should appear random and natural. This may occur less frequently in subalpine zones, where tree growth is extremely slow. Avoid an abrupt, artificial, clear-cut appearance at the view site by saving or adding vegetation and replicating a natural, mixed-height, mixed-age, and otherwise ecologically appropriate vegetation community.

## Turnouts and Overlooks

- Renovation of turnouts with historic walls or other historic features should conform to *The Secretary of the Interior's Standards for the Treatment of Historic Properties* guidance on compatibility.
- When turnouts are eliminated, the site should be restored to natural conditions and vehicle access should be physically blocked. Vegetative berms, such as those installed along Glacier Point Road, may be used for this purpose. Materials used for blocking access should fit in with immediately adjacent vegetation, soil, rock types, and topography. These could include plantings and unevenly distributed boulders; partially buried guard boulders, distributed in informal clusters parallel to the fog line and no greater than five feet apart; or log barriers. Avoid the unnatural appearance of evenly spaced and aligned boulders or logs.

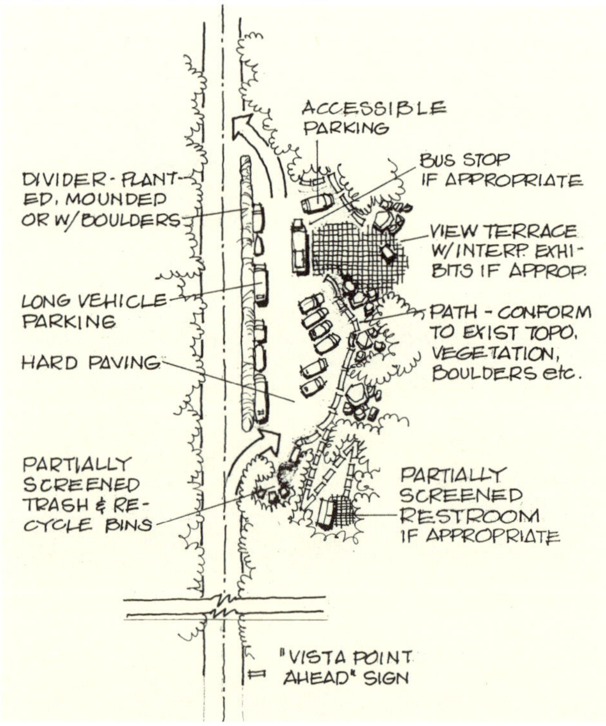


*Conceptual plan of turnout and overlook*

"IF YOU WANT TO ENJOY THE BEAUTIES OF SUCH LANDSCAPES AS YOSEMITE PRESENTS, YOU MUST SEE THEM SLOWLY." BRITISH AMBASSADOR JAMES BRYCE'S ADDRESS TO THE AMERICAN CIVIC ASSOCIATION IN 1912. **HARDY • 1990**

- The design of pedestrian zones at new overlooks should avoid formal geometries. After satisfying traffic and maneuverability standards, let the topography, boulder clusters, and vegetation dictate the shape and detailing of the outer or pedestrian edge of the overlook.
- Provide for adequate, clearly marked pedestrian zones separated from vehicle zones by such means as rough-worked granite curbs, boulders, and planted mounds or strips that appear to have been gathered from the immediate landscape surroundings.
- Provide universal access for pedestrians at new viewpoints, wayside interpretive exhibits, or other areas where visitors are likely to congregate.
- Masonry walls should be designed and placed to enhance views for all visitors. Interpretive exhibits and signs should be placed and scaled to avoid blocking or competing with popular views, including from a wheelchair or passenger car.
- In planning of roadside facilities, allow adequate space for future shuttle bus stops, where appropriate and practicable.
- Refer to "Landscape Uses + Structures—Sign Character" in the "Unifying Elements" chapter.

## Trailheads

- All elements of the trailhead should be designed to create a distinct transition from the roadway and adjacent parking area to the surrounding area. As trailheads occur at areas of different character due to elevation and forest type, improvements should strive to reflect the uniqueness of each site.
- Major trailheads in developed areas should be designed to be rustic in character while also providing more facilities and sometimes incorporating such features as paving and vault toilets. In addition to the items listed for minor trailheads, the following should be considered at major trailhead sites:

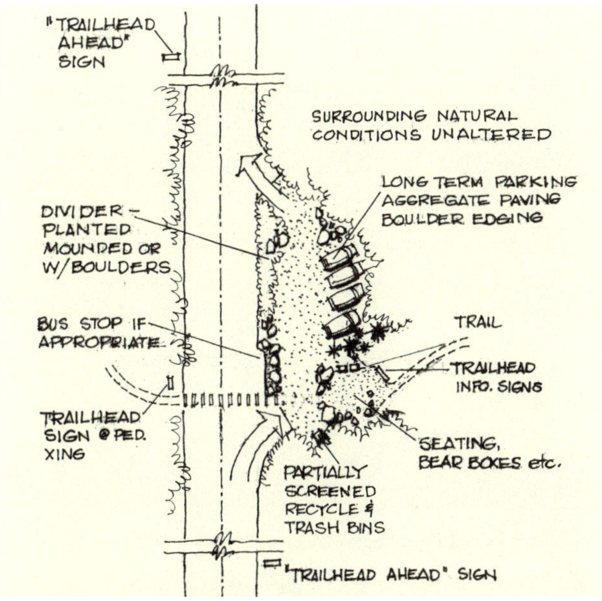


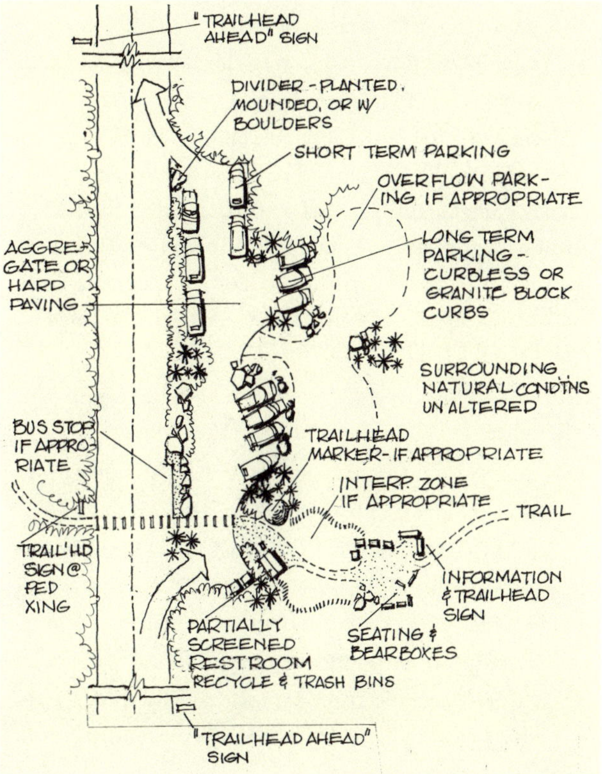


TOP *Conceptual plan of minor trailhead* BOTTOM *Conceptual plan of major trailhead*

(a) Paving of stabilized aggregate over an engineered base, unstriped and without curbs, except when near developed areas where asphaltic concrete paving already exists.

(b) Irregularly spaced boulder or cobble stops rather than concrete curbs.

(c) Partially buried cobbles to define spaces at asphalt-paved parking, using striping only at highly developed areas.

(d) A small, designated area for trash containers and bear-proof food storage boxes, located at logical nodes where they can be accessed by garbage trucks and where people gather, but without dominating the landscape (see plan diagram).

(e) Log benches where site conditions permit.

(f) Informally arranged and unevenly spaced, partially buried local boulders to define a pedestrian zone containing interpretive signs and kiosk clusters, log bench seating areas, and trash and recycle container clusters.

- Comfort stations should be designed to be as unobtrusive as possible, and should be simple, reflecting and making use of site-sourced materials where allowed. If not locally sourced, materials should be selected to match those found in the immediate environment. Refer to "Landscape Uses + Structures—Small Buildings" in the "Unifying Elements" chapter.
- Minor trailheads should be designed to be simple in character and should incorporate the following:

(a) An approach sign for oncoming vehicles, either 200–300 feet in advance of the trailhead or an appropriate distance dictated by traffic, geometrics, or surrounding landscape conditions.

(b) Aggregate for trailheads or trailhead parking that blends with the of surrounding ground color.

(c) A clearly marked trail entrance, ideally incorporating a marking device reflecting the unique cultural or natural characteristics of a particular trail, made of site-sourced materials where possible.

(d) A traditional trail destination mileage sign of prerusted metal with cutout letters and numbers mounted on a single prerusted metal stake.

(e) Informal seating of locally sourced boulders, logs, or other material, matching in appearance those at the site.

- Curbs and wheel stops should be avoided, where snow removal is expected. Partially buried boulders or cobbles, or logs with footings, can be used where wheel stops are needed for safety. Cobbles may be used to define spaces if needed. Striping should be minimized.
- Sign clutter at wilderness thresholds should be avoided. Refer to "Landscape Uses + Structures—Sign Character" in the "Unifying Elements" chapter.

## Masonry

- New guard walls, culverts, etc. should be rustic in nature and compatible with any design precedents in the vicinity. Some modern materials such as reinforced concrete may be appropriate. Avoid faux materials, finishes, or detailing. Use locally-sourced stone if available.

*Large-scale granite guard wall (2009) TP*

The design goal should be consistent with Rustic design principles, such as ensuring compatibility of design with the immediate natural surroundings.

- Refer to "Landscape Uses + Structures—Masonry Structures" in the "Unifying Elements" chapter.

## Roadside Landscape Structures

- If small landscape structures—including interpretive exhibits, informational signs, and benches—are deemed necessary, their scale, placement, design, and material should be compatible with existing features in the immediate vicinity and should blend with their surroundings.
- Roadside landscape structures should be sited to blend with their surroundings and avoid being silhouetted against the sky. They should also be painted or treated to blend with their surroundings. Refer to "Developed Areas—Building Exteriors" in the "Unifying Elements" chapter for guidelines on color.
- Refer to "Landscape Uses + Structures—Small Buildings" in the "Unifying Elements" chapter for guidelines on roadside landscape structures and above-ground utilities such as repeater towers, transmission towers, and light poles.
- When replacing or repairing park welcome signs or markers at the park boundary, use logs, masonry, and graphics that convey the strength and scale of the landscape the visitor is about to experience.
- Refer to "Landscape Uses + Structures—Sign Character" in the "Unifying Elements" chapter.

TOP *Historic masonry retaining walls and guard walls, Big Oak Flat Road (2008) GH* MIDDLE *Typical rough-worked granite boulders (2007) TP* BOTTOM *Granite seat wall and interpretive pedestal, Olmsted Point viewing area, Tioga Road (2011) RF*

IT HAS BEEN CALLED THE "ROAD TO BROKEN DREAMS." PERHAPS THOUGH, ITS MANY MILES OF UNEXCELLED SCENIC GRANDEUR HAVE FULFILLED THE DESIRES, THE DEEP FELT LONGING FOR A CONTACT WITH NATURE'S WILDERNESS, EVEN THE DREAMS OF MANY THOUSANDS WHO HAVE PASSED OVER ITS OFTEN TWISTING, EVER CHANGING COURSE. (REFERRING TO TIOGA ROAD) **TREXLER • 1980**

## TIOGA ROAD

The Tioga Road corridor extends 58 miles from Crane Flat in the west to the Tioga Pass Entrance Station at the eastern boundary of the park. It is both the highest highway in California—ascending to an elevation of 9,945 feet at Tioga Pass—and the southernmost auto-accessible pass in the Sierra Nevada range. In connection with Highways 120 and 140, this trans-Sierra route offers the unique experience of crossing a range of geological and forest types in spectacular scenic settings from California's Central Valley to the Mono Basin. The Tioga Road winds through a wide range of landscapes—dense forests, broad meadows, and vast slopes of polished granite—offering spectacular views and numerous interpretive opportunities. Extensive portions of the road follow American Indian trade routes that once extended from Yosemite Valley to Mono Lake. Significant lengths of the road follow the historic Great Sierra Wagon Road, built in the late 1800s. Backpackers and day hikers can access numerous trailheads and trail crossings along the road, including the famous John Muir and Pacific Crest trails. Because of its great beauty and significant history, the Tioga Road, as well as the adjacent section of Big Oak Flat Road, has been designated a National Scenic Byway and All-American Road.

Traveling east from Crane Flat, the Tioga Road ascends gradually from 6,250 feet through heavily wooded stands of lower montane conifers, curving along a series of creek swales. Exposed, cut banks of dark-brown soil and dense vegetation give way to occasional sunlit patches of grass and views to distant ranges. At about 7,000 feet the road transitions into several long, relatively straight segments, at first paralleling a tributary to the South Fork of the Tuolumne River. At Siesta Lake (8,000 feet), the road passes through a dense, mature red fir forest. Continuing eastward, the curving road hugs the steep slopes of Yosemite Creek canyon. Elevations vary from 8,000 to 9,000 feet, and masses of exposed and polished grey granite dominate the views from the road. At Porcupine Flat, vegetation thins to an upper montane forest. Road cuts are lighter in color because of the prevalence of granitic soils. After a long curve with several south-facing turnouts, the road winds in tight curves through dense forest until it comes upon the breathtaking openness of Olmsted Point, a scenic overlook constructed during the Mission 66 era.

Olmsted Point presents one of the most spectacular vistas in the park, with a view that stretches from Tenaya Lake to Half Dome. The predominantly grey landscape of granitic domes, massifs, and broad slopes is dotted with erratic boulders and punctuated with narrow, widely

*Granitic domes, Tioga Road (2008) GH*

*Tuolumne Meadows from west end, Tioga Road (2008) GH*

TOP *Parking at Olmsted Point, Tioga Road (2008) DV* BOTTOM LEFT *Tenaya Lake from Olmsted Point, Tioga Road (2008) GH* BOTTOM RIGHT *Tenaya Lake, Tioga Road (2008) GH*

spaced stands of whitebark pine. The large, recently renovated turnout and parking area accommodates about 60 vehicles, allowing visitors to access wayside exhibits and scenic overlooks. It is defined by orderly curbs, guard walls of varying height made of large, worked, rectangular granite blocks, and an extensive fill area stabilized by overcast unworked granite boulder riprap. Low guard wall sections avoid a sense of enclosure and enhance the grand scale of the open landscape.

From Olmsted Point, Tioga Road descends through steep, forested slopes to Tenaya Lake, the largest lake in the park and "the shining centerpiece of the Yosemite trans-Sierra corridor" (Rose 2006). Drivers often pull off the road and park on the narrow shoulder to view the pristine subalpine lake and the 10,000-foot peaks beyond.

Northeast of Tenaya Lake, the road ascends, threading between Pywiack and Medlicott and other grey granite domes that exceed 8,800 feet, the scale of which makes the road feel narrower.

Shortly after a long curve in the road, at 8,600 feet, the expanse of Tuolumne Meadows comes suddenly into view. This serene grassy plain—the largest subalpine meadow complex in the Sierra Nevada—consists of meadow vegetation bordered by lodgepole pine forests. Some succession of pines into the meadow is occurring. Fragments of riparian vegetation along the Tuolumne River and its tributaries thread in serpentine patterns through the meadows. Beyond the meadows loom the seasonally snow-covered peaks of the Sierra Nevada crest. Portions of the highway here follow the alignment of the historic Great Sierra Wagon Road.

Red fir (Abies magnifica)

Tioga Road passes in a relatively straight course along the edge of the meadows to a zone of heavily used visitor facilities. Leaving the meadows, the road crosses a bridge over the Tuolumne River and ascends past Lembert Dome through another lodgepole pine forest. At 9,000 feet, the vegetation transitions to scattered clusters of stunted conifers on vast slopes of granite. The sparse vegetation conveys a sense of the harsh and powerful winters at this altitude and strongly enhances a feeling of remoteness. At Dana Meadows (9,750 feet), the road turns north and ascends to the Tioga Pass Entrance Station (9,945 feet). The scattered, wind-sculpted subalpine vegetation of the meadow is dominated by the barren, rocky, and often snow-covered flanks of the Sierra crest, including Mount Dana, Mount Gibbs, and Gaylor Peak. Past the Tioga Pass Entrance Station (outside of the park), the road rapidly descends through the steep, towering slopes of Lee Vining Canyon, a landscape remarkably different from the gently sloping Dana Meadows.

**GUIDELINES**

- New road design should conform to *The Secretary of the Interior's Standards for the Treatment of Historic Properties* guidance on compatibility and the NPS Park Road Standards (Director's Order 87a).
- Refer to the "Unifying Elements" chapter for guidelines on parking areas.
- New overlooks along the road or at trailheads should ensure compatibility with rustic detailing and materials. Ensure minimal impact of design and visitor use on meadow vegetation and soils.
- Naturalistic barriers, such as guard boulders or logs, can be used to control visitor use and unsanctioned parking. The placement of such barriers should retain a rustic character, avoiding straight lines or even spacing. New barriers should be low enough to retain meadow views from private vehicles. Refer to the "Unifying Elements" chapter for guidelines on barriers and parking areas. Refer also to the "Tuolumne Meadows" chapter for more detail on specific sites.
- Design may consider selective tree thinning for designated roadside and turnout views along the many forested miles of Tioga Road. Refer to the "General Guidelines for Major Road Corridors" section in this chapter for guidelines on view management and road corridors.

Dana Meadows, Mammoth Peak, Tioga Road (2008) GH

Commemorative plaque, Tioga Pass Entrance Station (2008) GH

## EL PORTAL ROAD

El Portal Road runs for nine miles along the banks of the winding Merced River from El Portal (west of the park boundary) to Pohono Bridge. Near El Portal, the shape of the narrow canyon floor illustrates the cutting power of the river as it meanders through deep deposits of alluvial gravel and boulders. North of the river are steep, grass-covered, south-facing slopes, some of which show evidence of former mining operations. On the opposite side of the river, foothill belt vegetation dominates the cooler, north-facing slope. At points along the road are fine examples of well-crafted, random, angular, fitted-rock riprap.

Just east of El Portal, at the mouth of the Merced Gorge, the park boundary is marked by a stone pylon and sign. Here the character of the road changes. The road narrows and begins to ascend the granite slopes above the cascading river, with a retaining wall between the road and steep drop-offs. This is the westerly extent of the third and last glacial epoch. Steep canyon walls as high as 3,000 feet form a narrow, V-shaped valley floor. Frequent rockfalls and landslides in this geologically active area have littered the riverbed with house-sized boulders and rocks from the steep slopes above. Flooding has caused significant damage to the road over the years. Extreme floods in 1997 washed out numerous sections of the road, all of which have been rebuilt, widened, and/or straightened. Along the river's edge, long sections of rock-patterned, liner-formed concrete guard walls replaced the original hand-laid, worked-granite blocks. A few examples of original stonework of site materials remain, including hand-laid masonry guard walls at Arch Rock, lined ditches and culverts from the 1920s, and the granite rubble entry pylon and wooden sign from 1930 at the park boundary line.

*El Portal Road, Merced River (2010) RF*

From the Merced River Gorge the road follows the historic wagon road alignment. Along this route, riparian vegetation of varying density lines the more stable banks along the river. Views are limited by dense vegetation and the closeness of the canyon walls. However, glimpses of the boulder-strewn rapids and pools of the Merced are compelling, especially during the spring snowmelt. Rock cuts made to widen the roadway in the first half of the 20th century were carefully designed to blend with the surroundings. This has been enhanced by the growth of natural vegetation.

At Arch Rock there is an entrance station and parking for a picnic area and comfort station. Visitors stop to photograph Arch Rock and the often-wild

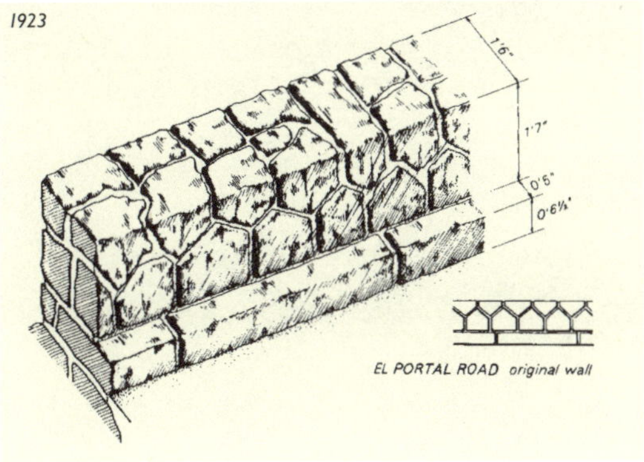

Merced River that cascades past the canyon's monumental walls. The narrow El Portal road ascends through Arch Rock, a dramatic and unique gateway to the park from the west, then past Cascade Creek, where a picnic area and overlook to Cascade Fall exist. The road continues to Fireplace Creek, where it connects with Big Oak Flat Road. At the eastern terminus of El Portal Road is the Pohono Bridge, constructed in 1920 (NPS 2007c). Here, at an elevation of 3,750 feet, El Portal Road meets the Valley Loop Road.

The El Portal Road exhibits a conscious alignment in relation to rockfall boulders and trees. Many of the masonry improvements in the 1930s along El Portal Road were based on "principles of naturalistic design and use of native materials" (NPS 2007c).

**GUIDELINES**

- New road design should conform to *The Secretary of the Interior's Standards for the Treatment of Historic Properties* guidance on compatibility.
- New design along the road should continue the use of slope stabilization techniques that encourage riparian vegetation, such as mechanically stabilized earth gabions.

*Boulders, Merced River Gorge (2011) RF*

- The use of faux-rock form-liner concrete retaining walls should be limited to the repair or replacement of such walls as they currently exist along the gorge segment of El Portal Road. New design should use historically compatible masonry or concrete retaining walls.
- Refer to "General Guidelines for Major Road Corridors" in this chapter for more guidelines on road corridors.

## BIG OAK FLAT ROAD

This 18-mile road extends from the Big Oak Flat entrance to the juncture with the El Portal Road near Fireplace Creek, one mile downstream from Pohono Bridge. It starts at an elevation of 4,750 feet at Big Oak Flat, rises to 6,250 feet at Crane Flat, and descends to under 4,000 feet at the El Portal Road junction. The alignment is called the "new" Big Oak Flat Road, having been built under the supervision of landscape architects in the 1930s to replace the original route that served horse and wagon traffic. The road's original incarnation was as one of the earliest routes into Yosemite Valley and is determined eligible for listing on the National Register of Historic Places. Some of the best examples of historic stonemasonry work in the park can be seen along this road. Because of significant cultural, visual, and scenic values, the section of Big Oak Flat Road from the entrance station to Crane Flat has been designated a National Scenic Byway and All-American Road.

From Big Oak Flat the road turns south and ascends slowly, past road cuts of dark-brown soil, to 6,000 feet, climbing through a heavily forested, lower montane, mixed conifer zone. The road then turns easterly and begins to descend, sometimes steeply, in a combination of straight sections and curves to Crane Flat. A gas station and store are located just off the junction with Tioga Road at Crane Flat, providing services for travelers that are otherwise unavailable for miles to the east or west.

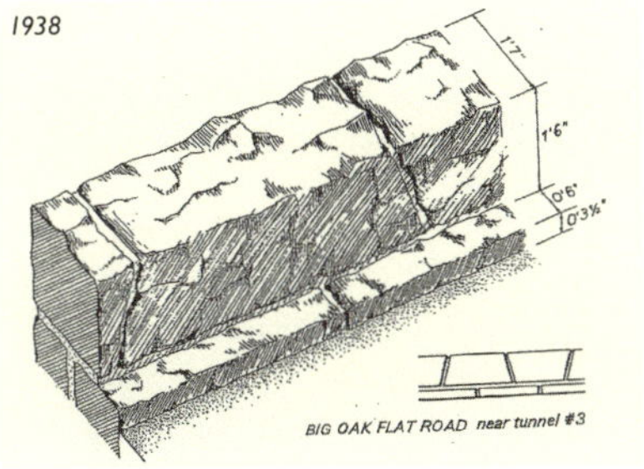


Past Crane Flat the road steeply descends along southwest-facing slopes through patches of chaparral. Here, there are sweeping, sparsely vegetated views of Big Meadow, Foresta, and beyond—a result of the A-Rock and Big Meadow fires. Westward views, especially at sunset, can be vast and colorful. There are narrow, unsanctioned turnouts and a few formal turnouts along this section of the road, including Big Meadow overlook.

Just east of the juncture with the historic Foresta Road is a small paved turnout with entry and exit lanes, known as Half Dome View. This spot provides a view of the impressive steep walls of the narrow Merced River canyon, with Half Dome in the distance. Partially buried boulders and scattered canyon oaks at the southern end of the turnout present a recognizable transition from the pavement edge to the wilderness beyond. This transition area forms an appealing and often-photographed foreground to the compelling view.

Along this section of the road, several large and small creeks intersect the road and cascade down the steep, forested slopes of the Merced River canyon. The steep slopes make the roadbed feel narrower and more constricted. Fine hand-laid guard and retaining walls of large, local, rough-worked granite blocks are set between house-sized boulders in narrow gorges. Three graceful bridges, built in the 1930s of reinforced concrete, cross Wildcat, Tamarack, and Cascade creeks. Three tunnels were cut through topographic shoulders to allow for a constant roadway gradient and to minimize scarring. The tunnel portals, characterized as "some of the finest stone work in the park," were flanked and topped with replanted native vegetation (Davis 2004). The masonry retaining walls and tunnel portals are "illustrative of landscape design and Rustic architecture principles" (NPS 2004b). Exiting the tunnels, the road continues to descend through oak-dominated foothill vegetation until it joins the El Portal road in a sharply angled intersection adjacent to the Merced River.

TOP *Tunnel portal, Big Oak Flat Road (2008) GH* BOTTOM *Old Big Oak Flat Road*

TOP *Fitted riprap, Big Oak Flat Road (2008) GH* MIDDLE *Half Dome View, Big Oak Flat Road (2010) DN* BOTTOM *Concrete bridge over Cascade Creek, Big Oak Flat Road (date unknown) YRL-RA*

**GUIDELINES**

- New road design should conform to *The Secretary of the Interior's Standards for the Treatment of Historic Properties* guidance on compatibility and the NPS Park Road Standards (Director's Order 87a).
- Refer to "General Guidelines for Major Road Corridors" in this chapter.

## GLACIER POINT ROAD

The historic 16-mile Glacier Point Road runs from Chinquapin to Glacier Point. The road ranges from 6,040 feet in elevation at Chinquapin to 7,750 feet in elevation between Ostrander Rocks and Washburn Point; it then descends to 7,214 feet at Glacier Point. At only 18 feet wide, it is narrower than some of the other main roads in the park. The road shoulder varies in width except at the switchback section near Glacier Point, where there are no shoulders (NPS 2007a). In the winter the road is closed to vehicle traffic from Badger Pass ski area to Glacier Point.

Glacier Point is not a through road. Visitors instead head for one or more of the destinations along the road, including Badger Pass, wilderness trailheads, Bridalveil Creek campground, Washburn Point, and Glacier Point. Turnouts designed to capture spectacular views include El Portal View, Clark Range View, Sentinel Dome, and Washburn Point. The road is a notable example of 1930s naturalistic road aesthetics. It was designed to take advantage of views and to fit comfortably within natural topography, and the road prism was naturalized by creating gradual side slopes and revegetating with native vegetation (NPS 2007a).

From Bridalveil Creek Bridge to Clark Range View, and again in the Pothole Meadows area to Glacier Point, significant segments follow the historic alignment of the Old Glacier Point Road. Trailheads at various points along the corridor provide access to McGurk Meadow, Buena

*Panorama view, Glacier Point Road (2011) RF*

Vista Crest, Alder Creek, the Clark Range, Ostrander Lake, Pohono, Sentinel Dome, and the Panorama trails.

Glacier Point Road was purposefully designed to meander through the forest and along the edges of vegetation communities in order to prolong the visitor's approach to the view of Yosemite Valley and its massive granite walls. Road designers removed shrubs and trees at turnouts and at other places along the road to enhance views. Through-cuts in the granite were sometimes covered with local soil and planted with site-appropriate vegetation. Specimen trees were planted at visually critical locations such as bends in the road. The large red firs near Summit Meadow are a good example. Today, large mature trees along the roadway tower over human-constructed features, immersing visitors in the natural world (NPS 2007a). This contributes significantly to a sense of remoteness.

Between Chinquapin and the entrance to the Badger Pass ski area, a mixed conifer forest of pine, cedar, and fir dominates the winding, relatively level road. Elsewhere, the curving road is characterized by relatively dense, mixed conifer forest that conceals all but a few glimpsed views where there are gaps in the trees or where tree density is lighter. Informal, sometimes narrow and unpaved turnouts can occur at these viewpoints (NPS 2007a).

As the road climbs gently east of Badger Pass, stands of red fir predominate for a distance of about eight miles. The wide spacing, limited understory, and dark trunks of these tall, mature specimens, as well as the dark soils they grow in, distinguish these groves from the mixed conifer stands back down the road (NPS 2007a). Beyond the restored Bridalveil Creek bridge, the road straightens, with only a few long curves. Here the road follows the historic alignment. Red fir gives way to mixed stands of Jeffrey and lodgepole pines with more shrubbery, including manzanita, Ceanothus velutinus (tobacco brush), and Ceanothus cordulatus (snow brush), providing a lighter, greener understory.

Near Mono Meadows, just before the Clark Range View turnout, the road turns 90 degrees toward the north, following the historic alignment, across the level Pothole Meadows, and descends through Sentinel Saddle toward Washburn Point.

Bridalveil Creek Bridge, Glacier Point Road (2007) TP

Vehicle barrier, Washburn Point, Glacier Point Road (2007) GH

Half Dome and Little Yosemite Valley, Washburn Point, Glacier Point Road (2008) GH

Approaching Washburn Point, stunning views of Half Dome, Little Yosemite Valley, the Illilouette drainage, and Tenaya Creek Canyon are visible before visitors even reach the parking lot. The long, sweeping views are visible from the parking area. Washburn Point provides a different experience from Glacier Point, where parking is separated from the pedestrian-oriented viewing areas.

Past Washburn Point, a series of switchbacks descends toward Glacier Point. Here the steep, winding road narrows a bit and reenters a forest of red fir. There is more light and greater spacing between these fir trees, in part because of the presence of granite boulders, outcrops, and shoulders. Long views are nevertheless limited, if not obstructed. At the base of the switchback zone the road ends in a loop at the Glacier Point parking area. A pedestrian loop leads from the parking area to Glacier Point, with its magnificent, sweeping views from northwest to east of Yosemite Valley, Half Dome, and scores of peaks and ridges of the Sierra crest.

**GUIDELINES**

- New design should follow compatibility guidance in *The Secretary of the Interior's Standards for the Treatment of Historic Properties* and the NPS Park Road Standards (Director's Order 87a).
- New design should take advantage of opportunities to manage, remove, thin, and plant native vegetation to create, restore, and retain significant views from turnouts.
- Design hardscape and plantings with a naturalistic approach and in a manner that creates an imperceptible transition from the constructed road edge to the natural areas beyond.
- Refer to "General Guidelines for Major Road Corridors" in this chapter.

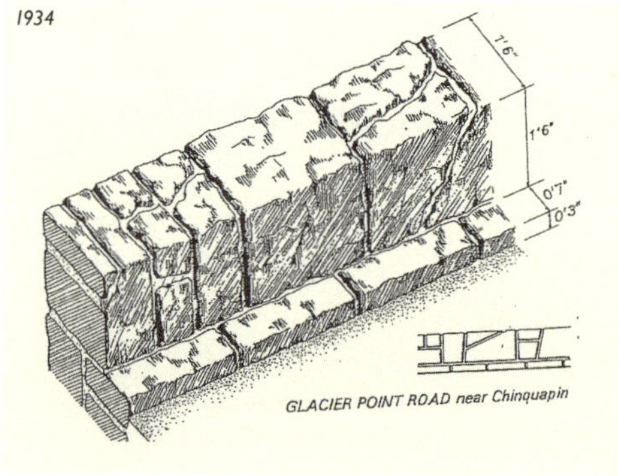

## WAWONA ROAD

Wawona Road runs 27 miles from State Highway 41 at the southernmost boundary of the park to its crossing with Southside Drive near Bridalveil Fall. A stone pylon and timber sign in the Rustic style marks the park's boundary near the South Entrance. From there the road winds gently for about a mile in a northerly direction through dense coniferous forest until it reaches the South Entrance Station. The South Entrance Station receives more vehicle traffic—in the form of automobiles, recreational vehicles, and trucks—than any other park entrance. The Mariposa Grove Road begins at the South Entrance and continues east toward the popular Mariposa Grove of Giant Sequoias. After leaving the South Entrance Station, the Wawona Road runs north and then predominantly northwest, ascending and winding slowly from an elevation of 5,000 feet through forests of mixed pine, cedar, and fir. There are few views and turnouts along this segment.

The road then descends slowly to below 4,000 feet, past the dense grasses of Wawona Meadow, paralleling a tributary of the South Fork of the Merced River. Dense coniferous vegetation surrounds the meadow, the nine-hole golf course, and the green foreground of the historic Wawona Hotel, all in full view from the road. Past the unique cluster of white buildings on its north side, the road crosses a contemporary masonry-faced bridge over the South Fork of the Merced. To the east, scattered on the flat floodplain valley and meadow, are facilities including the Wawona Hotel, the Pioneer Yosemite History Center, an administrative center, and a maintenance area. Chilnualna Falls Road leads east from here to Section 35, an area interspersed with private in-holdings, containing a mixture of NPS housing and vacation cabins. Mariposa Grove, Chilnualna Falls, and Meadow Loop trails converge on this area.

*Tunnel View, Wawona Road (2008) DN*

Within a quarter mile northwest of the bridge, at slightly under 4,000 feet, short views through roadside conifers open up to the river, riparian vegetation, and the Wawona Campground. On the low terraces above the river, U.S Army Cavalry Captain A.E. Wood built a sunny encampment for troops who patrolled the park in the early 1900s.

Ascending in a more northerly direction, the road winds past trails leading to Empire Meadows, Deer Camp, and the Sierra National Forest before ascending in a sharp bend at Mosquito Creek. There are few significant view gaps through the mixed coniferous trees crowding both sides of the road. In places, the road follows the historic alignment.

Wawona Road continues past the entrance to Yosemite West (a privately owned community inholding) before reaching the Chinquapin intersection with Glacier Point Road. At 6,000 feet, Chinquapin is comprised of a cluster of white buildings similar in character to those at Wawona. Leading from the broad paved intersection and winter chain-up area is the Glacier Point Road, which offers all-season access to the Badger Pass ski area and seasonal access to popular Glacier Point.

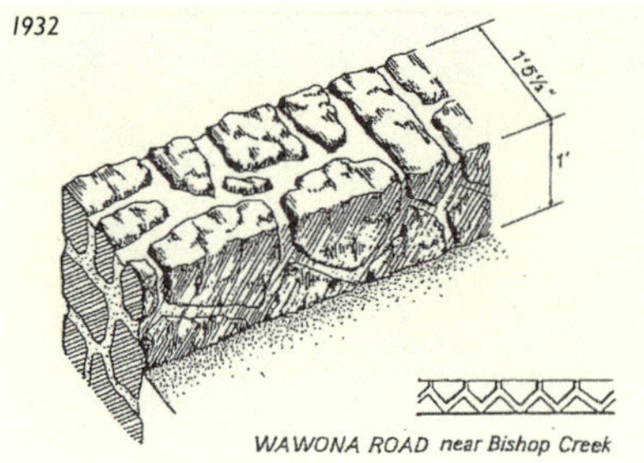

*WAWONA ROAD near Bishop Creek*

From Chinquapin, Wawona Road continues northward, descending gently and curving through miles of coniferous forest between 5,000 and 6,000 feet in elevation. Before reaching Turtleback Dome, roadside gaps in the forest vegetation begin to appear, followed by an abrupt opening of wide views to the west over a broad zone of chaparral, the result of past forest fires. Informal, unauthorized turnouts begin to appear along the west edge of the road.

The road continues to descend slowly north of Turtleback Dome in long curves. Views are largely limited by mixed coniferous vegetation, with the exception of a few gaps through which the steep walls of the Merced River Canyon can be glimpsed. After a short distance, and rather suddenly, the road turns toward the east, drops to about 4,200 feet, and reveals a partial view of Yosemite Valley and the west portal of the historic Wawona Tunnel. The east portal of the tunnel is hewn out of granite bedrock. The renovated Tunnel View overlook, just past the tunnel, offers a spectacular up-Valley view to Half Dome and attracts thousands of visitors daily. The handsome rustic stone retaining and guard walls built by skilled masons in 1933 are still in place.

From Tunnel View overlook, the road descends to the east through dense forest to its terminus in Yosemite Valley near Bridalveil Fall, at an elevation of 3,750 feet. Here Wawona Road merges with Southside Drive.

**GUIDELINES**

- New road design should conform to *The Secretary of the Interior's Standards for the Treatment of Historic Properties* for guidance to ensure compatibility and the NPS Park Road Standards (Director's Order 87a).
- Design new turnouts or improvements to existing turnouts between Wawona and the Wawona tunnel to take advantage of outstanding views.
- See "General Guidelines for Major Road Corridors" in this chapter for guidelines on trailheads.

## HETCH HETCHY ROAD

Hetch Hetchy Road begins at Camp Mather and travels eight miles past the Hetch Hetchy Entrance Station to the Hetch Hetchy Reservoir. Preceding Hetch Hetchy Road, visitors travel along Evergreen Road, which runs from Highway 120 near the Big Oak Flat entrance to Camp Mather. Beginning at 4,700 feet in the Stanislaus National Forest, Evergreen Road passes through gently rolling, lower montane coniferous forest. The forest is interrupted by several large meadows and a few simple homesteads and barns built in the attractive mountain rural vernacular.

After entering Yosemite National Park and passing the Hetch Hetchy Entrance Station, the road briefly ascends to Poopenaut Pass, then descends steadily toward O'Shaughnessy Dam. The road is very narrow, lacking a centerline and shoulders in many places. North of the entrance station the road changes character, breaking out of the coniferous forest, narrowing, and descending along the precipitous slopes above the Tuolumne River. Vegetation changes to a broadleaved, upland, woodland type, consisting of blue oak, foothill pine mix, and juniper. Impressive views to the northwest overlook the rugged and wooded Poopenaut Valley, the Tuolumne River, O'Shaughnessy Dam, Hetch Hetchy Reservoir, and adjacent granitic slopes.

The winding section of road just above and leading to the dam is narrower than most other major roads in the park, and it follows the original alignment of the rail line used in the construction of the dam. To avoid extensive upslope excavation and downslope overcasting in this steep terrain, slope retention was required. This resulted in some of the finest examples of granite guard walls, retaining walls, culverts, swales, and fitted riprap found in the park. The rectangular rough-worked blocks and fitted random angular stones match the dark-grey color of the surrounding granite shoulders and boulders. Some of the granite-faced culverts were rehabilitated after the 1997 flood, replicating the important handmade quality of the original work.

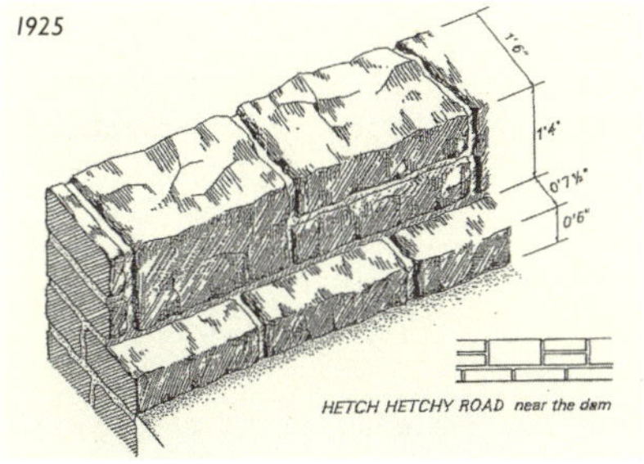


**GUIDELINES**

- New road design should conform to *The Secretary of the Interior's Standards for the Treatment of Historic Properties* guidance on compatibility and the NPS Park Road Standards (Director's Order 87a).
- Refer to "General Guidelines for Major Road Corridors" in this chapter.

TOP *Road above dam, Hetch Hetchy (2009) TP* BOTTOM *Masonry guard walls, Hetch Hetchy Road (2007) GH*

## VEHICLE BRIDGES

With the exception of the steel-truss second Sentinel Bridge, erected in 1879, most of the 19th and early 20th century bridges in Yosemite were either simple spans of large logs or trusses of timber. Compared to the surrounding granite cliffs in Yosemite Valley, the early bridges of wood and steel trusswork appear fragile and even temporary when compared to modern bridges. Given the frequent flooding of the Merced River, the natural erosion and migration of the riverbed through the relatively soft alluvium of the Valley floor, and the geological dynamics of Yosemite, this temporary appearance may be appropriate.

The early bridges were initially designed for the lighter loads of pedestrians, horses, and horse-drawn wagons. With the exception of the rebuilt covered bridge over the South Fork of the Merced River at Wawona, none of these early bridges survives in original form. Most were built with locally available materials. The military who patrolled the park at the turn of the 19th century were responsible for the more complex truss structures. The 20th century brought heavier vehicles to the park, leading to wider paved roads, and with them, a greater need for wider, stronger structures spanning greater distances. Reinforced concrete spans began to appear in the 1920s in the Valley. Built in the 20th century and distributed throughout the park, these bridges span numerous seasonal and perennial creeks in addition to the Tuolumne and Merced rivers and their tributaries. They are found in widely differing settings, both visually

Streamlined concrete bridge at Cascade Creek, Big Oak Flat Road (date unknown) RA

Bridalveil Creek Bridge, Glacier Point Road (2007) GH

and historically, at elevations ranging from 4,000 feet at the South Fork of the Merced at Wawona to 8,600 feet at the Tuolumne River in Tuolumne Meadows (Davis, Croteau, and Marston 2004).

Yosemite's historic vehicle bridges can generally be divided into two broad categories:

- *Historic reinforced concrete open spandrel arches.* Good examples of this type include Cascade, Tamarack, and Wildcat Creek bridges, which seem to sit lightly but tenaciously in their rugged settings. Graceful primary arches spring from abutments, and smaller arched forms support the roadway. The simple concrete guard rails with evenly spaced openings and stout top and bottom rails are low enough so that seated passengers can see over them to the scenery beyond. These bridges, designed in the 1930s, were considered streamlined, and are appropriate for steep terrain spanning deep ravines or gorges.
- *Rusticated.* The Rustic style emphasized a handmade look, and most early structures were in fact built with hand tools. Only relatively unrefined local materials or materials matching local sources were used for the rustic appearance. Structures were designed to reference natural forces such as gravity and severe weather conditions such as heavy snows. For example, wet or dry masonry walls involved careful but straightforward nesting of interlocking stones with the largest stones at the base of the walls, thereby expressing gravity and the limitations of hand labor. The walls were always visually anchored to the ground at the base (or, in the case of arched bridges, sprung from the riverbanks), typically being battered or splayed at the ground line. The large scale and relatively crude shaping of materials and the irregularity of repeated features (such as with stone guard and retaining walls) all expressed the apparent limitations of handwork and hand tools, but also, and more importantly, hinted at a relationship to the grandeur of the surrounding mountain landscape.

Applied specifically to vehicle bridges, rustication involved hand-shaped granite stones for self-supporting guard walls, with spandrel cladding as an extension of wing wall cladding that sprang from grade, often engaging huge site boulders. Piers and abutments were likewise clad with stone and hand-hewn timber or log members. Even though the rustication was intended to portray a historic appearance while covering reinforced concrete or steel support structures, the materials used were not artificial, and the construction was essentially by hand labor or convincingly conveyed that quality. Rustication of functional structures such as bridges in the classic Rustic style can be distinguished from more contemporary attempts at copying past styles or looks (such as faux rock walls).

Many of the park's creeks, rivers, and ravines are spanned by steel or reinforced concrete beams or arches clad with various types of stonemasonry or concealed beneath timber falsework. The guard rail designs and heights for bridges rusticated with masonry vary from crossing to crossing, as does the provision of a sidewalk. The rustic arched masonry-clad concrete bridges included hand-shaped ring stones of granite quarried in the park. More recent contemporary rustic bridges, incorporating new standards such as higher guard walls, have had varying degrees of success in meeting the aesthetic standards of the 1930s rustic styles.

With respect to views from the road, most older bridges had guard rails or parapet walks, which were low enough (generally 24–36 inches) to see over from a seated position in a private automobile. Newer bridges have high guard walls or large-diameter pipe or timber railings wherever there is a dropoff of more than 30 inches high and where pedestrian traffic is expected. Some pipe railings employ reflective metals and have been given a streamlined appearance with curved support brackets.

**GUIDELINES**

- For design of new bridges, designers should consult *The Secretary of the Interior's Standards for the Treatment of Historic Properties* for guidance to ensure compatibility and the NPS Park Road Standards (Director's Order 87a).
- In areas of steep terrain, deep ravines, or gorges, the 1930s-era, streamlined, reinforced concrete arch and guard rail system bridges could serve as appropriate models.
- Masonry cladding for new bridges should only be applied from the ground up—for example, masonry cladding should not be applied only to suspended spandrels or railings without also being applied to piers, abutments, pylons, and wing walls.
- Masonry cladding on concrete arch and spandrels, as well as parapet guard walls on new bridges, should retain the historic patterns found in the park. Use practical, simple, timeless-looking stone patterns that were typical of rusticated structures of the 1930s, and not designed patterns such as Ashlar, a style unrelated to the practical, structurally based use of natural, locally found stone of past eras. Continue the use of ring stones on stone-clad arched spans. Mortar joints should be narrow and deep-raked to the extent possible, to give an appearance similar to that of a dry-laid wall.
- Where little or no pedestrian use is anticipated, low, masonry-clad, solid parapet guard walls are preferable to taller open ones with metal or timber top rails on arched spans.
- Log or rough-cut timber post and rail systems are preferred to metal piping guard rails. Where no pedestrian use is anticipated, consider large-diameter unpeeled logs secured as guard rails on concrete or steel-girder deck bridges.

## ENTRANCE STATIONS

Yosemite's entrance stations function as doorways where uniformed park staff welcome visitors and provide them with information to enrich their time in the park. Rather than being located exactly at the park boundaries, stations occupy sites that enhance the sense of arrival in a unique and special place. At the same time, the entrance stations are meant to be symbols of the National Park Service's authority and oversight. This helps to remind visitors that their enjoyment of the park also carries with it the responsibility to help protect Yosemite's wonders.

Shifting park boundaries and road alignments mean that Yosemite has had entrance stations—or "checking stations," as they were originally termed—at a number of different locations over the years. The current stations are: Hetch Hetchy near Camp Mather, Big Oak Flat in the Hodgdon Meadow area, Arch Rock on the El Portal Road, the South Entrance at the intersection of the Wawona Road and the Mariposa Grove Road, and Tioga Pass on the eastern boundary of the park. The facilities themselves have been repeatedly modified in response to changing traffic patterns, administrative needs, and, in some cases, natural disasters. The stations are typically made up of one or more kiosks, a comfort station, and a residence unit (in some cases converted to an office).

*Tioga Pass Entrance Station (2007) GH*

*Arch Rock, El Portal Road (date unknown) YRL*

Arch Rock Entrance Station, dating from 1926 and partially reconstructed in 2009, is the oldest entrance station in use. It was built in conjunction with the All Weather Highway through the Merced River canyon, and was sited to take advantage of the natural granite arch that formed a suitable entry point to the park. The location—immediately adjacent to the Merced River—has made the station vulnerable to periodic flooding.

The Tioga Pass Entrance Station was built during 1931 and 1932 to replace an earlier facility in Tuolumne Meadows. It is a notable example of Rustic design, using rugged stone and log construction to blend in with the scenery of the High Sierra.

The 1934 South Entrance complex reflects a different expression of Rustic design, with low wood-frame buildings with rubble foundations for harmony with the heavily wooded site. This included using stones that were specially selected for their worn and weathered appearance in the foundations. The layout of the station has been changed on several occasions to better handle traffic or to protect the buildings from the traffic—problems compounded by narrow lanes and tight curves (NPS 1999b).

The Hetch Hetchy Entrance Station buildings have a design similar to those at the South Entrance, Chinquapin, and Crane Flat. This includes the kiosk, which was originally built in the 1950s and reconstructed in 2010 to be compatible with adjacent Rustic style buildings. By contrast, the Big Oak Flat Entrance Station complex, which was originally built in 1966 and reconstructed in 2010, reflects the simplified architecture of the Mission 66 period.

## GENERAL GUIDELINES

- For new design at entrance stations, designers should consult *The Secretary of the Interior's Standards for the Treatment of Historic Properties* for guidance to ensure compatibility.
- Entry markers are an important first opportunity to present a welcoming image of the national park and to communicate to the visitor the experience beyond the point of entry. Refer to "Landscape Uses + Structures—Entrance Markers" in the "Unifying Elements" chapter.
- At fee kiosk medians it is essential to retain the NPS Rustic character in the design and detailing of vehicle barriers. Median designs for entry stations—including choices for color and texture—should relate to and draw from natural conditions flanking the station. These include soil type and color; vegetation type, color, and pattern; boulders; cuts into granitic or soil slopes; and outcrops. Unfinished natural materials, such as boulders, timbers, or rough-formed concrete in the form of stout, oversized, rounded or square bollards with

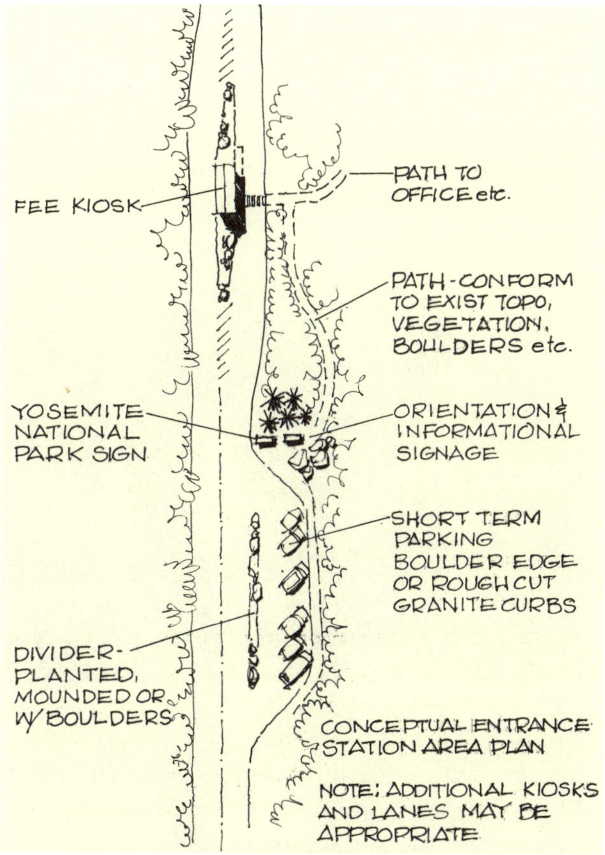


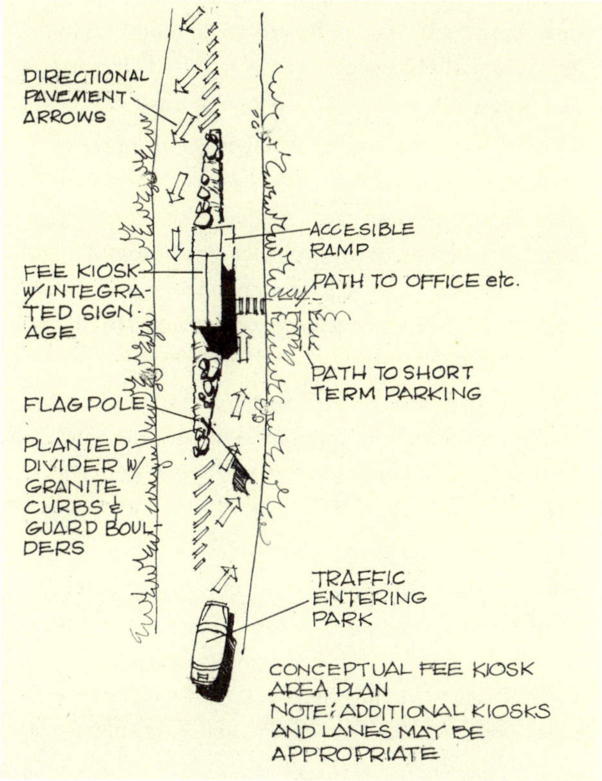


TOP *Conceptual entrance station plan* BOTTOM *Conceptual fee kiosk plan*

Fee kiosk (2007) GH

Tioga Pass entrance gates (2008) GH

integrated shielded lighting, are appropriate. If large boulders are used, they should be buried at least one-third of their height and anchored at the approach and departure ends of the kiosks, and they should be distributed and clustered with smaller boulders in random and naturalistic patterns as required for security and pedestrian safety.

- Medians should be uniformly enclosed by large-scale, worked, single-course granite block curbs forming long, narrow, asymmetrical median zones shaped to direct traffic flow to the reception and departure windows. Use pavement markings and colored reflectors on the curb face to direct oncoming traffic around and to the right of kiosks.
- Medians should be planted with low-growing shrubs and/or grasses of the appropriate vegetation zone. Vegetation should not block views to and from the kiosk.
- Entry signs—such as the NPS arrowhead logo and informational signs that include entrance fees, fees at work, and "campgrounds full" signs—should be designed with the NPS Rustic architectural style in mind. Refer to "Landscape Uses + Structures—Sign Character" in the "Unifying Elements" chapter.
- Give special attention to interior lighting in order to avoid glare and reflection on the viewing windows. The use of task lighting is an effective technique to control the interior environment. The pass-through windows require special attention; control the relative brightness of interior space with the adjacent outdoor area so that there is a transparency between the two. Observe the principles of night-sky practice. Refer to the park lighting guidelines and "Landscape Uses + Structures—Lighting" in the "Unifying Elements" chapter.
- At some entry stations such as Tioga Pass, Big Oak Flat, and South Entrance, it will be appropriate to provide for an approach parking area and pedestrian plaza within a short walking distance of the entrance kiosk, with a safe, clearly marked walking path to the kiosk. Refer to

Tioga Pass Entrance Station (2008) GH

"General Guidelines for Major Road Corridors" in this chapter for a discussion of trailheads and turnouts.

- A desirable rustic character for the kiosk can be achieved by the use of wood-post-and-beam framing. Masonry, as the protected base, is a desirable and useful treatment, as the splash caused by vehicles as they proceed past the kiosk can be considerable. Sash and doors should be painted in NPS Rustic colors.
- Refer to "Landscape Uses + Structures—Small Buildings" in the "Unifying Elements" chapter.
- The roof slope should reflect the slope found in adjacent structures, particularly those that are historic, such as the office or rangers' quarters. Because the traditional alignment of the ridge is parallel to the direction of the traffic, it becomes necessary to control and collect rain and snow so that it does not interfere with the visitor–ranger interface and function. Roofing material of fire-retardant sawn shakes, weathering metal, or properly bonded color coatings are appropriate.
- Wall cladding should be of wood with resawn surface, trimmed with members that are a minimum of ⅞ inches in thickness. Shingle or shake sidewalls with corner boards can be an effective treatment. Use transparent stain finish.
- Design structures so that the occupant of the kiosk structure will have clear views in every direction.
- Entrance gates such as the Tioga Pass log gate which pivots with reflectors to warn approaching motorists, are still an effective solution for low-key control. These gates can also function as markers, reminding visitors that they are passing over the threshold to a very special environment.

*South Entrance Station (2008) GH*

- Security equipment or features included in the median and kiosk designs should be integrated into the structures so that they do not detract from the character at each of these entrances.
- Light poles, where needed, should be placed to the sides of the roadway. Poles can be prefinished metal, bronze or dark brown, or wood, blending as much as possible with the surrounding site.
- See also the "Unifying Elements" chapter for guidelines on lighting.

## TIOGA PASS ENTRANCE STATION

After departing the Mono Basin east of Yosemite and negotiating Highway 120's narrow, winding road that ascends through the steep walls of Lee Vining Canyon, motorists finally arrive at the summit of Tioga Pass, at 9,945 feet. There they find the Tioga Pass Entrance Station. Set at the northeast end of Dana Meadows, the entrance station is surrounded by majestic bulwarks of the central Sierra crest, including Mt. Dana (13,053 feet) and Mt. Gibbs (12,764 feet) to the south and Gaylor Mountain to the north. Looking west is the spectacular, snow-covered Kuna Crest, with bright blue tarns and golden meadows in the foreground. This extraordinary view, along with the rarified air, wind, and white daylight, present a sense of stark isolation at this remote entrance to the park. The fragile high-altitude subalpine vegetation is particularly vulnerable to damage from pedestrian traffic, evident in several areas around the ranger's office.

Tioga Pass is the highest automobile pass in California. The first winter storm closes the road sometime between mid-October and mid-December. The deep drifts usually cannot be plowed clear until late May or June. Often snowbanks still line the road into July and snow can be seen on the surrounding peaks well into the summer.

The Tioga Pass complex consists of recently reconstructed entrance gates made of peeled logs that are supported from the original 1934 masonry piers, the ranger station and comfort station dating from 1934, and a Mission 66 era fee kiosk.

The ranger station, built in 1934, was the first stone building of the NPS Rustic architectural style built by the National Park Service in the Tuolumne Meadows/Tioga Pass area. It was listed on the National Register of Historic Places in 1978. According to NPS landscape architect John Wosky, it set the precedent for use of the Rustic style in this area of the park; other Rustic stone buildings were erected in Tuolumne Meadows at the same time. Initially the building was a combined one-bedroom residence and ranger station. Today it is used entirely as an office. It stands on the north side of the highway adjacent to the fee kiosk. It is a predominantly stone building, roughly 28 feet square, with a porch across its south facade. The entrance door at the eastern end of the porch opens into a lobby with a finely scaled

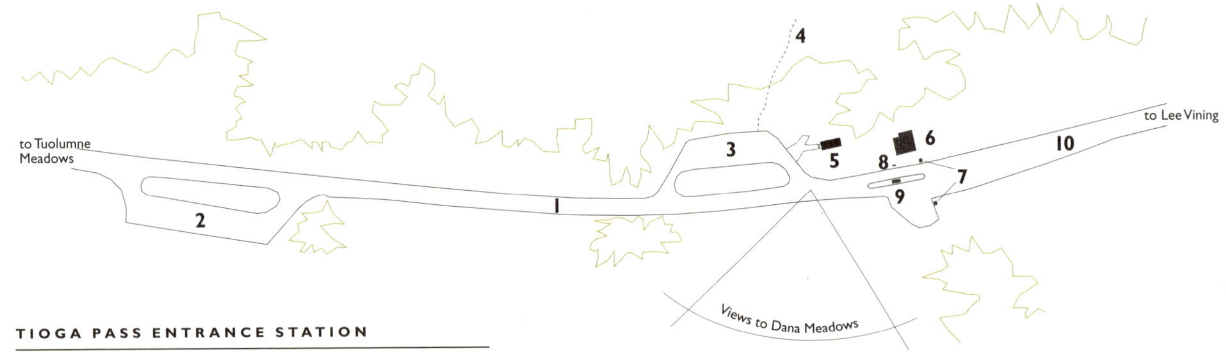


**TIOGA PASS ENTRANCE STATION**

1 Tioga Road
2 Parking Area
3 Parking Area
4 Trail to Gaylor Lakes
5 Comfort Station
6 Ranger Office
7 Stone Pylon and Gate
8 Memorial Stone
9 Entrance Kiosk
10 Highway 120

N

SCALE IN FEET
0 100 200 300 400 600

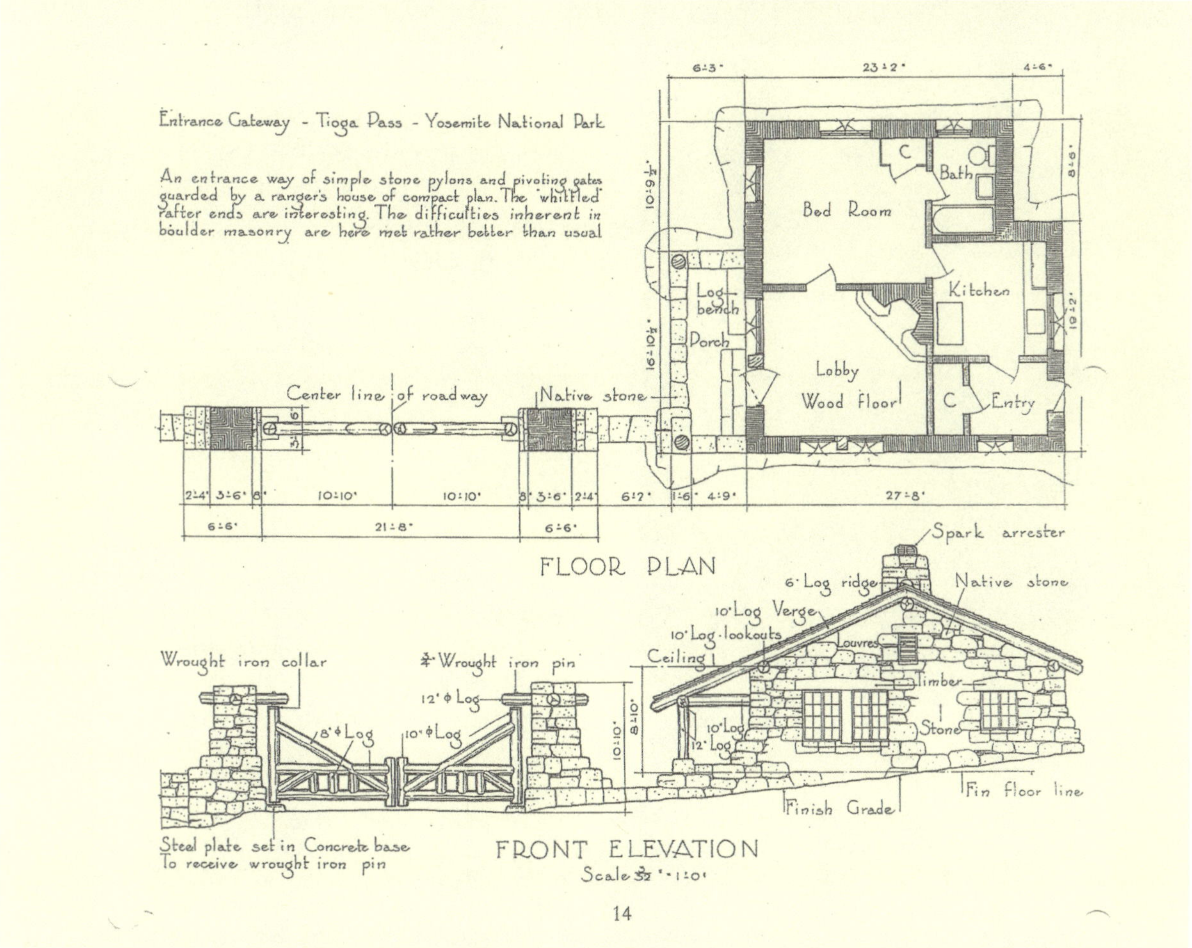


TOP LEFT *Porch, Tioga Pass Entrance Station (2008) GH* TOP RIGHT *Masonry pier and gate support, Tioga Pass Entrance Station (2008) GH* MIDDLE LEFT *Tioga Pass Entrance Station from the east (2008) GH* BOTTOM *Tioga Pass Entrance Station; from* Park and Recreation Structures *(1938) Good*

TOP *Comfort station, Tioga Pass Entrance Station (2007) GH* BOTTOM *Tioga Pass Entrance Station (2008) GH*

stone corner fireplace. The building has large-scale masonry walls with added wood beams for window lintels. The roof is framed with logs of about eight inches in diameter that support a shingled roof. The entrance porch, enclosed with a low stone wall, has two peeled-log columns that mark the entrance. Hunkered down into the hillside, the station appears to emerge from the uphill sloping grade, its masonry walls blending with the boulder-strewn hillside. The white flagpole adds an elegant vertical accent to the setting. The architectural drawings of the station were included in the highly regarded *Park and Recreation Structures* (Good 1938). The text states that "the difficulties inherent in boulder masonry are here met rather better than usual."

A few yards to the northwest, surrounded by a group of young trees, is the comfort station, built with the same materials as the ranger station. The comfort station was also constructed in 1934, and measures roughly 11 feet by 26 feet. The structure has battered, large-scale stone walls and a jerkinhead gable roof covered with shingles.

> *...The Tioga Pass region has inspired millions of visitors over the years. The late Ferdinand Castillo of the National Park Service became possessed by the area. Until his death in 1993, Ferdinand reigned as the "keeper of the gate," working in the small entrance station at the top of the Sierra.*
>
> *"Welcome to Yosemite," Ferdinand would intone as he greeted incoming visitors. Often he added a "travelers' advisory" to his message. "The sun is low. Watch for deer on the road," was a common warning. For those leaving the park and headed toward the Blue Slide area of Lee Vining Canyon, it was "Look out for rocks on the road. Please come back again."—Reprinted by permission from Gene Rose,* Yosemite's Tioga Country, *2006*

**GUIDELINES**

- New design should use stone materials for paving and rough-cut, random-length, granite for curbing, compatible with the masonry found on the building and the gate structure. Granite boulders should be placed in informal clusters as barriers to vehicles at pathway turning points, terminations, and at the intersections with pedestrian plazas. Refer to the "Unifying Elements" chapter for guidelines on circulation and pathways.

## SOUTH ENTRANCE STATION

The South Entrance Station is about one mile north of the park boundary on the Wawona Road, at an elevation of 5,150 feet. The landscape is characterized by dense groves of large incense-cedar trees, medium-green foliage, and a shaded forest floor of dark-brown soil thick with duff.

In July 1934, federal relief funds became available to build the South Entrance Station, a comfort station, and nearby housing for the rangers employed year-round in the Wawona District. The buildings were all constructed using locally available materials and were designed to blend harmoniously with the setting. The buildings are set on a gentle southwest-facing slope in a dense, mature, lower montane coniferous forest. They consist of a restored entrance station building, a ranger residence, a comfort station, and two non-historic fee kiosks.

The ranger residence is a wood-frame structure, approximately 36 feet by 68 feet, with two separate living quarters. The exterior steps and the foundation of the structure are made of rubble masonry. Workers transported the stone and sand needed to build the steps and foundation some six miles from the Wawona Basin. Originally, the gable roof was covered with shingles that were hand-brushed with a green creosote shingle stain. Today it is a standard cedar shingle, weathered a dark grey. A porch is at each end of the structure. The asymmetrical gable on the south elevation is worth noting. A garage was also constructed at this time, sited uphill at the end of a narrow drive to the rear of the residence. The garage structure also has a stone foundation and a gable roof, with the ridge running the long axis of the structure. Both the house and the garage are clad with bevel siding. The National Park Service used this same plan for the ranger residence at Crane Flat.

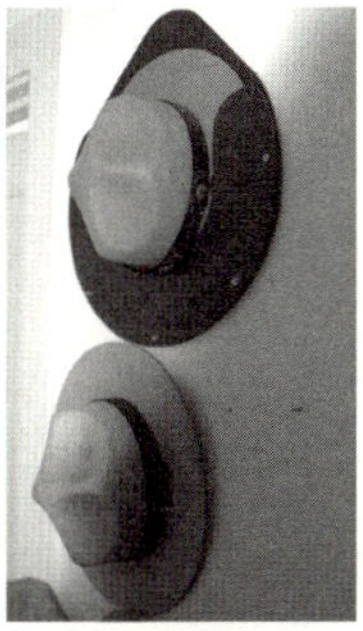

*Flat hats at entrance station (2007) GH*

The comfort station, measuring approximately 19 feet by 32 feet, is adjacent to the entrance kiosks on the east side. The wood-frame building has bevel redwood siding and a gable roof. The foundation consists of the same rubble masonry from the Wawona Basin—specifically from the bed of the South Fork of the Merced River—similar to the foundations of the ranger quarters and the entrance kiosk. Marked, river-washed, worn specimens were chosen for this purpose. Stone steps lead to entrances on either end of the building. The stone base extends approximately 30 inches above grade to the windowsills. This feature—the protected base—is a key element in Rustic design; in this instance, it is an important, character-defining element of the building. Designed for year-round use, the comfort station originally had a gas heating system and was lit with gas lamps. North of the comfort station is a stone drinking fountain.

The recently renovated historic entrance station (now used as an office) is a wood-frame structure with rubble granite foundation and a wood shingle gable roof. The building also originally had a gas heating system and gas lamps providing illumination. Like the ranger residence, the stone for the foundation came from the Wawona Basin.

The South Entrance layout has undergone numerous changes through the years. Landscape architects, especially John Wosky, believed it never fulfilled the park's needs with regard to traffic and circulation control (NPS 1987b).

Today the South Entrance is the most heavily used entrance in Yosemite. Despite the inconvenience of traffic delays, the handsome Rustic-style structures of the South Entrance continue to announce to visitors that they are entering a place where natural beauty abounds, and where the Valley's massive granite walls and the Mariposa Grove's stately giants continue to delight and inspire visitors since their protection in 1864.

TOP RIGHT *Comfort station, South Entrance (2008) GH*

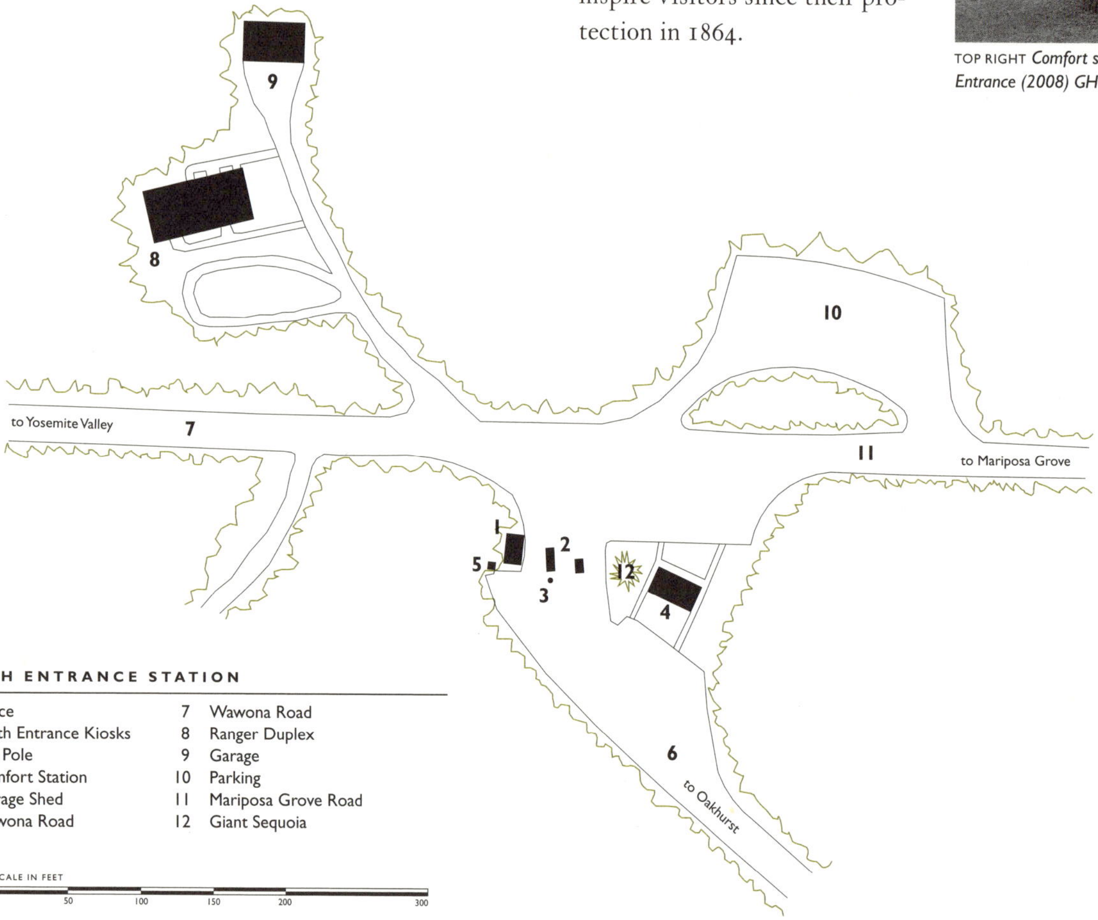


**SOUTH ENTRANCE STATION**

| | | | |
|---|---|---|---|
| 1 | Office | 7 | Wawona Road |
| 2 | South Entrance Kiosks | 8 | Ranger Duplex |
| 3 | Flag Pole | 9 | Garage |
| 4 | Comfort Station | 10 | Parking |
| 5 | Storage Shed | 11 | Mariposa Grove Road |
| 6 | Wawona Road | 12 | Giant Sequoia |

N

SCALE IN FEET
0 50 100 150 200 300

*Detail, ranger residence, South Entrance (2008) GH*

**GUIDELINES**

- Cluster recycle and trash containers adjacent to the pedestrian plazas in areas with low visual impact.
- New fences for separating pedestrian and vehicle traffic and protecting planted areas should be rustic, split-timber, double-post barrier fences.
- New log benches should be arranged to allow for social interaction. Refer to "Landscape Uses + Structures—Barriers, Fences, and Benches" in the "Unifying Elements" chapter.
- Consider the use of stabilized soils where feasible for all areas not subject to snow removal.
- New signs should be limited to those that are essential to entrance function at the fee kiosk. The scale and character of necessary signs should not distract from the kiosk structure. Refer to the "Unifying Elements" chapter for guidelines on sign character.
- Primary light sources should not be visible or overly bright and should reflect the historic character of the area. Warning lights, although essential, should be kept to a minimum.
- Refer to "Developed Areas—Building Exteriors" in the "Unifying Elements" chapter.

TOP LEFT *Entrance kiosks, South Entrance (2008) GH* TOP RIGHT *Ranger residence, South Entrance (2008) GH* BOTTOM LEFT *Comfort station, South Entrance (2010) RF* BOTTOM RIGHT *Office, South Entrance (2008) GH*

TOP *Entrance kiosk, Arch Rock Entrance Station (2010) RF*
BOTTOM *Office, Arch Rock Entrance Station (2007) GH*

## ARCH ROCK ENTRANCE STATION

At an elevation of approximately 3,000 feet, this entrance station is the lowest in the park. It sits on a narrow shelf at the bottom of a river-cut canyon. The buildings are set amid house-sized boulders, close to the roaring rapids of the Merced River. The character of this landscape reflects the geologically unstable canyon walls and the power of the river as a cutting agent. The kiosks (one of which was completely rebuilt in 2010) and nearby historic ranger residence and offices are appropriately secondary in this setting. For visitors entering the park, there is a small, oak-shaded parking and picnic area overlooking the rapids and the adjacent riparian vegetation. At the river's edge are the remains of a handsome worked-granite footbridge abutment, swept away in the flood of 1938, that contrasts with the dynamic, wild setting.

### GUIDELINES

- All new signs should be of the same architectural character as the existing station.
- Refer to "Landscape Uses + Structures—Sign Character" in the "Unifying Elements" chapter.
- Refer to "General Guidelines for Entrance Stations" in this chapter regarding clustering of signs and median design.
- Refer to the "Unifying Elements" chapter for guidelines on the layout of parking areas and masonry.

TOP *Merced River, Arch Rock Entrance Station (2008) GH* MIDDLE *Guard wall incorporating existing boulder, Arch Rock Entrance Station (2007) GH*
BOTTOM *Roof bracket at office, Arch Rock Entrance Station (2007) GH*

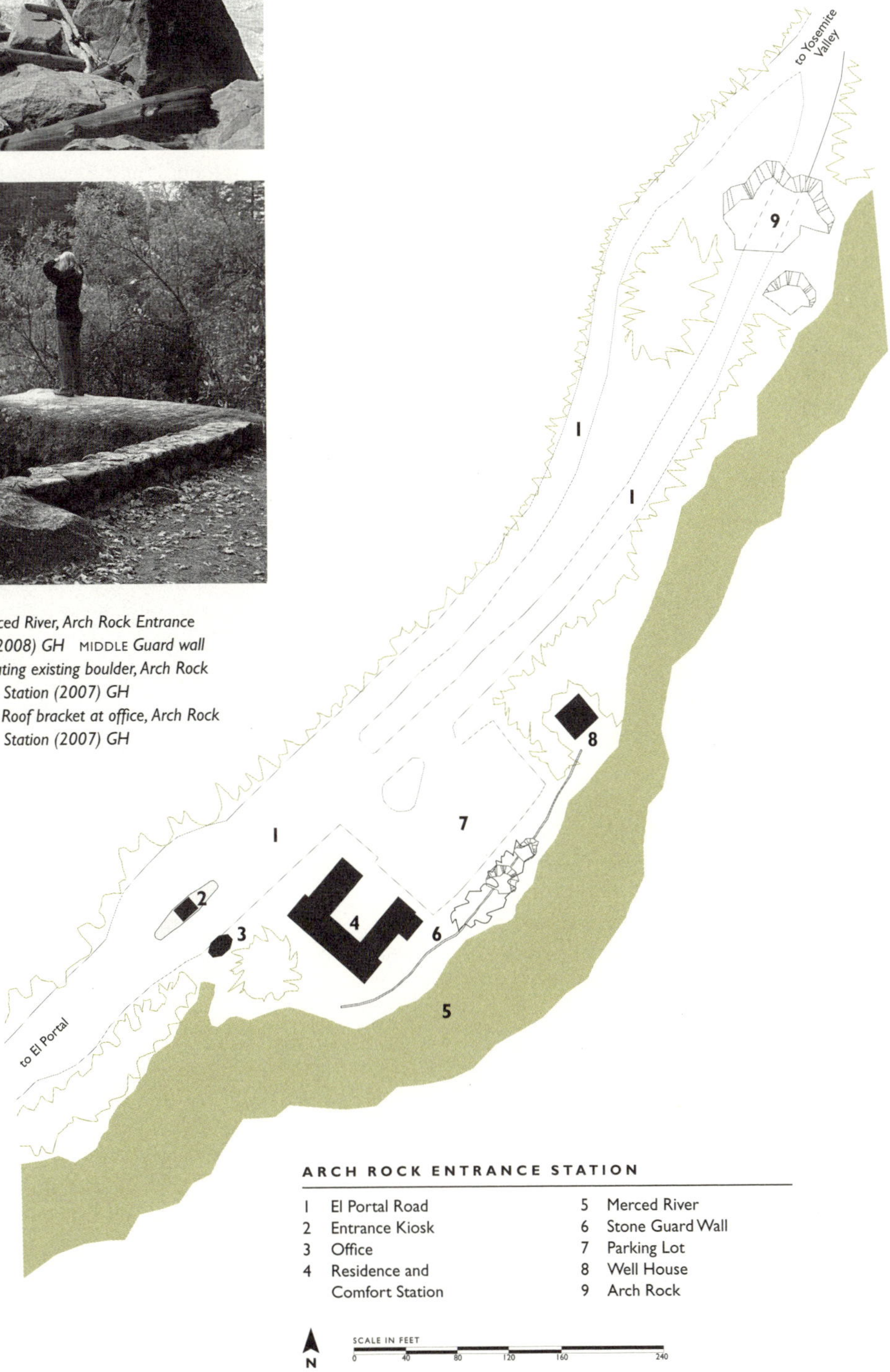

## BIG OAK FLAT ENTRANCE STATION

The Big Oak Flat Entrance Station is set in a gently undulating, densely forested landscape of ponderosa pine, sugar pine, and Douglas fir at 4,900 feet. Second to the South Entrance, it receives many visitors and is an area of intense vehicle and pedestrian activity. The road almost doubles in width at the approach to the three fee kiosks, which were completely rebuilt in 2010, replacing the Mission 66-era kiosks. A generous parking area to the right is the foreground for a group of buildings of various sizes, ages, and shapes. These include a comfort station, offices, and other visitor service buildings.

### GUIDELINES

- A unified architectural style, compatible with the 2010 fee kiosks, should be used.
- There is an opportunity to closely mass buildings to provide a view and connection to the forest behind the complex of visitor service buildings.
- New plantings should be protected by split-timber barriers, either pierced-post or zigzag. Refer to "Landscape Uses + Structures—Barriers, Fences, and Benches" in the "Unifying Elements" chapter.
- When planning new buildings or facilities, consider the use of porches and verandahs to gather various functions under a unified architectural motif.

*Fee kiosks, Big Oak Flat Entrance Station (2010) RF*

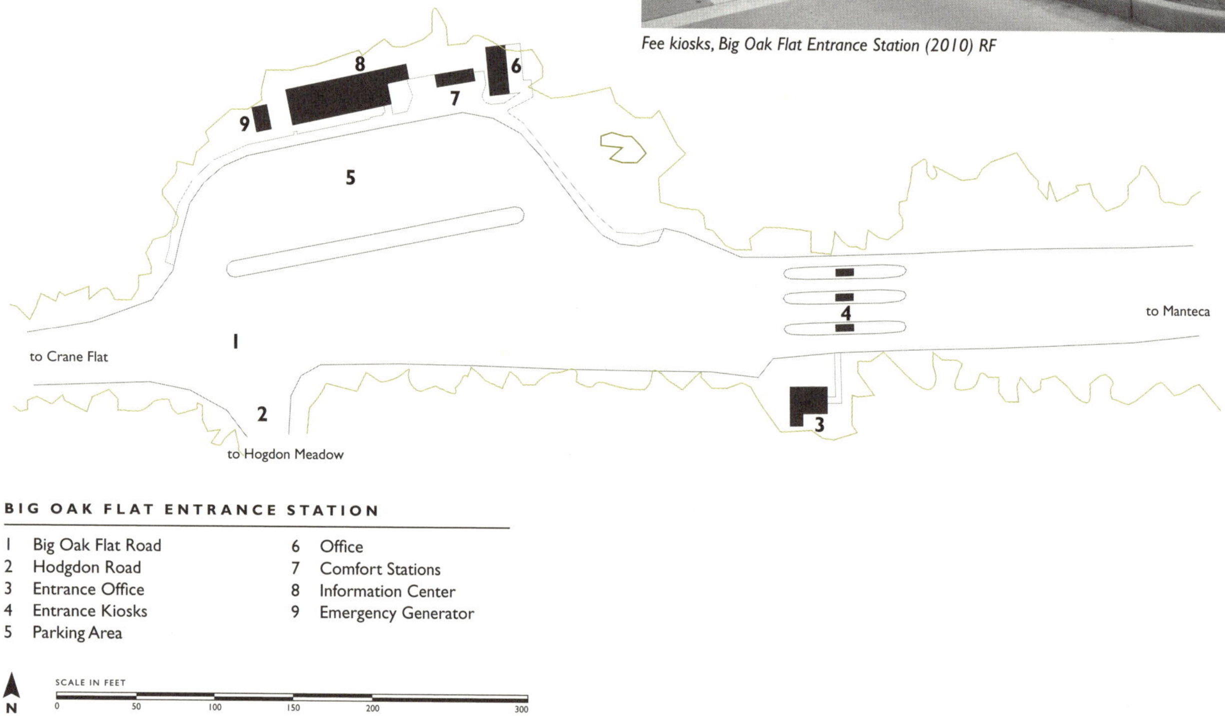


**BIG OAK FLAT ENTRANCE STATION**

1 Big Oak Flat Road
2 Hodgdon Road
3 Entrance Office
4 Entrance Kiosks
5 Parking Area
6 Office
7 Comfort Stations
8 Information Center
9 Emergency Generator

*Ranger office and residence, Hetch Hetchy Entrance Station (date unknown) YRL*

## HETCH HETCHY ENTRANCE STATION

This remote, lightly visited entrance station is found in a heavily shaded, dense mixed pine and fir forest. It sits on a level bench at an elevation of approximately 4,200 feet, south of Poopenaut Valley. Beyond the Mission 66 kiosk (rehabilitated in 2010) are two historic Rustic buildings—a ranger residence and an office with a porch overlooking the station entrance and a garage to the rear. The site plan is similar to that found at Chinquapin. The station evokes the feeling of a settlement in a clearing—quiet and peaceful. An old corral and cabin are hidden among conifers behind and at some distance from the ranger residence and office. Across the road, recessed into the forest, is a cluster of small plywood cabins for seasonal employees. The Hetch Hetchy Road overlays the historic route of the rail line used in the construction of the Hetch Hetchy Dam.

### GUIDELINES

- Future employee housing should be located away from the road and screened from the view of visitors.
- Refer to "General Guidelines for Entrance Stations" in this chapter.

TOP *Fee kiosk, Hetch Hetchy Entrance Station (2007) RF* BOTTOM *Ranger office and residence, Hetch Hetchy Entrance Station (2008) GH*

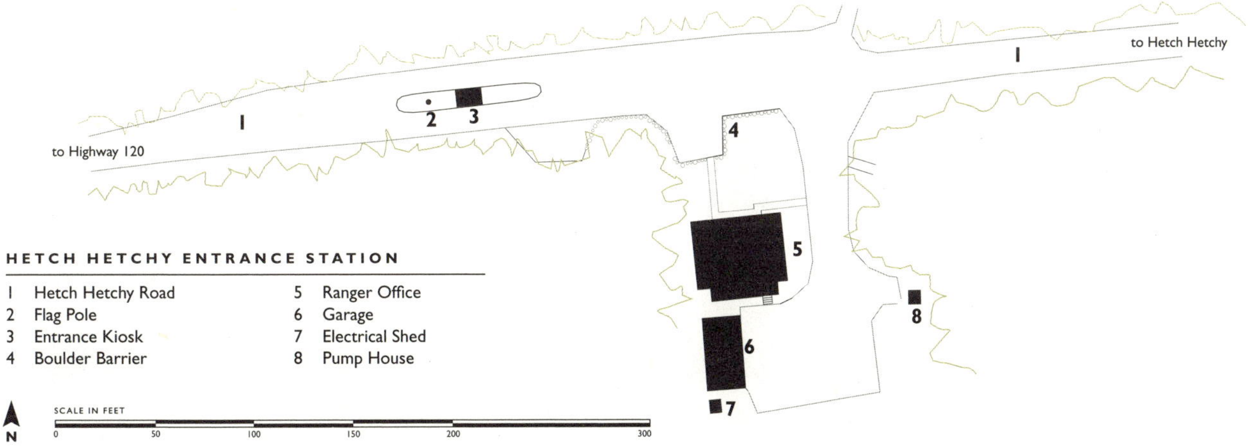

## SHUTTLE BUS STOPS

Shuttle bus stops by their very nature should be easily recognizable yet also recede and blend as much as possible into the landscape. To preserve the visual tranquility of the setting, extra care must be given to the design of these structures. In some areas a structure such as a porch can provide the necessary shelter required for a bus stop, thus eliminating the need for an additional structure in the environment.

The key design elements of shuttle bus stops include the shelter structure design; the waiting area; transitions to pathways; and the treatment of vegetation, benches, barriers, lighting, and signs.

Most Valley shuttle bus stops have been redesigned to integrate site work into their natural and architectural surroundings. Details include a consistent system of site furnishings such as benches, fencing, information signs, and lighting. (The detailing of several of these shelters relates stylistically to nearby structures.)

Shuttle bus stops outside the Valley, often in high-country settings, may not need the level of development found in the Valley, yet they should provide shelter during inclement weather.

## Setting

Some Valley shuttle bus stops were refurbished in 2009, with new maps, schedules, and interpretive signs added; others were improved with new shelters and benches.

The setting for each new shuttle bus stop in Yosemite is different. Some are at the edges of open meadows, some are in the forest, and those planned for developed areas such as Yosemite Lodge and Curry Village will be located next to buildings. Some stops have shelters and others do not. The new shuttle bus stop at Yosemite Falls incorporates ease of maintenance and flexibility of access. The old bus stop at Curry Village, while it embodied the visual spirit of the original complex, did not satisfy current requirements for shuttle bus stops.

The old shuttle bus stop at Sentinel Bridge, because of its simple, nonintrusive structure, has been adapted to new functional requirements.

### GUIDELINES

#### *Site Design*

- Shuttle bus stops should be designed for convenient connections with adjacent circulation pathways. Multiple entry points will provide easy access and allow approaches from different directions. The new Yosemite Falls stop is an example of a shuttle bus stop with multiple entry points.
- Pedestrian zones associated with each shuttle bus stop waiting area must be integrated with surrounding pedestrian trails or gathering areas. They must also relate to adjacent bike trails, providing for appropriate separation, caution indicators, and bike racks. For example, incorporate adjacent trails or sidewalks into the shuttle bus stop pavement instead of separating them with narrow planting areas.
- Allow generous space for the free flow of pedestrians and multiple entry points in areas of high pedestrian traffic.
- Use boulder and cobble clusters, tree drip lines, and grade changes to define the edges of pavements. This allows for informal transitions to adjacent planted or natural landscapes.
- Lay out leading edge curbs or warning strips in transitional curves to ensure that safety and functional requirements for buses are not compromised.
- With either a raised or a flush waiting area, the use of a granite edge element is recommended. If there is a curb, the granite should be split-face with a flame finish. If there is no curb, the edge of the waiting area should be defined by a flush granite paver strip with flame finish.
- Shuttle bus shelters and their surroundings should incorporate a set of standard elements throughout the Valley. The roof shape proportions and ridge and eave

*Shuttle bus stop at Tuolumne Meadows store (2008) GH*

*Valley Visitor Center shuttle bus stop (2005) RF*

height should be the same, as should curb/warning strip treatment, benches, timber barriers, and signs. Where appropriate, incorporate some elements that are unique to the specific site.

- In addition to sizing the platform for passenger load, the width and length of the shelter should be sized to provide proper protection from the weather.
- Several smaller shelters with space between them may be preferable to one long shelter. Smaller shelters have a modest scale and allow the layout to be easily adapted to local site conditions.

#### Landscape Elements

- Concrete is recommended for the platform and the braking pad areas. The concrete should include a color admixture to reduce the contrast with the roadway (the color is to be determined site by site). The platform paving should have a light, exposed-aggregate, finished surface. The braking pad should have a shuddered surface texture. Shape the concrete braking pad to conform to the zone required for buses to exit the adjacent roadway—in most cases, a rectangle with tapered ends. Refer to the Yosemite Falls shuttle stop as an example.
- At stops with curbs, place accessible ramps at the ends of the loading platform parallel to the alignment of the curb. Where feasible, use straight ramps instead of the truncated ramps that are typical in urban settings.
- Where asphalt pedestrian pathways are being renewed or replaced, finish with sand-impregnated asphalt. Refer to the Yosemite Falls shuttle bus stop.
- Use barriers sparingly and where necessary for safety reasons or to prevent trespass onto planted areas. Around planted areas, use the pierced-post system. Refer to "Landscape Uses + Structures—Barriers, Fences, and Benches" in the "Unifying Elements" chapter.
- Use barriers to separate shuttle seating areas and bicycle traffic. The shuttle bus stop at Yosemite Falls uses a series of low stone walls that can also be used for seating.
- Trash and recycling cans should be enclosed with the appropriate material and clustered at key points on the platform to maximize use. Where the back edge of the platform abuts natural or planted areas, partial enclosures made of low granite walls or large boulders (backed with plantable mounded soil) may be appropriate.

- Two types of wood benches are recommended for shuttle bus stops: one type for outside the shelter, and another type for within the shelter. Benches outside shuttle bus shelters should be arranged in clusters of two or three in orthogonal relationships (instead of end-to-end rows). Refer to "Landscape Uses + Structures—Barriers, Fences, and Benches" in the "Unifying Elements" chapter for more guidelines on benches.
- Signs for wayfinding and transit information should comply with the NPS graphic identity.

***Structures***

- The roof of the shelter should be framed using saw-sized lumber with resawn surfaces.
- For the standard design, roofing material should be either wood shingle or asphalt shingle, depending on local context and approval of the fire marshal.
- The bus shelter roof must divert rainwater and snow melt from the loading area (where passengers interface with the bus). Because the typical roof is a gable running parallel to the curb, gutters and leaders are required to conduct rainwater and snowmelt away from the loading area and sidewalk. This will prevent ice from forming on the loading area in winter.
- In more developed areas, columns should be rough-sawn, oversized timbers that are supported on concrete bases with concealed connectors. Log columns may be more appropriate in forested areas or in historic properties with buildings of a strong rustic character. When logs are used for columns, they should not appear too finished—tight knots are desirable, similar to lodgepole pine with bark peeled.

*Mirror Lake shuttle bus stop (2008) RF*

- Columns should have a generous plinth to separate the wood column from water that might collect on the pavement. Board-formed concrete is recommended for typical structures. Granite masonry is also recommended where it is compatible with the architectural context.
- Wood elements should have a protective stain in a color that blends with the surrounding landscape.
- Lighting: Surface-mounted ceiling fixtures are recommended for the shelter area. Electrical conduit should be concealed in the roof assembly. Area lighting for the platforms should have fixtures shielded with sharp cut-offs. A pole-mounted area light is required for waiting areas without shelters. Signs should incorporate lighting as required, primarily in developed areas. Refer to "Landscape Uses + Structures—Lighting" in the "Unifying Elements" chapter.

GUIDELINES. AFTERNOON 2:00 – 4:00 (along

DON McCLARY / JEANNETTE / DON NELSON / LARRY STRAND / BURTON / HENRY S...

[SEIGAL + STRAND]

INDIAN CULTURAL CENTER – WAH HOGA

OUR CONCERN MOSTLY W/ COMMUNITY BLDG, LIGHTING, SITE DETAILS ETC.

## ENDNOTES



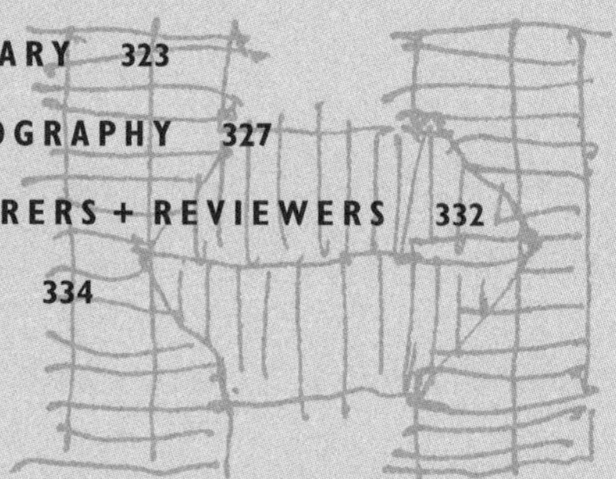

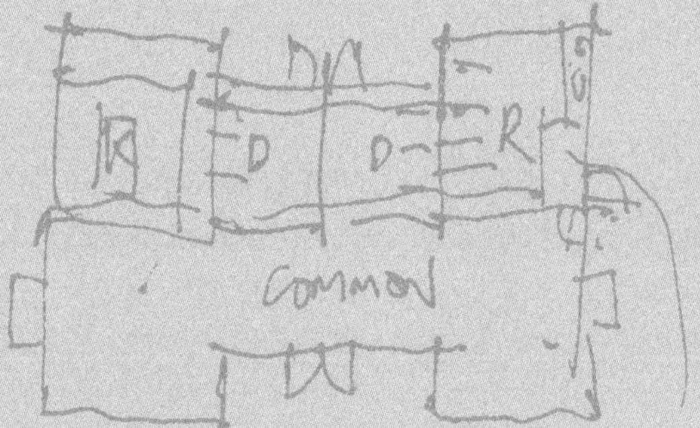


REALLY A BU... DIAGRAM.

exterior publi... to restrooms (encourage NPS

IN REFERENCE TO HOUSE THEY ARE MOVING! NOT THIS)

SH – "LOOKS A BLDG IN NORTH BERKELEY"

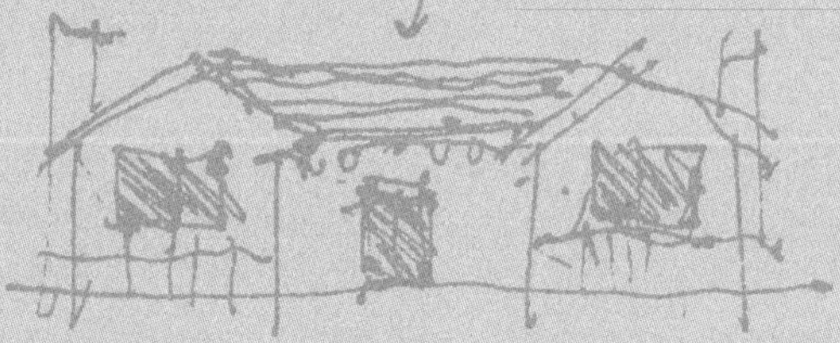

THE NEW BLDG SHOULD MAKE REF...

RIGHT DIRECTION....

THAT CABIN USED TO BE ON THAT SITE.
SECRETARY STNDS APPLIED
TREATED AS "HISTORIC" EVEN THOUGH NOT.

USED AS ADMIN & WILL BE ADAPTIVELY RE USED.

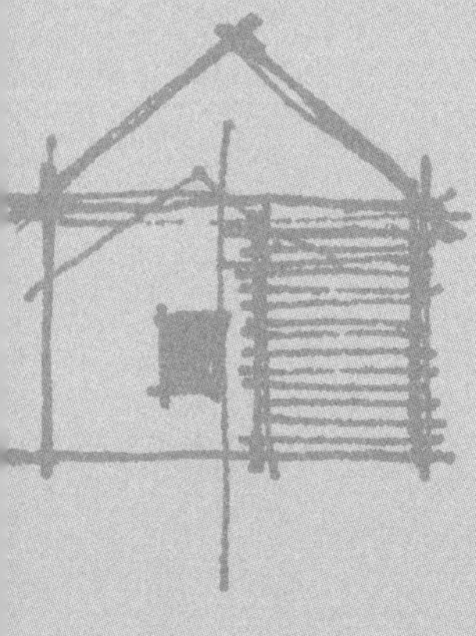

OVERLEAF *Black Oaks, Yosemite Valley (1938) YRL-RA*

# GLOSSARY

**100-year floodplain** The land adjacent to a river corridor that would be covered by water during a 100-year flood event. A 100-year flood event has a 1% probability of occurring during any given year.

**Abutment** A structure that supports the ends of a bridge or dam.

**Adaptive reuse** A new use for a structure or landscape other than the historic use, normally entailing some modification of the structure or landscape. Also see Rehabilitation (cultural resources).

**Alluvial** Processes by which sediment is deposited by running water.

**Alluvium** Sediment deposited by a stream or other body of running water.

**Alpenglow** A reddish glow on mountain peaks at sunset or sunrise, caused by reflected weak sunlight.

**Ambient noise** The existing sounds at a given location coming from all sources, both near and far.

**Background noise** The all-encompassing sound associated with a given environment at a specified time, usually a composite of sound from many sources and directions. Background noise remains in a given location in a given situation when all uniquely identifiable, discrete sound sources are eliminated, rendered insignificant, or are otherwise not included.

**Bank** The slope of land adjoining a body of water, especially a river, stream, lake, or channel.

**Base of talus** See Talus slope zone.

**Biodiversity** Or biological diversity. Includes genetic diversity within species, species diversity within a community, and diversity in a full range of biological communities. An area is considered biologically diverse when it includes rich and stable populations of native species that are naturally distributed across the landscape.

**Biological community** An association of plants and animals in a region dominated by one or more prominent species or by a physical characteristic (e.g., California black oak community).

**Bond** An arrangement of masonry units to provide strength, stability, and in some cases, beauty.

**Braided stream system** A stream pattern that is characterized by the division of water flow into more than one channel. A basic characteristic of this pattern is the diversion of a single trunk channel into a network of interconnected branches and the formation of interspersed islands.

**California black oak woodland** A vegetation community dominated by California black oak (Quercus kelloggii). Other species that may be present include canyon live oak, California buckeye, Douglas fir, incense cedar, and ponderosa pine. The canopy can be continuous, intermittent, or savanna-like. Shrubs may or may not be common. Ground-layer vegetation is sparse or grassy (Sawyer 1995).

**Cabin (cultural resource)** A small, rustic residential structure, usually occupied seasonally.

**Cabin (lodging)** A structure containing one to four lodging units, as defined in the 1992 Concession Services Plan/EIS.

**Chukah** A Miwok granary.

**Colluvial soils** Loose earth material (such as rock fragments, sand, etc.) that accumulates on steep slopes or at the base of talus slopes through the action of gravity.

**Community** When used in a social or political context, refers to the group of people living in a particular area. When used in a biological context, any group of interacting organisms belonging to a number of different species that occur in the same habitat. Also see Biological community.

**Concessioner** A private commercial entity that conducts business under contract with the National Park Service in Yosemite National Park to provide food, lodging, retail, recreation, and other services to park visitors.

**Conifer invasion** The progressive growth of coniferous trees, such as pines and incense cedars, into areas that formerly did not support these species. Over the last 150 years, human-caused changes (such as alteration of soil moisture and suppression of a natural fire regime) have encouraged unnatural rates of conifer spread, reducing the size and continuity of meadows in Yosemite Valley.

**Cottage** A lodging structure containing five to eighteen lodging rooms, as defined in the 1992 Concession Services Plan/EIS.

**Cultural landscape** A geographic area, including both cultural and natural elements, associated with a historic event, activity, or person, or exhibiting other cultural or aesthetic values.

**Cultural resources** Properties such as landscapes or districts, sites, buildings, structures, objects, or cultural practices that are usually greater than 50 years of age and possess architectural, historic, scientific, or other technical value. By their nature, cultural resources are non-renewable.

**Day visitor** Any visitor who does not spend the night in the park.

**Debris flow** Soil, rock, and other materials that are rapidly transported by water and gravity. Debris flows occur in a variety of environments throughout Yosemite, ranging from steep ephemeral and perennial stream channels below cliffs to nearly flat alluvial fans.

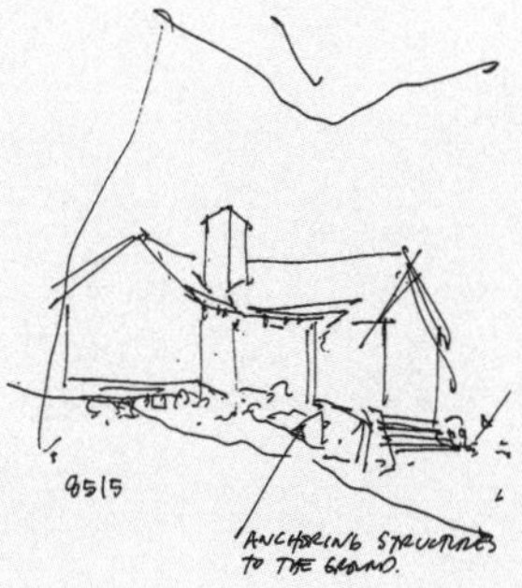


**Degradation (natural resources)** Refers to negative impact(s) to natural resources or natural processes. The impact may be singular or cumulative; the extent may be local or ecosystem-wide. The term degradation is used broadly and may refer to: reduction in habitat size, reduction in extent of plant populations, declining species vigor exhibited as reduced population numbers, reduced reproductive success, increased mortality rates, and/or decreased percent of available habitat utilized.

**Ecological restoration** See Restoration (natural).

**Ecosystem** A system that involves the interaction of organisms with their physical environment.

**Ecotone** A vegetation transition zone between different habitat types, such as the area between meadows and California black oak woodlands.

**Environmental Impact Statement (EIS)** A detailed statement required by the National Environmental Policy Act (NEPA) when an agency proposes a major action that significantly affects the quality of the environment. This document describes and analyzes the activities that might affect the environment.

**Exotic species** See Non-native species.

**Facilities** Refers to buildings, houses, campgrounds, picnic areas, visitor-use areas, operational areas, and associated supporting infrastructure such as roads, trails, and utilities.

**Faux** A French word used to describe something made to resemble something else, such as pre-cast concrete made to look like granite.

**Fen** A unique wetland type, possessing a water source that originates from alkaline ground water. Typically fens possess unique wetland vegetation adapted to saturated alkaline growing conditions.

**Fire return interval** The typical period of time between naturally occurring fires. Fire return intervals vary by vegetation type and location.

**Floodplain** Land on either side of a stream or river that is submerged during floods.

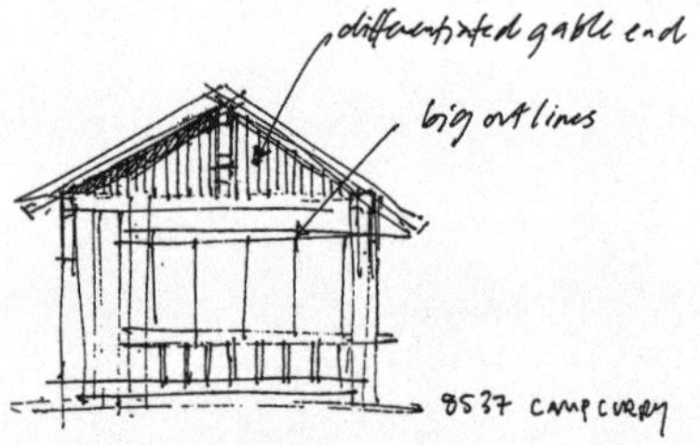


**Footprint** The land area covered or occupied by a function or structure.

**Free-flowing river** A body of water existing or flowing under natural conditions without impoundments, diversions, straightening, riprapping, or other modification of the waterway (as defined in the Wild and Scenic Rivers Act–16 USC 1286 [b]). Also see Riprap.

**Geographic information system (GIS)** A unique assemblage of hardware, software, and personnel that integrates digital databases, spatial technologies, and analytical methods in order to capture, store, edit, analyze, and display geographic data.

**Geologic hazards** Natural geologic processes (i.e., rockfall) that occur or could potentially occur in locations that present a threat to humans or developed areas.

**Geomorphic** Refers to the shape of the earth, or the shape of features on the earth's surface.

**Glaciation** A collective term for geologic processes of glacial activity, including erosion, deposition, and the resulting effects of such action on the earth's surface.

**Groundwater** All water found below the surface of the ground. Also see Surface water.

**Hazard trees** Any tree, either alive or dead, which due to outwardly visible defects could fall down (in part or in entirety) and strike a person or property within any designated portion of a development zone.

**Hazardous waste** Hazardous materials that no longer have practical use, such as substances that have been discarded, spilled, or contaminated, or that are being temporarily stored prior to proper disposal.

**Headwaters** The point or area of origin for a river or stream.

**Herbaceous** Refers to plants that lack a woody structure.

**Historic American Buildings Survey (HABS)/ Historic American Engineering Record (HAER)/Historic American Landscape Survey (HALS)** A documentation program that produces a thorough archival record of buildings, engineered structures, and cultural landscapes significant in American history and the growth and development of the built environment.

**Historic character** The sum of all visual aspects, features, materials, and spaces associated with the historic nature of a site, structure, or landscape.

**Historic district** A geographically definable urban or rural area, possessing a significant concentration, linkage, or continuity of sites, landscapes, structures, or objects united by past events or aesthetically by plan or physical developments. A district may also be composed of individual elements separated geographically but linked by association or history.

**Historic topography** The physical features and contours of a place or region as they existed during historic time.

**Hotel** A structure containing more than eighteen lodging rooms, as defined in the 1992 *Concession Services Plan/EIS*.

**Housekeeping unit** A type of rustic accommodation found within Housekeeping Camp in Yosemite Valley. The unit is composed of a concrete, three-walled structure with canvas roof and door, a small patio, and a common bathroom.

**Housing support facilities** Amenities required by a typical residential community (i.e., post office, food preparation and service, recreational facilities, barber shop, childcare, etc.).

**Hydrologic response** The response of a watershed to precipitation, often the resulting streamflow from a precipitation event or snowmelt.

**Hydrology** The science dealing with the properties, distribution, and circulation of water on the surface of the land, in the soil and underlying rocks, and in the atmosphere.

**Infrastructure** The various systems and facilities needed to support park operations and visitor services (e.g., sewer and water systems, electric systems, communication lines, roads and trails, and various support buildings).

**Jerkinhead roof** A gable roof that ends with a clipped ridge in the form of a small hip.

**Life zone** Bands of characteristic vegetation occurring along elevation gradients.

**Liquefaction** A process by which water-saturated soils lose strength and liquefy during ground-shaking events.

**Lithic** Of or relating to stone or stone tools.

**Lodging unit/room** Concessioner-operated facilities for overnight visitors. A lodging unit may be a single structure, such as a tent cabin, or a series of rooms grouped into larger motels or hotels. Lodging rooms in Yosemite are available at a range of prices that correspond to the type of structure as well as the amenities provided.

**Mechanical treatment** The alteration of the landscape using hand implements, power tools, and heavy equipment.

**Microclimate** The distinct yet uniform localized climate of a small site or habitat.

**Mission 66 style (architecture)** Refers to buildings developed in national parks between 1956 and 1970, during a period of experimentation with new structural forms, modern materials, and machine-driven methods of construction. The intent was to provide low maintenance, economical, permanent structures.

**Mitigation** An activity designed to avoid, minimize, rectify, eliminate, or compensate for impacts of a proposed project. A mitigation measure should be a solution to an identified environmental problem.

**Mixed conifer zone** Plant communities consisting of a mix of conifers such as pine, fir, incense cedar, and Douglas fir. The zone includes lower montane, montane, and upper montane coniferous forests. California black oak and other hardwoods are common associates.

**Moraine** An accumulation of mineral material, such as boulders, stones, and sediment, that is transported and deposited by a glacier.

**Mosaic** A descriptive term for vegetation where the mix of species types and ages creates a diverse assemblage of vegetation or vegetation communities. This term can also be used to describe diversity in habitat types.

**Multi-use paved trail** A trail that is intended for pedestrian and bicycle use. Occasionally, short segments of multi-use trails may also be used for horses, maintenance, and emergency access by motor vehicles.

**Museum collection** Objects, works of art, historic documents, and natural history specimens collected according to a rational scheme and maintained so they can be preserved, studied, and interpreted for public benefit.

**National Environmental Policy Act (NEPA)** The federal act that requires the development of an environmental impact statement (EIS) for federal actions that might have substantial environmental, social, or other impacts.

**National Historic Landmark (NHL)** A district, site, building, structure, landscape, or object of national historical significance designated by the Secretary of the Interior under authority of the Historic Sites Act of 1935 and entered in the National Register of Historic Places.

**National Register of Historic Places** The comprehensive list of districts, sites, buildings, structures, and objects of national, regional, state, and local significance in American history, architecture, archeology, engineering, and culture. This list is maintained by the National Park Service under authority of the National Historic Preservation Act of 1966.

**Natural process** A collective term for processes, including hydrologic, geologic, biologic, and ecosystemic, that are not the result of human manipulation.

**Natural quiet** The absence of human-caused sounds.

**Natural resources** Features and values that include plants and animals, water, air, soils, topographic features, geologic features, paleontologic resources, natural quiet, and clear night skies.

**Natural topography** The natural shape or contour of the land.

**Non-native species** Species of plants or animals that do not naturally occur in a particular area and often interfere with natural biological systems. Also known as alien, introduced, or exotic species.

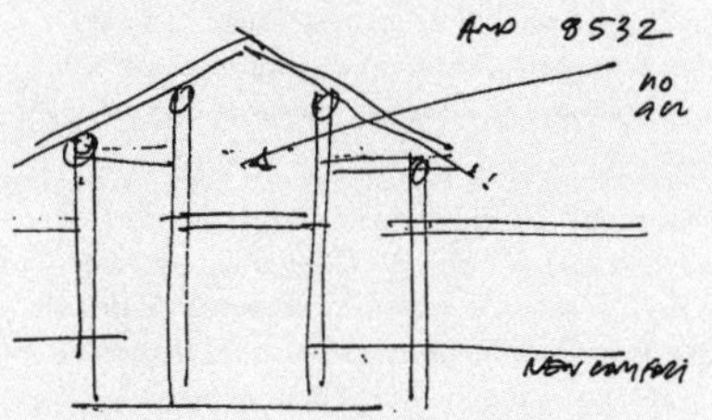

**Off-season** Refers to a period of year when Yosemite visitation is lowest, usually from late autumn to early spring.

**Ordinary high water** That line on the shore established by the fluctuations of water and indicated by physical characteristics such as a clear, natural line impressed on the bank, shelving, changes in the character of the soil, destruction of terrestrial vegetation, the presence of litter and debris, or other appropriate means that consider the characteristics of the surrounding areas.

**Overnight visitor** Refers to visitors who spend the night in Yosemite. This includes those that who in lodging, campgrounds, and wilderness areas.

**Oxbow** A bend in a meandering river channel that is abandoned as the river shifts its course over time. Oxbows can remain saturated with surface water or groundwater for some time, providing diverse wetland habitats for vegetation and wildlife.

**Palustrine** A term relating to vegetated wetlands (e.g., marsh, swamp, fen, bogs) and small, shallow ponds.

**Pedestrian/stock trail** Mostly unpaved trails intended to accommodate both pedestrians and stock users. (Use of bicycles on unpaved trails is prohibited.)

**Point bars** Areas along the inside bends of a meandering river where material is deposited.

**Pool-riffle** The relationship, usually expressed as a ratio, between the surface area of pools and that of small rapids (riffles) in a given portion of a stream or river.

**Post-flood conditions** Describes the environment in Yosemite Valley following the January 1997 flood. Post-flood conditions include any subsequent clean-up activities, such as the removal of flood-damaged facilities at Yosemite Lodge and the closure of Upper and Lower River campgrounds.

**Prescribed fire** Fires that are intentionally ignited under controlled conditions to meet management goals for natural resources and processes, wildland fire protection, and cultural resource preservation.

**Preservation (cultural resource)** The act or process of applying measures to sustain the existing form, integrity, and material of a historic structure, landscape, or object. Work may include preliminary measures to protect and stabilize the property, but generally focuses on the ongoing preservation, maintenance, and repair of historic materials and features rather than extensive replacement and new work.

**Preservation (natural resource)** The act or process of preventing, eliminating, or reducing impacts to natural resources and natural processes.

**Protected species** See Threatened and endangered species.

**Radiating impacts** Human activity and associated foot traffic that originates in visitor focal points, such as parking lots, and spreads into adjacent areas.

**Reconstruction** The act or process of depicting, by means of new work, the form, features, and detailing of a nonsurviving historic structure or landscape for the purpose of replicating its appearance at a specific time and in its historic location. (The term also refers to the resulting structure or landscape.)

**Redevelop** A term that applies to areas that are currently developed, where all or part of the existing development is removed and replaced, modified, or adaptively reused.

**Rehabilitation (cultural resources)** The act or process of making possible an efficient, compatible use for a historic structure or landscape through repair, alterations, and additions while preserving the portions or features which convey the historical, cultural, and architectural values. Also see Adaptive use.

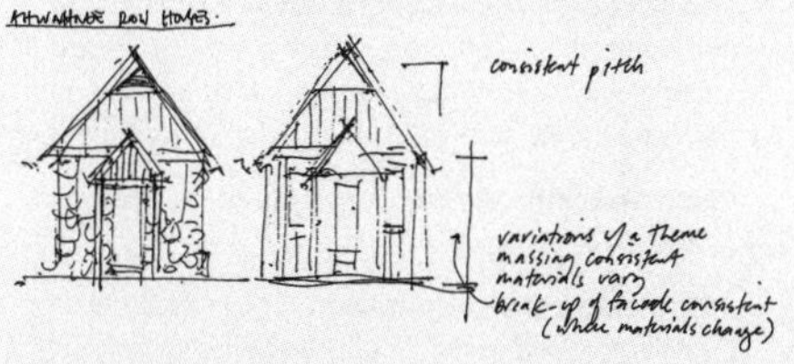


**Rehabilitation (natural resources)** All activities conducted to improve the quality or biologic function of an impacted natural resource. The term rehabilitation connotes a less extensive process than restoration. Site impacts may preclude a full restoration, but project work is undertaken to enhance the extent or function of natural processes.

**Restoration (cultural)** The act or process of accurately depicting the form, features, and character of an existing historic structure, landscape, or object as it appeared at a particular period of time, by removing modern additions and replacing lost portions of historic fabric, paint, or other elements.

**Restoration (natural)** Work conducted to remove impacts to natural resources and restore natural processes, and to return a site to natural conditions.

**Revegetation** Replacement or augmentation of native plants in an area largely or entirely denuded of vegetation.

**Riparian areas** Areas that are on or adjacent to rivers and streams; these areas are typically rich in biological diversity (flora and fauna).

**Riprap** Any hardening of a shoreline (with rocks or cement) to stabilize river banks for the protection of facilities on or near the bank.

**Rockfall** Associated forms of mass movement such as rock avalanches, rockslides, debris slides, and debris flows (Wieczorek, et al. 1998).

**Rockfall shadow zone** A distance calculated to determine outlying boulder locations beyond the extent of talus. The limit of the shadow zone is determined by a procedure based on the apex of the talus and a minimum shadow angle of 22 degrees (Wieczorek et al. 1998).

**Rockfall talus zone** See Talus slope zone.

**Root rot (Armillaria root rot)** A native plant disease primarily affecting oaks, but other tree species as well; sometimes exacerbated by management activities. It can also result in tree hazards.

**Rubble bond** A random pattern of irregularly sized masonry units.

**Rustic style (architecture)** Refers to a building style developed in the 1920s and 1930s in national parks. The Rustic style emphasized the use of natural materials and textures, and thoughtful integration with the natural landscape.

**Sediment** A particle of soil or rock dislodged, transported, and deposited by surface runoff or a stream. The particle can range in size from microscopic to cobble stones.

**Sense of arrival** An emotional and mental state that accompanies the end of a visitor's travels and the beginning of their park experience. For many visitors, arrival in Yosemite marks the end of a considerable journey involving both lengthy planning and travel. For some, a sense of arrival is created by the clear opportunity to park their car, learn about and plan activities in the park, and begin their exploration of the park with the assistance of exhibits, signs, guidebooks, trails, shuttle buses, etc. For others, this sense of arrival begins with the first sight of Yosemite icons (e.g., Tunnel View, El Capitan, Half Dome). For returning visitors, this sense of arrival may occur as they check into their campsite, cabin, or lodging room.

**Stewardship** The responsibility of caring for the park. This often grows from an understanding of and respect for the principles of the National Park System and the needs of the park's natural, social, and cultural environment.

**Stock** This term generally refers to horses and mules used for riding or carrying packed supplies on established trails.

**Succession** The process by which vegetation is either re-established following a disturbance or by which it initially develops in an unvegetated site. This term also refers to the entire process from initial colonization to the development of vegetation typical of that geographic area.

**Surface-treated asphalt paving** A method of modifying the finish of freshly-laid asphaltic concrete to accelerate blending with the surrounding ground by broadcasting and brooming the surface with fine soil from the installation site.

**Surface water** Water that naturally flows or settles on top of natural landforms and vegetation, often as rivers, streams, lakes, ponds, and other bodies of water.

**Sustainable design** Sustainable design is a concept that recognizes that human civilization is an integral part of the natural world and that nature must be preserved and perpetuated if the human community itself is to survive. Sustainable design articulates this idea through developments that exemplify the principles of conservation, particularly of nonrenewable resources, and encourages the application of those principles in our daily lives. Sustainable design results in development that meets the needs of the present without compromising the ability of future generations to meet their own needs; they do not permanently reduce the natural resources available to humanity.

**Talus** An accumulated mass of rock fragments (broken rock formed by falling, rolling, or sliding) of various sizes derived from and lying at the base of a steep slope (Wieczorek, et al. 1998).

**Talus slope zone** The area where the majority of accumulated rock debris is deposited at the base of a steep slope following a mass movement event (i.e., rockfall) (Wieczorek et al. 1998).

**Threatened and endangered species** Species of plants and animals that receive special protection under state and federal laws. Also referred to as listed, endangered, or protected species.

**Traffic check station** A location where vehicle access is regulated; typically requires buildings, multiple traffic lanes, and staffing.

**Transit bus** A mode of transportation that operates on a schedule along routes with established stops. Transit buses do not require daytime parking in Yosemite Valley, as they continuously pick up and drop off passengers along their established routes.

**Umacha** A Miwok structure made of cedar bark and used for shelter.

**Understory** An underlying layer of vegetation, specifically the vegetative layer, and especially the trees and shrubs, between the forest canopy and the ground cover.

**Upland community** The vegetation found where soil conditions are average to dry and where soils are only infrequently flooded or saturated.

**Visitor experience** The perceptions, feelings, and interaction a park visitor has in relationship with the environment. The visitor experience is influenced by general access, facilities, visitor services, interpretation and orientation, and recreational opportunities. Other elements also contribute to the quality of the visitor experience, such as the condition of natural and cultural resources, air quality, transportation, and noise.

**Walk-in campground** A campground with consolidated parking areas separated from the individual campsites. Campers walk a short distance from the parking area to their campsites (e.g., Camp 4).

**Weathering steel** A type of steel that oxidizes naturally over time, giving it an orange-brown color and a rough texture. It has a very high tensile strength, and in spite of its rusted appearance it is actually more resistant to damaging corrosion than standard forms of carbon steel.

**Wetland areas** Areas inundated by surface or groundwater with a frequency sufficient to support, under normal circumstances, vegetation or aquatic life that requires saturated or seasonally saturated soil conditions for growth and reproduction.

**Wilderness** Areas protected by provisions of the Wilderness Act of 1964. These areas are characterized by a lack of human interference in natural processes; generally, there are no roads, structures, or installations, and the use of motorized equipment is not allowed.

# BIBLIOGRAPHY


Allaback, Sarah
2000 *Mission 66 Visitors Center: The History of a Building Type*. Washington, DC: Department of the Interior/National Park Service.

Architectural Resources Group
1995 *Badger Pass Day Lodge Evaluation Draft*. Report prepared for the National Park Service under contract.

Bates, Craig and Martha Lee
1990 *Tradition and Innovation, A Basket History of the Indians of the Yosemite–Mono Lake Area*. Yosemite National Park: Yosemite Association.

Bitterroot Restoration Inc.
1999 *Comprehensive Landscape and Revegetation Plan: Reconstruct Yosemite Lodge Project, Yosemite National Park, California*. Report prepared for the National Park Service under contract.

Blodgett, Peter J.
1990 "Visiting the 'Realm of Wonder': Yosemite and the Business of Tourism, 1855–1916," *California History*, Summer 1990: 118–133.

Brown, Vinson and Robert Livezey
1962 *The Sierra Nevadan Wildlife Region*. Happy Camp, CA: Nature Graph Publishers, Inc.

Browning, Peter
1988 *Yosemite Place Names: The Historic Background of Geographic Names in Yosemite National Park*. Lafayette, CA: Great West Books.

Browning, Peter, ed.
1988 *John Muir in His Own Words: A Book of Quotations*. Lafayette, CA: Great West Books.

Bunnell, M.D.
1990 *Lafayetter Houghton, Discovery of the Yosemite*. Yosemite, CA: Yosemite Association.

California Historical Society
2000 *California History*, LXXXIX, No. 2, Summer 2000.

Carr, Ethan
1998 *Wilderness by Design: Landscape Architecture & the National Park Service*. Lincoln, NE: University of Nebraska Press.

2007 *Mission 66: Modernism and the National Park Dilemma*. Amherst: University of Massachusetts Press.

Chronic, Halka
1989 *Pages of Stone: Geology of Western National Parks and Monuments: Sierra Nevada, Cascades and Pacific Coast*. Seattle: Mountaineers Books.

Club Alpin Suisse
1928 *Cabanes*. Lausanne, Switzerland.

Davis, Timothy, Todd Croteau, and Christopher Marston, eds.
2004 *Americas National Park Road and Parkways: Drawings from the Historic American Engineering Record*. Baltimore, MD: Johns Hopkins University Press.

Demars, Stanford E.
1991 *The Tourist in Yosemite, 1855–1985*. Salt Lake, UT: University of Utah Press.

Ditton, Richard
1989 *Yosemite Road Guide*. Yosemite National Park: Yosemite Association.

Ehrlich, Gretl
2000 *John Muir, Nature's Visionary*. Washington, DC: National Geographic Society.

Everhart, William C.
1972 *The National Park Service*. New York: Praeger Publishers.

Farabee, Charles R.
2003 *National Park Ranger: An American Icon*. Lanham, MD: Roberts Rinehart Publishers.

Farquar, Francis D.
1966 *The History of the Sierra Nevada*. Berkeley, CA: University of California Press.

Federal Highway Administration
1995 "National Scenic Byways Program," *Federal Register*. Vol. 60, No. 96.

Fletemeyer and Lee Associates
n.d. *Camp Wawona: Master Plan and Design Guidelines*. Report prepared for the National Park Service under contract.

Fornoff, Susan
1999 "It's time to worship at the Wawona Altar." *San Francisco Examiner*, May 2.

Fox, Stephen.
1986 *The American Conservation Movement: John Muir and his Legacy*. Madison, WI: University of Wisconsin Press.

Freudenheim, Leslie Mandelson and Elizabeth Sussman
1974 *Building with Nature: Roots of the San Francisco Bay Region Tradition*. Santa Barbara, CA: P. Smith.

Frissell, Sidney S., Robert G. Lee, George H. Stankey, and Ervin H. Zube
1979 *A Framework for Estimating the Consequences of Alternative Carrying Capacity Levels in Yosemite Valley*. Report prepared for the National Park Service under contract.

Gibbens, Robert P. and Harold F. Heady
1964 *The Influence of Modern Man on the Vegetation of Yosemite Valley*. Davis, CA: University of California, Division of Agricultural Sciences.

Gill, Kent, ed.
1967 *Sierra Club Bulletin: A Handbook*. December.

Gilligan, David
2000 *The Secret Sierra: The Alpine World Above the Trees*. Bishop, CA: Spotted Dog Press.

Godfrey, Elizabeth
1977 *Yosemite Indians*. Yosemite National Park: Yosemite Association.

Good, Albert H.
1938 *Park and Recreation Structures*. Boulder, CO: Graybooks. (1990 reprint of 1938 edition published by the National Park Service.)

Greene, Linda Wedel
1987 *Yosemite: The Park and Its Resources. A History of the Discovery, Management, and Physical Development of Yosemite National Park, California*. Washington, DC: Department of the Interior/National Park Service.

Griswold, Stephen S.
1996 *A Handbook on Trail Building and Maintenance: For National, State, and Local Natural Resource Managing Agencies*. Sequoia National Park: Sequoia Natural History Association.

Gruell, George E.
2001 *Fire in Sierra Nevada Forests: A Photographic Interpretation of Ecological Change Since 1849*. Missoula, MT: Mountain Press Publishing Co.

Hardy, Hugh.
1990 "Towards an Architecture of the Valley," *Places: A Quarterly Journal of Environmental Design*. Vol. 6, No. 3, Spring: 28–31.

Harris, Charles and Nicholas Dines
1988 *Timesaver Standards for Landscape Architecture*. New York: McGraw Hill Professional.

Harvey, H. Thomas
1991 *The Sequoias of Yosemite National Park*. Yosemite National Park: Yosemite Association.

Haulenbeek, Rod
1994 *Tree Adventures in Yosemite Valley*. Carnelien Bay, CA: Wide-Eyed Publications.

Hill, Edwin G.
1990 *In the Shadow of the Mountain: The Spirit of the C.C.C.* Pullman, Washington: Washington State University Press.

Hinds, Norman E.A.
1952 "Evolution of the California Landscape," *Bulletin 158*, Division of Mines, Department of National Resources, State of California.

Horn, Yvonne.
1990 "A Distinctive Course with a Distinctive History," *Golf Journal*, Vol. XLIII, No. 4.

Huber, N. King
1989 *Yosemite Road Guide.* Yosemite National Park: Yosemite Association.

Hyde, Anne F.
1990 "From Stagecoach to Packard Twin Six: Yosemite and the Changing Face of Tourism, 1880–1930." *California History*, Summer 1990, 154–169.

Jackson, Louise A.
2004 *The Mule Men, A History of Stock Packing in the Sierra Nevada.* Missoula, MT: Mountain Press Publishing Company.

Johnston, Hank, ed.
1971 *John Muir in Yosemite.* Yosemite, CA: Flying Spur Press.

1995 *Yosemite Grant 1864–1906: A Pictorial History.* Yosemite National Park: Yosemite Association.

2000 *Ho! For Yo-Semite.* Yosemite National Park, CA: Yosemite Association.

Kaiser, Harvey H.
1997 *Landmarks in the Landscape: Historic Architecture in the National Parks of the West.* San Francisco: Chronicle Books.

Kirker, Harold
1973 *California's Architectural Frontier: Style and Tradition in the Nineteenth Century.* Santa Barbara: Peregrine Smith.

Klett, Mark, Rebecca Solnit, and Byron Wolfe
2005 *Yosemite in Time: Ice Ages, Tree Clocks, Ghost Rivers.* San Antonio, TX: Trinity University Press.

Kurutz, Gary F.
2000 "Popular Culture at the Golden Shore," *California History Magazine*, Summer: 2000, 280–309.

Law, James
1993 *Memories of El Portal.* Mariposa, CA: Mariposa Heritage Press.

Laws, John Muir
2007 *The Laws Field Guide to the Sierra Nevada.* Berkeley, CA: Heyday Books.

LeConte, Joseph
1875 *A Journal of Ramblings through the High Sierra by the "University Excursion Party."* (Reprint: San Francisco: Sierra Club Books, 1930.)

1889 *A Yosemite Camping Trip.* (Reprint: Berkley, CA: Friends of the Bancroft Library, University of California, 1990.)

Litton, R. Burton Jr., Joe B. McBride, et al
1990 "Perceptions and Reflections on Yosemite Valley," *Places: A Quarterly Journal of Environmental Design.* Vol 6, No 3, Spring: 32–36.

Litton, R. Burton Jr., Joe B. McBride et al
1990b "Yosemite's Meadows," *Places*, Vol. 6, No. 3, Spring.

Louter, David
2001 "Glaciers and Gasoline: The Making of a Windshield Wilderness, 1900–1915," *Seeing and Being Seen: Tourism in the American West.* Edited by David M. Wrobel and Patrick T. Long, 248–270. Lawrence, KS: University Press of Kansas.

Matthes, Francois E.
1950 *The Incomparable Valley, A Geologic Interpretation of the Yosemite.* Berkeley, CA: University of California Press.

McClelland, Linda Flint
1997 *Presenting Nature: The Historic Landscape Design of the National Park Service, 1916 to 1942.* Darby, PA: Diane Publishing Co.

1998 *Building in the National Parks: Historic Landscape Design and Construction.* Baltimore: Johns Hopkins University Press.

McHugh, Paul
2003 "Downhill Slide." *San Francisco Chronicle*, December 5.

Medley, Steven P.
2002 *The Complete Guidebook to Yosemite National Park.* Yosemite National Park: Yosemite Association.

Meyerson, Harvey
2001 *Nature's Army.* Lawrence, KS: University Press of Kansas.

Muir, John
1874–75 *John Muir's Studies in the Sierra.* (Reprint: San Francisco: Sierra Club Books, 1950.)

1890 Article in Alaska Fragment.

1898 *The Wild Parks and Forest Reservations of the West.* Altlantic Monthly.

1912 *The Yosemite.* (Reprint: San Francisco: The Sierra Club Books, 1988.)

1938 *John of the Mountains.*

1976 *Discovering Yosemite: Historic Photographs by Pioneer Photographers.* New York: Eakins Press Foundation.

1992 *The Eight Wilderness Discovery Books.* Seattle, WA: Mountaineers Books.

Munz, Philip A. and David D. Keck
1973 *A California Flora and Supplement.* Berkeley, CA: University of California Press.

NPS (National Park Service)
1935 *Park Structures and Facilities.* Unpublished report.

1965 *Maps of High Sierra Camps and Utilities.* (Revised 1975.) Yosemite National Park, CA.

1976a *The Ahwahnee Hotel National Register of Historic Places Nomination.* Yosemite National Park, CA.

1976b *Glacier Point National Register of Historic Places Nomination.* Yosemite National Park, CA.

1976c *Old Coulterville Road and Trail National Register of Historic Places Nomination.* Yosemite National Park, CA.

1977a *McCauley Cabin National Historic Register Nomination.* Yosemite National Park, CA.

1977b *National Park Service Rustic Architecture: 1916–1942*, by William C. Tweed, Laura Souliere and Henry Law. San Francisco: Western Regional Office, Division of Cultural Resource Management.


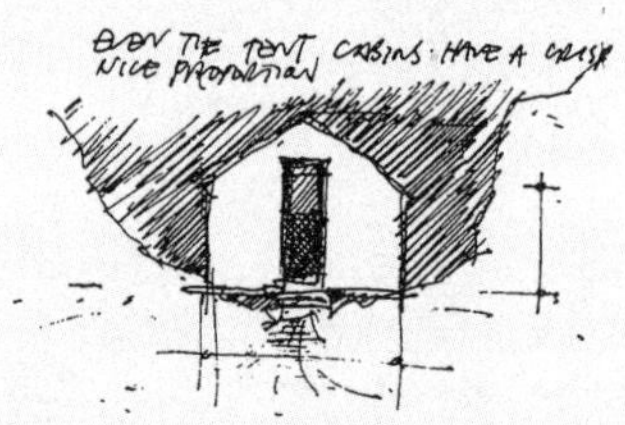


1977c. *Tioga Pass Station National Register of Historic Places Nomination.* Yosemite Park, CA.

1977d *Yosemite Village Historic District National Register of Historic Places Nomination.* Yosemite National Park, CA.

1978 "Vegetational Changes in Yosemite Valley," *National Park Service Occasional Paper No. 5.* Yosemite National Park, CA.

1979 *Camp Curry Historic Site National Register of Historic Places Nomination.* Yosemite National Park, CA.

1980a *Design Criteria for the Curry Village Historic District.* San Francisco: Division Cultural Resources Management, Western Regional Office.

1980b *General Management Plan.* Yosemite National Park, CA.

1983 *Administrative History: Expansion of the National Park Service in the 1930s.* Denver, CO: U.S. Department of the Interior, National Park Service, Denver Service Center.

1984a *Best's Studio Historic Structures Report.* San Francisco: Park Historic Preservation Division, Western Regional Office.

1984b. *Park Road Standards, Director's Order #87A.* Washington, DC.

1984c. Memorandum from Associate Director, Park Operations, to Director U.S. Dept. of Interior regarding park road standards, 9 July 1984. Yosemite National Park, CA.

1985 *LeConte Memorial Lodge National Register of Historic Places Nomination.* Yosemite National Park, CA.

1986a *Architecture in the Parks: National Historic Landmark Theme Study.* Unpublished report.

1986b *Merced Lake Ranger Station National Register of Historic Places Nomination.* (Revised 2002) Yosemite National Park, CA.

1987a. *Parsons Memorial Lodge National Register of Historic Places Nomination.* Yosemite National Park, CA.

1987b *Historic Resource Study: Yosemite: The Park and its Resources. A History of the Discovery, Management, and Physical Development of Yosemite National Park, California.* 3 volumes. By Linda Wedel Greene. Washington, DC: Department of the Interior/ National Park Service.

1988a *Historic American Buildings Survey, "HABS CA-1805, Wawona Hotel, Wawona, Mariposa County, California.* Yosemite National Park, CA.

1988b *National Park Service Trail Management Handbook.* By Lennon Hooper. Denver, CO.

1989a *Arch Rock Retaining Walls and Entrance Sign National Register of Historic Places Nomination.* Yosemite National Park, CA.

1989b *Architectural Character Guidelines, Sequoia & King's Canyon National Parks.* By Laura Soullière Harrison. Sequoia and King's Canyon National Parks, CA.

1989c *Inventory of Significant Structures, Architectural Character Guidelines, Sequoia & King's Canyon National Parks.* By Laura Soullière Harrison. Sequoia and King's Canyon National Parks, CA.

1990 *Yosemite: Official National Park Handbook 138, A Guide to Yosemite National Park.* Division of Publications, National Park Service.


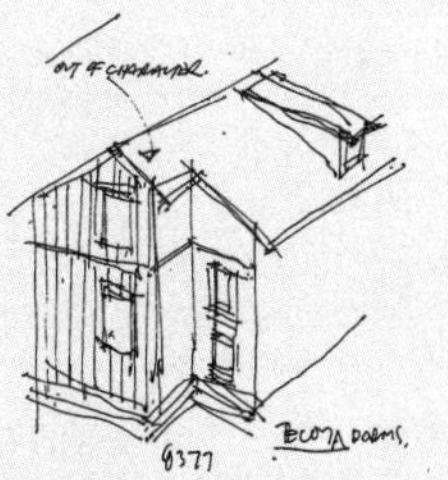


1991a *Historic American Engineering Record: Wawona Road, Yosemite National Park. HAER CA-148.* Washington, DC.

1991b *Historic American Buildings Survey: Chinquapin Service Station and Lunchroom HABS CA-2299.* Washington, DC.

1991c *Mather Memorial Way, Mt. Rainer National Park Development Guidelines.* Denver, CO.

1994a *Grand Canyon National Park Architectural Character Guidelines.* Prepared by Oz Architecture, Denver, CO.

1994b *Guiding Principles of Sustainable Design.* Denver, CO: Denver Service Center.

1995a *Presenting Nature: The Historic Landscape Design of the National Park Service.* Washington, DC: Government Printing Office.

1995b *The Secretary of the Interior's Standards for the Treatment of Historic Properties with Guidelines for Preserving, Rehabilitating, Restoring, and Reconstructing Historic Buildings.* Washington, DC.

1995c Wilderness Historic Resources Surveys, 1988–1995. Yosemite National Park. Manuscript on file at Yosemite National Park Research Library.

1996a *The Ahwahnee Landscape Maintenance Plan.* Yosemite National Park, CA.

1996b *The Secretary of the Interior's Standards for the Treatment of Historic Properties with Guidelines for the Treatment of Cultural Landscapes.* Washington, DC.

1996c *Tioga Road–Big Oak Flat Road National Scenic Byways and All-American Roads Nomination.* Yosemite National Park, CA.

1997 *Vegetation Management Plan.* Yosemite National Park, CA.

1998. *Evaluation of the Historical Significance and Integrity of the Hetch Hetchy Road for Determination of Eligibility for the National Register of Historic Places.* Denver, CO.

1999a *Mariposa Grove Cultural Landscape Inventory.* Yosemite National Park, CA.

1999b *South Entrance Station Cultural Landscapes Inventory.* Yosemite National Park, CA.

2000 *Mission 66 Visitor Centers, The History of a Building Type.* Washington, DC.

2001a *Camp 4 National Register of Historic Places Nomination.* Yosemite National Park, CA.

2001b *Residential Yard Care Policy, Housing Management Plan.* Chapter 6, Policies, Yosemite National Park, CA.

2002 *Cultural Landscape Treatment Recommendations, Yosemite Village Historic District, Housing Area, 85% Draft.* Unpublished report. Yosemite National Park, CA.

2003a NPS Correspondence, Jim Snyder, Park Historian, December.

2003b "Natural Resources at Yosemite National Park," *Yosemite National Park Fact Sheet*, April. Yosemite National Park, CA.

2004a *Buck Camp National Register of Historic Places Nomination.* Yosemite National Park, CA.

2004b *New Big Oak Flat Road National Register of Historic Places Nomination.* Yosemite National Park, CA.

2004c *Ostrander Ski Hut National Register of Historic Places Nomination.* Yosemite National Park, CA.

2004d *Snow Creek Cabin National Register of Historic Places Nomination.* Yosemite National Park, CA.

2004e *Snow Flat Cabin National Register of Historic Places Nomination.* Yosemite National Park, CA.

2004f *Yosemite National Park Fire Management Plan/ EIS.* Yosemite National Park, CA. Available at http://www.nps.gov/yose/parkmgmt/fireplan.htm.

2004g *Yosemite National Park Geology Overview.* Yosemite National Park, CA. Available http://www.nps.gov/archive/yose/nature/geology.htm.

2004h *Yosemite Valley Historic District National Register of Historic Places Nomination,* Yosemite National Park, CA.

2006a *Wawona's Lost Garden—Buffalo Soldier Arboretum Restoration Feasibility Study.* By Charles Palmer, Robin Pan and Brenda Hanley. Yosemite National Park: Division of Resource Management and Science.

2006b *Management Policies.* Washington, DC.

2007a *Glacier Point Road Cultural Landscape Inventory.* Yosemite National Park, CA.

2007b *Draft Hetch Hetchy Cultural Landscape Inventory.* Yosemite National Park, CA.

2007c *Segment D, El Portal Road Addendum to 1997 Determination of Eligibility.* Yosemite National Park, CA.

2007d *Soda Springs Historic District Cultural Landscapes Inventory*. Yosemite National Park, CA.

2007e *Tunnel View Overlook Rehabilitation—Environmental Assessment*. Yosemite National Park, CA.

2007f *Tuolumne Meadows Historic District Cultural Landscapes Inventory*. Yosemite National Park, CA.

2008 *Wawona Historic District Cultural Landscape Inventory*. Yosemite National Park, CA.

2010a *Badger Pass Cultural Landscape Report*. Yosemite National Park, CA.

2010b *Cultural Landscape Report Camp Curry Historic District*, Yosemite National Park, CA.

2010c *Administrative Draft Tuolumne River Plan*. Yosemite National Park, CA.

2011a *The Ahwahnee Historic Structures Report*. Yosemite National Park, CA.

2011b *The Ahwahnee Cultural Landscape Report*. Yosemite National Park, CA.

2011c *Wawona Hotel Complex Historic Structures Report and Cultural Landscape Report*. Yosemite National Park, CA.

2011d NPS *Yosemite Scenic Vista Management Plan*. Yosemite National Park, CA.

2011e White Wolf Lodge Main Building and Duplex Cabins Historic Structures Report. Yosemite National Park, CA.

2011f *Long Range Interpretive Plan*. Yosemite National Park, CA.

2011g *Lighting Guidelines Final Report*. Yosemite National Park, CA.

Neider, Susan M.
2007 *Wild Yosemite: Personal Accounts of Adventure, Discovery and Nature*. New York: Skyhorse Publishing.

Nordhoff, Charles
1973 *California: For Health, Pleasure and Residence: A Book for Travelers and Settlers*. Berkeley, CA: Tenspeed Press.

Obata, Chiura
1993 *Obata's Yosemite: The Art and Letters of Chiura Obata from his Trip to the High Sierra in 1927*. Yosemite, CA: Yosemite Association.

Ogden, Kate Nearpass
1990 "Sublime Vistas and Scenic Backdrops: Nineteenth-Century Painters and Photographers at Yosemite." *California History*, Summer, 134–153.

Olmsted, Frederick Law
1865 *Yosemite and Mariposa Groves: A Preliminary Report, 1865*. (Reprint: Yosemite National Park: The Yosemite Foundation, 1993.)

1930 *Suggested Revisions and Appropriate Draining and Planting*. (Drawing.)

O'Neill, E.S.
1993 *Meadow in the Sky: A History of Yosemite's Tuolumne Meadows Region*. Groveland, CA: Albicaulis Press.

O'Neill, E.S. and Carroll J. O'Neill
2002 *Tioga Tramps: Day Hikes in the Tioga Pass Region*. Groveland, CA: Abicaulus Press.

Orsi, Richard J., Alfred Runte and Marlene Smith-Baranzini
1990 "Yosemite and Sequoia, A Century of California National Parks." *California History, the Magazine of the California Historical Society* (Summer).

Page & Turnbull
1997 *The Ahwahnee Historic Structure Report: Yosemite National Park, California*. Unpublished report, November.

2008 4711 *Badger Pass—Prepare Rehabilitation Program*. San Francisco, CA.

Palmer, Charles
2006 "Parkitecture." *Yosemite Historic Journal*, Spring.

Paruk, Jim
1997 *Sierra Nevada Tree Identifier*. Yosemite National Park: Yosemite Association.

Pavlik, Robert C.
1990 "In Harmony with the Landscape: Yosemite's Built Environment, 1913–1940." *California History*, Summer, pp.182–195.

Perrottet, Tony
2008 "John Muir's Yosemite," *Smithsonian Magazine*, July.

Phillips, Thomas Bruce
1999 *Bridges of Wawona*. Mariposa, CA: Mariposa County Friends of the Library.

Pioppi, Anthony
2006 *To the Nines*. Ann Arbor, MI: Sports Media Group.

Pusateri, Samuel J., Ph.D.
1963 *Flora of our Sierran National Parks, Yosemite, Sequoia and Kings Canyon*. Tulare, CA: Carl and Irving Printers.

Rose, Gene
1999 *Magic Yosemite Winters*. Coldstream Press.

Rose, Gene
2006 *Yosemite's Tioga Country*. Yosemite National Park: Yosemite Association.

Rothman, Hal K.
1998 *Devil's Bargains: Tourism in the Twentieth-Century American West*. Lawrence, KS: University Press of Kansas.

Royston, Hamamoto, Alley & Abey
2002 *Wahoga Yosemite Indian Cultural Center*. Unpublished report.

Runte, Alfred
1990 *Yosemite: The Embattled Wilderness*. Lincoln, NE: University of Nebraska Press.

Russell, Carl Parcher
1992 *One Hundred Years in Yosemite* (reprint edition). Yosemite National Park: Yosemite Association.

Sargent, Shirley
1971 *John Muir in Yosemite*. Yosemite, CA: Flying Spur Press.

1977 *The Ahwahnee: Yosemite's Classic Hotel*. Yosemite, CA: Yosemite Park and Curry Company.

1979 *Yosemite's Historic Wawona*. Yosemite, CA: Flying Spur Press.

1993 *Enchanted Childhoods: Growing Up in Yosemite, 1864–1945*. Yosemite, CA: Flying Spur Press.

1997 *Yosemite's High Sierra Camps*. Yosemite National Park: Flying Spur Press.

2000 *Yosemite's Innkeepers: The Story of a Great Park and Its Chief Concessionaires*. Yosemite, CA: Ponderosa Press.

Schaffer, Jeffrey P.
2003 *The Geomorphic Evolution of Yosemite Valley and Sierra Nevada Landscapes: Solving Riddles in the Rocks*. Berkeley, CA: Wilderness Press.

Schlichtmann, Margaret E. and Irene D. Paden
1955 *The Big Oak Flat Road to Yosemite*. (Reprint edition: Fredericksburg, Texas: Awani Press, 1986.)

Schlichtmann, Margaret and D. Paden, Irene 1986
*The Big Oak Flat Road to Yosemite*. Awani Press, Fredricksburg, TX.

Scott, Amy, ed.
2006 *Yosemite: Art of an American Icon*. Berkeley, CA: University of California Press.

Sellars, Richard West
1997 *Preserving Nature in the National Parks: A History*. New Haven: Yale University Press.

Shaffer, Marguerite S.
2001 *See America First: Tourism and National Identity, 1880–1940*. Washington, DC: Smithsonian.

Sierra Club
1917 *Sierra Club Bulletin* 10(2):202–209.

Smith, Genny, ed.
2003 *Sierra East, Edge of the Great Basin*. Berkeley, CA: University of California Press.

Snyder, Gary, Tom Killion and John Muir
2002 *The High Sierra of California*. Berkley, CA: Heyday Books. Yosemite Association, Yosemite, California.

Sontag, William, Linda Griffin and Paul Schullery
1991 *National Park Service: A 75th Anniversary Album*. Lanham, MD: Robert Reinhardt Publishers.

Storer, Tracy I., Robert L. Usinger
1989 *The Sierra Nevada Natural History: An Illustrated Handbook*. Berkeley, CA: University of California Press.

Swedo, Suzanne
2005 *Hiking Yosemite National Park: A Guide to Yosemite National Park's Greatest Hiking Adventures*. Guilford, CT: Falcon Guides.

Temko, Allan
1987 "Show of Architectural 'Treasures,'" *San Francisco Chronicle*, 23 January.

Thomas, Bruce Phillips
1999 *Bridges of Wawona*, for Mariposa County Friends of the Library.

Trexler, Keith A.
1980 *The Tioga Road—A History, 1883–1961*. Yosemite National Park: Yosemite Natural History Association.

Treib, Marc, ed.
1996 *An Everyday Modernism: The Houses of William Wurster*. Berkeley, CA: University of California Press.

USDA (U.S. Department of Agriculture)
2007 *Built Environment Image Guide: Image and Identity*. San Dimas, CA.

USDI (U.S. Department of the Interior)
1918 *Annual Report of the Department of the Interior*. Washington, DC: Government Printing Office.

USDOT (U.S. Department of Transportation)
2007 *National Scenic Byways Program*. Available at http://www.bywaysonline.org/program/iq.html.

USEPA (U.S. Environmental Protection Agency)
1971 *Effects of Noise on Wildlife and Other Animals*. Washington, DC: U.S. Government Printing Office.

USFS (U.S. Forest Service)
1908 *Forest Trees of the Pacific Slope*. Washington, DC: U.S. Department of Agriculture.

2001 *The Built Environment Image Guide for the National Forests and Grasslands*. Washington, DC.

2006a *Accessibility Guidebook for Outdoor Recreation and Trails*. Washington, DC.

2006b *Forest Service Outdoor Recreation Accessibility Guidelines*. Washington, DC.

USGS (U.S. Geological Survey)
1985 *Bedrock Geologic Map of Yosemite Valley*, Yosemite National Park, CA.

Orr, Howard R.
n.d. *Design and Layout of Recreational Facilities*. Division of Recreation and Watershed, Southern Region, U.S. Forest Service, Atlanta, GA.

Vincent, Stephan, ed.
1990 *Oh California: 19th and 20th Century California Landscapes and Observations*. San Francisco: Bedford Arts.

Whitney, Josiah D.
1871 *The Yosemite Guide Book: A Description of the Yosemite Valley and the Adjacent Region of the Sierra Nevada, and of the Big Trees of California*. Cambridge: University Press, Welch, Bigelow and Co.

Willard, Dwight
2000 *A Guide to the Sequoia Groves of California*. Yosemite National Park: Yosemite Association.

Winter, Robert, ed.
1997 *Toward a Simpler Way of Life: The Arts and Crafts Architecture of California*. Berkeley, CA: University of California Press.

Wirth, Conrad, L.
1980 *Parks, Politics, and the People*. Norman, OK: University of Oklahoma Press.

Wurm, Ted
2000 *Yosemite's Hetch Hetchy Railroad*. Fish Camp, CA: Stauffer Publishing.

Yosemite Sentinel
1961 "Pilot Unit Erected in Housekeeping Camp," August 25.

Zaitlin, Joyce
1989 *Gilbert Stanley Underwood: His Rustic, Art Deco, and Federal Architecture*. Malibu, CA: Pangloss Press.

# PREPARERS + REVIEWERS


A SENSE OF PLACE
DESIGN GUIDELINES FOR
YOSEMITE NATIONAL PARK

*Second Edition, Expanded*




**National Park Service,**
**Yosemite National Park**

Don L. Neubacher, *Superintendent*

Mark Butler, *Former Chief of Project Management*

## PREPARERS + PROJECT TEAM

**National Park Service,**
**Yosemite National Park**

Gretchen Stromberg, *Project Manager/ Landscape Architect*

Randy Fong, *Chief of Project Management*

Bernadette Barthelenghi, *Former Project Manager*

Kimball Koch, *Landscape Architect*

Daniel Schaible, *Historical Landscape Architect*

Erik Skindrud, *Editor*

**Pacific West Region**

Charles Palmer, *Historian*

**Denver Service Center**

Christy Fischer, *Editor*

Carla McConnell, *Architect*

**Consultants**

George Homsey, *FAIA, Esherick Homsey Dodge & Davis*

Tito Patri, *FASLA, Landscape Architect*

Katherine Whitney, *Editor, Katherine Whitney & Associates*

Madeleine Corson with Rachel Griffiths, Lucy Kirchner, Stuart Silberman, *Book Design, Madeleine Corson Design, San Francisco*

Melissa Harris, *Architect, Associate Professor, University of Michigan*

Diana Vanderburg, *Editorial Support, Esherick Homsey Dodge & Davis*

Johanna Hauser, *Editorial Support, Esherick Homsey Dodge & Davis*

Amy MacKay, *Editorial Support, Esherick Homsey Dodge & Davis*

Kari Holmquist, *Editorial Support, Esherick Homsey Dodge & Davis*

## REVIEWERS + ADVISORS

Lisa Acree, *Botanist, Resources Management & Science*

Jim Benya, *Benya Lighting Design*

Sueann Brown, *Former Historical Architect, Resources Management & Science*

Linda Eade, *Research Librarian, Interpretation & Education*

Jennifer Hardin, *Native American Liaison, Resources Management & Science*

Dave Humphrey, *Branch Chief, History, Architecture, and Landscapes, Resources Management & Science*

George Jaramillo, *Historical Architect, Resources Management & Science*

Laura Kirn, *Branch Chief Archeology & Anthropology, Resources Management & Science*

Mary Kline, *Branch Chief, Visitor Services, Interpretation & Education*

Shawn Lingo, *Historical Architect, Resources Management & Science*

Kristina Rylands, *Former Planner, Planning Division*

Jennifer Self, *Architectural Historian, Resources Management & Science*

Jeannette Simons, *Former Native American Liaison, Project Management/Compliance*

## PHOTOGRAPHY CREDITS

CW: Carson White
DN: Doug Nelson
DNC: Delaware North Companies
DNC-KW: Delaware North Companies, Keith Walklet
DV: Diana Vanderburg
GH: George Homsey
GS: Gretchen Stromberg
HJ: Hank Johnston
JM: James McLane
LH: Laura Hartman
ML: Mark Lazzaro
NPS-DD: National Park Service Night Sky Team, Dan Duriscoe
RF: Randy Fong
SA: Sasaki Associates Inc.
TH: Thomas Heinser
TP: Tito Patri
YRL: Yosemite Research Library
YRL-EM: Yosemite Research Library, E.F. Menning
YRL-HW: Yosemite Research Library, H.D. Wulzen
YRL-OW: Yosemite Research Library, Onas Ward
YRL-RA: Yosemite Research Library, Ralph Anderson
YRL-ST: Yosemite Research Library, Steve Thompson
YRL-TH: Yosemite Research Library, Thomas Houseworth

FRONT COVER PHOTO Geology Hut, Glacier Point (2011) Thomas Heinser

BACK COVER PHOTO Ahwahnee bungalow, chimney detail (2004) Randy Fong

## ILLUSTRATION CREDITS

Hand sketches by Melissa Harris unless noted otherwise

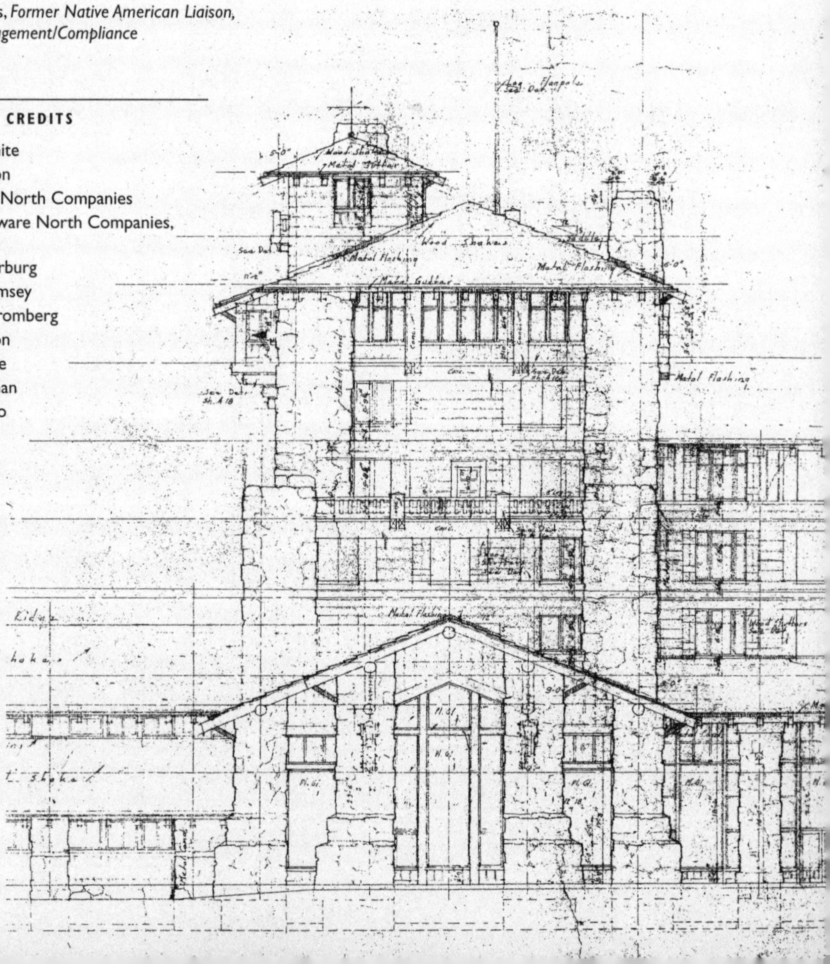

# A SENSE OF PLACE

DESIGN GUIDELINES FOR YOSEMITE VALLEY

*First Edition*



**National Park Service, Yosemite National Park**

Michael J. Tollefson, *Superintendent*

Kevin Cann, *Deputy Superintendent*

Bill Delaney, *Chief of Project Management/Compliance*

Russell Galipeau, *Former Chief of Resources Management & Science*

Jerry Mitchell, *Former Acting Chief of Resources Management & Science*

**DNC Parks & Resorts at Yosemite, Inc.**

Jerry Ernest, *Director of Facility Services*

Tim Smith, *Director of Operations*

## PREPARERS + PROJECT TEAM

**National Park Service, Yosemite National Park**

Randy Fong, *Project Manager/Architect*

Paul Chattey, *Historical Architect*

**Consultants**

George Homsey, *FAIA, Esherick Homsey Dodge & Davis, Architects*

Jim McLane, *Architect, James McLane & Associates*

Tito Patri, *FASLA, Landscape Architect*

Katherine Whitney, *Editor, Katherine Whitney & Associates*

Madeleine Corson with Supreeya Pongkasem, *Book Design, Madeleine Corson Design, San Francisco*

Melissa Harris, *Architect, Associate Professor, University of Michigan*

David Robbins, *Graphic Support, Esherick Homsey Dodge & Davis, Architects*

## REVIEWERS + ADVISORS

**National Park Service, Yosemite National Park**

Sue Beatty, *Biologist, Resources Management & Science*

Ed Billington, *Division Liaison, Facilities Management*

Linda Eade, *Research Librarian, Interpretation & Education*

Dave Forgang, *Museum Curator, Interpretation & Education*

Don Fox, *Landscape Architect/Accessibility Coordinator, Facilities Management*

Sue Fritzke, *Vegetation Ecologist, Resources Management & Science*

Phyllis Harvey, *Division Liaison, Visitor Protection*

Laura Kirn, *Archeologist, Resources Management & Science*

Carol Knipper, *Division Liaison, Resources Management & Science*

Victoria Mates, *Writer/Editor, Interpretation & Education*

Barbara Moritsch, *Division Liaison, Resources Management & Science*

Bob Roney, *Interpreter, Interpretation & Education*

Bill Rust, *Concession Facility Manager-Engineer, Business & Revenue Management*

Kristina Rylands, *Editor-in-Chief, Interpretation & Education*

David Siegenthaler, *Interpreter, Interpretation & Education*

Jeannette Simons, *Park Historic Preservation Officer, Project Management/Compliance*

Jim Snyder, *Historian, Interpretation & Education*

Craig Struble, *Historic Preservation Specialist, Facilities Management*

Kim Tucker, *Division Liaison, Business & Revenue Management*

**National Park Service, Pacific West Region-Oakland Office**

Michael Crowe, *Architectural Historian*

Robbyn Jackson, *Historical Architect*

Kimball Koch, *Landscape Architect*

**National Park Service, Pacific West Region-Seattle Office**

Cathy Gilbert, *Historical Landscape Architect*

David Louter, *Historian*

**DNC Parks and Resorts of Yosemite, Inc.**

Don Evans, *Project Manager*

Bill Hunsaker, *Project Manager*

Bridget Rabon, *General Manager, Yosemite Lodge*

**Independent Reviewer**

Jim Benya, *Benya Lighting Design*

Ethan Carr, *Assistant Professor, Department of Landscape Architecture and Regional Planning, University of Massachusetts, Amherst*

Gretchen Stromberg, *Planner, Newfields, LLC*

**Valley Project Firms**

East Valley Site Plan, Curry Village Cabins, and Employee Housing, *Architectural Resources Group, Inc.*

Lower Yosemite Fall, *Office of Lawrence Halprin*

Valley Shuttle Bus Stops, *David Evans and Associates, Inc.*

Yosemite Lodge/Camp 4/Northside Drive, *Sasaki Associates Inc.*

---

## PHOTOGRAPHY CREDITS

DNC: Delaware North Companies
DNC-KW: Delaware North Companies, Keith Walklet
GH: George Homsey
JM: James McLane
NPS-DD: National Park Service Night Sky Team, Dan Duriscoe
RF: Randy Fong
SA: Sasaki Associates Inc.
TP: Tito Patri
YRL: Yosemite Research Library
YRL-EM: Yosemite Research Library, E.F. Menning
YRL-HW: Yosemite Research Library, H.D. Wulzen
YRL-OW: Yosemite Research Library, Onas Ward
YRL-RA: Yosemite Research Library, Ralph Anderson
YRL-ST: Yosemite Research Library, Steve Thompson
YRL-TH: Yosemite Research Library, Thomas Houseworth

FRONT COVER PHOTO Bird-walk group along Merced River (1936) YRL-Ralph Anderson

BACK COVER PHOTO Ahwahnee bungalow, chimney detail (2004) Randy Fong

## ILLUSTRATION CREDITS

Hand sketches by Melissa Harris unless noted otherwise

OPPOSITE *Original architectural drawing of The Ahwahnee (1926)*

# INDEX